CARE OF SOULS, CARE OF POLIS

CARE OF SOULS, CARE OF POLIS

Toward a Political Pastoral Theology

Ryan LaMothe

CASCADE *Books* • Eugene, Oregon

CARE OF SOULS, CARE OF POLIS
Toward a Political Pastoral Theology

Cascade Books
An Imprint of Wipf and Stock Publishers
199 W. 8th Ave., Suite 3
Eugene, OR 97401

www.wipfandstock.com

PAPERBACK ISBN: 978-1-4982-0521-4
HARDCOVER ISBN: 978-1-4982-0523-8
EBOOK ISBN: 978-1-4982-0522-1

Cataloguing-in-Publication data:

Names: LaMothe, Ryan, author.

Title: Care of souls, care of polis : toward a political pastoral theology / Ryan LaMothe.

Description: Eugene, OR: Cascade Books, 2017 | Includes bibliographical references.

Identifiers: ISBN 978-1-4982-0521-4 (paperback) | ISBN 978-1-4982-0523-8 (hardcover) | ISBN 978-1-4982-0522-1 (ebook).

Subjects: LCSH: Public Theology | Pastoral Care.

Classification: BV4012.2 L35 2017 (print) | BV4012.2 (ebook).

Manufactured in the U.S.A. 07/24/17

For Cindy

and

for those who seek justice and care in a polis marred by cruelty and indifference

CONTENTS

PREFACE

We must love one another or die.[1]

It is true, as psychoanalysts continually point out, that people do often have the 'increasing sense of being moved by obscure forces within themselves which they are unable to define.' But it is not true, as Ernest Jones asserted, that 'man's chief enemy and danger is his own unruly nature and the dark forces pent up within him.' On the contrary: 'Man's chief danger' today lies in the unruly forces of contemporary society itself, with its alienating methods of production, its enveloping techniques of political domination, its international anarchy—in a word, its pervasive transformations of the very 'nature' of man and the conditions of his life.[2]

More than two decades ago, while studying at Vanderbilt University, I heard Gerda Weissman Klein give a lecture on her experiences in a Nazi concentration camp. I recall two stories she told the audience.[3] In the first story, Gerda said that after a long day, weary from work and lack of food, she sat against the wall of the barracks. Gerda's childhood friend came up to her and opened her hand, revealing a small raspberry that she had found in the street earlier in the day. Knowing it was Gerda's birthday, her friend wrapped the raspberry in a leaf and offered it to Gerda as a gift. The second story: as the war drew to a close, the Nazi guards were intent on killing as many Jews as possible. Gathering all the remaining Jewish women of Gerda's camp, the Nazi soldiers forced them into a warehouse

1. Auden, https://www.poets.org/poetsorg/poem/september-1-1939.

2. Mills, *The Sociological Imagination*, 13.

3. I wish to stress that these are my recollections and that I may have some of the details wrong. That said, I think the core points of the stories are accurate.

that was rigged with explosives. The Nazi guards fled, believing the building would explode, but an afternoon rain had shorted the electrical connections. Gerda, frail and thin, was able to squeeze out of the building and, as she stepped out, Gerda saw a U.S. Army jeep moving toward the building. An American officer jumped out and greeted her. Gerda bowed and said she was a Jew and the officer bowed in return and said he was Jewish as well. As they walked to the door of the warehouse, the American officer reached out and opened the door for her. She stated that, in that act, he had restored her humanity. These were two simple acts of care and, yet, when seen against the backdrop of profound and pervasive alienation and depersonalization, they were powerful moments of care.

Typically, we do not think about or remember simple gestures of care, because they are all too common. And we rarely see simple acts of care as heroic, such as giving a friend a dusty raspberry. Care is like the air we breathe—not noticed until it is absent. When natural disasters and instances of human malevolence occur—revealing not only human vulnerability, desperation, and cruelty—we become exquisitely attuned to even the smallest gestures of care and remember them because of their novelty against the background of deprivation. We become awakened, during these times, to the necessity of routine acts of care for individual human and collective survival and flourishing.

Consider also the thousands of mundane, necessary acts of care involved in parenting. Children are not turtles that need no parental care when they hatch and then crawl off to the sea to fend for themselves. To survive and flourish, children must receive consistent care from parents, teachers, coaches, and so forth. But it is not just children, as Winnicott noted,[4] who need care. To care, parents need to be cared for as well. And so we see that a family, even as it provides care, needs care to survive and flourish. We could stop here, but it would be premature. As Gerda and other Holocaust survivors knew, individuals, families, and communities cannot survive, let alone flourish, in a state and society that has institutions, policies, and programs that weaken or obliterate care. A state and its social, economic, and cultural institutions can undermine (or promote) care. To complicate this further, a state can promote care for one segment of the population while at the same time undermining care for a marginalized group. So, in stable, less violent societies, some individuals and families struggle to survive because they are kept from the resources needed to care for themselves and their families.

Of course, we know that human cruelty and indifference have been present throughout history and across the world, but in most instances

4. Winnicott, *Playing and Reality.*

there is sufficient care to keep individuals, families, and societies functioning. Even during periods like the 1930s and 1940s, when evil seemed to have the upper hand in Europe, care, as Gerda's story reveals, could not be completely extinguished. Indeed, the resilience and resistance of care in even the direst circumstances of human cruelty is evident in a key story for Christians. In the midst of being tortured, Jesus forgives his tormentors—an incredible act of care in the very presence of political forces that sought his demise.

Indeed, the prevalence of care (and love) threatens every totalitarian regime and empire, because care lays bare the falsehoods and injustices they promulgate. Yet, as the stories of Jesus reveal, despite attempts to snuff out care and love, they keep being resurrected. This is not a counsel for complacency—for care needs to be cultivated if a society and its citizens are to flourish. Indeed, we live in a society where poets such as W. H. Auden and sociologists such as C. Wright Mills saw leaders and institutions overtly or covertly promoting, not care and love, but cruelty, indifference, and hatred. We live in an era when it becomes even more important for theologians, philosophers, public intellectuals, and artists to reflect critically on the importance of care (and justice) for the survival and flourishing of individuals, families, societies, and the earth. Care, then, becomes the hermeneutical frame for a critique of powers and principalities as well as a vision for a world where everyone cares for each other so that the polis flourishes.

But I am getting ahead of myself. The title of this book needs to be unpacked. "Care of Souls" naturally points to religion and, more particularly, the field of pastoral theology. While pastoral theology is a relatively recent academic discipline, pastoral care has always been the concern of Christian churches. For instance, in Acts (6:1–6) we read about how people were selected to ensure that widows received what they needed. More broadly, John McNeill,[5] as well as William Clebsch and Charles Jaekle,[6] depict in detail the various types and methods of care in the cure-of-souls traditions. In the care-of-souls traditions, care is not restricted to those within the community of faith. Communities of faith are to care for those outside the confines of the church, though of course churches often fail both inside and outside. The notion of care will be addressed more fully in the first few chapters, but here I turn to the other term in the phrase "care of souls," which has different meanings. It is not necessary to delve into the various meanings and history of the term "soul," because I am using it in the title to refer to something ineffable about individual human beings. "Care of souls" implies that a soul

5. McNeill, *A History of the Cure of Souls.*

6. Clebsch and Jaekle, *Pastoral Care in Historical Perspective.*

is conditioned or affected by the material world, yet a soul is related to the unconditioned—God—and the *unconditional* love of God. Human beings can care for souls and, in not caring, can harm souls, but they do not have the power to create or destroy them. There is, then, something ineffable, something beyond our ability to circumscribe with our thoughts and actions vis-à-vis the notion of souls. While I say more about this in chapter 2, it is this ineffable (or ontological) feature of being human that gives rise to the existential demand—theologically understood—to care for others, a demand that we can, of course, refuse.

While I use the term "soul" in the title to hearken to the religious roots of care, I recognize it can be restrictive in the sense that it simply falls within the province of theology or, more broadly, religion. Yet, care and its existential demand are obviously not confined to Christianity and religion. So, while I use it in the title to point to the ineffable aspect of human beings, I use the term "person" when discussing care and justice. Like the notion of soul, "person," in my view, is also existentially ineffable and particular, in the sense that each individual person is unique and conditioned by time, history, and culture. Also, like the concept of soul, "person" places an existential demand to care. To see the Other as a person necessarily means one is existentially obliged to care, though again one has the freedom to eschew this demand. So, while the use of "soul" in the title serves to point to the care-of-souls tradition and to the ineffable feature of being human, the use of "person" in the following chapters serves to shift to a more existential and expansive view—a care-of-persons tradition, if you will. My underlying aim in shifting viewpoints is to expand rather than restrict the conversation about care. I add that I am not suggesting these nouns are identical, but each in its own way highlights the ineffable reality of being human and, correspondingly, the existential demand to care.

Let me move on to the next phrase in the title—"care of polis." We often restrict the notion of care to individuals and families. This narrow focus leaves aside the larger society or polis, which I address in greater detail in chapter 1. For the moment, though, I note that care for souls or persons also means caring for the society and vice versa. We cannot talk about one without including the other, because human beings are social and communal beings. The social and communal nature of being human includes the social, political, and economic stories, rituals, and institutions that human beings create to organize life and to administer good enough care and justice so that the polis survives and thrives. A polis that does not have institutions that promote care is a dystopian and dying polis.

The last part of the title highlights the provisional nature of this project. Pastoral theologians and caregivers have long been interested in political matters, because we see the suffering and struggles of people in society and in our congregations. Yet, we have spent less time formulating our interpretive (if not diagnostic) frameworks vis-à-vis more macro political-economic systems and structures. Moreover, we have been less involved publicly as a guild, which has also meant we have not been part of the conversations taking place in the larger public square and, more specifically, in political theology. As I argue in chapter 1, pastoral theologians have much to offer the public at large, and political theology in particular, because of our work in reflecting on contexts and issues of care and justice. This book is a step toward joining and adding to this public and scholarly discourse.

The book is structured in two parts. The first four chapters focus on building a hermeneutical framework with which to envision and critique current political, economic, and social structures and systems. The first chapter sets out to define some of the terms such as *polis*, *politics*, and the like, as well as to situate this book in the larger political theological discourse. I conclude the first chapter with an overview of what I mean by political pastoral theology and how it can contribute to political theological discourses. The second chapter focuses on the notions of care and pastoral care, and how they are political concepts. Here I lay the foundation for a critical and visionary hermeneutical framework that I use in the latter part of the book.

Since the notion of justice is in the foreground of political theological discourses, chapter 3 sets out to differentiate between the ethics of care and the ethics of justice, and to explore why we need both in analyzing what is taking place in the polis and in constructing responses. Chapter 4 is concerned with our methods of communication and action vis-à-vis engaging contested public-political matters. Here I argue that while civil discourse is necessary for a viable and vibrant democratic polis, redemptive discourse aims toward an ethics of care and an ethics of justice that invites the repair of social relations marred by injustices and carelessness. Redemptive discourse is a *just* and *care-full* discourse. These chapters set the foundation for a hermeneutical framework for analyzing macro political-economic realities.

The second part of the book comprises a political pastoral analysis of various macro issues in the United States and of how faith communities can resist systems, structures, and groups that erode care and justice. Chapter 5 addresses the United States Empire and its long history of violence that continues into the present, undermining care and justice not only for peoples from other nations but for U.S. citizens as well. Since the U.S. Empire is inextricably yoked to economics, chapter 6 is concerned with a critical analysis of neoliberal capitalism and its contributions to weakening care and justice in the polis. I briefly propose, in chapters 5 and 6, that *alterempire* and *altercapitalist* faith communities can both resist and defy the powers and principalities that distort and undermine care in the polis. Because empire and capitalism are wedded and inevitably create class hierarchies and inequalities, chapter 7 shifts to the notions of class, class conflict, and classism and their relation to both care and justice. I argue that a neoliberal market society breeds class, classism, and class conflict, all of which reflect distortions of care and justice in the polis. The final chapter addresses five other pressing macro matters vis-à-vis care (and justice) in the polis, namely, global warming, healthcare, education, the penal system, and finally the politics of exclusion.

One aim I had in writing this book was to develop a hermeneutical framework for analyzing systemic issues. My hope here is to further a critical and constructive conversation among pastoral theologians, political theologians, pastoral caregivers, and interested members of faith communities (religious and otherwise) about the serious issues that face our society and the world. This aim and hope have been aided and sustained by numerous people who deserve my deepest thanks. I first wish to thank the editorial staff at Cascade Books, in particular, Matt Wimer, Jeremy Funk, and Brian Palmer. Special thanks to the editorial acumen and labor of Jeremy Funk. He corrected numerous mistakes and offered many helpful editorial changes. Cindy Geisen and Mary Jeanne Schumacher merit my deep gratitude for patiently reading and editing numerous drafts of each chapter. I want to thank Dr. Lewis Rambo, editor of the *Journal of Pastoral Psychology*, for his long and abiding interest in my work in engaging political matters. I am not alone in appreciating Lewis's numerous contributions to the psychology of religion and pastoral psychology and his encouragement to scholars in these guilds. By way of a personal example, Lewis supported Dr. Bruce Rogers-Vaughn and me in publishing a special issue on politics and pastoral care in the *Journal of Pastoral Psychology*. This leads me to offer my gratitude to Dr. Rogers-Vaughn, who has similar interests and passions and is an engaging conversation partner. I have learned much by listening to him and reading his works. My friends and colleagues in New Directions of Pastoral Theology have listened to, offered helpful critiques of, and sustained my forays into economics and politics. I especially want to thank Dr. Robert Dykstra and Dr. Nathan Carlin for their friendship, insights, and good humor. All who have consistently participated in New Directions of Pastoral Theology mourn the loss of Donald Capps, who died tragically in the summer of 2015. I am deeply grateful for Don and the conversations we had, particularly about our shared interest in Malcolm X. My intellectual home for the last twenty-five years has been the Society for Pastoral

Theology (SPT). There are so many accomplished scholars in this group, and I have benefited from their work and wisdom. I also wish to mention the Postcolonial study group of SPT for addressing matters of empire, neoliberal capitalism, and class. I also wish to thank Professor Marcos Villatoro McPeek for his friendship and shared conversations and rantings about the injustices the U.S. commits and the frustrations at the willed ignorance of many of our citizens.

I end my litany of thanks with the person who has supported me in numerous ways during our time together, my wife, the Reverend Cindy Geisen. Since the first days we met over thirty years ago, Cindy's passion about marginalized and oppressed peoples has challenged me to reconsider many of my perspectives. This book's dedication is a small token of my appreciation for her and for those who quietly resist and defy powers and principalities that undermine care and justice in society.

1

POLIS, POLITICS, AND POLITICAL THEOLOGIES

God's Care among Us

As soon as any [individual] says of the affairs of the State, What does it matter to me? the State may be given up for lost.[1]

It has been my conviction ever since reading Rauschenbusch that any religion that professes concern for the souls of men and is not equally concerned about the slums that damn them, the economic conditions that strangle them, and the social conditions that cripple them is a spiritually moribund religion only waiting for the day to be buried.[2]

The summer heat is relentless, even brutal, Sally thinks, as she hands out water bottles and ice to homeless persons at the downtown Lutheran Ministry Outreach Office. Miles away, Rabbi Benjamin listens to the Coopers tearfully lament the insurmountable medical bills and the looming specter of bankruptcy. In her parish office, Reverend Anita greets several parishioners who express concerns about the rising violence in their inner-city neighborhood, as well as a recent report detailing negative environmental and health impacts of a nearby power plant. Each of these ministry moments represents direct acts of pastoral care: the problems are immediate, emotional, demanding pastoral ministers' attention, concern,

1. Rousseau in Curtis, *The Great Political Theories*, 32.
2. King, *The Autobiography of Martin Luther King, Jr.*, 18.

empathy, reflection, and response. Frequently overlooked in these challenging situations are the systemic political-economic and social forces and structures that are implicated in individuals' particular sufferings. Perhaps it is not so much that these forces are not considered as it is that pastoral ministers often feel helpless about what to do about them, especially given the immediate, proximate need for care. Sally readily recognizes that the downturn in the economy and so-called austerity measures have wreaked havoc among the poor. Rabbi Benjamin knows that the Coopers are not an anomaly in a society where the highest rate of bankruptcy results from people being unable to pay huge medical bills. As Reverend Anita listens to her parishioners, she knows that politicians, in collusion with the local power company, have lessened environmental regulations, leading to health problems of people within her community. Of course, knowledge of larger systemic forces and structures implicated in the immediate suffering of individuals and communities may not lead to pastoral actions, which may mean collusion with the status quo.

Some ministers are political activists, taking seriously the impact of politics and economics on the life of the church and surrounding community. For instance, Pastor Anita works assiduously with local leaders to agitate for change in community policing and in holding power companies accountable. Similarly, many pastoral theologians consider the impact of macroforces on the particular needs and sufferings of individuals, families, and communities.[3] Like the pastoral caregivers above, though, pastoral theologians typically focus on a specific issue (for example, domestic violence), and then consider how systemic forces and structures contribute to the problem. The gravitational pull is toward more immediate issues of suffering and how to respond adequately to heal, sustain, or liberate people. The pastoral method not usually adopted is a pastoral theological analysis of more abstract, macro structures, systems, and forces.[4] For example, there is little in the way of a pastoral theological analysis of capitalism, capitalism and political governance, the relation between capitalism and empire, and capitalism and class.[5] To be sure, pastoral theologians do address capitalism

3. For example, see Graham, *Care of Persons, Care of Worlds*; Miller-McLemore, *Also a Mother*; Miller-McLemore, "Children and Religion in the Public Square"; Poling, *Render unto God*; Scheib, *Challenging Invisibility*.

4. For exceptions see Rumscheidt, *No Room for Grace*; Mercer, "Economics, Class, and Classism"; Smith, *The Relational Self*.

5. For exceptions see LaMothe, "Empire Matters"; LaMothe, "The Spirits of Capitalism and Christianity"; LaMothe, "Neoliberal Capitalism"; Mercer, "Economics, Class, and Classism"; Rogers-Vaughn, "Powers and Principalities." There are instances of churches and church organizations that critique and resist capitalism. The Lutheran World Federation in 2003 released a statement highly critical of capitalism, which

and politics when examining particular contextual issues of suffering, though not an analysis of economics and politics as an object of pastoral theological study. One of the consequences of this is that pastoral ministers and pastoral theologians have not contributed to or been participants in political theological discourses. Likewise, political theologians have, in general, not used the research of pastoral theologians. Indeed, in my review of the literature, I have not come across a single political theologian who has cited the research of pastoral theologians; this indicates that pastoral theological literature is not considered relevant to political theological discourse. Also noted is the relative absence of pastoral theologians in this discourse.

Someone may wonder why ministers and pastoral theologians need to develop a political pastoral theology and engage in political theological discourse. How will a pastoral political theology inform or help ministers who are struggling with the immediate and concrete needs and sufferings of their congregants? Why should pastoral theologians and ministers turn their attention to macro issues, relying on the notion of care and community—theologically understood? What does a pastoral perspective contribute to political theological discourse? The last question is the focus of this book, but as to the former questions, I have five brief responses.

First, ministers who dismiss or overlook the very real impact of economic and political realities vis-à-vis individual, family, and communal suffering, survival, and vitality will likely collude unwittingly with those forces that lead to harm, instead of devising interventions aimed at resisting and changing these forces and structures.[6] This means, not only being aware of political-economic forces, structures, systems of meaning and how they contribute to suffering (or to life-enhancing ways of being in the world), but also analyzing and critiquing them, relying on pastoral concepts as well as research from human and natural sciences.

A second reason, to turn our attention to macro forces, is that pastoral theologians and ministers now face unique historical challenges. For the first time in history, human beings are on the threshold of what Elizabeth Kolbert calls the sixth extinction.[7] Unlike previous mass extinctions, this

was followed by a similar critique from the World Alliance of Reformed Churches (in Rieger, *No Rising Tide*, 124–25). Recently Pope Francis released an encyclical (*Evangelii Gaudium*) that, in line with previous church documents (e.g., Pope Leo XIII, *Rerum Novarum*; and United States Conference of Catholic Bishops, *Economic Justice for All*), is critical of the excesses of capitalism.

6. For an analysis of the subtle ways citizens and professional caregivers collude with macroeconomic forces and systems of meaning, see Connolly, *The Fragility of Things*; Cushman, *Constructing the Self, Constructing America*; Illouz, *Cold Intimacies*; Illouz, *Saving the Modern Soul.*

7. Kolbert, *The Sixth Extinction.*

one is clearly caused by human activity and is well underway. Extinctions and climate warming will accompany vast social and political upheavals as peoples and nations compete for declining resources.[8] It is likely that conflicts, wars, and violence will increase, as well as illness, social dislocation, and political oppression. Indeed, evidence of this is already mounting.[9] Pastoral theologians and ministers do not have the luxury of ignoring political and economic issues at the macro level and their relation to the sixth extinction (Anthropocene extinction), because, as Naomi Klein recently argues, some of these macro systems (e.g., global neoliberal capitalism) are implicated in the rapid trajectory toward climate change and mass extinction.[10] Pastoral ministers and theologians need to move out of the ship's sick bay and consider the very ship itself, its systems, and their contribution to harm or health. Of course, we need, we *must* continue to deal with the particular sufferings of individuals, families, and communities, but we are obliged to develop analyses of macro forces and structures and devise pastoral interventions. Failure to do so may mean we are simply caring for the sick while the *Titanic*'s captain (captains of industry) decides to increase speed, denying or ignoring the signs of peril.

A third reason for becoming more intentional about political theological discourse is the presence in the United States of what seems to be, first, a growing brutality and, second, an indifference to violence, both of which reveal a lack of caring imagination.[11] To be sure, cruelty and carelessness, within and between societies, have been present since the dawn of civilization. Yet, some societies descend into greater brutality and depravity over time. Given this, it is intriguing that during the 1980s some feminist scholars began addressing the issue of care vis-à-vis the political realm and, to my mind, this was not an accident, because care theories emerged at the same time an expansion of neoliberal capitalism as a way of organizing societies.[12] In other words, the rise of a market society corresponded the growth of both violence and indifference to violence in the United States. The most egregious current example is the sociopathic cruelty and indifference observed in many politicians who advocate torture and in a large percentage of citizens who agree with them.[13] A barbarism and cruelty is also evident in

8. See Klein, *This Changes Everything*; Sassen, *Expulsions*.

9. Hedges and Sacco, *Days of Destruction, Days of Revolt*; Sassen, *Expulsions*; Parenti, *Tropic of Chaos*.

10. Klein, *This Changes Everything*.

11. For instance see Giroux, *Disposable Youth*; Parenti, *Tropic of Chaos*.

12. See Harvey, *A Brief History of Neoliberalism*; Sandel, *What Money Can't Buy*.

13. See Giroux, "America's Addiction to Torture"; Danner, *Stripping Bare the Body*.

political, polarizing speech, whether from the Left or Right.[14] Pastoral theologians and caregivers have a responsibility to confront the diverse forms of brutality in the public sphere and to facilitate more caring public relations.

A fourth reason for a more deliberate attention to political concerns is theology itself. Daniel Bell asserted "that theology is always already political," which, to my mind, certainly includes pastoral theology.[15] To be sure, we recognize that part of pastoral theology, historically speaking, addresses governance (pastoral leadership), though this is usually located within the *ecclesia* and its polity, rather than larger political arrangements (e.g., democratic, socialist governments). Pastoral theology and, by implication, pastoral care are political not only because both are tied to a *mythos* and its vision of living together, but also because suffering and care are inextricably bound to political and economic realities. For instance, the politically, religiously marginalized Good Samaritan cared for the injured Jewish man by binding his wounds and providing the financial support necessary for his recovery. This parable of care illustrates both the immediate political-religious context and the underlying mythos of the kingdom of God where care is not restricted by religious (or any other) affiliation—a *mythos* of care that undermines and critiques the immediate political-religious reality that excludes Samaritans from being recognized as worthy of inclusion. If one agrees that every pastoral theology is a political theology, then pastoral theologians and ministers need to be more deliberate about constructing a political pastoral theology.

A final reason is that pastoral theology offers a unique and helpful perspective to political theological discourse, which is a focus of subsequent chapters.

To argue that pastoral theology can contribute to ongoing political theological discourse requires, as an initial step, a description of the terrain, much of which is contested. More precisely, I begin by addressing the meanings of *polis*, *political*, and *public*. From here I can move toward addressing the question, what is political theology? What subjects are the foci of political theology? What interpretive frameworks do political theologians use? Once the contours of the terrain have been described, I provide a general definition of "political pastoral theology," which highlights some of the important differences that the next three chapters illuminate further.

14. See Hetherington and Weiler, *Authoritarianism and Polarization in American Politics*; McCarty et al., *Polarized America*.

15. Bell, "State and Civil Society," 423.

CLARIFYING TERMS: POLIS, POLITICAL, AND PUBLIC

One of the wonderful yet sometimes frustrating aspects of human discourse, which colleagues of Socrates discovered, is the elusive if not illusive nature of the meanings of concepts. More often than not, the words we choose to grasp complex realities are, by their nature, polysemic, contingent on their varied cultural and historical contexts. We can conclude, then, that definitions are not definitive or timeless or universal, which allows for a certain amount of creativity and contestation when clarifying terms. In what follows, I am concerned not so much with concise definitions of contested terms than with descriptions of the contours of these concepts—concepts that are central to political theological discourse in general and this book in particular. Another important point to identify is that these terms—*polis*, *political*, and *public*—are distinct, yet intimately joined, and they accompany other key terms such as justice, power, and so forth, which I address at different points in this book.

Aristotle argued that the polis was prior to the individual and necessary for the individual's survival and for his/her flourishing in living a life with others.[16] Indeed, the polis, he posited, "grows for the sake of mere life, but it exists for the sake of a good life."[17] In Aristotle's view, the polis, which was the city-state of his day, is a "sphere of conscious creation," which is allied with humankind's nature to associate together—life lived in common.[18] The polis, in other words, reflects the given and the made. What is given is human beings' social nature and what is made or constructed is the city-state and its institutions, laws, and regulations that order a life lived in common—the polis. This suggests that while human beings by their nature form associations, the actual form of governance vis-à-vis the polis can vary widely and dramatically because of human freedom and creativity. Indeed, Aristotle's disciples researched numerous constitutions and Aristotle, with his penchant for taxonomy, identified six basic forms of governments or regimes.[19] Echoing Aristotle, Scottish philosopher John Macmurray argued that governments are human creations and, as such, can be altered or overthrown.[20] Put another way, for Macmurray "The State has no rights, no authority, for it is an instrument, not an agent; a network of organization, not

16. Lord, "Aristotle."
17. Ryan, *On Politics*.
18. Barker, ed., *The Politics of Aristotle*, xlix.
19. Lord, "Aristotle," 139.
20. Macmurray, *Person in Relation*, 137.

a person."[21] The state, Macmurray noted, "exists to make society possible, to provide mechanisms through which the sharing of human experience may be achieved."[22] This is analogous to Arendt's view of political power as citizens acting together—space of appearances, which I will attend to in greater detail below.[23] The state, in other words, has a function vis-à-vis a space of appearances and the sharing of human experience. This said, for Macmurray, the "State is merely a mechanism, and therefore a means to an end . . . it has no value in itself," and it is assessed in terms of whether it facilitates the sharing of human experience, acting together, and the flourishing of its citizens—the common good.[24] This highlights the socially constructed reality, the impermanence of political institutions, and the necessity that these institutions be secondary and subordinate to persons-in-community.[25] Also implicit here is that loyalty is due primarily to members of the polis and not necessarily to the created entity that we call the state. The state is created for the people, for the polis, and not the people for the state, though human beings often make the mistake of placing the survival of state before the survival and flourishing of the people. This would be both an epistemological error and problem of differentiation, both of which have real political consequences.

To further clarify the notion of polis vis-à-vis society and the state, Leo Strauss and Joseph Cropsey indicate that modern people tend to view the state "in contradistinction to 'society.'"[26] This distinction is inconceivable, they argue, to classical political philosophers like Plato and Aristotle. The polis "is a kind of partnership, association, or community, that is, a group of persons who share or hold certain things in common"[27] and, while distinct from the state, is inseparable from it. For Macmurray, a society "is a group of persons co-operating in the pursuit of a common purpose. The common purpose creates the association; for if the purpose should disappear, the society will go into dissolution. It also dictates the association; since members must co-operate in the way which secure the common end."[28] The state or body of governing institutions, as indicated above, is created and assessed in terms of how it contributes to society as an organic unity of individuals

21. Macmurray, "The Conception of Society," 106.

22. Ibid.

23. Arendt, *The Human Condition.*

24. Macmurray, "The Conception of Society," 106.

25. See Kirkpatrick, *Community.*

26. Strauss and Cropsey, *History of Political Philosophy*, 6.

27. Lord, "Aristotle," 134.

28. Macmurray, *Conditions of Freedom*, 35.

cooperating together vis-à-vis survival and the good life. The state, then, has a role in the pursuit of and cooperation toward achieving common purposes that contribute to an organic unity. While society and the state are distinct terms, the notion of the polis brings them together. Consider that a well-functioning society depends on well-ordered and well-administrated institutions of the state and, in classical political philosophy, a well-ordered state depends on the citizens expressing and living out virtuous lives—virtues that are encouraged and supported by the State.[29] Thus, the concept of polis includes both the state (e.g., public and governing institutions) and society. To confirm this, we need only look to failed states (e.g., Syria, Iraq, Honduras) that disrupt society, but also how corruption in a society (e.g., capitalistic ethos where greed is an elevated good in a market society) can lead to a corrupt state (e.g., the United States as a plutocracy or oligarchy).[30]

Included in this formulation are the functions or aims of the polis. Political theorist Hannah Arendt, following though amending Aristotle's view, wrote that the polis is "the public-political realm in which [human beings] attain their full humanity, not only because they are (as in the privacy of the household) but also because they appear."[31] While I will say more about "appearing" vis-à-vis the political realm, for now I simply point out that the notion of polis refers "not to the city-state in its physical location" but more importantly to "the organization of the people as it arises out of acting and speaking together."[32] This association of people living a life in common ideally involves collective cooperation so that the aims of survival as well as the fullness of humanity or personhood-in-community are possible. Of course, this organization of people, which clearly has a physical location, comprises particular created institutions and accompanying rules, regulations, and laws that order lives lived in common. In addition, living a life in common attends the key aims that are associated with Arendt's metaphor of appearing, and these aims are dynamic. Arendt, like Aristotle, stresses that political and public institutions, which facilitate individuals living together, possess, ideally, the aims of surviving and thriving. That is, as social or political animals, we need to create the polis's institutions wherein the common good reflects both survival and the pursuit of the good life for society's members.[33]

29. Lord, "Aristotle," 122–26.

30. See Mander, *The Capitalism Papers*; Stiglitz, *The Price of Inequality;* Stiglitz, *The Great Divide.*

31. Arendt, *The Promise of Politics*, 21.

32. Arendt, *The Human Condition*, 198.

33. Naturally, the meaning of the good life varies, even within the same polis, yet the idea of the good life becomes part of the discourse that attempts to arrive at some

I add that these aims of the polis point to the necessity of care and justice. To survive as individuals and as a society requires a basic level of care and concern for each other. To thrive requires an even more expansive and deeper reality of care, and the state, as a creation of a people, plays a role in promoting and sustaining both care and justice.[34] Put differently, the polis is conditioned by and conditions care and justice, and both make possible the very existence of the polis. Consider the family as the basic unit of the polis. The family comprises parental behaviors (attunement to the child's needs and desires) that are caring, which includes repairing relational disruptions—what we may call a form of justice. These caring and repairing actions are aimed at a child's survival and for thriving—becoming more fully person-in-community. The polis, with its institutions and accompanying narratives, depends on and supports these aims by facilitating cooperative caring behaviors of others outside the family and between families toward individual and communal survival and flourishing. This includes rituals or repair mechanisms when care and cooperation fail and when behaviors threaten the existence of citizens, undermine caring cooperation, or undermine meaningful living. Social disruption and repair usually fall under the heading of justice. While chapters 2 and 3 deal more specifically with these concepts, for now I suggest that care and justice are found the polis and both are central to the aims of the polis, namely, survival and flourishing. Without care and justice, human beings cannot survive together, let alone thrive. Briefly, we see evidence of the undermining of care and justice in a polis (e.g., the United States) and the corresponding corruption of society when a society becomes a market society, wherein everyone cares for him- or herself and no others.[35]

With this rudimentary beginning, one may wonder whether the term *polis* refers to a village, town, city, or nation-state, given that each possesses institutions, rules, and laws that regulate social relations and, in varying degrees, each ostensibly seeks to establish the common good.[36] In my view,

---

degree of consensus. Also, in reading Aristotle's *Politics*, it becomes clear that we consider who has the power to decide not only what is the good life, but who participates in and who is excluded from the public-political discourse. Thus, the idea of and discourse about the good life is closely connected to political power and who is allowed to engage in the political realm.

34. Thomas Hobbes rejects Aristotle's view of the aim of the common good or the good life. The state for Hobbes is created to keep human beings in a society from warring against each other as they pursue their own self-interests or desires. In a Hobbesian society care is only for oneself, and justice is aimed at preventing people from warring against each other. See Ryan, *On Politics*, 430–39.

35. See Ryan, *On Politics*, 430–38; Sandel, *What Money Can't Buy*.

36. The concept "common good" is contested and raises questions. What person

one's local municipality is a polis, but it is one that resides within and is inextricably linked to state and national government institutions—institutions that are political in the sense of comprising elected officials, as well as institutions that are bureaucratic, regulating diverse economic and non-economic activities (e.g., U.S. Patent Office, Federal Bureau of Investigation). The term, then, can refer to the local city or township in which one resides as well as to the larger state, whether that is one's state or province or the nation-state in which one is a citizen.

I wish to address two additional features of the polis. First, it seems to me that discourse regarding polis implies a bidirectional relation between the polis and individual citizens. Carnes Lord notes, for example, that for Aristotle a good citizen helps preserve the political partnerships that are necessary for a well-ordered state and society.[37] More specifically, he points out, the virtue of the citizen is integral to the health of the state. The polis, then, comprises a reciprocal relationship between the state and the citizen, each depending on and influencing the other. The implication of this relation is noted in what Leon Trotsky observed: "You say you are not interested in politics; but politics is interested in you."[38] I interpret this to mean that one can ignore or deny one's role as a citizen in relation to the larger society and the State, but the society and the state have an interest in the individual citizen—for good or ill. To live in the polis is to be caught in the drama of society and the state.

A second aspect of polis that I would add is its geographical location. By this I mean not only the particular, locally lived reality and ethos of a people, but more importantly the dependence of the polis on the well-being of the earth—locally and universally. Geography is ecology, and the common good of the citizens of a polis depends on a good environment. In short, habitable life in the polis depends on the health of the habitat. This has become increasingly clear in the twentieth and twenty-first centuries.

---

or group defines what the common good is? Who benefits and who does not? What composes the common good? Additionally, even if the common good is achieved, it likely means that some people may be left out. For example, public education is generally considered to be a common good in many Western countries, yet not everyone has access to quality education. I conclude with a quote regarding the common in a Vatican II document, *Gaudium et Spes*, #26. "Because of the closer bonds of human interdependence . . . we are today witnessing a widening role of the common good, which is the sum total of social conditions which allow people, either as groups or as individuals, to reach their fulfillment more fully and more easily . . . Every group must take into account the needs and legitimate aspirations of every other group, and still more of the human family as a whole."

37. Lord, "Aristotle," 138.

38. Ryan, *On Politics*, 95.

The aims of a polis—survival and thriving of the common good—cannot be separated from nature, from the well-being of the earth. Of course, we have long recognized that natural disasters can harm or even destroy a city (e.g., New Orleans, Lisbon, Pompeii), and we know that wars can do this as well (Nagasaki, Hiroshima, Dresden, Tokyo, and so forth). Yet often subtle human actions can harm the local environment and can in the process make habitation and health precarious among citizens of a polis. For instance, mountaintop removal (MTR) has had deleterious health effects on local populations.[39] Jason Howard writes that MTR is a "radical form of strip mining that has left over 2,000 miles of streams buried and over 500 mountains destroyed. According to several recent studies, people living near surface mining sites have a 50 percent greater risk of fatal cancer and a 42 percent greater risk of birth defects than the general population."[40] Local municipalities are left to handle soaring medical costs as well as population decline. The polis, then (both individual citizens and governing institutions) has a vested interest in the well-being of the earth if the aims of survival and human flourishing are to be realized.

Geography and the polis are important in another sense. A city and its people may take solace that they do not live near environmental hazards. We are not near the mountains. Our water is clean, and the air mostly so. Centuries ago, this collective belief would more than likely fall under the heading of truth or fact. Today, however, it is a stark illusion, if not delusion. Geography is both local and universal, and increasingly so. Habitable habitat is no longer simply local. As an example, what do Chicago and Beijing have to do with each other? They are thousands of miles apart. Beijing has some of the worst air pollution of any city in the world, yet Chicago also contributes to pollution. The local polis is part of the larger biosphere and thus has a part not only in the common good of its citizens but also in the survival and the common good of people throughout the world. We can no longer simply care about *our* polis and the local geography/ecology, because ultimately the health of the local polis and its geography are contingent on global realities—a global polis that depends on a healthy biosphere. Unlike Aristotle, today's and tomorrow's city-state must also be concerned about its impact on the whole and the whole's impact on the local population. In brief, the aims of the polis—the common good as survival and flourishing—must include the health of the earth as well as the survival and common good of other cities both near and far.

39. Hedges and Sacco, *Days of Destruction, Days of Revolt*, 116–75.

40. Howard, "Appalachia Turns on Itself."

As the notion of the polis takes shape, the concept of the political likewise emerges, begging for clarification. Above I noted, the polis is made up of particular created institutions, rules, regulations, and laws for ordering life lived in common, and all of this creative activity depends on *politics*—broadly, the actions and communications of its citizens. A more precise definition of politics or the political is a challenge. Most of us know what it is when we see it, and that is probably because the political is in our marrow, our DNA. Indeed, politics has been a reality of human life since we started organizing ourselves into tribes or clans millennia ago. We might say that politics began in the travails of loss, scarcity, disappointment, and hope from the earliest days of human life. The loss of paradise and the impolitic murder of Abel represent the first mythic glimmers of a group trying to come to terms with the harsh realities of finitude and the need for and vicissitudes of civilization. Who are we, who will lead us, how will we protect ourselves, how will we survive together, who will care for the orphans and widows, how will we organize ourselves? These are some of the latent political questions found in the Torah,[41] as well as questions we see in the writings of the Greek philosophers, such as Plato and Aristotle.

These questions, implicit or explicit, are part and parcel of living a life in common. Hannah Arendt viewed the political as "an organization of people as it arises out of acting and speaking together, and its true space lies between people living together for this purpose."[42] For Arendt, characteristics of the political space of speaking and acting are the stories and storytelling that aid in unifying and organizing the polis. Indeed, for Arendt the "organization of the polis . . . is a kind of organized remembrance"[43] manifested in the public-political space of shared narratives, rituals, and institutions. This communicative space, this space of appearances, encompasses a complex web of economic, political, and social rules, roles, values, beliefs, obligations, fantasies, and expectations/goals expressed and lived out in collective, secular and religious rituals, institutions, and narratives. These social rituals, structures, narratives, disciplines, and discourses inform citizens (and noncitizens) about whom to trust and where loyalties ought to lie; they provide a shared identity crucial to making ethical decisions or assigning standards to social practices;[44] they signify and make licit, for good or ill, the kinds of authority, power, privilege, and prestige that are

41. Walzer, *In God's Shadow*.

42. Arendt, *The Human Condition*, 198.

43. Ibid., 197.

44. See Nealon, *Alterity Politics*.

meted out in diverse social contexts;[45] they represent the good aims citizens are to pursue and the sanctions that result when one fails (e.g., justice);[46] they determine and distribute various social goods;[47] they shape who we care for and how we care in the public sphere.[48] This intricate economic, social, and cultural web serves as the political milieu that gives rise to and shapes citizens' experiences and identity.[49]

In brief, I offer a functional definition. By political, I mean socially held and publicly expressed symbols, narratives, and rituals that are embodied in a polis's institutions and social-symbolic spaces that function to

a. organize a person's experiences and legitimate an individual's actions in the public realm[50]
b. facilitate collective discourse and action in the public realm[51]
c. distribute power and resources[52]
d. legitimate authority and governance
e. adjudicate claims and discipline and repair breaches of both social order and the laws governing social arrangements and the distribution of resources
f. provide an overarching social-political identity that supports collective action and discourse, and provides for a shared sense of continuity and cohesion
g. facilitate mutual care of citizens (and noncitizens) for the sake of survival and flourishing

The notion of politics, then, refers to groups of people, not necessarily or always citizens, who are engaged in public action and discourse pertaining to the common good and to decisions being made about (a) who is allowed to participate in public-political discourse (citizenship and identity), (b) who should govern, (c) what type of institution(s) should be the instrument of governing, (d) the kinds of policies and programs that administer

45. See Foucault, *Power/Knowledge*; Kertzer, *Ritual, Politics, and Power.*

46. See Benhabib, *Situating the Self.*

47. Miller, *Market, State, and Community.*

48. See Hamington, *Embodied Care*; Noddings, *Caring.*

49. Samuels, "Politics on the Couch?"

50. See Arendt, *The Human Condition.*

51. See D'Entreves, *The Political Philosophy of Hannah Arendt*; Young, *Justice and the Politics of Difference.*

52. Ransom, *Foucault's Discipline.*

and regulate economic and social affairs, (e) care of citizens and strangers, and (f) the enactment and adjudication of laws that order the society and repair social disruptions.

I wish to stress that the "political," in all its varied arrangements and expressions, is inextricably yoked to the notion of power and its relation to the space of appearances. Having lived in and later fled Germany in the 1930s, Hannah Arendt, a political philosopher, was well acquainted with political "power," force/coercion, and violence. Arendt contended that power "exists only in actualization . . . where word and deed have not parted company."[53] Positively stated, actualization of power refers to the space of appearances where men and women of the polis are acting and speaking together—where they are politically engaged in varied ways. The metaphor, "space of appearances,"[54] denotes the mutual recognition and treatment of others as persons—unique, valued, inviolable, and responsive/agentic.[55] Individuals ideally appear in the political space as persons (unique, valued, inviolable, and agentic), as having a voice, and as being able to join together in corporate action. The mutual recognition and treatment of others as persons, which implies the presence of social care and justice, secures social trust, confidence, and fidelity necessary for cooperation toward political aims—for shared speaking and acting together. In other words, mutual recognition of persons reflects political power whereas force and coercion represent the decline of political power and the attenuation of the space of appearances.

It is also important to point out that power, for Arendt, is both actual and potential, because power cannot be stored up like instruments of violence. Power and space of appearances, then, are dynamic, needing to be continually exercised. Stated differently, the polis's space of appearances and, therefore, personhood, are not static, not guaranteed, always being created or diminished. Likewise, speaking and acting together must be exercised to exist, to be a reality. Even when actualized, power can already be in decline (or changing into force, violence, and coercion) as the space of

53. Arendt, *The Human Condition*, 200.

54. Ibid., 179.

55. See Macmurray, *Persons in Relation*. The concept of person is, for Macmurray not necessarily a legal concept, rather it is primarily a philosophical concept pointing to an ontological reality. This said, the notion of universal personhood accompanies the local realities of sexism, racism, and other forms of discrimination and exploitation—realities that involve the denial of personhood. See Brown, *Politics Out of History*, 13–15. All of this suggests that personhood, as Macmurray recognized, is both a matter of fact and a matter of intention. In other words, human beings must continually create personhood in the face of the human tendency to deny personhood to those constructed as Other.

appearances wanes. This implies that political power is not something associated simply and solely with the institutions of the state, though the state plays a particularly important role in making possible the actualization of power (or not) as speaking and acting together. A negative example of this is a tyrannical state that uses force and violence to secure adherence and to control social relations, corrupting the space of appearances, undermining trust and fidelity, debasing care and justice, and distorting the common good. In these contexts, power is not actualized because people are not free to speak and act together, though power is potential, which is why tyrannical political elites must continually use force, coercion, propaganda, and violence to keep power from being actualized in the political space.

It is easy to point to tyrannies as illustrations of the corruption of power into force and violence and the corresponding attenuation of the polis's space of appearances. The situation becomes more complex when we take note of democracies, where there is an ideal of citizens speaking and acting together. Many people believe that a democracy is a reality, a static thing, something that exists. Yet for Arendt, political power is always potential, and even democracies can move toward corrupting political power into force and coercion, even though citizens may continue to hold the belief that the polis is a democracy. Consider, for instance, the United States, where various groups of people (e.g., women, African Americans) were denied the vote, denied participation in political space. On some occasions the state used force and violence to restrict dissenting speech and action (e.g., in the cases of Eugene Debs and Emma Goldman). Moreover, during the last forty years we have seen the political influence of corporations increase so that corporations have been deemed to be persons who have free speech (in the Citizens United Supreme Court case); the U.S. democracy has been transformed into a plutocracy or oligarchy.[56] Here we have the appearance of a democracy whereby the state is captive to corporate interests, using propaganda, coercion, and force to secure benefits for the few at the expense of the many. As Sheldon Wolin argues, the United States exhibits an inverted totalitarian system, with networks of power instead of a single source of power.[57] In these cases, the space of appearances at the state level is largely limited to the wealthy and corporations, and the state and corporations demonstrate little interest in expanding the space of appearances wherein citizens act and speak together. Instead, a corporatocracy is interested in the good (survival and thriving) of corporations, rather than the common good. What is complicated is that the space of appearances

56. See Mander, *The Capitalism Papers*; Stiglitz, *The Price of Inequality*.

57. Wolin, *Democracy Incorporated*. See also, Hardt and Negri, *Empire*.

and corresponding political power continue to remain both actual and potential among the citizenry. That is, people can still speak and gather and act (consdier, e.g., the Occupy Wall Street movement), which is why corporate interests must continue to use the state to adopt measures to ensure their economic and political privileges and to use propaganda to deflect citizens from taking note of the corruption of the political system and society.

Political power, then, is associated with who is recognized as being able to speak and act together in the public-political realm. For Aristotle, only men of property had power; slaves and women were barred from politics. In a democracy, the ideal is that all adult citizens can speak and act together in the public-political space. It is the dynamic nature of power and the space of appearances that make democracy always potential and actual, never permanent. In reality, political power can easily devolve into coercion, force, violence, and propaganda to enforce cooperation and to restrict the space of appearances and corrupt the common good.

Arendt's notion of the space of appearances includes the concepts "polis" and "political," as well the idea of public. The notion of "public" is broader than the concept "political." For Arendt, the public sphere comprises the space of appearances or the space of political freedom, which I have associated with the political, and the *common world*, "a shared and public world of human artifacts, institutions, and settings."[58] The public square, this common space, is where people can raise and discuss issues and concerns, as well as participate in other shared activities.[59] This common world certainly includes political realities, but it is broader, including cultural and religious artifacts and activities. There are many examples of the public realm. The mall, restaurants, sports venues, theaters for movies and plays, spaces for camping and hiking, and the zoo, are just some examples. To be sure, each of these has political tendrils in the sense that laws and regulations are associated with the (a) market (the mall), (b) safe food, (c) care of animals, and so forth, but these laws and regulations are not in the foreground when the public gathers in these spaces. This distinction is important when we come to differences between political and public theologies.

Public theologians may address the political, but they may also focus on theological analyses of common world realities related to culture, such as music or media (and offer, for instance, a theological analysis of bluegrass or a theology of *The Simpsons*). A political pastoral theology will focus on the analysis of specific political realities.

58. D'Entreves, *The Political Philosophy of Hannah Arendt*, 15.

59. Arendt, *The Human Condition*, 22–76; see also Hardt and Negri, *Commonwealth*.

POLITICAL THEOLOGIES

With this broad overview of some key concepts, we can now turn to the notion of political theology. What is political theology? What questions or issues do political theologians address? What is the relation between political theology and the life of the *ecclesia* or the *ecclesia's* role vis-à-vis the public-political realm? There are many possible answers to these questions, which indicate both plasticity and contestation with regard to Christian theology and the social-political world. My intention is to offer a brief overview of the various features of political theology. This sets the stage for distinguishing between a political pastoral theology and political theologies and, more specifically, denoting political pastoral theology's contributions to this political theological discourse.

Hent de Vries notes that the "term *political theology* dates to Marcus Terentius Varro" (in the first century BCE), who used "the Stoic tripartition of theology (*theologia tripertita*), in which a political theology (*theologia politikē*) is juxtaposed with the mythical (*mythikē*) and cosmological (*kosmikē*) theologies."[60] The concept, de Vries points out, disappears until the seventeenth century, though this does not imply that theologizing about political questions and issues went underground or were of little concern to theologians. Indeed, as Daniel Bell contends, "every theology is always already political," because "every theology embodies, either explicitly or implicitly, a mythos, a vision of how communities ought to be organized"; this suggests that theologians long before and after Varro directly or indirectly addressed questions of living a life in common.[61] De Vries makes a similar point, arguing that "the theologico-political problem is perceived and lived well before being theorized and named as such."[62] For instance, Bell argues that early theologies of the Torah are political theologies because they represent the myths of a people who find ways to organize themselves in space and time and, thus, are concerned with issues of power, authority, the common good, care, and justice.[63] While Christian *political theology* has its roots in Jewish Scriptures, as a concept it makes its first appearance in the second century and becomes prevalent in the twentieth century after the devastation of World War I, perhaps beginning with Carl Schmidt's book, *Political Theology*.

60. De Vries, "Introduction," 25.

61. Bell, "The State and Civil Society," 423. Note also that Carl Schmidt reversed this, arguing that all key secularized concepts of the state are theological: see Hollerich, "Carl Schmidt," 111.

62. De Vries, "Introduction," 29.

63. Bell, "The State and Civil Society," 424.

The idea that theologies are also political theologies can be further understood in terms of theological anthropology. Every theology is an anthropology, which is used to interpret or make sense of the routine and extraordinary interactions and events of a particular age and cultural context. That is, a Christian mythos becomes the lens for perceiving and interpreting not only life in the church but also society and the larger world. For example, Augustine's theological anthropology was the interpretive lens he used to address political questions and concerns of his day. Human beings, Augustine posited, are fallen creatures; this fallenness results in an existential tension between *caritas* (love/care) and *cupiditas* (desire). This existential tension, theologically understood, is present not only in the *ecclesia* but in all of human life, including political arrangements. From this, Augustine drew a sharp distinction between the earthly city and God's kingdom, which was intended, in part, to strip away "the sacral patina given to the Roman Empire by Christian apologists such as Eusebius of Caesarea."[64] Augustine's theological anthropology, then, was the lens through which he engaged, understood, and critiqued political realities of his day.

It is important to note that theological anthropologies can be used to support or critique political orders and that theologians on different sides of the political spectrum can use the very same mythos to promote decidedly divergent political views. Egregious examples of this are Roman Catholic leaders and theologians who supported the Nazis[65] and those who buttressed the oppressive military juntas in Central America.[66] These theologians and religious leaders used the anthropology of the Christian mythos to give legitimacy to reprehensible political governments and the force, violence, coercion, and propaganda they used to maintain economic, social and political privileges. By contrast, Dietrich Bonhoeffer and liberation theologians, using the very same mythos, critiqued and resisted religious and political leaders who sought to secure power and privilege for the few.[67] As Roland Boer notes, Judeo-Christian religious myths, while often used to oppress, contain a seed of subversion.[68]

The diversity of theological anthropologies, political theologies, and their concomitant interpretations vis-à-vis a particular social-political milieu means that we often use them to create, not only a world that is

64. Hollerich, "Carl Schmidt," 120.

65. Krieg, *Catholic Theologians in Nazi Germany.*

66. Hewitt, "Critical Theory," 456.

67. See Hauerwas, "Dietrich Bonhoeffer"; Gutiérrez, *A Theology of Liberation*; Segundo, *The Liberation of Theology*; Sobrino, *The True Church and the Poor.*

68. Boer, *Criticism of Heaven*, 27, 32–36.

meaningful, but also one that conforms to our values, prejudices, and desires. There are three implications here. First and foremost, the diversity and complexity of past and present political theologies should encourage the virtue of humility when proposing one's own political theology. No political theology and no form of the polis are sacrosanct, as Augustine seemed to suggest when distinguishing between the *imperium* and the City of God. Put differently, we are all creatures of time and geography and, of course, finitude, which means that we are prone not only to error (theologically to sin, missing the mark) but also self-deception. Second, a variety of political theologies is a necessary outcome of Christians and Christian communities not only living in community but engaging people of other religious and existential faiths, as everyone participates in the social-political realities of their day. A diversity of political theologies reflects the complexity of human life, and this diversity, while at times troubling and conflicted, can lead to both humility, and mutual enrichment. Third, the diversity of political theologies points to the importance of the theological reflections of citizens vis-à-vis the public-political sphere. Augustine, for example, was not merely interested in the life of the church. As a citizen of the Roman Empire, he was understandably concerned with the political-public realities of his time. To be a citizen of the earth and heaven necessarily means participating in civil discourse with all of its disputations and agreements, whether in the confines of the *ecclesia* or the larger social-political realm. Disciples—citizens of the earth and the kingdom of heaven—are not to retreat in the face of diversity and complexity, but to embrace both as we engage people within our own polis and people of other nations. In my view, this is a moral demand that is even more critical today than at any time in history, because the stakes are so high: existence and life on earth.

We have moved a bit closer to unpacking the notion of political theology by indicating that: (1) every theology has a mythos and anthropology that inform followers about how to organize themselves, (2) the very same mythos can be used to support and critique a variety of political arrangements and realities, and (3) as disciple-citizens we ought to be concerned about and participate in this diverse, complex discourse and public action. Given these general contours, how are we to understand political theology, and how is it distinct from other theological enterprises? Cavanaugh and Scott offer a broad depiction of political theology: "What distinguishes all political theology from other types of theology or political discourse," they write, "is the explicit attempt to relate discourse about God to the organization of bodies in time and space."[69] More narrowly, Cavanaugh and Scott

69. Scott and Cavanaugh, "Introduction," 3.

summarize political theology as "the analysis and criticism of political arrangements (including cultural-psychological, social and economic aspects) from the perspective of differing interpretations of God's ways with the world."[70]

As a theological discipline, political theology, then, involves two interrelated activities—reflection and action (praxis). In terms of reflection, Christian political theology uses of the Judeo-Christian Scripture and tradition to interpret political realities, which includes analysis and criticism as well as construction, in the sense that a political theologian can imagine a political vision that includes kinds of political institutions distinct from present political arrangements. Some political theologians, such as Augustine and Aquinas, reflected, in part, on questions about the relation between human political arrangements and the kingdom of God. Other political theologians seek to construct theocracies wherein God's rule is intertwined with political arrangements at all levels of society; we note this in Iran today and in Christian Reconstructionism and Dominionism.[71] Still, some political theologians, such as Sobrino, Rieger, and Cone, critique political, economic, and cultural institutions, policies, and narratives that oppress people, whether within their country or in other places in the world.[72]

Analytic, critical, and constructive reflections, to be sure, are not simply beholden to theological frameworks. The political theologies of Augustine, Aquinas, Barth, and Gutiérrez, for example, rely on philosophers such as Plato, Aristotle, and Marx. In addition, political theologians may rely on the human sciences to help in their analyses, critiques, and constructions. So, while a political theologian relies principally on the Christian mythos as an interpretive framework in analysis, critique, and construction, s/he also may use other bodies of knowledge.

While one may rightly argue that all theologies have something to do with action, in the sense of influencing current realities, political theological reflection in particular is aimed at critiquing, influencing, supporting, or changing current political structures, policies, and programs. For example, South American liberation theologians in general critique: (1) government leaders and political structures and programs, (2) economic colonization by the U.S. Empire, and (3) religious leaders who support dominant political systems complicit in the oppression of indigenous peoples. Similarly, black and feminist political theologians critique religious, cultural, and political narratives, structures, and rituals implicated in systemic violence aimed

70. Ibid., 2.

71. See for example the website of Chalcedon: http://chalcedon.edu/about/.

72. Cone, *A Black Theology of Liberation*; Rieger, *Opting for the Margins*; Sobrino, *The True Church and the Poor*.

toward people of color and women. These political theologians, in general, seek to influence and to be involved in political and public discourses and direct actions that aim to influence or change current organizations of bodies in time and space.

Let me pause here and clarify that a political theologian may be someone such as Augustine, Aquinas, or Barth. These towering theologians spilled considerable amount of ink developing their theologies and engaging various ecclesial and societal issues. On the reflection-action scale, they are clearly on the left side of the equation. We might say they spent more of their time in their offices. By contrast, Martin Luther King Jr., Malcolm X, Desmond Tutu, and Cornel West (to name only a few) are, in my view, political theologians who have not written systematic treatises, yet are deeply involved in political actions aimed at changing dominant political-economic structures and policies that foster injustice, marginalization, and oppression. These political theologians spent and spend more time on the streets and less time in their offices. In between are political theologians such as Reinhold Niebuhr[73] and John Courtney Murray,[74] who clearly shaped political discourse, yet who did not take to the streets. Political theologians, then, all engage in reflection and action, though the degree of their direct political action and influence may vary considerably.

Political theologians' reflection and action are, in general, concerned with numerous public, political, and economic questions and realities. How should a people organize themselves, and who or what group decides this? What kind of government is best in leading people toward a particular vision of the common good? Who should lead and how does this person/group attain and retain leadership? What is the responsibility of the citizen to the state? What is the responsibility of the state to the citizen and non-citizen (or stranger)? What composes the common good? Who decides or has the authority to decide what the common good is? What economic arrangements and structures benefit society? Who administers justice? Who crafts law and who enforces it? Who is a citizen? How much authority do citizens have in participating in public-political life? What are the rights and obligations of citizens and what are the rights and obligations of political leaders? What political-economic structures contribute to just or unjust relations? What is the relation between the *ecclesia* (with its narratives and rituals) and the larger political milieu? What is the relation between the household and the political arrangements of the state? To be sure, political theologians address many other questions, and implicit in these and other

73. Werpehowski, "Reinhold Niebuhr."

74. Baxter, "John Courtney Murray."

questions are topics of power, authority, legitimacy, sovereignty, rights, obligations, and justice—topics of the political-public order that impact the daily life of citizens.

In summary, political theologies, generally speaking, are concerned with how human beings organize themselves in time and space, as well as with how human beings survive and flourish. The political theological activities of reflection and action presuppose not only a particular religious mythos but also other knowledge systems (e.g., philosophy, human sciences) used to examine and critique political institutions, realities, and issues of a particular societal context and era: all of this points to the implicit limitations and diversity of political theologies. And the bread and butter of political theologians are issues such as the common good, political-economic power and authority, sovereignty, justice, citizenship, and so forth.

A BRIEF OVERVIEW OF A POLITICAL PASTORAL THEOLOGY

It follows that if, as Daniel Bell posits, all theologies are political, then pastoral theologies are as well, because they are linked to a mythos. To be sure, most pastoral theologians and caregivers are overtly or tacitly concerned about political-economic realities precisely because these realities impact the survival and well-being of people in the church and the larger society. Domestic violence, adequate medical care, food insecurity, widespread incarceration and economic poverty, and numerous other areas of concern, reflection, and care are intertwined with political-economic factors, though these issues may not be in the foreground of pastoral theological focus. Nevertheless, for pastoral theologians and ministers, the underlying Christian mythos is a central interpretive framework for understanding the needs and sufferings of individuals and communities. Yet this mythos, which is an ethos, is more than simply an interpretive framework. It also includes beliefs and practices rooted in the core belief in God's care for us and for creation, and it is God's care for us that commands us to care for each other and for the earth. *Care is a central hermeneutical framework for pastoral theological reflection and action.*

This said, as indicated above, pastoral theologians have generally not been involved in developing a "political" theology. A deliberate critical and constructive attention toward political-economic issues, structures, and institutions not only shifts pastoral theology's focus but also alters how we might think about political theology in general. A way to begin defining a political pastoral theology is to identify what I consider to be its four interrelated tasks, which are followed by three principles evident in the cure-of-souls traditions.

As I indicated above, the activities of a political theological enterprise are reflection and action aimed at addressing issues and questions about political-public matters. This is true for political pastoral theology, yet I will address reflection and action in terms of four tasks. The first task of a political pastoral theologian is a critical, systemic examination of political-economic governance, policies, programs, and structures *vis-à-vis the concept of care*—theologically understood and informed by the human sciences. Here we see the Judeo-Christian mythos and tradition that informs the meanings and visions of care with regard to individuals, families, communities, societies, and the earth. It is a mythos and ethos of God's care for us incarnated in our care for others and the earth. More specifically, *care is a political concept*, understood in light of God's care for creation and for human beings in particular. In short, care is a theological-existential core of a viable, thriving polis.

Pastoral theologians have long relied on additional disciplines to understand human suffering and needs, as well as how best to care for individuals and communities. Like other political theologies that borrow from different fields of knowledge, a political pastoral theology uses the human sciences to deepen and expand the understanding of care with regard to political-economic context. Together these fields of knowledge provide additional and necessary interpretative frameworks to examine, assess, and critique political-economic arrangements, institutions, policies, and programs.

While the next chapter addresses care as a political concept in greater depth, here I briefly portray three overarching criteria associated with care, which one can derive from the Judeo-Christian mythos, the human sciences, and political theologies. The first is the *survival* of individuals, families, communities, societies, and the earth. To be sure, this is a minimum requirement of care vis-à-vis political-economic realities. We can, for instance, critique the government and political parties that create and support a medical system that negatively impacts the physical survival and well-being of poor people and people of color.[75]

Survival is an important feature of caring actions, yet in the history of pastoral care there is also a concern for the *flourishing* of individuals and communities, which is the second criterion of care.[76] In Scripture this is

75. Sommers et al. "Mortality and Access to Care among Adults after State Medicaid Expansions."

76. See Clebsch and Jaekle, *Pastoral Care in Historical Perspective.*

evident in the image of a land of milk and honey and in the words of Jesus: "I came so that they may have life and have it in abundance" (John 10:10) And it is seen in the history of pastoral care wherein ministers ideally seek to provide care that leads to human well-being.[77] Assessment and critique of political realities, using the framework of care, involves determining whether political-economic policies contribute to the thriving of individuals, families, and communities. Care, then, is not simply associated with survival; it is also aimed at living a meaningful, purposeful life in the company of others. In this sense, the notion of the common good is understood as both survival and flourishing.

Finally, care has, at times, a *liberative* dimension. Traditionally, this is seen when persons are cured of their illnesses—physical, mental, or spiritual. They are freed from physical and mental torments. Liberation is also seen when persons are freed from the terror of violence—political or otherwise—as well as from the anxious suffering of politically enforced poverty. Indeed, I suggest that liberation theologies, while generally focusing on issues of justice, reflect a deep care for freeing people from economic, political, cultural, and religious oppression, which I address in greater detail in chapter 3. These three features of care, then, serve as a primary lens for analyzing political realities. Put another way, the notion of the common good vis-à-vis the notion of care is understood in terms of survival, flourishing, and liberation. In addition, the notion of care as a political concept is a key departure from political theologies that tend to focus on justice, and this difference serves as a contribution to political theological discourse.

Under the rubric of reflection and action, the second task of a political pastoral theology involves assessing and facilitating cooperation and collaboration with diverse others to cultivate public spaces of appearances. Hannah Arendt coined the term "space of appearances" to refer to a public-political space wherein individuals[78] can express their needs and desires while being recognized and treated as unique, inviolable, valued, responsive subjects—persons.[79] Implicit in this notion of space of appearances is cooperative communication that has at its core respect and care for others, even amid vigorous disagreement. A society made up of diverse individuals and communities can survive and thrive only with cooperative discourse and action. This means that attention must be directed toward political commu-

77. See also Kittay, *Love's Labor.*

78. I have deliberately avoided the term *citizen* because it restricts political space to those who are recognized as citizens. The use of the term *individual,* then, includes people who are not citizens but who nevertheless participate in the larger public-political-economic sphere, though often on the fringe or in the shadows.

79. See Macmurray, *Persons in Relation.*

nicative processes, because societies can devolve into what John Courtney Murray called barbarism—a barbarism that undermines civil society, care, and the common good. He wrote:

> Barbarism likewise threatens when men cease to talk together according to reasonable laws. There are laws of argument, the observance of which is imperative if discourse is to be civilized. Argument ceases to be civil when it is dominated by passion and prejudice; when its vocabulary becomes solipsist, premised on the theory that my insight is mine alone and cannot be shared; when dialogue gives way to a series of monologues; when the parties to the conversation cease to listen to one another, or hear only what they want to hear, or see the other's argument only through the screen of their own categories . . . When things like this happen, men cannot be locked together in argument. Conversation becomes merely quarrelsome or querulous. Civility dies with the death of dialogue.[80]

The barbarism Murray refers to can be understood as an attenuation of the space of appearances, wherein communication reflects mere disrespectful contestation with little hope for cooperation—the mark of a careless society marred by rampant narcissism. The second task of a political pastoral theology, then, is to critically and constructively attend to the dialogic space between individual citizens and groups, because the attenuation of the space of appearances represents the decline of social care, the presence of injustice, and the diminishment of civil discourse. A political pastoral theology, then, necessarily attends to public-political communication, which I address more fully in chapter 4.

Part of any analytic reflection and action with regard to a political pastoral theology involves proffering concrete plans to meet the needs of particular individuals and communities, which is the third task. Throughout the history of pastoral care, we note the interrelation between answering the diagnostic question, what is going on? and the attending prescription that aims to relieve symptoms, meet needs, facilitate meaning, and so forth. Similarly, a political pastoral theology includes working with others toward developing policies, programs, and interventions aimed at the survival, flourishing, and liberation of individuals and communities. The fact that pastoral theologians and caregivers are not "experts" in economics, politics, and foreign relations is not an excuse for neglecting to engage or failing to offer ideas and plans that focus on care and justice.[81] Indeed, pastoral theo-

80. Murray, *We Hold These Truths*, 14.

81. Reinhold Niebuhr, for instance, was a prominent public theologian and clearly

logians need to be engaged in political conversations and in the construction of solutions, especially in light of the catastrophic consequences of climate change and the widespread cruelty fostered by the hegemony of neoliberal capitalism.

The construction and critique of possible solutions or interventions, which are aimed at survival, flourishing, and liberation, need to be accompanied by assessment of the implementation of these solutions. This fourth task necessarily involves the use of quantitative and qualitative analyses conducted by independent researchers—analyses that a political pastoral theologian would interpret in terms of the three criteria of care, namely, survival, flourishing, and liberation. A political pastoral theologian, then, is concerned with whether programs actually meet the particular needs of individuals, families, and communities, especially considering times when the prevailing vision of the common good excludes some individuals or groups (e.g., persons in the United States illegally).

This task is important because, all too often, research is skewed because of political and economic ideological interests and political-economic gains. For example, states enact legislation and programs ostensibly aimed at creating more jobs, such as right-to-work legislation, yet these same laws foster conditions that lead to lower incomes and lower benefits for workers.[82] Consider also the work of Elizabeth Kolbert and Naomi Klein, which provides numerous illustrations of public-political figures who overlook, deny, or reject the massive amount of data and research that points to increase in greenhouse gases and the effects of global warming.[83] The failure to consider and rely on research to construct and assess programs and policies has led to, and will lead to, in the case of global warming, injustices and catastrophic failures to care for individual human beings, communities, and other living creatures.

These four tasks of a political pastoral theology, in my view, are shaped by three guiding principles: principles, I argue, are inherent in the cure-of-souls traditions and evident in the ministry of Jesus Christ. The first principle is compassionate realism, which, in my view, depends on caring dispositions and practices evident in the ministry of Jesus and a central feature of Christian discipleship. By realistic compassion, I mean: (a) an accurate recognition and understanding of the experiences and needs of persons and communities, (b) a willingness to be with and share, to some

not an expert, yet he threw himself into political, economic, and foreign policy matters throughout his long career and is often cited today by Democrats and Republicans.

82. Murphy, "Fact Sheet."

83. Klein, *This Changes Everything*; Kolbert, *The Sixth Extinction*.

degree, in the suffering of particular persons in need, and (c) the development of competent, caring policies and actions aimed at addressing the needs of particular others, as well as communities. Compassion is a necessary attitude and practice when it comes to issues of justice and notions of the common good. It is all too easy (on the one hand) to advocate for justice, either for a group's or an individual's rights, or for punishing those who have harmed others and at the same time (on the other hand) to see, construct, and treat Others negatively. Felons, for example, are often treated in very punitive ways by the criminal justice system, demonstrating the lack of compassion from the larger public.[84] With a similar lack of compassion, political protests can collapse into us versus them, furthering a deep divide. Two political pastoral theologians who practiced compassionate realism were Martin Luther King Jr. and Desmond Tutu. These men were realistic about the political-economic obstacles of their context. Both experienced a great deal of animosity from opponents, yet each advocated love and compassion for all people. Both demonstrated that care, as compassion, is not relegated simply to those of our group. All human beings, as God's children, merit respect and compassion.

Realistic compassion, as seen in the lives and ministries of King and Tutu, does not overlook injustices and harm done by other persons, which moves me to the second principle, namely, *prophetic* discipleship. The pastoral care tradition has included the prophetic features of care. Care of persons and communities often requires those who speak truth to power. Biblical prophets afflicted the powerful by speaking the truth while also offering consolation and hope to the afflicted. Martin Luther King Jr. was a modern prophet, exemplifying a type of political pastoral theology. King's pastoral concern or compassion led him to the truth that Vietnamese people are children of God and that they were suffering and dying as a result of U.S. military interventions. He was, at the same time, profoundly concerned about the souls of Americans who accepted and supported militarism and the arrogance of American economic and military power.[85] During the last year of his life, King criticized political leaders and sought to reveal the ugly truths about capitalism and American militarism. King's stance garnered considerable criticism from white and black leaders, resulting in further political isolation.[86] Nevertheless, King maintained his compassionate and prophetic stance. Developing and living out a political pastoral theology

84. See Alexander, *The New Jim Crow*; Gilligan, *Why Some Politicians Are More Dangerous than Others*.

85. King, *The Autobiography of Martin Luther King, Jr.*, 337–40.

86. Smiley and Ritz, *Death of a King*.

ideally involves adhering to the prophetic dimension of care—speaking truth to power while maintaining compassion realism.

This is, perhaps, most clearly seen in King's Riverside speech. He said, "I believe . . . the Father is deeply concerned especially for His suffering and helpless outcast children . . . We are called to speak for the weak, for the voiceless, for the victims of our nation, for those it calls 'enemy,' for no document from human hands can make these humans any less our brothers."[87] Practicing compassion and speaking truth to power means that political pastoral theologians have a special duty to care for those on the fringe of society, those who have no voice in the public sphere, those who lack political-economic means to participate in the public space of appearances, those who do not benefit from or who are excluded from the common good. The third principle, then, is *solidarity with the politically and socially disenfranchised*, including those who are harmed by the political and economic policies and the actions of their nation. The principle of solidarity requires an empathic imagination that can be indirect or direct. For instance, King did not have to travel to Vietnam to know the pain and suffering of the Vietnamese people, or of the soldiers fighting the war. More direct empathic imagination and solidarity comes across through King's participation in political protests and in his living with black people who suffered from segregation and racism.

A political pastoral theology, then, is best when conducted on the fringe of society. Some political theologians, such as Carl Schmidt,[88] were concerned about sovereignty. Schmidt's reflections came from the center of power and authority. The same could be said for Aristotle and Aquinas: both tended to provide philosophical and theological supports for already well-established political systems while also critiquing aspects of the political order. These three principles, grounded in the Christian mythos, necessarily move one away from merely focusing on centers of political and economic power. Instead, a political pastoral theology considers political-economic powers, structures, and institutions from the perspective of the "least of these." If the poor are surviving, thriving, and being liberated, then it is assured that the larger polis is functioning well. Of course, a political pastoral theologian can conduct the four tasks from the centers of power, but from those places it is more likely that s/he will be co-opted by and collude with these powers, neglecting or paying less attention to the poor and voiceless in society. Also, I do not think those who wield political and economic power need a political pastoral theologian to be in solidarity with them, given that

87. King, *The Autobiography of Martin Luther King, Jr.*, 339.

88. Hollerich, "Carl Schmidt."

they have a voice: they already possess political and economic influence; they construct and possess their own space of appearances. This does not mean, however, that political elites and the wealthy, as children of God, do not need respect and compassion, but they hardly need someone to speak for them or to lend support to their political and economic views.

Just as pastoral political theologians must work from the fringe of society, so political pastoral theologians must maintain what philosopher Simon Critchley calls an "interstitial distance" (a critical distance) from the state.[89] I am wary of providing theological justifications for a specific kind of political governance or institution. Instead, I see pastoral political theology as a theological, critical reflection on political matters and not as an attempt to construct a City of God on earth. Put another way, the goal of a political pastoral theology is not to baptize a set of political institutions: political institutions have plasticity; that is, "political institutions are anyway too fluid to assume an ideal form."[90] A political pastoral critique, however, may include a condemnation, theologically justified, of an entire political system, such as totalitarian political entities. In making these remarks, I confess to having a clear preference for democratic institutions, though I make no attempt to provide theological justifications for democracy. Instead, I focus on using the notion of care, theologically understood, to critique some of the political realities of our time.

In summary, a political pastoral theology, grounded in the Christian mythos, aims to understand and assess current political-economic narratives, issues, institutions, and structures, and to develop programs and policies that are themselves assessed and critiqued. A central interpretive framework for these aims is the notion of care, informed by the Christian tradition and the human sciences and aimed at the survival, flourishing, and liberation of individuals, communities, societies, and the earth. Care of the polis necessarily includes a concern about cooperation of diverse others, and thus a political pastoral theology must attend to the communicative practices of a society. In addition, a political pastoral theology aims to construct interventions or offer solutions to vexing public-political issues and to assess the effectiveness of these interventions. Finally, a political pastoral theology is rooted in three principles of the pastoral care tradition, namely, compassionate realism, speaking truth to power, and solidarity with society's disenfranchised. These three principles suggest that a political pastoral theologian reflects and acts from the fringe, away from the centers of political-economic power, with the premise that if the "least of these" are cared for, the polis will thrive.

89. Critchley, *Infinitely Demanding*, 111–14.

90. O'Donovan, "Political Theology, Tradition, and Modernity," 277.

2

CARE AND PASTORAL CARE AS POLITICAL CONCEPTS

It [the ideal of the personal] is a universal community of persons in which each cares for all the others and no one for him.[1]

As a farmer engages in varied actions of care in relation to the soil and its products according to the varying seasons of the year, so God administers entire ages of time, as if they were, so to speak, so many individual years, performing during each one of them what is requisite with a reasonable regard to the care of the world.[2]

The continuity of life and a sense of security in people's day-to-day lives are impossible without relations and networks of care and responsibility.[3]

Society has relinquished its caretaking function, demolished its institutions for supporting emotional development, and shifted priorities from the mental and emotional to the material. In the increasing violence around us, we may be seeing the causalities of this cavalier approach.[4]

1. Macmurray, *Reason and Emotion*, 159.

2. Origen, *Against Celsus*, chap. LXIX, *ANF* IV. 528, http://www.clerus.org/bibliaclerusonline/DE/gst.htm/.

3. Robinson, *The Ethics of Care*, 44.

4. Fonagy, "Male Perpetrators of Violence against Women," 1–17.

Love serves as the basis for our political projects in common and the construction of a new society. Without love, we are nothing.[5]

THERE IS A ROMAN fable about the creation of human beings that illustrates the relation between care and politics. The god Cura (Care), in the early morning hours, ambles along the river's edge. Where the water has receded, she notices some wet clay and in a burst of creativity molds a figure. Jupiter, also out for his morning constitutional, strolls by, and Cura asks him to breathe spirit into the clay figure, which he readily agrees to do. Delighted it is alive, Cura decides to name the creature, which annoys Jupiter because he believes he has the naming rights. The dispute heightens when the god Tellus jumps into the fray, arguing that since the creature was made of the earth, she should name it. To name the creature was not simply a divine narcissistic endeavor, but one that indicates who would have responsibility for the creature. Well past noon, with tempers flaring, it became evident that they were getting nowhere and they asked Saturn to come up with a solution, which he did:

> Jupiter, since you have given the spirit, take the soul after death: Tellus, since she provided the body, should receive the body. And since Cura first molded him, let Cura possess him as long as he is alive.[6]

The creation of the first human being was a political act, initiated by Cura, assisted by spirit and earth, argued about who had responsibility, and resolved by the wisdom of Saturn. Politics, in this fable, accompanies creation, and the very nature of this political creation and corresponding dispute is inextricably yoked to care. Care's creation initiates a political act, crisis, and resolution. In other words, care precedes politics and is an inevitable feature of it.

In this chapter, I consider the relation between care and politics. More particularly, I argue, along with care theorists,[7] that care and pastoral care are political concepts, though they are rarely in the foreground of political analyses. Toward this end, I begin by defining care and depicting its various features. This is followed by a discussion of pastoral care and how its specific characteristics align with and deepen philosophical understandings of care. By defining and describing care and pastoral care, I am in a position

5. Hardt and Negri, *Multitude*, 352.

6. In Hamilton, *Security*, 3–5.

7. See Held, *The Ethics of Care*; Noddings, *Caring*; Noddings, *Starting at Home*; Oliner and Oliner, *Toward a Caring Society*; Robinson, *The Ethics of Care*.

to discuss care as a political concept. In short, this chapter establishes the notion of care and its attributes as a hermeneutical and evaluative lens for assessing political-economic realities, which I make use of in later chapters.

CARE AND ITS ATTRIBUTES

Leonardo Boff indicates that the notion of care is derived from the Latin *cura*, and "in its most ancient form . . . was used within the context of relations of love and friendship."[8] Yet, in the Roman fable we learn that care precedes and makes possible human friendship and love. Indeed, care is essential to the very act of creation, and Cura is charged with the responsibility of caring for her creation until it dies, all of which suggests that care is a key anthropological category. Put differently, the Roman fable reveals the relation of care to both birth or natality and death.[9] Arendt makes a similar point when writing, "In this sense of initiative, an element of action, and therefore of natality, is inherent in all human activities [and] since action is the political activity par excellence, natality . . . may be a central category of political . . . thought."[10] Care, then, is necessary for creation, giving birth, sustaining life, and human flourishing.

In the Roman fable, the initiation of Cura and the resulting action of Jupiter were necessary for creating and sustaining the creature. Cura, along with Jupiter, created a space for the creature to appear as a human being. Moving away from the Roman gods, consider good enough parents who are involved in the creation of a baby—physically and psychologically. Even before birth, a good enough parent expresses care by taking care of her body, by preparing a place for the newborn, by taking pains to come up with a fitting name. Once the baby is born, the parents' care takes the forms of attunement, mirroring, and repair, all of which are necessary for sustaining life as well as fostering psychosocial growth. Indeed, parental care is necessary for the development of the capacities for self-reflection, social intelligence, and affect regulation.[11] Philosophically, one could say

8. Boff, *Essential Care.*

9. Hamilton, *Security*, 72–73.

10. Arendt, *The Human Condition*, 9.

11. There has been a great deal of infant-parent research during the last three decades that addresses the relation between care and psychosocial development. See Beebe et al., "Mother-infant Interactions"; Beebe and Lachmann, *Infant Research and Adult Treatment*; Bowlby, *A Secure Base*; Fonagy and Target, "Attachment and Reflective Function"; Fonagy et al., *Affect Regulation, Mentalization, and the Development of the Self*; Jurist, "Mind and Yours"; Sroufe, *Emotional Development*; Stern, *The Interpersonal World of the Infant.*

that the parents' attunement creates a space of appearances for the baby to express an unique, valued, inviolable sense of self. The withdrawal of care is traumatic, diminishing this interhuman space of appearances and human capacities for reflexiveness, psychological mindedness, and social engagement.[12] Worse, the loss of care leads to physical death.

The fable and the reality of a child's birth reveal the existential truth about care and human beings. We are dependent on the care of Others—Others create and sustain us psychologically and physically and we see this most clearly in birth (and in dying). To rephrase Descartes, "You care, therefore I am." Or "You care and therefore I am able to think 'I am.'" What precedes the very ability to say "I think therefore I am" is care. Care and knowledge (self and other) are inextricably related, which I discuss in greater detail below.

There are three other points I wish to raise about the illustrations of a child and the Roman fable. First, the child, like the clay creation, is born vulnerable, resilient, and dependent. As philosopher Ortega y Gasset indicates, babies are born open or existentially receptive to the parents' care, without which there is no survival, let alone thriving.[13] From a psychoanalytic developmental perspective, the infant's unadaptiveness to life aligns well with the parents' adaptation to the infant's needs.[14] While our ability to care for ourselves progresses and we hold onto the illusions of independence, existential vulnerability and dependence are never far away. In other words, if birth awakens us to the fact of our finitude and need of care, so too does the reality of dying and death. It is only in death that Cura is relieved of her charge, handing over the responsibility to Jupiter and Tellus. The second point is that infants are obviously unable to care for themselves or others. Human beings learn and develop the capacity to care because we have been cared for. This suggests that if there are "caring" genes, they would be akin to genes associated with language. For language to be activated, a child must be introduced to the spoken and written word, otherwise the ability to communicate will be significantly impaired. By analogy, our "caring genes" must be activated by the caring activities of others. This means that even our ability to care is dependent on the care of others. Third, care is fundamentally relational, which reveals the social and communal reality of being human. Human beings are not turtles, which are precocial; they hatch, crawl to the ocean, and develop without the aid of other turtles. We are altricial beings

12. See Corrigan and Gordon, "The Mind as an Object"; Hesse and Main, "Second-Generation Effects"; Schore, *Affect Regulation and the Repair of the Self.*

13. Ortega y Gasset, *Man and People*, 106.

14. See Winnicott, *Playing and Reality*, 10–12.

that are necessarily relational and in need of Others who care for our survival and psychosocial development.

In this creation fable, another sign of the existential reality of care is death. In the fable, after death Tellus receives the body and Jupiter the spirit. Across cultures and over the millennia, human beings care for their dead. Elaborate rituals, physical memorials, prayers are found in every society, expressing individual and collective concern for the dead. We, who consign the dead to the earth, offer hope that the spirits of the dead find rest. The point here is that the dead are beyond being the beneficiaries of our care, yet the motivation and disposition to care do not cease with death. The reality of death, in other words, cannot overcome the reality of human care.

Given these general comments about care and human existence, what is meant by care and what are its attributes? Milton Mayeroff offered a terse general definition of caring, writing that caring is helping the other person to grow,[15] which requires accurately seeing the actual condition.[16] This definition focuses on the individual, and the notion of growth is, as Mayeroff noted, admittedly vague.[17] Care theorist Joan Tronto's definition, while broad, moves away from a simple dyadic view of care and includes other important aims beyond growing. Caring, she argues, "is a species of activity that includes anything we do to maintain, continue, and repair our 'world' so that we can live in it as well as possible. That world includes our bodies, ourselves, and our environment."[18] Like any general definition, this covers a large swath of human activity, ranging from a nurse tending to an infant to public policies that make health care affordable and available to all. Building on and critiquing Tronto's definition, Daniel Engster suggests that care is "everything we do to help individuals meet their vital biological needs, develop or maintain their basic capabilities, and avoid or alleviate unnecessary or unwanted pain and suffering, so that they can survive, develop, and function in society."[19] In these definitions, care is an action, an activity that aims to sustain and develop individuals, families, communities, societies, and the environment.

There are other points to consider. First, it is important to highlight that Tronto and Engster acknowledge that the aim of caring activities is not mere functioning within a society. There may be occasions when helping people function within a society is not an act of care, either with regard to

15. Mayeroff, *On Caring*, 7.

16. Eagleton, *After Theory*, 131.

17. Ibid., 12–15.

18. Tronto, *Moral Boundaries*, 103.

19. Engster, *The Heart of Justice*, 28.

the individual or the larger society. For instance, aiding someone to function and adapt to a racist society or totalitarian regime would not fall under the heading of care. Caring activities, given this context, would include a critique of and political resistance toward sociopolitical structures and policies that inhibit care (and justice) and, as a result, undermine human flourishing. Second, these and other care theorists do not restrict the responsibility to care for a particular group or gender. All human beings are responsible for caring activities that contribute to human survival and flourishing—not mere functioning or adaptation.[20]

When we consider definitions of care, it can appear that care is understood in terms of the individual's survival and flourishing. This is a mistaken view given the necessity of families and communities in caring for individuals. That is, care necessarily requires caring for groups—families and communities—by which care emerges and depends. In the Roman Catholic tradition, for instance, the family is considered the cell or basis of community and society, which is addressed more fully below.[21] A brief example is helpful in illustrating this. In the late nineteenth century, the Vatican was critical of Western societies and capitalism because of the negative impacts on many parents who did not earn enough money to care for their children. Tragically, many desperate parents had their children work so that the family could survive.[22] Capitalism's undermining the family as an institution of care also undermined communities and their ability to care for members. Government leaders, in these documents, were obliged to develop policies, programs, and legislation to enable families and communities to care for their children.

I add here that care includes being concerned about the survival and flourishing of communities. There are manifold examples of political leaders creating legislation and policies that have crippling effects on communities. For instance, Jonathan Lear writes about the devastating effects of the United States government in relation to the Crow people.[23] Policies of ethnic

20. Held and Engster point out that care has often been feminized and restricted to what women do. Women are involved in activities that maintain, sustain, and repair selves, bodies, and so forth. This is, they rightly argue, a distortion of care because care is mostly restricted to one gender, indicating injustices within the larger sociopolitical system.

21. See, *Familiaris Consortio*.

22. See for example, Leo XIII, 1890, *Sapientiae Christianae*; Leo XIII, 1891, *Rerum Novarum*. Of course, these documents make use of a patriarchal and essentialized view of family life where the wife was to remain at home and care for the children. Regardless, the importance of a just wage and the survival and flourishing of families and communities were, in part, the aims of these pre–Vatican II documents.

23. Lear, *Radical Hope*.

cleansing, the forced education of indigenous children, and the denial of traditional practices were instituted across the United States and harmed individuals, families, and communities. A more recent illustration of the state's failure is seen in the justice system's treatment of African Americans, which Michelle Alexander details in her book *The New Jim Crow.*[24] In this work, Alexander describes the rise of legislation after the civil rights movement that disproportionately affected African American communities through the incarceration of black men, as well as punitive aftereffects once people leave prison. Two positive examples of how government leaders construct policies that help families and communities care for their members are the Earned Income Tax Credit (EITC) and the Women, Infants, and Children (WIC) program.

Another feature of care in Tronto's and Engster's definitions is that care is not necessarily restricted to direct interpersonal encounters. In an earlier work, Bubeck argued that "caring for is the meeting of the needs of one person by another person, where face-to-face interaction between the carer and cared-for is a crucial element of the overall activity and where the need is of such a nature that it cannot possibly be met by the person in need."[25] This is a narrow understanding of care, because, like Mayeroff's definition, it restricts care to face-to-face encounters. Of course, our deepest experiences of caring and being cared for are dependent on these interpersonal encounters, but care can also be indirect, especially when we consider global political realities and climate change. That is, I can care deeply about people in Sudan and work to find ways for them to have basic necessities for survival, yet never have met any Sudanese people. I can also care about unborn children of the next generation as I engage in activities aimed at caring for the well-being of our planet. Care, while in most cases is direct, can also involve indirect actions, which necessarily include those political actions that indirectly lead to concrete caring actions aimed at helping particular individuals and groups in need.

The definitions above highlight the fact that care is an activity, which raises a question about what makes up this activity. Caring activities entail five interconnected features, namely knowledge, motivations, dispositions, practices/skills, and virtues. Maurice Hamington writes that knowledge "is a *necessary condition* of care."[26] If knowledge is necessary for care, then what kinds of knowledge are fitting? This is a difficult question to answer because of the manifold contexts of human needs, yet at the most basic existential

24. Alexander, *The New Jim Crow.*

25. Bubeck, *Care, Gender, and Justice*, 129.

26. Hamington, *Embodied Care*, 44 (italics original).

level of caring knowledge is the knowledge of the Other as person—personal knowing.[27] Indeed, the foundation of all caring knowledge vis-à-vis human beings requires recognition of other human beings as persons.[28] It is this type of knowing that makes possible the space of appearances, and the space of appearances, I contend, necessarily implies caring activity. A good enough parent, for example, believes and knows that an infant is a person—without question. This knowledge is a necessary human construction that undergirds all forms of caring knowledge associated with appropriately attending to the infant's assertions. Occasions when this knowledge is absent abounds in human life and inevitably accompanies a lack or absence of care and, correspondingly, a collapse of the space of appearances. More egregious illustrations are the Holocaust, ethnic cleansings, and racism for instance. Less egregious but also damaging is the treatment of workers as objects, as cogs in the machine of a market society. In this scenario workers serve the market, and the market does not serve the flourishing of all persons. These negative examples show not only the essential connection between care and the knowledge of the Other as person, but also that this personal recognition is a human construction. The space of appearances, wherein the Other is invited to appear as a person—unique, valued, inviolable subject—is a human construction. Therefore, the space of appearances can also collapse, giving rise to acts of depersonalization that by definition are devoid of care and caring knowledge.

Another important feature of this existential personal knowledge undergirds direct and indirect caring activities. Recognizing the Other as a person involves attending to each individual's uniqueness, particularity, and immeasurability. By this I mean in the space of appearances the Other is particular in his or her uniqueness and value. The parent's recognition of her baby as a person contains both particular knowledge and an existential knowledge that the baby is beyond all representations and calculative quantification (immeasurable). Additionally, the notion of person carries with it immeasurability. That is, personal recognition points to the unrepresentable nature of the Other as person, and it is this immeasurable aspect of the Other as person that becomes the very condition for the receptivity of being moved by the Other's unique communications—knowing the particular Other as a person.[29] The parent's recognition of her baby as a person contains both particular knowledge and an existential knowledge that the baby

27. See Macmurray, *Persons in Relation*.

28. While here I am restricting care to human beings, I would argue that care for animals and for the earth requires a fundamental respect for the unique integrity of animals and inanimate objects of the earth.

29. See Ganis, *The Politics of Care in Habermas and Derrida*.

is beyond all representations and calculative quantification (immeasurable). Both particular knowledge and existential knowledge are foundational for a space of appearances. Indeed, existential immeasurableness of care is the ingredient that creates the space for the parent to be receptive to the baby's assertions. This, I contend, is a necessary foundation of caring activities where there is particular knowledge of the Other and the Other's needs, as well as an accompanying, usually hidden, knowledge that the Other as person is beyond being represented.[30] In this sense, care is unconditioned. There are, in other words, no strings attached; it is a gift.

Recognition vis-à-vis the Other as person includes general and specific or contextual physical, psychological, and cultural forms of knowing. A physician, for instance, has general knowledge of the workings of the human body, as well as specific knowledge of a patient's body—a patient who is recognized and treated as a person. This general and specific somatic knowledge is necessary if she is to care for the patient. Of course, knowledge of the body would also pertain to the nonexpert parent who has particular knowledge of a baby's body and concomitant needs—physical and psychological. Similarly, the psychotherapist possesses general knowledge of the working of the human psyche, which he obtained in graduate school and post-graduate internships. This general knowledge is made more specific when the therapist encounters a particular patient who suffers from depression and who has a unique history and psychology. Likewise, the nonexpert parent has knowledge of his/her infant's psychological world, which enables the parent to respond to the infant's unique psychological needs. I add here that psychological and physical knowledge accompanies cultural forms of knowledge. To recognize and meet the psychological and physical needs of people from other groups also requires knowledge of their culture. Implicit here is the notion that physical and psychological knowledge, while broadly speaking are universal, are also particular to an individual and the individual's culture. For instance, depression and schizophrenia are found in all cultures, yet the meanings associated with each and the activities of care surrounding both are culturally contingent.[31] For caring activities to be appropriate requires both general and specific forms of knowledge.

Psychological, somatic, and cultural knowledge are usually associated with the direct and immediate needs of persons. Other forms of knowledge are directly and indirectly necessary, at times, in caring activities. For example, Habitat for Humanity is an organization of volunteers who

30. Naturally, each person is represented by a name or names, yet no representation can capture the person.

31. See Frank, *Persuasion and Healing*; Sass, *Madness and Modernism*; Solomon, *The Noonday Demon*.

gather to construct homes for people in need. The homes provide shelter necessary for survival and human flourishing. Different types of knowledge are needed to meet families' needs for housing—engineering, electrical, construction, logistical, and administrative. These forms of knowledge are not typically considered caring forms of knowledge. Instead, they are forms of knowledge indirectly related to caring for particular persons. Another example is a lawmaker who writes a bill that will make it possible for citizens who cannot afford medical insurance to receive the medical care they need. The elected official has knowledge of the law, the insurance business, government, and the group of people who are without health care. We may imagine further that she does not know anyone directly who is in need of medical care, yet the lawmaker knows these people are persons who have medical needs. The forms of knowledge, which are contingent on the knowledge of Others as persons, the lawmaker uses are indirect yet directly impact the lives of others. These types of knowledge are necessary, but they are associated with indirect activities that meet the particular psychological and somatic needs of families. We might categorize these as ancillary forms of knowledge sometimes necessary in caring activities.

Direct and indirect knowledge of the Other qua person is a necessary feature of caring activities, yet it is also, from a developmental perspective, necessary for self-knowledge related to self-care. A child comes to know him- or herself because the parents recognize and treat the child as person, which includes attuning to the child's particular needs. Using Winnicott's notion of mirroring,[32] the good enough parent's caring activities include reflecting back to the child who the child is, which is necessary for the development of self-knowledge needed for the capacity for self-care. In addition, the child in relation to a caring parent eventually learns to recognize him- or herself and Others as persons, along with ways to care for Others. Children who grow up in relation to depriving and impinging parents not only have difficulty possessing accurate knowledge of themselves, but they also have difficulty accurately recognizing and acknowledging their needs and meeting them. Indeed, because of this deprivation, they develop negative self-representations (I am worthless—not a person), which accompany distortions vis-à-vis their needs (e.g., needs are equivalent to shame) and diminishment in their capacities for self-care. In addition, children who have been deprived of care have difficulty recognizing and treating others as persons, which accompanies the lack of capacity to care for others. For these people, therapy, in part, becomes a long process of the therapist consistently recognizing and treating the patient as a person, which can lead to

32. Winnicott, *Playing and Reality*, 111–18.

increased self-care capacities in the patient: these capacities include more positive and accurate self-representations and needs, along with behaviors aimed at meeting those needs.

Implicit in this discussion of the knowledge associated with caring activities is the notion of empathy. To recognize the Other as a person and to be receptive to the Other's unique expressions of needs, desires, and experiences points to the capacity for empathy.[33] I argue that all caring activities, whether direct or indirect, are dependent on the capacity to recognize the emotional experiences and needs of Others—empathy. As Maurice Hamington notes, since "the other's experience is not primordial to me, my imagination must create empathy to bridge the gap of alterity."[34] This bridge is connected to human imagination and is an ability inextricably yoked to knowledge of the Other as person[35] that is dependent on the Other's verbal and nonverbal communications. The parent, for instance, empathically imagines what her infant's cries of distress mean and then acts to meet the child's needs. The lawmaker who has no direct contact with the needs of the poor possesses empathy as she works with other lawmakers to enact legislation that will help poor persons survive and obtain assistance in finding meaningful work. Empathy, in short, is associated with direct and indirect caring activities. It also exists on a continuum from low to high. A surgeon who lacks bedside manner may have little empathy, but he must have some empathy in order to care effectively for the patient and the family.[36] The lawmaker may have only a little bit of empathy for poor people as she crafts a bill to meet their needs, but she must have some, even if it is screened by political ambitions. Without some empathy, caring activity does not seem possible.

33. See Hamington, *Embodied Care*, 70–72.

34. Ibid., 72.

35. Hamington cites Edith Stein's work on empathy, indicating that empathy is necessary for "knowledge of the existing outer world." I argue that it is more accurate to say that empathy is necessary for knowledge of the Other as a human being and, more particularly, as a person. Clearly, there are types of knowledge of the world that are not connected to being human or personhood. I would add here that empathy is necessary for caring activities, which, in the case of child development, leads to positive self-knowledge and capacities to care.

36. It is possible to imagine a robot that does surgery—a machine without empathy. Could we consider this a caring activity, given the robot's particular knowledge of the patient and general knowledge of the human body and surgery? I suspect that inventors will try to develop a machine that mimics empathy, because human beings, who are vulnerable, desire and need empathy. I would suggest that this situation would be care by proxy and an uncanny experience. The robot is merely a tool, which can meet some needs, but not the fundamental need to be recognized and treated as a person by other persons, especially when one is vulnerable.

Of course, we are aware that our empathic knowledge of the other and the psychosocial context can be incorrect. We may, in other words, recognize the Other as a person and empathically imagine his/her needs yet miss the mark. This is why Hamington argues that caregiving activities must include critical reflection vis-à-vis one's knowledge of the Other and the activity itself.[37] We see this in many caring professions where practitioners engage in critical reflection so that they may provide what we now call best practices. This is also true for good enough parents who listen and attend to their children's communications, consciously and unconsciously assessing the effectiveness of their caring actions. There is also critical reflection when we consider state and national policies intended to provide care for individuals and families. For instance, there is research on the effectiveness of SNAP (the Supplemental Nutrition Assistance Program).[38] Research, of course, can be manipulated for political purposes or not used to amend or add to programs or policies. Consider the fact that plenty of research reveals rising productivity of workers since the early 1980s, the stagnation of wages, and huge income inequality, all of which are due to neoliberal political-economic policies and laws beginning with the Carter and Reagan administrations.[39] This research is not used to help raise wages and benefits for working and middle-class people so that they can have the means to better care for their families and others. In this case, knowledge is not used to develop "best practices" and, worse, knowledge gained from critical research is even distorted by the imaginations of neoliberal advocates.[40]

In this discussion of knowledge of the Other as person vis-à-vis care I have neglected to mention object-oriented care. Human beings also care for various material things, as well as animals. For the moment, I depict care of material objects as object-care. The knowledge associated with object care should inform and be subordinate to the knowledge vis-à-vis care of other human beings as persons. For instance, a parent cares about maintaining the house, which may include keeping it relatively neat and clean. This requires object knowledge and should be aimed at providing a safe environment for the children. If a parent places object care in the foreground and children as persons in the background, then care for the children is distorted—as if the house and its condition are more important than the needs of the children. Of course situations emerge when object care may be primary, such as in an emergency room full of machines; here, knowledge of and

37. Hamington, *Embodied Care*, 75–78.

38. See fns.usda.gov/.

39. See Piketty, *Capital in the Twenty-First Century*; Reich, *Supercapitalism*.

40. See for instance Vauhini, "Tom Perkins and Schadenfreude in Silicon Valley."

care for machines may prevail for a time so that the machines function to save as many human lives as possible. As chapter 6 will note, care of objects and associated knowledge can undermine the knowledge necessary to care for persons. For instance, a business owner may care more about company profits, and care for workers is primarily in terms of their role in attaining surplus value. Object knowledge and care in this situation are fundamentally depersonalizing.

While object knowing is part of all forms of knowledge, personal knowledge, Maurice Hamington writes, "is a *necessary condition* of care," though it "is not a *sufficient condition*."[41] Other ingredients in caring must accompany knowledge. We must have knowledge in order to care for others, and we must have the motivation to use the knowledge for the sake of the other. I can recall occasions as a pastoral psychotherapist when I had the requisite knowledge to intervene effectively, yet because of fatigue and irritation, I lacked motivation, which resulted in a failure to care. This is also the case from more systemic perspectives. Knowledge is available and widespread about human behavior that is causing climate change, which, in turn, is harming and will continue to harm human beings and other species.[42] Yet many politicians and citizens do not act on this knowledge because, for a variety of reasons,[43] they do not have the motivation to do so. In some cases it is not only a lack of motivation. It is also, in my view, a deliberate attempt to distort knowledge. For example, proponents of the Keystone Pipeline and of the fracking fad disregard environmental degradation or distort information about its severity.[44] The distortion of knowledge corrupts or undermines motivation. Lack of motivation, then, can arise for many reasons, including self-deception and the distortion of knowledge necessary for care.

The motivation to care is closely allied to disposition. The *Merriam-Webster Dictionary* defines *disposition* as a "tendency to act or think in a particular way."[45] The foundation of any caring disposition is a receptivity to attend, listen to, and be moved by the expressed needs and experiences of persons and groups of people. This openness to learn from and respond to the Other(s) as persons can be both direct and indirect, as well as something shared with others. "Unless we are ready, receptive—and also, possibly, vulnerable," philosopher Gemma Corradi Fiumara writes, "the experience

41. Hamington, *Embodied Care*, 44 (italics original).

42. See Kolbert, *The Sixth Extinction*.

43. See Klein, *This Changes Everything*.

44. Ibid., 143–52.

45. http://www.merriam-webster.com/dictionary/disposition/.

of listening appears to be impossible."[46] Listening and caring, in this sentence, are synonymous—both depend on being receptive and open. A local church, for instance, listens to the news about the devastating earthquake in Haiti. After learning of the specific needs of the people of Haiti, the community sends relief supplies. The group's caring activities are contingent on being motivated and disposed to learn about and respond to the particular needs of the people of Haiti. Another example is a politician who, while also having other motivations, genuinely listens to her constituents and their needs, which, in turn, leads her to take to political actions that address their needs. I suspect we can all recall occasions when someone was genuinely receptive to our spoken or unspoken needs, as well as painful occasions when someone was lacking this disposition to care.

A motivation to care and a caring disposition are necessary for caring, but they are not always enough. At times people in an organization volunteer to care, and they have the knowledge, motivation, and even the disposition yet lack the skills. Similarly, people who are beginning in a helping profession may have the motivation, disposition, and some knowledge, but do not yet have the skills to effectively employ their knowledge. Care theorists, therefore, highlight the importance of skills/practices if care is to be effective. Nel Noddings suggests that one's motivation to care "pushes me to acquire skills in caretaking. But it is important to recognize that they *are* skills."[47] The intern, for instance, is motivated to develop skills as well as to deepen knowledge, so as to be effective. Virginia Held brings up another point. She argues that care "is a practice involving the work of care-giving and the standards by which the practices of care can be evaluated. Care must concern itself with the effectiveness of its efforts to meet needs, but also with the motives with which care is provided."[48] We want to know whether our caring actions are effective, and effectiveness is due largely to how skillful one is in employing requisite knowledge to care. Of course, skills are in many ways context dependent. For instance, the skills (and knowledge) necessary to meet the developmental needs of an infant are different from the skills required to treat a person's broken femur. Even within a particular caring profession, like psychotherapy, skills vary according to a particular diagnosis. For example, the skills needed to work effectively with people struggling with addictions are distinct from skills needed to aid psychotic patients. To be sure, there are areas of overlap, even as skills vary.

46. Corradi Fiumara, *The Other Side of Language*, 191.

47. Noddings, *Caring*, 122–23.

48. Held, *The Ethics of Care*, 37.

Caring skills do not simply fall under the heading of helping professions and their notions of best practices. Caring activities are routine. They are inextricably part of the web of mundane, daily activities necessary for both survival and flourishing. In general, we learn rudimentary skills of caring by being cared for and by caring for others as we grow up in our families. A father learns the skills to care for his daughter by being brought up by loving parents. As I indicated above, we are not born with skills to care but develop them by being cared for and caring for others. Individuals can also learn to improve their caring skills by recognizing a lack and deliberately attempting to alter their behaviors. The father of a daughter, for instance, recognizes that he had a distant relationship with his father and mother and he wants to have a closer relationship with his daughter. He may seek out the assistance of his partner, books, and therapy to deepen his knowledge and skills vis-à-vis his daughter. In addition, his critical reflection on his care and his daughter's response will serve to hone his skills. Effectiveness, in this instance, is assessed by whether the relationship deepens and whether the daughter flourishes in her relationship with him.

Several care theorists consider that internal to effective skills or practices are a number of virtues. Alasdair MacIntyre states that virtue is "an acquired human quality the possession and exercise of which tends to enable us to achieve goods which are internal to practices and the lack of which prevents us from achieving any such goods."[49] Virtue, we note, is something that someone possesses and exercises. The failure to exercise the virtue will result in its loss. Given this, what virtues are needed for effective caring actions? Daniel Engster argues that three virtues are central to caring activities, namely, attentiveness, responsiveness, and respect.[50] Attentiveness is being aware when someone is in need. Closely associated with attentiveness is responsiveness, which for Engster "means engaging with others to discern the precise nature of their needs and monitoring their responses to our care."[51] Here responsiveness suggests a collaborative interaction aimed at understanding and meeting the needs of the Other. The third virtue is respect and this, for Engster, involves recognizing the Other as an equal, worthy of our attention and care. In my view, coming from a different angle, this virtue is part of our recognizing and treating Others as persons—as unique, valued, inviolable, and agentic.

I have no quibble with Engster's three virtues. However, he neglects other important virtues. According Milton Mayeroff, there are essential

49. MacIntyre, *After Virtue*, 191.

50. Engster, *The Heart of Justice*, 30–31.

51. Ibid., 30.

features of our caring activities, which he simply calls ingredients of care, but these can also be understood as virtues.[52] Mayeroff notes eight features of care, five of which I consider to be virtues, namely, patience, honesty, humility, hope, and courage. A skillful caregiver possesses and exercises these virtues depending on the needs, experiences, and contexts of the person(s) in need. Let me briefly comment on each of these. John Keats's notion of negative capability is an excellent way to understand the virtue of patience. In a letter to his brother, Keats wrote that negative capability "is when a [human being] is capable of being in uncertainty, mysteries, doubts, without irritable reaching after fact and reason."[53] Care is the exercise of patience whereby one can contain not-knowing, which creates a space for the Other to appear, to express needs and experiences. Without the virtue of patience, it is unlikely that one can obtain accurate knowledge of the Other. The lack of patience is a common source of mistakes in caring.

The virtue of honesty, for Mayeroff, involves seeing oneself and the other clearly, as well as being accountable for one's mistakes, which usually requires the virtue of courage. Honesty means seeing clearly and being appropriately and sensitively forthright. Dishonesty, even for a good cause or for ostensibly good reasons, rarely results in effective care, and lying is more likely to reflect the caregiver's difficulty and not necessarily the other person. Recently a gentleman said that his older brother died and the siblings decided not to tell their mother, who would be turning 100 years old later in the summer. They feared the news of the death of her beloved son would kill her. They were understandably concerned about their mother and wished her to live longer. They overlooked the fact that she had lived through the Great Depression, World War II, the Korean War, and the deaths of her husband and friends. They did not see her as emotionally resilient and, as a result, were not making it possible for her to express her care and love for her son by grieving. In this situation, the virtue of courage was needed to overcome anxiety and fear represented in their being dishonest. Stated differently, courage is not the absence of fear and anxiety but the ability to act for the Other's good despite fear. To care often requires honesty and courage to be attentive and responsive.

Closely associated with the virtues of courage and honesty is that of humility. Humility means facing and accepting oneself as one is, which includes acknowledging strengths, limitations, and mistakes. Indeed, humility is necessary for creating a space to accept and learn from the Other—the

52. Mayeroff, *On Caring*, 23–35.

53. Letter John Keats wrote to George Keats, quoted in Bion, *Attention and Interpretation*, 125.

space of appearances. Negatively stated, arrogance forecloses the space of appearances and undermines care. An arrogant person may have the knowledge and motivation to care, but an arrogant disposition means the person will have difficulty recognizing and taking accountability for mistakes. Put another way, an underlying motivation to retain a sense of superiority will interfere with creating a space for the Other to express desires, experiences, and needs, as well as to offer needed corrections. In his recent book *The Tyranny of Experts*, William Easterly provides numerous examples of concerned people who "know" what will help poor people without really listening to them.[54] The experts have ostensibly good intentions and dispositions, which hide an underlying hubris. This top-down approach, in other words, reveals the occult arrogance of people of privilege who believe they know better and therefore do not need to gather direct knowledge from individual poor people. Easterly was not arguing that these groups were complete failures, because there were also some important successes. However, a lack of specific, local knowledge of the people they sought to serve led to unintended failures and, in some cases, created more problems, which experts overlooked or denied. Their lack of humility, then, impeded their knowledge of the people in need and their resulting acts of care.

Finally, genuine care embodies the virtue of hope, even in situations of hopelessness. In routine acts of care, hope is necessarily present because without hope one would not have the motivation or disposition to care. Something as simple as a parent hearing her child cry and responding with comfort and food displays the hope that the mother's knowledge and skills will meet the need. In more rare situations, where there is no hope that a need will be met (someone will not survive or flourish), the virtue of hope is still necessary to care. There were occasions when, as a chaplain, I sat with people who were dying from cancer. There was no hope for cure. Some patients had hope they would be with God, while others did not possess this hope. In each instance, my hope was not in any idea that my caring acts would lead to cure. Rather, my hope was to be with them in the fear, uncertainty, and anguish of dying without giving false assurances. Put another way, my hope, theologically understood, was that I might in some small way incarnate the love and compassion of God in the face of darkness and the mystery of death.

In summary, care refers to activities or practices that are aimed at meeting individuals' and families', vital biological needs, developing or maintaining "their basic capabilities, and avoid or alleviate unnecessary or unwanted pain and suffering, so that they can survive, develop, and function

54. See Easterly, *The Tyranny of Experts*.

in society."[55] Care, I argued, is aimed not simply at persons' survival and flourishing but also at families and communities—those social entities from which the individual emerges. There are key features in any effective caring activity. To care effectively necessarily requires *personal* knowledge of the individual, family, or community and their particular needs, experiences, and cultural beliefs and values. Personal knowledge entails the view that the Other, as person, is immeasurably valued and that care, in an ideal sense, is unconditioned. Other forms of knowledge (somatic, psychological, social, cultural) are necessary for caring activities. Lack of knowledge or inadequate knowledge is a prelude to acts of care that fail to achieve the aim of survival or flourishing. Nevertheless, as Hamington notes, knowledge is necessary but not sufficient, which means there are other crucial features of caring activities. One also needs to have the motivation and disposition to care—a desire to care and the receptiveness to be moved by the experiences and needs of the Other(s). Naturally, one can imagine instances when an individual has the knowledge, motivation, and disposition to care, but lacks the skills. While skills are often transferrable from one context to another, it is important to recognize that a caregiver needs to adjust or make alterations in skills given the particular knowledge gained in relation to a unique individual. Last, effective caring skills are contingent on the possession and exercise of five virtues, namely, patience, honesty, humility, hope, and courage.

PASTORAL CARE

The above philosophical depiction of care and its attributes can easily fall under the umbrella term of *pastoral care*, though, of course, framed in theological language. I do not feel the need to repeat the above, grounding it in a theological anthropology. Instead, I provide a definition of pastoral care and a few theological concepts that expand and deepen our understanding of care, which will also serve as a foundation for understanding care as a political concept.

In their historical survey of the Christian traditions, Clebsch and Jaeckle define pastoral care as "the ministry of the cure of souls [which] consists of helping acts, done by representative Christian persons, directed toward the healing, sustaining, guiding, and reconciling of troubled persons whose troubles arise in the context of ultimate meaning and concerns."[56] While not stated in this definition, it is clear that pastoral care is likewise concerned

55. Engster, *The Heart of Justice*, 28.

56. Clebsch and Jaekle, *Pastoral Care in Historical Perspective*, 4.

about persons' survival and flourishing. Their definition, however, appears to restrict caring activities to those who are recognized and authorized to do so. These representative persons, we presume, possess the requisite knowledge, disposition, habits, and skills to perform acts of healing, guiding, sustaining, reconciling, and resisting.[57] To be sure, churches do set apart people to serve in varied ministries of care, but it is also important to recognize that by virtue of baptism and discipleship, all Christians are, to the extent of their abilities, obliged to care for Others, regardless of the Other's religious faith or absence of religious faith. This obligation to care is not rooted simply in the fact of our existential dependency[58] and vulnerability[59] but rather in creation's dependence on the creator. To care is an ontological obligation.

I want to say a bit more about obligation by taking a quick detour to French philosopher Emmanuel Levinas, who has influenced such theologians as Edward Farley[60] and John Zizioulas.[61] This detour will help highlight some of the differences between the philosophical notion of care above and pastoral care. Levinas, eschewing religious language, though clearly influenced by his Jewish education and faith, attempts to move beyond ontology to express the human obligation to respect and care for the Other. Using the metaphor of face, he contends that the face of the Other imposes an infinite obligation to care. For Levinas, "The face to face is a final and irreducible relation which no concept could cover."[62] As an irreducible relation, "The face," Levinas writes, "opens the primordial discourse whose first word is obligation."[63] Using more colloquial language, he states that the "face of a neighbor signifies for me an unexceptionable responsibility, preceding every free consent, every pact, every contract. It escapes representation."[64] The Other is irreducible to any concept or representation and, for Levinas, this fact of being beyond language accompanies an infinite obligation to care. It is this obligation that opens a space for the face of the Other to appear—unconditionally.

Before moving to another feature of Levinas's philosophy, I consider his notion of the face in light of the Judeo-Christian idea of *imago dei* and its

57. The pastoral function of resisting refers to acts of caring compassion whereby people confront and resist oppressive forces and institutions. See, Ramsay, "Compassionate Resistance," 217–26.

58. Engster, *The Heart of Justice*, 48–52.

59. Pulcini, *Care of the World*, 165.

60. See Farley, *Divine Empathy*.

61. See Zizioulas, *Being as Communion*; Zizioulas, *Communion as Otherness*.

62. Zizioulas, *Communion as Otherness*, 291.

63. Levinas, *Totality and Infinity*, 201.

64. Levinas, *Otherwise Than Being*, 88.

relation to the obligation to care. Levinas's philosophy, in my view, is closely linked to and, in many ways, emerges out of his Jewish faith, which is why I believe Jewish and Christian theologians have found him so amendable to their own work. The notion of *imago dei* implies that there is an un-representable aspect of being human—an Otherness that defies thematization—a transcendent Otherness. The Other as created in the image and likeness of God places an obligation to respect, be concerned about, and care for the Other's inherent dignity. Here is where the Roman fable falls short. The created, passive being is cared for by the gods, but there is no sense of any obligation to care from other human beings. By contrast, the Judeo-Christian stories of creation suggest that human beings, as created in the image and likeness of God, are obliged to care for each other precisely because each human being retains this spark of God—the face of God, if you will. We are created to care for each Other, and it is our obligation to care that points to human agency in participating in ongoing creation. Acts of care vis-à-vis Others reveal God's ongoing creation—incarnation as creation. While on earth, we are all Cura to each other.

Obligation, then, does not emerge simply from our existential dependency (I am obliged to care for Others because I needed, and need, their care to survive and thrive). The idea that obligation extends from our dependency is articulated in Daniel Engster's book *The Heart of Justice*. In his view, an individual is indebted by virtue of the fact that others cared for that individual. I care because you cared for me, which has a hint of a contractual obligation. Certainly there is an element of this in life, but Levinas's notion of the face and the idea of *imago dei* go beyond dependency and contract. Our obligation to care is infinite in the sense of being part of our very existential DNA as human beings. It is, then, woven into our very agency and in the fact that the Other as Other obliges our concern, our respect, our hospitality. And this obligation to care is not discriminate or conditioned. We are obliged to care for our family members, our fellow citizens, those who are like us. But the radical command and obligation includes caring for any human being, including enemies and those who are not like us. This is evident in Judeo-Christian Scriptures where God commands us to love not only our neighbors but our enemies. To have an enemy does not, then, negate this ontological obligation, though to be sure we can use our agency to deceive ourselves that we do not need to care, which, more often than not, we tend to do. This is a more radical sense of obligation than noted in care theories that focus on dependency and vulnerability as sources of our obligation to care.

There is another key point in this formulation of care. The un-representable face of the neighbor and the responsibility to care for the neighbor are, for Levinas, inextricably joined to the family and social (fraternity) life. He writes, "The relation with the face in fraternity, where in his turn the Other appears in solidarity with all others, constitutes the social order, the reference of every dialogue to the third party by which We encompasses the face to face opposition, opens the erotic upon a social life."[65] In my view, Levinas's face (or *imago dei*) points to an infinite obligation that founds social forms of living. Put another way, caring for the Other, which involves recognizing and treating the Other as a person—an inviolable, valued, unique, and agentic subject—*founds societal and communal life.*[66] This is fitting in any definition of pastoral care, because pastoral care emerges from and is inextricably linked to the *ecclesia*. It is not, in other words, simply that care is necessary for survival and flourishing of community; it is that care and community, from a Judeo-Christian anthropological perspective, are entwined. Care founds community, yet care also emerges from community. This particular view is absent from care theorists' notions of care.

Levinas's view of obligation and Judeo-Christian commands to love one's enemies and to care for widows and orphans (those on the fringe of society) suggests that while care is foundational to human survival and flourishing, it can also be refused. While finite, human beings have agency and some measure of freedom. Illustrations abound in the present and past of people refusing to care. The parable of the Good Samaritan reveals the all-too-common reality of people who should care but do not. When we turn to the present and our own lives, we find instances when we chose not to care, whether that involved someone we were in direct contact with or those suffering from afar. Pastoral care and its specific activities of care (healing, guiding, and so forth) contain a command or infinite obligation as well as the human freedom to care. This freedom to ignore or reject one's obligation to care, while individual, is also communal. The *ecclesia* can decide to not care for a group of people within or outside the group. For example, some Christian communities have rejected gay and lesbian persons, going so far as to actively deny them certain civil rights. More positive examples are churches that were involved in the sanctuary movement during the 1980s, caring for people from war-torn countries such as Nicaragua and El Salvador. These churches illustrate the collective aspects of freedom and obligation vis-à-vis care.

Before moving to the last two features of pastoral care that broaden the discussion of care above, I want to say a bit more about the communal dimension of care, which is evident in scriptural metaphors, such as the

65. Levinas, *Totality and Infinity*, 280.

66. See Zizioulas, *Communion and Otherness*.

body of Christ and the kingdom of God. These metaphors have often been used in relation to discussions about the community of faith and its polity. In my own Roman Catholic tradition, Church documents are peppered with these metaphors, which highlight the communal aspects of Christian life, the political organization of this community, and the belief and hope that present communal realities have some connection to the kingdom of God in heaven. Despite the many failed attempts at community and their polities, there is an anthropological truth, and it is that human beings are not simply social animals; we are communal. The metaphors body of Christ and kingdom of God, in my view, represent both the promise of God's care for human beings in community and the necessity of human care vis-à-vis each other. John Macmurray, echoing Saint Paul, remarked about the ideal community where "each cares for all others and no one for himself."[67] It is in caring for one another that God's concern is incarnated in the present beloved community.

Two more related features of pastoral care help round out this discussion. Paul exhorts the congregation "not to look to your own interests, but to the interests of others. Let the same mind be in you that was in Christ Jesus, who, though he was in the form of God, did not regard equality with God as something to be exploited, but emptied himself, taking the form of a slave, being born in human likeness."[68] In this passage, the term "emptied" is taken from the Greek *kenosis*, which is used in conjunction with the notion of incarnation. God becomes human and, in the process, there is a decision, an action, to empty Godself in order to create a space to become fully human. This is what theologian Edward Farley calls divine empathy.[69] Divine empathy is an act of divine communicative care and one where there is a decision to empty Godself of anything that would interfere with becoming embodied. That is, divine empathy creates a space of appearances that makes possible, in fragmentary ways, forms of communion between human beings and God. Care as communion necessarily means recognition of the Other as a unique, inviolable, valued, responsive subject—theologically, *imago dei*—and this means emptying oneself of any representations that interfere with the reality of the un-representable, immeasurable Other. Metaphorically, divine empathy involves a self-emptying to take on the

67. Macmurray, *Reason and Emotion*, 159. This is, of course, an ideal that Macmurray recognized. Moreover, he was not suggesting that individuals not care for themselves. We are to care for ourselves, but Macmurray's comment is an attempt to move us away from our preoccupation with egoist concerns. I will say more about this in chapter 3 in the discussion of care and justice.

68. Phil 2:4–7.

69 Farley, *Divine Empathy*.

emotional experiences and needs of being human. It is a radical receptivity, a radical openness to create a space where the need for communion can be partially realized.

Nel Noddings, while ignoring the religious dimensions of Simone Weil's work, quotes Weil: "This way of looking is first of all attentive. The soul *empties itself* of all its contents in order to receive the being it is looking at, just as he is, in all his truth. Only he who is capable of attention can do this."[70] Weil is pointing out the human necessity of *kenosis* for one to encounter and receive the Other as is and not as one wishes or expects to know the Other. While it is laudable to include a religious figure in her discussion of care, Noddings ignores important dimensions of care and *kenosis* crucial to understanding pastoral care. That said, the human ability to empty oneself, to be empathic, is a feature of the *imago dei* and, thus, divine empathy.

While I addressed the notion of empathy above, *kenosis* is a disposition and virtue necessary for empathy expressed in compassion. In terms of pastoral care, *kenosis* and empathy have three implications. First, care is not simply an existential reality related to human life. Care has transcendent roots in acts of creation and the incarnation of God's love and compassion in the life and ministry of Jesus Christ. It is God's self-emptying that makes possible the incarnation of God's embodied love or care. Second, as pastoral caregivers, we are, in our own limited ways, called to incarnate God's care by deciding to empty ourselves of anything that impedes us from being empathic, which, theologically speaking, requires God's grace to courageously accept and appreciate the incommensurate reality of the Other as person.[71] While we need categories and representations of Others to care, we are obliged to empty ourselves of representations that interfere with our ability and willingness to recognize the Other as a person, *imago dei*—un-representable and immeasurable. It seems, then, that empathy and compassion are possible only if we are willing and able to empty ourselves or set aside representations that interfere with recognizing the Other's needs and experiences. Theologically, grace provides the strength and courage for *kenosis* and for encountering the Other as mystery without the irritable reaching after fact (representation) and reason. Third, empathy is fundamental to the creation of the space of appearances wherein the Other is invited to be cared for and to develop a form of communion. It is this space of appearances that inaugurates, theologically stated, the social covenant of care between God and humanity, as well as social and communal relations between and among human beings.

70. Noddings, *Starting at Home*, 35.

71. Cook, "Empathy," 29–38.

It is necessary to move from this high plane of theological, abstract discourse vis-à-vis *kenosis* to the more mundane, difficult realities of human life and care, For a human being to be able to empty oneself or to set aside beliefs, concepts, or representations that will impede empathy requires the disciplines of self-awareness and making use of oneself for the sake of the Other, and both are contingent on grace. Effective pastoral care, in other words, means that one is aware of one's representations of the Other and is able to set those aside when they interfere with an act of care. The Samaritan's ability to care for the wounded man meant he had to set aside any representations that would interfere with his caring and to set aside his agenda (business aims) to make time to care. In other words, to the Samarian the wounded man was a person, immeasurably valued, and thus his care was unconditioned. It was his empathic care—his emptying himself of anything that would obstruct care—that led to treating wounds and insuring the victim's recovery. Put another way, in emptying himself, the Samaritan empathically created a space for the Other to appear as a person in need of care. Implicit in this story is the grace the Samaritan relied on to empty himself of hindrances to care.

This view of *kenosis* and empathy parallels theorists' views on caring activities; yet philosophical renderings of care do not have a spiritual/transcendent or religious dimension. From my perspective, theological groundings of care bring forth the transcendent aspects of care and a corollary view of the need for grace and conversion in our caring for Others. That is, to care, individually and collectively, requires going beyond ourselves and embracing the un-representable, immeasurable reality of the Other—the mystery of the Other that obliges our unconditional respect and care. I add here that the transcendent feature of care suggests that to care, in many instances, is dependent on grace that strengthens motivation and the disposition of receptivity. Similarly, grace gives one the temerity to set aside one's representations of the Other for the sake of creating a space for the Other to appear, to express needs, experiences, and gifts. Empathy, then, entails the grace to handle the paradox of knowing and not-knowing, and this not-knowing is the self-emptying that is requisite for one to develop the knowledge of the Other as person. Implicit in the parable of the Good Samaritan is his faith in God, which gives him the strength to be receptive to the suffering of another human being, the motivation and knowledge to stop, bind wounds, and ensure that the man has the resources to heal. In pastoral care, there are times when care is the grace of conversion. In seeing the Other, the caregiver (or community) draws on grace to set aside preconceived representations of the Other and to be receptive to the Other's assertions and self-representations, which gives one the knowledge necessary to care. There is, from a pastoral care perspective, something transcendent and unconditional about the activity of caring, and in acts of care we are often changed.

In summary, a pastoral care perspective highlights the ontological obligation to care as seen in the notion of *imago dei* and the commands to love one's neighbors and enemies. The un-representable and immeasurable face of the Other and the corresponding obligation to care are inextricably yoked to community. Individual obligation and freedom (to care or not) are located in a community free to accept and act on this ontological obligation inextricably joined to the unconditioned aspect of care. Put another way, care is required for a viable community, and yet care also emerges from community. The foundation of the concrete activity of care involves *kenosis*—self-emptying—and *kenosis* is a feature of empathy, which invites a space of appearances for the Other to assert and express unique, inviolable, subjectivity and to have needs respected and, if necessary, met. I claimed that self-emptying and empathy, which requires a degree of selflessness and courage, depend on grace. In short, there is a transcendent aspect of the activity of caring.

CARE AND PASTORAL CARE AS POLITICAL CONCEPTS

We have finally arrived at a place where we can consider the relation between politics and care or, more specifically, the issue of care as a political concept, though there have been allusions to care as a political concept above. Care theorists have argued that care is a political concept for the last three decades and have sought to use care as a hermeneutical and critical lens vis-à-vis government institutions and social-political policies and programs. This critical lens is aimed at bolstering state institutions in their efforts to foster caring activities in the society, as well as to develop programs that foster the common good.[72] As Nel Noddings argues, government institutions should be "instrumental in establishing the conditions under which caring-for can flourish."[73] These care theorists are attempting to alter the discourse in political theory to include the concept of care.[74] This

72. See Engster, *The Heart of Justice*, 70–75.

73. Noddings, *Starting at Home*, 22.

74. Michael Hardt and Antonio Negri in their book *Commonwealth* argue that love is an essential concept for politics, because it is central in the establishment of what they call the common—the shared material and created resources. Similarly Terry Eagleton (*After Theory*) and Martha Nussbaum (*Political Emotions*) contend that love is a necessary political concept. I view love and care as related but distinct concepts. Love includes care, but care does not necessarily include love. I can care about people I

said, they, by and large, are not arguing that care has not been a part of the political-social fabric and attending institutions. Indeed, governments and many other social institutions implicitly have some elements of care with regard to the populace, simply because the absence of care would not only highlight a failed state but a failing society.[75] Of course, typically the discourse is centered on whether the state is fostering a just society, respecting and promoting rights, and attempting to address the common good. The notion of care, however, is nearly nonexistent in public-political discourse, though it may be latent in some government policies that help families and communities care for their children. Care theorists, in my view, are arguing that the notion of care, while implicit in political realms, should be an overt, intentional framework for analysis of a society and its institutions; a concept used in the development of laws, regulations, policies, and programs that address the needs of citizens; and an aim that leaders of government and social institutions seek to foster vis-à-vis social relations.[76]

This brief background does not yet address what is peculiar with regard to care as a political concept and value or how and why it should be a concept we use vis-à-vis the political realm. While I rely on care theory discourse, I do not seek to repeat it in detail or demonstrate the strengths and weaknesses of the arguments, which has been done elsewhere.[77] Instead, from the perspectives on care and pastoral care above, I outline my own argument for care as a political concept and value.

The discussion above on care and pastoral care reveals that care is a foundational reality of human life and is, therefore, a constitutive feature of philosophical and theological anthropologies. Care, in other words, founds interpersonal relations wherein individuals recognize and treat each other as persons, which, for every individual human being, begins at birth and

---

have never met, while sending them aid. The Samaritan cared for the injured man, but I do not think he loved him. Some might try to make the case that he did love him, but this is love in the abstract. A physician or nurse can care for someone who she thinks is despicable. There is care, but no love. Care, then, from my perspective is more a fundamental human reality and a more fundamental political concept. I believe, then, that developing and maintaining caring attitudes and behaviors in society are more realistic goals than love. Care for others, for neighbors, is more likely and more common than love. See Hardt and Negri, *Commonwealth*, 179–88; Eagleton, *After Theory*, 168–70.

75. For instance, many countries have governments that have knowledge of impoverished citizens who struggle to afford food and health care and use this knowledge in developing programs to meet some of those needs.

76. I wish to note that some care theorists extend the notion of care to global settings and the interactions between nation-states. See Pulcini, *Care of the World*; Robinson, *Globalizing Care*.

77. Engster, *The Heart of Justice*, 67–116.

ends at death.[78] From the beginning of life, then, a child is thrown into a family wherein good enough parents create a space of appearances so that the child will survive and thrive. It is through the good enough care of the parents that the child eventually comes to experience him- or herself as an individual who is joined to other individuals—persons. The most basic unit of human association, where we see the essential existential reality of care, is the family.[79] Yet families rarely exist as isolated units.

Throughout human history, families are part of larger units, such as clans or tribes. These larger human associations are formed usually for reasons of protection and security—survival. Indeed, it is difficult to imagine a lone family of four trying to survive relying on their own resources. Thus, care that founds the interpersonal relations within a family, similarly, as Levinas argues, founds the social relations of larger entities such as clans. As clans and tribes form, they must have ways of organizing themselves, developing leadership roles and institutions for regulating group life, which are enshrined in group rituals and narratives. A group of elders, for example, may function as a council to a chief or tribal leader who has been chosen by the council or the members of the clan. When human beings began forming into tribes and clans, it was the beginning of the polis: they were and are political entities. Of course, tribes can, and often do, form alliances, gradually merging into more complex societies and more intricate political realities. In short, families cooperate with other families and form tribes or clans, which, in turn, form a more complex social entity—polis.

In chapter 1, I indicated that Hannah Arendt, like Aristotle, stresses that political and public institutions involved in individuals living together possess, ideally, the aims of surviving and thriving. That is, as social or political animals, we need to create the polis's institutions wherein the common good reflects both survival and the pursuit of the good life.[80] This polis is made up of particular created institutions, rules, regulations, and laws for ordering life lived in common, and all of this creative activity depends

78. It is more accurate to say before birth and after death. Good enough parents are already constructing the infant as a person before birth and caring families, and communities treat the dead with dignity, honoring the person who died.

79. The definition of family varies from time to time and culture to culture, but every culture has some notion of family wherein children are born and taken care of.

80. Naturally, the meaning of the good life varies, even within the same polis, yet the idea of the good life becomes part of the discourse that attempts to arrive at some degree of consensus. Also, in reading Aristotle's *Politics*, it becomes clear that we consider who has the power to decide not only what is the good life, but who participates in and who is excluded from public-political discourse. Thus, the idea of and discourse about the good life is closely connected to political power and to who is allowed to engage in the political realm.

on *politics*—broadly, the actions and communications of its citizens. In addition, I pointed out that a polis comprises social rituals, structures, narratives, disciplines, and discourses that inform citizens (and noncitizens) about whom to trust and where their loyalties lie; they provide a shared identity that is crucial to making ethical decisions or assigning standards to social practices; they signify and make licit, for good or ill, the kinds of authority, power, privilege, and prestige meted out in diverse social contexts; they represent the good aims citizens are to pursue and the sanctions that result when the pursuit fails (e.g., justice); they determine and distribute various social goods; they shape who we care for and how we care in the public sphere.

Care, then, is not only foundational for the survival and thriving of a family; it is, as well, for the larger community and society—the polis—in which the family resides. This is not unidirectional. The society or polis depends on the survival and thriving of those basic cells of social life—families—and families depend on a functioning polis. Consider less complex[81] societies or groups depicted in Erik Erikson's book *Childhood and Society* and Jonathan Lear's book *Radical Hope*.[82] Erikson describes the Yurok tribe and the collectively held narratives and attending social practices around caring for children. These narratives were not simply tied to caring for infants, but were part of the tribe's identity and vision for living a life in common. That is, Yurok parental care of their children was linked to larger social structures and ways of governing and ordering their society. There was an interdependence between the individual family and the larger Yurok polis. A similar example is Lear's depiction of the Crow people, who suffered terribly at the hands of white European invaders who, in various ways, undermined their rituals and stories, as well as the tribe's resources to provide care for its members. Nevertheless, the Crow people struggled to retain the social practices and structures (e.g., the structure of chief and elders) that had helped the tribe survive. Evident in these examples of less complex societies is the underlying reality of care manifested in each group's stories, rituals, and institutions, all overtly or covertly aimed at fostering survival and flourishing of the tribe and, in particular, its families. Perhaps the relation between care and the polis is more evident in smaller, "primitive" (oral tradition–based) groups where actions of members have clearer connections to the actual survival and thriving of its members.

81. The notion "less complex" has nothing to do with the odious term primitive. Less complex means non-pluralistic and ideologically homogenous societies, which have with greater face-to-face interactions.

82. Erikson, *Childhood and Society*, 176–84; Lear, *Radical Hope*.

The necessity of care vis-à-vis families and the larger social group's narratives, rituals, and institutions is also evident in Jewish Scripture. We read the stories of God's covenant with Israel, wherein God cares for this group of people vis-à-vis survival and well-being (leading the people to a land of milk and honey). God's covenant of care founds the caring relations of the people of God—the tribes of Israel. In addition, struggles and changes in how this group organizes and governs itself (e.g., through judges and kings) were inextricably linked to this covenant of care.[83] Of course, the theological renderings of God's care for the chosen people also reflect, at times, the troubling absence of care for non-Israelites, as well as those who broke the covenant. Nevertheless, the covenant reflects God's ongoing care for the Israelite people, and it is this care that was/is integral for the survival and flourishing of Jewish community and society.

Christian scriptures also reflect in part the notion of care vis-à-vis families and the larger social group. In the book of Acts, we read the story of how a fledgling religious group is faced with the question of governance, survival, and care.[84] Members are to give their money, gifts, and talents to the group so that individuals and families may survive and thrive.[85] And we learn the dire consequences when a couple decides to withhold goods that could be used for those in need of resources to care for their families. The letters of Paul are also concerned about group organization and care of its members. God's care, then, experienced in the incarnation reflects a promise of care for individuals who share life in an *ecclesia*. In the stories of the Torah and Christian Scriptures we note the prevalence of care in relation to individuals and families, but more importantly to larger political entities.

In more complex, pluralistic, and ideologically diverse societies, care can become less clear as a political concept or value, perhaps because the notions of justice and rights take prominence as diverse individuals and groups compete for resources and power. The notion of care, in other words, can get easily lost in the politics of the day. Nevertheless, there is a latent thread of care in politics, even if it expressed rhetorically (e.g., by politicians who express concern about their children's children).

Whether we are talking about a clan or a nation-state, the basic cell of each is the family, and the family exists and has its being in care vis-à-vis the larger group. Without support from the larger society and its institutions, many families, especially those with few resources, will struggle to care for each other. Put differently, without good enough parents who possess the

83. Walzer, *In God's Shadow*.

84. Boer, *In the Vale of Tears*, 112–21.

85. Capper, "Jesus, Virtuoso Religion, and the Community of Goods," 76–80.

material and psychological resources to create a space of appearances in caring for their children's survival and flourishing, the family will fail or cease to exist. As child psychiatrist Donald Winnicott noted, parents who hold and handle their infants need to have the support of the community and society so that they can care for their children.[86] Failed or failing families mean that children will struggle in adulthood to care for their own children. Care is foundational for interpersonal life, and the family is the basic human association where this is realized. Any larger human collective, whether a tribe or a more complex diverse society, cannot survive or thrive without direct and indirect care of families. To be sure, care will continue to occur in families where tribal institutions or government institutions fail to be concerned about the common good and the needs of families. This said, a failed or failing state, while not obliterating the possibility of care, will make care much more difficult to realize, because parents and other family members will not have the necessary resources to care.

So, there are four key points in my argument. First, care is central to human life—interpersonal relations. Second, care is most profoundly experienced and realized in associations we call families, though care is not limited to families. Third, larger human groupings, such as tribes and more complex communities and societies that have institutions that regulate daily life, are political entities that have families as their basic foundations. Families are not political units themselves;[87] nevertheless, they are foundational to political entities and, therefore, families are inextricably yoked to larger social institutions and societal-political narratives and rituals. The implication here is that care is a necessary reality of political life, even if it is latent, because families are the cells, if you will, of tribes and larger, more complex societies. Finally, there is an interdependent relation between families and the polis. A well-functioning polis is dependent on thriving families, and families need a well-functioning polis to have the resources to care for its members.

This line of reasoning does not mean that care vis-à-vis larger political institutions is simply top-down. This relationship between families and larger social-political realities is more complex. As I stated above, families will continue to care for their members even in failed states, but usually with many more difficulties. And government institutions can have numerous programs that contribute to care or provide resources to families so that they can care for children and aging parents, but resources and aid do not

86. Winnicott, *Home Is Where We Start From*, 123–27.

87. While not political units, families nevertheless internalize and live out the political values and expectations found in social rituals, narratives. See Coontz, *The Social Origins of Private Life*; Mintz and Kellogg, *Domestic Revolutions*.

mean a family will provide good enough care for its members. Nevertheless, this relation is an important one, because a society's survival and viability depends on the well-being of families and their ability to care for members, and families depend on the care of the polis.

Implicit in this view is the notion that governments and attending institutions are obligated to create social and political conditions where families and other small groups have the resources, dispositions, knowledge, and skills to care for members of their families and others. Above, I argued that the obligation to care is ontological and not, as Engster argued, rooted merely in our shared experience of dependency. It appears that this perspective means that individuals are obliged to care, which is true, but I also argue that the obligation to care extends to larger institutions, such as the state. Some may argue this leads to a so-called nanny state, but I am not arguing here that the government and other institutions should take *over* caring activities. Rather, governments and other social institutions,[88] which the state creates and supports (e.g., corporations), not only have a vested interest in the psychological and physical health of its citizens, they are also obliged to aid, when necessary, families so that members can care for each other. Consider a simple example of the government promoting regulations that inform consumers about the ingredients of the food they are feeding to their children, as well as scientific information about what makes up a healthy diet for children and adults. The regulations and general information is for all citizens, though some groups of citizens may not have the resources to purchase fresh vegetables and fruits. That is, some citizens have fewer resources to provide healthy food for themselves and their children. Competent governments and other social institutions address this issue, creating policies, regulations, and resources for these citizens (and I would include residents who are not citizens). Of course, parents and nonparents can possess this knowledge and these resources yet fail to have the disposition and motivation to care adequately for themselves and their family members.

88. Social institutions include corporations. One may argue that corporations are economic entities that have as their aim economic profit and not care of citizens, let alone the thriving of their workers. It would seem naïve at best to suggest that they are obliged to care for citizens and families. To be sure, in a society dominated by neoliberal capitalism, corporations seek market expansion and profit to the exclusion of the common good. Yet this does not have to determine how we understand the aims and responsibilities of corporations. Some corporations possess the aim of caring for their workers so that workers can, in turn, care for their families and others. In addition, local, state, and national governments could find ways to encourage an ethos and to regulate corporations and businesses so that they include care of the workforce and community. See Wolff, *Occupy the Economy*.

To clarify further, caring for fellow citizens is rooted in our ontological obligation to care for Others. This individual obligation is also political in the sense that we live in a polis—a complex polis where we are interdependent. States have a role in facilitating this social care. An exemplary illustration of this is the Danish government's refusal to accede to the Nazi demands to deport its Jewish citizens, and the government's encouragement of all Danish citizens to care for Jewish citizens. Their collective caring actions led to the survival of thousands of Jews. This moving story, of course, takes place against the backdrop of governments (in Austria, Poland, Czechoslovakia, and elsewhere) that handed over their Jewish citizens, thus ignoring their obligation to promote care for all citizens. So we know that political institutions can ignore obligations to care, just as individuals can deny their obligations to care. In brief, care is a political concept because (1) states have an interest in the survival and well-being of citizenry and (2) states and their attending institutions cannot escape, though they may ignore, the ontological obligation to care, which is realized in policies and programs that assist citizens to care for family members and other fellow citizens.

Let's turn to a brief illustration of care as a political concept. There has been much public discussion about the minimum wage for the last several years. Those who advocate for raising it may frame this argument in terms of justice or rights, while those operating out of a capitalistic ethos may argue that boosting the minimum wage will actually help the economy, because workers will have more money to purchase goods. Of course, other capitalists will argue against it, saying that people will lose their jobs and employers are forced to pay more to their workers. These advocates, using different concepts, believe the government needs to find ways to enact legislation to aid workers, though exactly what form this takes may be hotly debated. Those who advocate leaving the minimum wage alone or getting rid of it altogether operate out of a neoliberal capitalistic narrative and its associated values. They argue that the government should not interfere with the invisible hand of the market. If workers want more money, in this narrative, they need only work harder to succeed or get an education that will make them more marketable. The group that uses rights or justice language, at times, hints at or points to the need for workers to have enough money to take care of their families (e.g., housing, food, health care, education). Providing a livable minimum wage is, in other words, not simply an issue of justice, but one of care. If individuals work full time on part-time wages, they can barely care for themselves, let alone family members. And two parents who work sixty hours a week do not have the time to provide the kind of psychosocial care their children need. The neoliberal capitalist who argues for the invisible hand of the market is not primarily concerned with justice or care. Instead, s/he is primarily concerned about the survival and flourishing of the market and, perhaps secondarily, the welfare of workers—but usually in relation to how they contribute to profit. The underlying belief, in other words, is that if the market is thriving, so are the workers. Of course, any cursory examination of the last thirty years will show that this is an illusion, if not a collective delusion.

The point here is that while we can engage in public conversations about the minimum wage in light of the concepts of rights and justice, there is an underlying key political concept that should be included and that is care. Citizens (and noncitizens) should be able to fulfill their responsibilities to care for family members and others. Moreover, the government and other institutions (including corporations) should, through legislation and regulations, foster the conditions that make it possible for citizens to care for family members (and others), which in this instance means facilitating the conditions where they are paid a wage sufficient to meet the aims of care—survival and flourishing.

There is one other important point in this discussion. The notion that care is a political concept tends to focus on the individual or family. This is well and good, but pastoral care has also emphasized the communal dimension of human life, represented in the notion of *ecclesia*, or what Martin Luther King Jr., following the Gospel of John, called the beloved community. Viable communities are made up of families that care for their members, but viable communities also include families that care for the larger community. There is a reciprocal, interdependent relationship between families and the community, which one notes in the narratives throughout Scripture. I add here that a well-functioning society is made up of well-functioning families and communities. Care as a political concept vis-à-vis communities is especially vital when we consider the decline during the last four decades of what Robert Putnam calls social capital.[89] Indeed, as I have argued elsewhere, one of the main issues of the twenty-first century will be the struggle of community.[90] And if communities struggle, we will see significant problems with regard to care in families and society. An implication here is that the state ought to facilitate care not only with regard to individuals and families but also with regard to communities.

I offer a negative example to make my point. Chris Hedges and Joe Sacco travelled around the United States "to take a look at the sacrifice zones, those areas in the country that have been offered up for exploitation

89. Putnam, *Bowling Alone.*

90. LaMothe, *Missing Us.*

in the name of profit, progress, and technological achievement."[91] Welch, a mining town in West Virginia, was a sacrifice zone where mining companies were given carte blanche to conduct mountaintop removal operations that have had severe environmental impacts that have harmed the health of local communities. As they note, "coal companies write laws. They control local and state politicians. They destroy water tables, suck billions of dollars' worth of coal out of the state, and render hundreds of acres uninhabitable."[92] Nearly 30 percent of the people make less than ten thousand dollars a year, and community members suffer from a variety of health problems in a place with inadequate health care.[93] This community is devastated economically and environmentally, which means also that its families face numerous obstacles in caring for each other. This is a clear example of the failure of the state to care for its citizens and these communities. More starkly stated, it is one of many examples of the "legal" corruption of state-elected officials and institutions by large mining corporations that are more concerned with profits than the care of individuals, families, and communities. A state is corrupt not simply when it is unjust in its dealings with citizens, but also when it fails in its obligations to care for its citizens and the communities in which citizens survive and thrive.

In summary, care is a political concept not because of the joint creation by Roman gods but by the existential reality that care is constitutive of human survival and flourishing. When we consider this in broad terms, we note that individual survival and flourishing depend on families or take place within the context of caring family relations. Families, while not a political unit, are foundations of a larger human collective or polis. A viable polis depends on the survival and flourishing of families, and families depend on how the state organizes itself to make possible the knowledge, resources, and skills for families to care for its members and others. The state and its institutions, then, are obliged to care, which suggests that states can ignore, deny, or refuse to live out this existential, political obligation. I also noted that this interdependent, reciprocal relationship between the state and families-individuals includes individuals' obligation to care for the state to the degree to which it facilitates social-political care and justice. Finally, I argued that in the pastoral care tradition, the *ecclesia* is a central concept and is related to care. Ideally families and individuals thrive in well-functioning communities. The state is obliged to foster the conditions in which communities can survive and thrive. A sign of a corrupt or failing

91. Hedges and Sacco, *Days of Destruction, Days of Revolt*, xi.

92. Ibid., 128.

93. Ibid., 156–75.

state is seen whenever states and state actors and institutions are concerned more about power, prestige, and privilege than the needs of individuals, families, and communities.

CONCLUSION

Personal caring is an essential existential reality of being human, whether we view this in terms of the individual who is dependent on the care of her parents for survival and flourishing or whether we consider that human beings are social and communal animals. When we move from a general statement to more concrete instances of care, we note complexity and diversity of knowledge, skills, and motivations vis-à-vis contexts of care. At the same time, we realize that while care is an essential feature of human life, it can be refused, denied, or ignored. We are obliged to care, but we have the freedom to refuse. This obligation to care is often framed in individual terms, but in this chapter I argued that the state and other nongovernmental institutions are obliged to care for and to facilitate care among citizens (and noncitizens), communities, and the larger society. It is this obligation and the anthropological reality that is foundational to individuals' survival and flourishing, as well as to the survival and flourishing of families and communities. Care, then, is foundational to the polis and its institutions and, therefore, a crucial political concept to be used in the analysis of political discourse and institutions, as well as in the construction of policies, regulations, and programs that shape the lives of citizens and communities.

3

CARE AND JUSTICE

Necessary Political Concepts for a Viable Polis and World

Care combines seeking to enhance someone's flourishing with seeking to secure their just treatment.[1]

Justice is a radical idea, because if people's sense of fairness is strained too far, their very sense of belonging and commitment to a common political community may snap.[2]

And earthly power doth then show likest God's,
when mercy seasons justice.[3]

When Malcolm X was a young boy living in Lansing, Michigan, he heard the tragic and devastating news that his father was found dead, a likely victim of racial murder. In the months that followed, Malcolm's mother strived hard to care for her children, despite the harsh economic depression of the 1930s and even more cruel obstacles imposed

1. Wolterstorff, *Justice in Love*, 101.
2. Lane, *The Birth of Politics*, 55.
3. Portia in Shakespeare. *Merchants of Venice*, Act IV, Scene 1.

by a culture of racism and sexism. Slowly, the challenges and hurdles in caring for her children, exacerbated by seemingly well-meaning state Welfare people, overwhelmed her. "As my mother talked to herself more and more," Malcolm X wrote, "she gradually became less responsive to us. And less responsible."[4] Soon after that she was taken to the State Mental Hospital at Kalamazoo, and most of the children became wards of the state. About his experience Malcolm X concluded, "I truly believe that if ever a state social agency destroyed a family, it destroyed ours. We wanted and tried to stay together. Our home didn't have to be destroyed. But the Welfare, the courts, and their doctor, gave us a one-two-three punch. And ours was not the only case of this kind."[5]

This tragic story poignantly portrays the intersection of the ethics of care and the ethics of justice in a polis, albeit a failure in both. The political and cultural milieu of rampant structural racism, sexism, and classism revealed the daily realities of injustice, of marginalization, oppression, and humiliation. It may be more accurate to say nonjustice, because African Americans were largely not recognized and treated as persons, let alone as full citizens meriting justice. The death of Malcolm X's father, for instance, was not investigated as a murder: so his life did not matter; he was misrecognized in life and not recognized in death. The systemic injustices of racism and sexism rained down on Malcolm's mother after her husband's death, making it difficult for her to care for the well-being of her children. To be sure, we have an example of the state providing some food relief and of state workers who seemingly care about the welfare of children, yet all of this takes place against the background of systemic, structural racial injustices that created the conditions that made it necessary for the state to step in and care for the children. So, we have racism that gives rise to injustices that harm people; this injustice in turn motivates the state welfare people to care for the family. Political and economic injustices, as pastoral theologians have long noted,[6] breed the conditions of desperate need for care, and the care is itself further entwined with systemic racism, which, in this case, led to a distortion of care—carelessness—and more instances of injustice. In a polis where there are systemic failures in the ethics of justice, there will also be systemic failures in the ethics of care.

4. X, *The Autobiography of Malcolm X*, 19.

5. Ibid., 22.

6. See for example, Kujawa-Holbrook and Montagno, *Injustice and the Care of Souls*; Smith, *The Relational Self*; Stevenson-Moessner and Snorton, *Women Out of Order*.

Stories like Malcolm X's, which are more common than we wish to admit,[7] bring to the foreground questions about the political concepts of care and justice. What does justice mean? What is the relation between care and justice? Does an ethic of care complement and ethic of justice? Does justice complement care? Can someone be just, impartial, and not care?[8] Can someone care and not be just? Are there instances of care that have nothing to do with justice? Does care precede justice? In a just society, is the notion of care as a political concept necessary? In a caring polis, is the concept of justice necessary? What is the relation of both concepts to political and economic power?

These are important questions to try to address, because any notion of care as a political concept inevitably runs up against the more pervasive discourse regarding the ethics of justice. More specifically, a political pastoral theology cannot simply rely on the notion of care as a hermeneutical lens in critiquing political-economic structures and practices. To do so would be to ignore contexts of need that arise out of hidden or overt systems of injustice, as in the case of welfare workers who ostensibly sought to care for Malcolm X's family while ignoring the economic racism, sexism, and classism that gave rise to their desperation. Also, by attending to these and other questions, we can gain a better understanding of notion of care as a political concept and how the concepts of justice and care are necessary if there is to be any change of a viable and lively community and society. Indeed, when justice is separated from care, justice easily slides into an uncritical mercilessness and aridity, and when care is split off from justice, care can devolve into myopic, naïve sentimentality that inadvertently colludes with hidden systems and structures of oppression and marginalization. As I will argue, these concepts need to be in creative tension if there is to be a good enough community or society.

I begin with an overview of care theorists' discussions about the ethics of care and the ethics of justice. This discourse had its beginning in the research and work of Carol Gilligan and has continued for the last four decades, addressing the intersection and tension between the ethics of care and justice.[9] While I begin with care theorists, I need to mention that care-justice discourse parallels the centuries-old theological discourse on love and justice. I will not take up this discourse, however, because it will take us

7. See Alexander, *The New Jim Crow*; National Center for Children in Poverty, "Child Poverty."

8. I am pointing to John Rawls's beliefs or, more aptly, illusions in the possibility of impartiality and the veil of ignorance vis-à-vis the possibility of universal justice. Rawls, *A Theory of Justice*.

9. Gilligan, *In a Different Voice*.

too far afield in differentiating between care and love, which would require a chapter or two.[10] I also need to mention that many pastoral theologians have been interested in situations when injustices have given rise to the need for care. However, in general, pastoral theologians, unlike care theorists, have not focused specifically on articulating the relation between care and justice, though many have clearly noted the relation.[11] After this discussion, I proffer a brief depiction of political theologies and their view of justice. I especially focus on liberation theologies because the notion of care is latent in their important attention on political and economic injustices that give rise to oppression, marginalization, and desperate poverty. In addition, these political theologies are attentive to and critical of structures and systems of political-economic power that harm persons and communities. And these political theologies, unlike care theories, highlight the importance of community for both justice and care—an emphasis also made in pastoral theology. Also, I argue that a pastoral political theology necessarily includes both concepts in any critical analysis of current local and global contexts. Finally, I address both concepts from the perspective of the notion of spaces of appearances, indicating that they are existentially distinct and inseparable.

While the focus of this chapter is on articulating the relation between care and justice with the aims of further clarifying care and its necessary partner justice in a political pastoral theology, I want to stress briefly a reason why this will become even more important in the future. The scientific research regarding global warming is overwhelming. The NASA website on climate change refers to a report by the Intergovernmental Panel on Climate Change—a group of independent scientific experts from countries all over the world—that "concluded there's a more than 90 percent probability that human activities over the past 250 years have warmed our planet."[12] Human activities the report refers to are those that heighten CO_2 emissions, as well as other greenhouse gases.[13] Wagner and Weitzman note that

10. Briefly, though let me say that care, in my view, is a broader concept than love. To be sure love necessarily involves care, but not all forms of care involve love.

11. See for example, Graham, "From Relational Humanness to Relational Justice"; Orr, "Ministry with Working-Class Women"; Ramsay, "When Race and Gender Collide"; Wimberly, *Counseling African American Marriages and Families*; Wimberly, *African American Pastoral Care and Counseling.*

12. National Aeronautics and Space Administration, "A Blanket around the Earth.".

13. Wagner and Weitzman, *Climate Shock*, 45. They point out that hydrofluorocarbons (HFCs) are "10,000 times as potent as carbon dioxide when it comes to global warming." So the Montreal Protocol that banned gases (chlorofluorocarbons—CFS) that were harming the ozone layer led to the production of HFCs. The ozone layer is expected to be healed by 2050, but we continue to use HFCs, though in smaller emission numbers than CO_2.

current carbon dioxide levels are at 400 parts per million (ppm) and the last time they were that high was over 3 million years ago during the Pliocene Era when "sea levels were up to 20 meters higher and camels lived in Canada."[14] Scientists have also discussed the diverse likely consequences of global warming, which range from rising sea levels, displaced populations, diminishing resources and heightened demand, declining fish populations, more extinctions, and more frequent catastrophic weather events.[15] These future events are taken very seriously by the Pentagon. Davenport writes that the "Pentagon . . . released a report asserting decisively that climate change poses an immediate threat to national security, with increased risks from terrorism, infectious disease, global poverty and food shortages. It also predicted rising demand for military disaster responses as extreme weather creates more global humanitarian crises."[16] One can only imagine the global violence, material deprivation, and suffering implied in these reports. Saskia Sassen and Christian Parenti have depicted injustices and desperate need that have already appeared because of global climate change.[17] All of this is to say that both the ethics of care and the ethics of justice are vital to present and future analyses of political, economic, and social structures, policies, and programs, both at the local and global levels. The consequences of climate change, in short, impel us to frame our analyses and constructive interventions in terms of both care and justice.

CARE THEORISTS AND THE ETHICS OF JUSTICE AND CARE

Carol Gilligan's research into the moral reasoning of girls and women and moral reasoning's connections to care and particular relationships initiated a lively debate regarding the ethics of care and the ethics of justice. In her seminal work, Gilligan contrasted the moral reasoning of women with the generally accepted male view of abstract moral reasoning associated with principles of justice and rights—a perspective reflected in Lawrence Kohlberg's work.[18] Gilligan finds a sharp distinction between the ethics of

14. Ibid., 10.

15. See Klein, *This Changes Everything*; Kolbert, *The Sixth Extinction*; Parenti, *Tropic of Chaos*; Sassen, *Expulsions*; Wagner and Weitzman, *Climate Shock*.

16. Davenport, "Pentagon Signals Security Risks of Climate Change."

17. Parenti, *The Tropic of Chaos*; Sassen, *Expulsions*.

18. Gilligan, *In a Different Voice*. For a more detailed discussion see Friedman, "Beyond Caring."

justice that emphasizes abstract, universal rules and principles, and an ethics of justice that focuses on particular persons, relationships, and contexts. Nel Noddings, another pioneer in care theory and a contemporary of Gilligan's, similarly argued for a sharp differentiation between care theory and justice,[19] though in later works she modified her views.[20] Both theorists[21] were reacting to the Rawlsian and neo-Kantian abstract and universalizing notions of justice, which tended to overlook particular cultural contexts and gender biases.[22]

Later care theorists critiqued Gilligan's research and the bifurcation of care and justice. They moved the discussion, acknowledging difference between the ethics of care and the ethics of justice, yet also seeing that these concepts overlapped and complemented each other. In her critique of Gilligan, Marilyn Friedman found that "women and men do not show statistical differences in moral reasoning along the lines of a care/justice dichotomy," which "should not be thought surprising since the concepts of care and justice are mutually compatible."[23] Joan Tronto similarly argues that the assumption that care and justice arise from two different metaethical starting points and are thus incompatible is false. "This argument," she notes, "presumes that care is particular, justice universal; that care draws out of compassion, justice out of rationality."[24] For Tronto, "justice without a notion of care is incomplete."[25] While compatible, these concepts, Sara Ruddick contends, are distinct and "unassimilable ways of identifying, interpreting, and responding to moral phenomena that can be seen from two perspectives, as a single figure can be seen alternatively as a duck or rabbit, a vase or two faces."[26] Each notion is moral and "neither can be replaced by or subsumed under the other; each covers the moral domain and can therefore check and inform the other; there is no third, 'mature,' single interpretive moral perspective within which each orientation has its place."[27]

Virginia Held follows this view and provides helpful clarifications and distinctions regarding justice and care. She writes:

19. Noddings, *Caring.*

20. Noddings, *Starting at Home.*

21. Both Gilligan and Noddings later changed their views, arguing that while the ethics of care is distinct from the ethics of justice, both are necessary and compatible.

22. See Benhabib, *Situating the Self*, 148–64.

23. Friedman, "Beyond Caring," 61.

24. Tronto, *Moral Boundaries*, 166.

25. Ibid., 167.

26. Ruddick, "Injustice in Families," 204.

27. Ibid.

> An ethic of justice focuses on questions of fairness, equality, individual rights, abstract principles, and the consistent application of them. An ethic of care focuses on attentiveness, trust, responsiveness to need, narrative nuance, and cultivating caring relations. Whereas the ethics of justice seeks a fair solution between competing individual interests and rights, an ethics of care sees interests of carers and cared-for as importantly intertwined rather than as simply competing. Whereas justice protects equality and freedom, care fosters social bonds and cooperation.[28]

Held remarks further that in dominant moral theories of the ethics of justice "the values of equality, impartiality, fair distribution, and noninterference have priority; in the practice of justice, individual rights are protected, impartial judgments arrived at, and equal treatment sought."[29] In care theory, by contrast, "the values of trust, solidarity, mutual concern, and empathic responsiveness have priority; in practices of care, relationships are cultivated, needs are responded to, and sensitivity demonstrated."[30]

The distinction regarding values is not meant to imply that these two domains of human life are separate. Held, in other words, argues that the context will determine the priority of values, suggesting that the other values are present but not in the foreground. For example, an individual breaks the law by robbing an old man walking down the street. Ideally, we would want the thief to have a fair trial overseen by an "impartial" judge, who would work to ensure that his rights would not be violated, even if he is to be eventually deprived of his liberty by going to prison. This scenario does not mean that care theory is ignored. We would want to ensure that the victim received care and the values of care apply as well to the man going to jail. Besides the routine needs for food, water, and the like, we would consider the individual's relationship needs (e.g., the need to stay in contact with family members) and perhaps other needs that might need to be met when he gets out of prison (e.g., the need for education, job training, or drug rehabilitation). The ethics of justice and care in this case can also be more expansive in the sense of critically evaluating the conditions that gave rise to this man's decision to rob. To return to Malcolm X, who was arrested for robbery, we would note the reality of an unjust legal system that doles out harsher sentences to African Americans. The injustice of racism is evident in the lack of education, job opportunities, and adequate wages for African Americans.

28. Held, *The Ethics of Care*, 15.

29. Ibid.

30. Ibid., 15–16.

And, of course, the ethics of care perspective reveals that many African Americans have a more difficult time obtaining the resources necessary to "help individuals to meet their vital biological needs, develop or maintain their basic capabilities, and avoid or alleviate unnecessary or unwanted pain and suffering, so that they can survive, develop, and function in society."[31]

Another important distinction that Held points out is how moral reasoning is understood vis-à-vis theories of justice and theories of care. She argues that "Kantian and utilitarian moral theorists focus primarily on rational decisions of agents taken as independent and autonomous individuals . . . In contrast, the ethics of care sees persons as enmeshed in relations with others. It pays attention primarily to relations between persons, valuing especially caring relations."[32] In addition, Kantian and Rawlsian theories of justice privilege reason in making moral decisions, placing in the background, often negatively, emotions or empathy. Care theorists have a different understanding of reason. Moral reasoning in an ethics of care indicates a need for empathy in making decisions. There is, in other words, reason in emotion and emotion in reason—a viewpoint argued by philosophers Susan Langer and John Macmurray and recent neuroscientific and childhood development research.[33]

Lest we think these views about moral reasoning vis-à-vis justice and care take place in the rarified domains of academic discourse, we need only recall the fierce discussions around the confirmation hearings of Supreme Court justice Sonia Sotomayor and President Obama's remark that "the critical ingredient is supplied by what is in the judge's heart" when making judicial decisions.[34] Sotomayor, when pressured by senators, proclaimed that she made decisions according to the law, which meant that she would be an impartial judge who would not make decisions on "emotions." To be sure, we want judges to strive toward impartiality—knowing, however, that impartiality like neutrality is an illusion—yet impartiality in this view is devoid of empathy (i.e., emotions). What Sotomayor (and others) overlooked is that laws are also made with emotions, biases, partiality, and in some cases empathy. Interestingly, an "impartial" judge is supposed to make a just decision based on laws that are often politically biased and may create suffering and harm to an underprivileged group. The denial of emotions and partiality in reasoning vis-à-vis justice (or care) lends itself to a Lady Justice who is

31. Engster, *The Heart of Justice*, 28.

32. Ibid., 156.

33. Macmurray, *Reason and Emotion*; Langer, *Philosophy in a New Key*; See also, Damasio, *Descartes' Error*; Goleman, *Emotional Intelligence*; Goleman, *Social Intelligence*; Sroufe, *Emotional Development*.

34. Shapiro, "Sotomayor Differs with Obama."

truly blind to unbalanced scales. Indeed, this denial is requisite in colluding with injustice. The examples are too numerous to list, but one example is the Dred Scott decision and the so-called rational arguments based in law that further solidified racial injustices toward African Americans. A little empathic imagination may have gone a long way toward opening the eyes of these "impartial" judges so that they might have recognized their own unseemly emotional biases and values that elevated white men, while insuring a political, economic, and social system that deprived African Americans of freedoms and other basic human needs. All of this is to emphasize that moral reasoning with regard to the ethics of care and the ethics of justice should not foreclose the reality of emotions in decision-making. In other words, we do not want to have reason overwhelmed by emotion, which can impair judgments with regard to care and justice, and we do not want reason to be devoid of emotion (as if Commander Spock were possible for human beings), because this would indicate a distortion of reason as well.[35] Perhaps we are looking for a kind of Aristotelian mean, the right amount of reason and emotion at the right time and in the right place with regard to both the ethics of care and the ethics of justice.

The emotional debate that President Obama launched by his remarks also reveals the close relation between discourse about justice (and care), gender, and the political realm. Seyla Benhabib notes that the "sphere of justice from Hobbes through Locke and Kant is regarded as the domain where independent, male heads of households transact with one another, while the domestic-intimate spheres are put beyond the pale of justice."[36] This social division is political and, she argues, is reflected the moral theories of Rawls and Kohlberg. "Rawls's and Kohlberg's work," Benhabib writes, "is based upon an implicit politics which defines the 'personal,' in the sense of the intimate/domestic sphere, as ahistorical, immobile, and unchanging, therefore removing it from discussion and reflection."[37] The bifurcation of the private (female, emotions) and public (male, reason) realms vis-à-vis values has other political consequences. Iris Marion Young also contends that "claims to impartiality feed cultural imperialism by allowing the particular experience and perspective of privileged groups to parade as universal. Second, the conviction that bureaucrats and experts can exercise their decision-making power in an impartial manner legitimates authoritarian hierarchy."[38] An impartial, objective, rational judge who adheres to universal

35. See Macmurray, *Reason and Emotion*.

36. Benhabib, *Situating the Self*, 155.

37. Ibid., 170.

38. Young, *Justice and the Politics of Difference*, 10.

principles of justice in the public is largely fictional, though it has very real political and social consequences with regard to gender (i.e., male privilege) and race. Put another way, Benhabib and Young are describing the close relation between conceptions of justice (and moral reasoning) to political and social realities of gender and race, and that in a patriarchal culture care becomes gendered (women do the care) and privatized (care takes place at home). All of this view lends itself to bifurcating care and justice, which recent care theorists argue forcefully against.

To focus more specifically on care ethics, we find that the emphasis on values of trust, social solidarity, mutual concern, and empathic responsiveness does not mean that reason and fairness are excluded or take a backseat. The ethics of care requires making reasoned judgments about the needs and experiences of others. Moreover, care requires reasoned judgments about the distribution of resources to meet needs. That reason and emotion are integral in care is brought out by Maurice Hamington. Recall that he contends that caring imagination, which is central to his ethics of care, comprises three features, namely, empathy, psychosocial context, and critical reflection.[39] Part of knowing vis-à-vis care requires empathy—the recognition of the other's needs and emotional experiences, which requires the capacities for reason and judgment. At the same time, accurate empathy depends on knowledge of the psychosocial context. Lack of knowledge of the particular psychosocial context often results in empathic failures and failures to be fair, because one does not grasp the particular meanings, beliefs, values, and expectations of the persons in need. An excellent example of this is Easterly's portrayal of NGOs (nongovernmental organizations) that design programs to address some needs, without first getting to know or understanding the particular needs and experiences of the people they are ostensibly trying to help.[40] His examples depict failures not only in accurate psychosocial knowledge and empathy but also in meeting needs.

Recall further that the third feature of caring imagination is critical reflection. Hamington recognized that imagination can be faulty. Our own subjectivity is partial and contains our own experiences, values, and biases. Subjectivity, even though it is limited, can aid us in our use of imagination to know someone empathically; on other occasions our subjectivity can be an obstacle to caring imagination. Put another way, our imagination, which involves both the capacities for reason and emotion, can be accurate at times and other times far off target, creating instances of carelessness and injustice. This is why Hamington stresses the necessity of a critical reflective

39. Hamington, *Embodied Care*, 75–84.

40. See Easterly, *The Tyranny of Experts.*

function vis-à-vis empathic imagination. In short, we use reason and imagination in empathically recognizing the Other's needs, and we use critical reflection, which includes being open to correction from the Other, to consider the accuracy of our perceptions, interpretations, and corresponding interventions. Critical reflection, then, includes reasoned judgments about our own biases and how these biases distort imagination and knowledge vis-à-vis the particular Other's needs and experiences.

While an ethics of justice and an ethics of care have different priorities and values that shape knowledge and guide behavior, both rely on reason and emotion in making judgments. Certainly, an ethics of care is more comfortable with relying on emotion as a form of knowledge in understanding a situation of care and using this to guide a response that meets particular needs. An ethics of justice is more reluctant to acknowledge the role of emotions in making laws, establishing rights, promoting freedoms, and making decisions about distribution of resources. Many of those involved in the ethics of justice want to shroud themselves in the values of impartiality, objectivity, and reason, holding emotions at arm's length. It would be interesting to account for this psychologically, but it is more important to stress that an ethics of justice that attempts to divorce itself from the reality of emotional cognitions in arriving at decisions will likely end up colluding with, if not creating, injustices. As I indicated above, the "reasoned justice" of the Dred Scott decision screened the underlying hostility toward African Americans and unjustly promulgated systemic white superiority that denied justice to African Americans for many decades, including the decades that followed the achievements of the civil rights movement.[41]

It is important to note the differences in priorities and values between care and justice, yet, as care theorists have noted, these differences can hide areas of existential agreement or identity. Thomas Aquinas, Frederick Bauerschmidt noted, considered that a "just society is one that is rightly or beautifully ordered by imitating God who, according to eternal law, 'gives to each thing its due to it by its nature and condition.'"[42] This view is echoed in Melissa Lane's discussion of Greek theories of justice where justice "is giving people what is owed,"[43] which in Aristotle's philosophy was the basis of political life.[44] To give people what they are due means recognizing that they have particular needs and these needs are necessary for not only survival

41. See Alexander, *The New Jim Crow*.

42. Bauerschmidt, "Aquinas," 56.

43. Lane, *The Birth of Politics*, 31.

44. Eagleton, *After Theory*, 142.

but also flourishing of the individual and community.[45] An ethics of justice and an ethics of care, then, are aimed at giving people what they are due or need. Of course, the different values of these discourses will shape what is meant by need or what is owed. For example, an ethics of care may highlight the medical needs of the poor, arguing that the state is ethically charged with meeting those needs so that people can reasonably care for themselves and if not be cared for by others. An ethics of justice may address the same issue from the perspective of citizens' rights to have access to health care and the state's duty to ensure local municipalities have the resources to provide health care to the poor. Moreover, an ethics of justice may point out that the absence of health care restricts an individual's freedom, interfering with self-sovereignty. Whether arguing from an ethics of care or ethics of justice viewpoint, giving persons what they are due is, at the base, the aim of both ethics.

There is something else important in the notion that care and justice involve giving to people what they are due. I argue that giving a person what the person is due according to the person's "nature and condition" is contingent on the recognition of the Other an inviolable and unique individual.[46] Recall in chapter 2 I indicated that care is founded on the recognition of the Other as person—unique, inviolable valued, agentic subject—that is integral to the space of appearances vis-à-vis the polis. In the ethics of justice discourse, we find John Rawls arguing that "each person possesses an inviolability founded on justice that even the welfare of society as a whole cannot override."[47] Both an ethics of care and an ethics of justice are founded on giving what is due to a person, which means acknowledging the inviolability and uniqueness of the Other. Put another way, the individual appears in the political space—the space of appearances—as a person who has particular needs (e.g., material, legal) and who is due an accurate response in meeting those needs for survival and flourishing. The foreclosure or attenuation of the space of appearances means that the individual's inviolability and uniqueness are disregarded, which necessarily leads to failures in both care and justice.

We know, then, that recognizing other human beings as persons and giving them their due for the sake of survival and flourishing are ideals that we often fall short of achieving. And our failures bring into stark relief the necessity of both justice and care. In other words, the notion of justice arises not simply in recognition of what is due a person, but more often than not

45. See Wolterstorff, *Love and Justice*, 101.

46. See Sandel, *Public Philosophy*, 151; Pulcini, *Care of the World*, 191.

47. In Sandel, *Public Philosophy*, 150.

against the realities of oppression, marginalization, powerlessness, cultural imperialism, and violence—realities where people are not recognized as inviolable and thus not given their due.[48] Likewise, the issue of care, while emerging in the face of the Other's needs and dependence, also comes to the foreground in situations where the needs of persons are misrecognized, denied, or overlooked. To refer back to Malcolm X, we read a story where his family experienced all kinds of injustices, injustices that were inextricably yoked to failures in care. Systemic racism distorted recognitions of blacks, which led to failures in justice and care. Abject failures in justice and care are also associated with not simply misrecognition but nonrecognition. From another perspective, Melissa Lane distinguishes between *un*just and *non*-just. The nonjust "marked the limits of where justice could apply."[49] Unjust, then, implied that the issue of justice applies and therefore the principles of justice vis-à-vis other persons had been violated. Nonjustice by contrast is a social-political space where principles and rules are not applicable—for example the slave or alien are terms to denote a space of nonjustice. Issues of justice do not apply to the slave, because the slave is property.

The same can be said of care. There are situations where there is carelessness (e.g., Malcolm X and the state)—care does apply but is distorted—and situations of noncare, because the Other is not recognized. The slave is cared for to the extent that s/he fulfills an economic function, but this is a space of noncare (and nonjustice) because the slave is not given his/her due with regard to flourishing.[50] The sacrifice zones that Chris Hedges and Joe Sacco address are examples of zones of nonjustice and noncare.[51] These people who suffer remain outside the space of appearances; they are outside the public-political imagination. The result is an absence of thought and just-care action.

Four points are to be garnered from this discussion. First, the ethics of care and the ethics of justice emerge out of an existential reality of human finitude and tragedy. Second, both are necessarily dependent on recognition of Others as persons, and, third, this recognition is integral to the political realm—space of appearances where Others' needs and experiences are acknowledge and they are given their due. Finally, because of human finitude and anxiety, there are examples of injustice and carelessness wherein

48. Young, *Justice and the Politics of Difference*, 9.

49. Lane, *The Birth of Politics*, 37.

50. One could argue that the slave is given his/her due with regard to survival, but this would be a distortion of both care and justice, because s/he is given his/her due not because s/he is a person—unique, inviolable, valued, subject—but because she is to perform an economic function.

51. Hedges and Sacco, *Days of Destruction, Days of Revolt.*

the space of appearances is distorted and attenuated because of prejudice, hostility,or the like. There are also areas of nonjustice and noncare where there is no space of appearances; there is no recognition of the Other as person and hence nothing is due. All of this highlights the necessity of cultivating a disciplined, ongoing critical attention to particular and *global* contexts of care and justice—or stated negatively, to instances of injustice and carelessness, as well to as zones of nonjustice and noncare.

This leads me to address another area of contention in care theory discourse regarding justice, which I mentioned briefly above, and that is the issue of universal principles or generalized other. Early on care theorists had been leery of abstract, universal principles of justice largely because they saw how the application of these universal principles led to overlooking particular sociocultural contexts and thus abjuring the needs and experiences of individuals. "The ethics of care . . . is skeptical of such abstractions and reliance on universal rule," Virginia Held writes, "and questions the priority given to them."[52] This skepticism is well founded. Annette Baier illustrates this, writing that the "moral tradition which developed the concept of rights is the same tradition that provided 'justification' of the oppression of those whom the primary-holders depended onto do the sort of work they themselves preferred not to do. The domestic work was left to women and slaves."[53] The generalized Other, then, has often been the compilation of projected biases that result in policies that violate both care and justice, while privileging other groups of people. I believe Easterly makes a similar point when he argues that experts who, having good intentions, make decisions about how to care for people they have not met often results in failures. These experts make assumptions—assumptions that are tacitly linked to universal principles or beliefs. In the process, they do not heed the particular needs and experiences of the very people they are interested in helping.

I can understand and appreciate the skepticism about discourse that uses universal principles or notions of a generalized other, whether that has to do with the ethics of justice or the ethics of care. Yet, we should not abandon discourse that involves universal principles, rights, and so forth, not only because human beings while diverse in language and culture are alike in many ways, but also because we are facing global challenges due to climate change—challenges that give rise to injustice, nonjustice, carelessness, and noncare. With regard to an ethics of care and an ethics of justice, we need to face the diverse particularities of people, as well as the similarities

52. Held, *The Ethics of Care*, 11.

53. Baier, "The Need for More Than Justice," 53.

we all share. Toward this end, Benhabib argues for an interactive universalism that "acknowledges the plurality of modes of being human, and differences among humans, without endorsing all the pluralities and differences as morally or politically valid . . . Interactive universalism regards difference as a starting point for reflection and action. In this sense, 'universality' is a regulative ideal that does not deny embodied and embedded identity, but aims at developing moral attitudes and encouraging political transformation that can yield a point of view acceptable to all."[54] She is careful to note that interactive universalism "is not the ideal of consensus of fictitiously defined selves, but a concrete *process* in politics and morals of the struggle of concrete, embodied selves."[55] To guard against the eclipse of the concrete other, "there must be a clear categorical distinction between each domain, such that the particularistic concerns of a given care ethos are in the end always subordinated to the question of universal justice."[56] The dialectical tension between the particular context and the universal principles is to remain dynamic and not be resolved.

Care theorist Fiona Robinson argues in a parallel fashion regarding the ethics of care vis-à-vis international relations.[57] From her perspective globalization has highlighted the increasing interrelatedness and interdependence among human beings, while also revealing significant differences. A universal ethics, she argues, "must address difference and exclusion."[58] In addition, a global ethics "must adopt a critical perspective on knowledge and power, rejecting the notion of impartiality and recognizing that the 'norm' is actually unstated but specific point of reference, and that the status quo cannot be unquestioningly accepted as natural, uncoerced, or good."[59] Perhaps Hamington's notion of caring imagination and its three attributes can also help ground interactive universalism or global ethics by emphasizing empathy, psychosocial context (embodied and embedded identities, experiences, and needs), and critical reflection, which would entail careful analysis of the impact of decisions and actions that arise from applying universal principles associated with care and justice.

A political implication of a vigorous discourse about universal principles vis-à-vis an ethics of care and an ethics of justice is that all human beings are to be included in the space of appearances—locally and universally.

54. Benhabib, *Situating the Self*, 153.

55. Ibid.; italics added.

56. Ganis, *The Politics of Care in Habermas and Derrida*, 29.

57. Robinson, *Globalizing Care*.

58. Ibid., 45.

59. Ibid., 46.

Within the borders of the United States, this is reflected in the recent slogans "Black Lives Matter" and "All Lives Matter." It is also seen in the drive to help immigrants obtain citizenship so that the state will, ideally, be required to give them their due so that they can care for themselves and others. But even more broadly, it is seen when nations and individuals recognize the rights and needs of all human beings and not simply those who are citizens. Indeed, a universal perspective views all persons as citizens of the cosmopolis and thus as all subjects of an ethics of care and an ethics of justice.

Before moving to the next section, I wish to emphasize a point about the intersection of an ethics of care and an ethics of justice. Nicholas Wolterstorff argues that care "combines seeking to enhance someone's flourishing with seeking to secure their just treatment."[60] For Wolterstorff and many care theorists an ethics of care includes an ethics of justice. As Wolterstorff notes that "Well-formed care does not wrong a person in the course of seeking to promote her good." In contrast, "Care about someone is malformed if it wrongs anyone."[61] Virginia Held possesses a similar view. "Care," she argues, "is probably the most deeply fundamental value. There can be care without justice . . . There can be no justice without care." For her, an ethics of care "provide[s] the wider and deeper ethics within which justice should be sought."[62] An ethics of care, from this perspective, necessarily includes an ethics of justice.

The reverse, these authors seem to suggest, is not the case. An ethics of justice, at least historically, has not included an ethics of care. It is often the case that the discourse and practices associated with justice do not address care, especially when one considers the legal system. For instance, there is a great deal of public discussion about bringing a person to justice, but when a person is imprisoned s/he resides in a place where care vis-à-vis the wider public is nearly absent. Prisoners are often forgotten and neglected, and when released face numerous obstacles in rejoining society.[63] To care about and care for prisoners would require attending to not only their needs for survival, but also their flourishing, which is very difficult to accomplish when there are few educational programs that will assist them in finding work when they are released. To emphasize justice without attending to an ethics of care inevitably means not giving people what they are due to care for themselves and others.

60. Wolterstorff, *Justice in Love*, 101.

61. Ibid., 102.

62. Held, *The Ethics of Care*, 17.

63. See Alexander, *The New Jim Crow*.

It appears, then, that when we care about and for people, we are giving them their due, which seems to imply that justice is being fulfilled. This does not mean that if we really focus on care or an ethics of care we need not concern ourselves with justice, because care appears to include justice. Both concepts, of course, have different emphases, priorities, and values, and therefore, both need to serve as hermeneutical lenses for critical analysis of particular and global contexts. We want both concepts when addressing areas of concern, whether we argue that care includes justice. For instance, the fact that poor women and men do not have enough resources to care for their own and their children's needs ideally motivates persons to find ways for them to obtain these resources. We can argue this from the perspective of care ethics, but also from the perspective of human rights—an ethics of justice.

To be sure, I can agree that if one cares for someone, then the Other will obtain what s/he is due, but we still need the notion of justice, because care can overlook issues of justice and thus collude with political and economic systems of oppression. For instance, a group of caring citizens works hard to meet the needs of people who are homeless and those that struggle to feed themselves and their kids because they are out of work or because they do not make enough money. This group of caring citizens is to be commended. However, if all they do is care without resisting or agitating against political-economic realities that give rise to the sufferings of the homeless and others, then they are tacitly facilitating the survival of an unjust system or a system that fosters unjust situations like these.

LIBERATION THEOLOGIES: GOD'S JUSTICE, CARE, AND COMMUNITY

I want to shift from care theorists' discourse on the relation between and distinctions of an ethics of care and an ethics of justice to liberation theologies. I do so for several reasons. First, liberation theologies are political theologies[64] that from my perspective are a subset of a political pastoral theology. I say this because liberation theologies, while focusing primarily on justice and liberation[65] of the oppressed and marginalized, also emerge out of a deep concern and care about the material, psychological, and spiritual

64. See Moltmann, "Political Theologies in Ecumenical Contexts," 4–11.

65. Another reason for suggesting that liberation theologies fall under the heading of pastoral theology is their focus on liberation, which, as Nancy Ramsay has noted, falls within the pastoral functions of resistance and liberation. See Ramsay, "When Race and Gender Collide," 331.

sufferings and needs of individuals, families, and communities. There is, in other words, an ethics of care embedded in liberation theologies—an ethics inextricably related to an ethics of justice. Second, liberation theologians bring a theological perspective vis-à-vis an ethics of justice, and this perspective, along with other interpretive frameworks (e.g., Marxism, human sciences, philosophy), is used to analyze and critique structures and systems of power that contribute to oppression, marginalization, and the denial or reduction of needed resources for people to survive and thrive. Third, liberation theology as a political theology serves as a bridge in depicting a political pastoral theology, because liberation theology tacitly includes an ethics of care perspective linked to the notion of community or *ecclesia* and care. Liberation theology also serves as a bridge between traditional political theologies that focus on rights, justice, freedom, and sovereignty and a pastoral political theology that brings a hermeneutic of care to all things political.

Of course, the topic of liberation theology covers a large and diverse territory. There are numerous liberation theologies (e.g., black, feminist, womanist, postcolonial, Asian, Latin American, and others) that have different emphases and social, political, and cultural contexts. Black liberation theologies in North America grew out of the suffering of African Americans in the face of rampant and systemic racism,[66] while in a different context of South Africa, liberation theology arose out of racist, violent policies of apartheid.[67] Feminist liberation theologies in the United States responded to patriarchal, sexist structures that contributed to forms of social, political, and economic oppression and marginalization of women and girls.[68] And postcolonial theologies address past and present forms of imperialism that have had and still have devastating impacts on the lives of individuals, communities, and societies in global south.[69] Latin or South American liberation theologies developed in relation to the exploitation of Central and South American nations by Western nations (principally the United States in the nineteenth and twentieth centuries) and by indigenous leaders (in business and government), which led to pervasive and desperate poverty.[70]

All of these theologies have developed in response to various subtle and overt forms of oppression and marginalization and the desire and hope for freedom from political, material, and cultural bondage. This said,

66. Cone, *A Black Theology of Liberation*.

67. Buthelezi, "Toward Indigenous Theology in South Africa."

68. See Graham, "Feminist Theology, Northern."

69. See Lartey, *Postcolonizing God*; Dussel, *A Philosophy of Liberation*.

70. See Gutiérrez, *A Theology of Liberation*; Gutiérrez, "Option for the Poor."

I primarily emphasize black liberation theology and Central, and South American liberation theology for several reasons. First, they give attention to the importance of community as a source of survival and resistance in the face of injustice. Second, these political theologies, in particular Central and South American theologies of liberation, emphasize preferential option for the poor, biblically and theologically understood. Third, these political theologies respond to political, economic, and cultural forms of oppression that denied resources to large segments of the population, making it difficult for individuals, families, and communities to care. That is, liberation in these political theologies is not simply about gaining political freedoms. It is also about restoring economic justice so that people can have the necessary resources for survival and for flourishing. These three features are the prisms through which I round out my discussion of the ethics of care and the ethics of justice.

Let me explain further these three features by beginning with preferential option for the poor. One of the fathers of liberation theology, Gustavo Gutiérrez, is a Peruvian priest who studied in Europe before returning to teach in his native country during the 1960s. Turning to Scripture, Gutiérrez noted God's preferential option for the poor,[71] which he claimed is at the very heart of Jewish Scriptures and the gospel.[72] "The ultimate basis for the privileged position of the poor," he writes, "is not the poor in themselves but in God, in the gratuitous and universality of God's *agapeic love*."[73] As Roberto Goizueta notes the preferential option for the poor does not mean exclusive love.[74] God's love is universal, though this "is not to say it is neutral."[75] From this perspective, to suggest that God's love is neutral would mean that God is supporting the status quo of injustice. Goizueta's, given his analysis of Gutiérrez's works, adds further clarifications. The "option for the poor is an option to place ourselves in a particular social location, to view reality from a particular perspective: the perspective of the poor, the

71. Gutiérrez noted three types of poverty, namely, material, spiritual, and voluntary. Material poverty is economic, and spiritual poverty represents a radical dependence on God. He made sure to critique facile notions of spiritual poverty, which functions to justify wealth and privilege. Gutiérrez, *A Theology of Liberation*, 287–306.

72. It is important to mention that Central and South American liberation theologies were critiqued by the Vatican for the tendency to equate liberation with salvation, which was not the case with Gutiérrez. He was also criticized by feminist theologians for not taking into account the oppression of women, which he later incorporated into his theology of liberation. See Gutiérrez, *Essential Writings*, 318.

73. Gutiérrez, *On Job*.

74. Goizueta, "Gustavo Gutiérrez," 291.

75. Ibid., 290.

outcast, the marginalized."[76] Moreover, Gutiérrez, recognizes that poor people "can be seduced by privilege and power; those without power can come to believe that their liberation will be achieved only when they themselves acquire power and wealth. The poor themselves, then, are called to place themselves on the side of the poor, not to abandon their own communities by 'opting' for the values of power, wealth, and violence."[77] Liberation from the oppressive effects of poverty, then, cannot come through the means of acquiring wealth and power or through opting for violent methods, because these aims and methods only serve to perpetuate further injustices and acts of dehumanization.

Another major contributor to liberation theology and a contemporary of Gutiérrez was Jon Sobrino, a theologian who lived and worked in Latin America for decades. Sobrino also focused on the poor, though he framed questions about the poor in terms of ecclesiology. What is the relation of the church to the poor? Does the notion of the poor alter how we understand the church? The church is not a church for the poor, he argued, because this would suggest a distinction of difference, suggesting the church stands apart from the poor. To be sure, a church "for the poor represents an ethical and therefore necessary approach, but it is not necessarily an ecclesiological approach."[78] Stated positively, the church "of the poor is not a Church for the poor but a Church that must be formed on the basis of the poor and that must find in them the principle of its structure, organization, and mission."[79] For Sobrino the church of the poor does not mean the church is "an agent of truth and grace because the poor are in it; rather the poor in the Church are the structural source that assures the Church of being really the agent of truth and justice."[80] In Sobrino the preferential option for the poor is viewed ecclesiologically.

My interest here is first to point out that liberation theologies' focus on the poor unites—theologically and ecclesiologically—an ethics of justice and an ethics of care. The "poor" are people who struggle to be able to care for themselves and others. They struggle to have sufficient food (in quantity and quality) to survive and thrive, and this struggle is oppressive—psychologically, spiritually, and materially. Lacking financial resources, the poor are unable to access educational opportunities, and this lack of opportunity traps them into low-wage jobs. The poor are also denied medical services

76. Ibid., 291.

77. Ibid.

78. Sobrino, *The True Church and the Poor*, 92.

79. Ibid., 93.

80. Ibid., 95.

and in countries where they are able to obtain medical services these are often of lesser quality.[81] And the poor are not represented politically, which means that they have little influence to address policy and programs that can improve their condition. For liberation theologians, the lack of material resources for the poor so that they cannot care for themselves and others results from structural and systemic political, economic, social, and cultural injustices. In brief, a political theology of liberation necessarily begins with concern about the material and immaterial needs of the oppressed and marginalized, analyzes and critiques—using theological, philosophical, and human science perspectives—the structural and systemic causes of poverty, and seeks interventions aimed at helping people participate in liberating themselves from their suffering. It is this focus on the poor that reveals the inextricable union between an ethics of care and an ethics of justice.

Before moving to the next point, I want to provide an illustration where we see the intersection of care and justice. Martin Luther King Jr. was not a liberation theologian, at least not in the technical sense, but clearly political and economic liberation were themes undergirding his speeches, decisions, and actions. When they were young adults, King and his wife, Coretta, were faced with a decision. The Kings had the chance to accept an offer of pastoring a church in the North or pastoring a church in the South where segregation and Jim Crow laws that made it difficult if not impossible for African Americans to vote in local, state, and national elections; to obtain good educations; and to attain good-paying jobs.[82] They decided to head south. After returning to the South, King became involved in NAACP and organized within his church a social and political action committee.[83] He and others worked assiduously to dismantle laws that supported segregation and kept blacks from participating in public-political life. For King, early on, the civil rights movement was about the confronting, resisting, and removing injustices associated with segregation and Jim Crow laws. In this regard, King was a liberation theologian who worked with others to free people from the bondage of systemic and structural racism.

King's focus on political freedoms did not mean that he failed to see and experience the struggles of economic poverty, but this only became a front-burner issue toward the end of his short life. President Johnson had declared a war on poverty and King recognized the tragedy "that our government declared a war against poverty, and yet financed a skirmish against

81. University of California, Davis, Center for Poverty Research, "How Is Poverty Related to Access to Care and Preventive Healthcare?"

82. King, *The Autobiography of Martin Luther King, Jr.*, 44–45.

83. Ibid., 47.

poverty."[84] Instead the attention and finances were going to fight a war in Vietnam. A year before King was murdered, he gave what is now a famous speech ("Beyond Vietnam") at Riverside Church. Here and elsewhere he criticized the involvement of the United States in Vietnam, arguing that the U.S. is "the greatest purveyor of violence in the world."[85] The injustice of violence, for King, is inextricably joined with the injustice of poverty. As a civil rights leader King said, "I have been concerned about justice for all people,"[86] which was the reason for his denunciation of the U.S. policies of aggression in Vietnam and elsewhere. But then he also makes the connection between justice and poverty. "I strongly feel," he wrote, "that we must end not merely poverty among negroes but poverty among white people,"[87] which is impossible to do in an imperial state bent on committing all manner of injustice. To avoid the specter of spiritual death that comes from a state "that continues year after year to spend more money on military defense than on programs of social uplift,"[88] King advocated a revolution in values. A revolution in values, for King, goes beyond a change in behavior to but a radical restructuring of society. In his speech he said "we are called to play the Good Samaritan on life's roadside, but that will be only an initial act. One day we must come to see that the whole Jericho road must be transformed . . . True compassion is more than flinging a coin to a beggar. It comes to see that an edifice which produces beggars needs restructuring."[89] A year later, King joined the Memphis sanitation workers, who were on strike, seeking living wages and just treatment. In this last speech, King offers encouragement for the weary workers to continue to strike for their freedoms and for the lifting of economic forces that materially oppressed them and made it more challenging to care for themselves and others.

King, a pastor, lived a liberation theology. He experienced and saw the numerous daily humiliations of blacks. The grinding, oppressive poverty of blacks was also a routine reality that King encountered. His speeches are peppered with a desire and demand for justice, as well as a demand that resistance be tempered with care for the enemy. That is, King's method of nonviolence reveals the intersection of an ethics of justice and an ethics of care. King's outrage at injustices emerges out of his care for his people, but also for all who are oppressed or marginalized, whether the white mine

84. Ibid., 336.

85. Smiley and Ritz, *Death of a King*, 17.

86. King, *The Autobiography of Martin Luther King, Jr.*, 343.

87. Ibid.

88. Ibid., 341.

89. Ibid., 340.

worker in Appalachia or the Vietnamese people suffering from the travails of war. Outrage, for King, was guided by an ethics of care for the very people who are implicated in unjust practices that have led to oppression and poverty. An ethics of care leads to a desire for justice in the face of suffering and unmet needs, and the demand for justice is tempered by an ethics of care informed by compassion—to include one's enemies. I believe for King care and justice could not have been separated without both being corrupted.

A second important feature of liberation theology is its attention on community.[90] Community, represented in the notion of church or *ecclesia*, is a central anthropological category for Christian theologies and, in particular, Latin American liberation theologies. The political and economic oppression liberation theologians saw and critiqued obviously affected individuals and families, but it also undermined and devastated communities. The church of the poor that Jon Sobrino discusses is a community that is aware of injustice and its sources; it is a community that cares for its own while concerned for the good of others.[91] The term often used for local church communities was *communidades de base*, which means basic ecclesial communities. These base communities exercise mutual care for their members while resisting social, political, and economic injustices that makes caring for oneself and others difficult. Base communities inform and educate the larger Church and its leaders, rather than simply passively receiving the teachings of the magisterium.[92] These communities, then, have their own authority in terms of interpreting Scripture from their experiences of suffering and needs. For Sobrino and other liberation theologians, the notion of community or *ecclesia* is central in any analysis and discussion of an ethics of justice and an ethics of care.

The importance of community in theological analysis of situations of oppression and marginalization is also evident in black liberation theologies. Black churches have been sources of consolation, care, and resistance long before the civil rights movement.[93] To return to Martin Luther King

90. Care theorists, many of whom are feminists, do mention community, though usually with some degree of wariness that stems from experiences of oppression and marginalization from communities. See, Tronto, *Moral Boundaries*, 30; Engster, *The Heart of Justice*, 10; Young, *Justice and the Politics of Difference*, 227–36. Liberation theologians, I believe, would not disagree with this. However, theologically community is a central feature of human life with regard to care and justice. The beloved community, while falling short of the ideals of justice and care due to sin, is at the same time the living, dynamic potential and reality of care and justice.

91. Sobrino, *The True Church and the Poor.*

92. Ibid., 111–16.

93. See Cone, *The Cross and the Lynching Tree*; Hendricks, *The Universe Bends toward Justice.*

Jr., the struggle for civil and economic justice began in and was sustained by black churches. These communities of faith cared for members and gave them strength to resist the daily racist humiliations and helped meet material needs that resulted from encountering economic forms of racism. The community of faith played a significant role in King's childhood. Understandably, the church was the center of his family's life and, I suspect, not simply because his father was the pastor. The community was a place, a sanctuary, of protection against racism. I contend that King's own strong sense of self-respect, dignity, and inner strength depended on both his family and his church community. I think we could characterize the church as a moral and caring community. That is, against the background of a caring community comes the recognition of injustice and the search for ways to resist succumbing to diverse forms of injustice. Put another way, the church as a moral community is a community where discourse and action embody an ethics of care and an ethics of justice.

In summary, Central and South American liberation theologies emphasize God's preferential option for the poor in guiding a critical analysis of political, economic, and social structures and systems that deny material and immaterial resources for individuals, families, and communities to care justly for themselves and others. Because these are theologians, they understandably anchor a theology of liberation in ecclesiology. Community, then, is a key concept in the pursuit of liberation from injustice. My brief discussion of liberation theology aims at elaborating further on the distinction between care and justice. The notions of the preferential option for the poor and base communities reveal the intertwining of an ethics of care and an ethics of justice vis-à-vis liberation, though the ethics of care is implicit in this discourse. The pursuit of liberation, in other words, comes out of a recognition of desperate poverty wherein people struggle to care for themselves and others. It is from the clear violations of an ethics of care that the passion for justice is given voice in theologies of liberation—liberation aimed at political freedoms as well as at just distribution of resources so that individuals, families, and communities can care for themselves and others.

POLITICAL PASTORAL THEOLOGY: CARE, JUSTICE, AND THE SPACE OF APPEARANCES

I believe liberation theologies fall under the heading of pastoral theology, in part because of their attention to responding to the needs and experiences of those suffering from various forms of political, economic, and cultural oppression and marginalization. One limitation of liberation theologies is that not all forms of human suffering and need in the polis fall under the metaphor of liberation. For instance, an ethics of care may involve the political actions aimed at making companies list on labels ingredients and calories from fat so that people can make decisions about what is healthy—caring for themselves and their families. Another example is noted when political activists work locally and nationally to enact legislation to reduce carbon emissions and for clean air and water—an issue of care for the well-being of human beings and the environment. A second limitation is that liberation theologies foreground the ethics of justice and only implicitly include the ethics of care—an ethic that is largely restricted by the notion of liberation. Pastoral theology is more expansive and foregrounds both the ethics of care and an ethics of justice.[94] In this last section of the chapter I frame political pastoral theology's notions of an ethics of care and ethics of justice by returning to the metaphor "space of appearances"—theologically understood.

In the previous chapter I mentioned two creation stories. While these stories are very different, what they have in common is that in the act of creation the human creature appears and is recognized by God or the gods as valued and unique. In the Israelite myth, value, uniqueness, and inviolability are ontologically anchored in the notion of *imago dei*: human beings are created in the image and likeness of God. Both stories also affirm that human beings are finite creatures that have needs throughout their existence, thus requiring care. Even in the Israelite myth Adam and Eve have their needs met in Eden, though without any apparent work on their part; they live in a womblike space. Regardless, both stories depict human finitude and dependency (or interdependency) for survival and flourishing.

In terms of the space of appearances, the act of creation involves recognition of the uniqueness, value, and agency of human beings. In the Roman fable, this creation and recognition accompanies a demand—the demand that the gods care for the creature. Cura cares for the creature while it lives and after death Jupiter cares for its spirit and Tellus for its body. The Israelite stories of creation place this demand to care not only on God but on human beings as well. Judeo-Christian Scriptures can be read as testaments to God's covenant of care, moving from a narrow concern for the chosen people to more expansive expressions of love and care for all human beings,

94. Many pastoral theologians, while not calling themselves political pastoral theologians, are very interested in issues of justice as they impact persons' and communities' ability to care for themselves and others. Moreover, like liberation theologians, they are interested in situations of oppression and acts of care that remove oppressive conditions. For example, see, Graham, "From Relational Humanness to Relational Justice"; Orr, "Ministry with Working-Class Women"; Ramsay, "When Race and Gender Collide"; Wimberly, *African American Pastoral Care and Counseling*.

for all creation. In addition, there are God's commands that the community is to care for widows, orphans, and neighbors. We also note the seemingly impossible command to love one's enemies. In the act of creation, then, there is the birth of a space of appearances, wherein the creature is recognized as valued, unique, agentic, and finite. And both uniqueness/value and finiteness that evoke the ontological demand for care and for justice.[95] The space of appearances is evident in the act of creation and in the acts of care.

Let's move, for a moment, to a more existential view of creation, space of appearances, and the demand to care. Human beings participate in creation in the process of giving birth. As depicted earlier, a good enough parent is already giving expression to the space of appearances prior to birth in naming the infant, fantasizing about who s/he is and will be, making room for the infant in the home. The parent's care is also evident in caring for her body—eating well, resting, and so forth. The child's uniqueness and value take on particular form after birth through the child's actions and preverbal speech. Any good enough parent makes room for, acknowledges, and affirms the child's assertions, though curbing those deemed to be harmful. And if there is any doubt about the existential demand to care, consider the routine stories of parents waking up in the middle of the night to feed and comfort a baby or to clean up and care for a sick child. The child's psychological, physical, and spiritual existence depends on the parents living out of this existential demand to care by creating a space of appearances wherein the child is recognized and treated as unique, valued, and agentic.

The space of appearances accompany this existential or ontological demand to care and the notion of demand implies the freedom to not care, to not recognize the Other as unique, valued, and inviolable. We note already in the Judeo-Christian creation stories the issue of human freedom and failings. To be sure, God created human beings, blessed them, and declared them and the rest of creation good. Not long after this pronouncement, we note that they cannot seem to keep the one rule God has commanded them to follow: that they cannot suggests that from the beginning human beings have agency. If there were no agency and freedom, there would be no need for the command to not eat the fruit of that one tree. After Adam and Eve are expelled from the garden, we read that their children do not get along; this is evidence of the trajectory of human existence. Theologically, human beings are created in the image and likeness of God, yet as Edward Farley notes, we are beset with anxieties related to separation from God (in the act of creation there is separation, not necessarily alienation) and human

95. See Farley, *Divine Empathy*; Levinas, *Totality and Infinity*; Zizioulas, *Being as Communion*.

finitude (loss, sickness, and death).[96] It is out of this anxiety that reason and emotion become distorted and we act in ways that alienate others and God. There is, then, an existential demand to care, but it accompanies freedom not to care, as well as our routine actions that miss the mark. This suggests that the space of appearances founded on acts of care between parents and children is dynamic and not static and, therefore, in need of restoration—an ethics of justice.

In many ways, good enough parents exhibit an ethics of care and an ethics of justice. Day in and day out, parents live out this existential demand to care for their children, recognizing them as persons and responding appropriately to their assertions and needs. Put another way, parents, as co-creators, give their children what they are due in material, psychological, and spiritual ways. Of course, family life is not Eden. Parents fail to care for all kinds of reasons, and hopefully these are not egregious events. Nevertheless, these quotidian failures give rise to another existential demand—an ethics of justice. A parent, for instance, recognizes that his/her child's behavior signals some distress, resulting from the parent's earlier failure of not attuning to the child's assertions. The child's preverbal behavior is a cry of injustice. "I am not being given what is due me." The parent who responds to meet the child's needs and to repair the relationship (the space of appearances) is acting from this existential demand for justice, which is inextricably joined to the parent's care. If the parent did not care, then s/he would not respond to the demand for justice. In this imaginary scenario, the ethics of care is what motivates the ethic of justice.

This analogy of a parent-child relationship can highlight how the ethics of care and an ethics of justice are existentially rooted and dynamic, yet the parent-child relationship is limited because it does not depict how both relate to the polis. To return to the Bible, by the sixth chapter of Genesis the story has moved from the first family to the human family apparently congregating in cities and given over to corruption and sin. I will bypass the image of a vengeful God who wipes out nearly all humanity and other creatures in order to consider the challenges of living in a polis and its relation to an ethics of care and an ethics of justice.

The Hebrew Scriptures contain many stories of how the people of God are to organize themselves, and stories about the accompanying infighting, corruption, murder, mayhem, and exile.[97] Broken relationships and harm fall under the heading of an ethics of justice, but there is more. The Hebrew Scriptures also feature numerous stories of care and commands to care for

96. See Farley, *Good and Evil.*

97. See Walzer, *In God's Shadow.*

those who struggle to care for themselves (widows and orphans). These same stories and commands we also find in the Christian Scriptures: in the book of Acts, people are to share what they have for the well-being of everyone in community; they are to practice what Roland Boer calls early Christian communism.[98] The demand to care is also extended to strangers and enemies—relations that exist outside the community and shared identity. Two points can be made here. First, the people of God, the *ecclesia*, the beloved community, the City of God and other metaphors reveal that the social-political reality of human life accompanies the dynamic and difficult circumstances of living a life in common. In terms of the space of appearances, human beings always struggle to recognize and treat each other as persons, even in families and beloved communities. Similarly, power as cooperation, which is a feature of the space of appearances and necessary for a viable polis, is easily corrupted by greed, lust, pride and other human vices.

Given this, the polis first depends on following the commands to love and care for the least. A viable if not thriving polis, wherein all are recognized as persons of immeasurable value, depends on a rigorous ethics of care. And yet the polis is also beset by human failings and the attenuation of the space of appearances. These human failings require an ethics of justice to correct wrongdoings and repair social relations. Second and relatedly, an ethics of justice cannot alone maintain community and the space of appearances. The ethics of care precedes an ethics of justice, as the creation stories noted, and care accompanies an ethics of justice, for in the Christian Scriptures forgiveness and enemy love are expectations.

What does this mean for a political pastoral theology? An ethics of care is grounded in the ontological reality of creation, and human beings are cocreators particularly through recognizing and treating Others as persons. This cocreation of the space of appearances ideally occurs in parent-child relations, family relations, communities, and societies. A viable polis, then, relies on an ethics of care, and it is an ethics of care that grounds an assessment and critique of political-economic institutions, structures, and policies. Of course, human beings are fallible creatures and through acts of commission or omission attenuate or obliterate the space of appearances, resulting in all kinds of destruction. Recognition of harm to individuals and the polis depends on an ethics of justice that aims at restoring, repairing the space of appearances wherein persons are given what they are due—physiologically, psychologically, and spiritually. What I have wanted to stress though is that the ethics of justice depends on the ethics of care. There must be some inner (existential) demand to care if we are to experience and live

98. Boer, *In the Vale of Tears*, 112–17.

out the demand for an ethics of justice. This means that a critical analysis of current political realities begins with the framework of an ethics of care that is necessarily joined to an ethics of justice that aims to restore the space of appearances so that people are given what they are due. To return to Malcolm X's story, restoring the space of appearances would have involved recognizing the personhood of all members of Malcolm's family, and this would have involved justice for his murdered father, genuine care for the material needs of his family, and correspondingly a rejection of racism. In his story, care was divorced from justice, which meant that care itself was distorted and thus inadequate. In summary, a political pastoral theology aims for an ethics of care that is informed by justice, and an ethics of justice that is formed by care.

4

CIVIL AND REDEMPTIVE DISCOURSE

Care of Souls and Care of Polis

When willingness to impose an image has replaced imagination, when calculation has replaced judgment, the life has gone out of politics.[1]

Power is actualized only where word and deed have not parted company, where words are not empty and deeds not brutal, where words are not used to veil intentions but to disclose realities, and deeds are not used to violate and destroy but to establish relations and create new realities.[2]

A POLIS IS A dynamic reality shaped by the vicissitudes of human creativity, aggression, vice, and virtue, as well as by nature. A polis comes into being, thrives, declines, rises, and, at times, fades into the pages of history. Given that it is a living entity, a necessary human creation, we may wonder, what is needed for a polis to survive and thrive? By contrast, we might query, what undermines a polis? The latter question is often easier to answer. Writing at the end of the 1960s, John Courtney Murray warns of a barbarism that undermines democracy and civil society. He writes,

> Barbarism likewise threatens when men cease to talk together according to reasonable laws. There are laws of argument, the observance of which is imperative if discourse is to be civilized.

1. Young-Bruehl, *Why Arendt Matters*, 116.
2. Arendt, *The Human Condition*, 200.

> Argument ceases to be civil when it is dominated by passion and prejudice; when its vocabulary becomes solipsist, premised on the theory that my insight is mine alone and cannot be shared; when dialogue gives way to a series of monologues; when the parties to the conversation cease to listen to one another, or hear only what they want to hear, or see the other's argument only through the screen of their own categories . . . When things like this happen, men cannot be locked together in argument. Conversation becomes merely quarrelsome or querulous. Civility dies with the death of dialogue.[3]

The polis begins to shrivel and die when civil discourse is replaced with self-certain, self-aggrandizing, intransigent monologues that aim at coercing the Other into acceptance of one's singular vision of the world.

Murray knows that a democratic polis relies on civil conversations. The term "civil" suggests respect, and "conversation" implies that partners listen to each other, which does not mean they agree with each other. Civil dialogue can range from a peaceful and relaxing conversation at a café regarding current political issues of the day to a vigorous argument over contested economic policies at a political gathering. In one sense, Murray is positing that the survival and flourishing of a democratic polis depends on *just* speech, whereby the speaker (and listener) is giving the Other his/her due, and what s/he is due is respect and understanding—not necessarily agreement. Just speech is foundational for a vibrant political space of appearances,

In this chapter, I consider discourse vis-à-vis the polis in terms of an ethics of care and an ethics of justice. That is, in this last of the theoretical chapters on a political pastoral theology, I attend to the foundation of any viable polis, and that is communication. What kind of discourse or communication is necessary for a polis to survive and thrive? What are the attributes of civil discourse? What virtues or practices are parts of vital civil discourse? How might an ethics of care and an ethics of justice frame how we think about civil discourse? These are important questions I want to consider, but in this chapter I also want to move beyond the notion of civil discourse, introducing the notion of redemptive discourse. I claim that the attributes of civil discourse are part of redemptive discourse, yet redemptive discourse is more demanding and radical than civil discourse. In the democratic society of the United States, redemptive discourse was demonstrated by Martin Luther King Jr. and others in facing hostile, uncivil monologues by racists. In South Africa, also a democratic society, redemptive discourse

3. Murray, *We Hold These Truths*, 14.

was manifested in the communications of Desmond Tutu and Nelson Mandela in the midst of vicious, nondemocratic apartheid. While civil discourse is necessary for a viable and vibrant democratic polis, redemptive discourse aims toward an ethics of care and an ethics of justice that invites the repair of social relations marred by injustices and carelessness, and makes possible a future space of appearances that is inclusive of diversity. Redemptive discourse is a *just* and *care-full* discourse. It is just because it intends to give the Other his/her due and care-full because it aims to establish relations of mutual care necessary for achieving the common good. Redemptive discourse embodies realistic hope that repair of political space, which is attenuated by fear, despair, and hostility, can occur.

With these general remarks, I begin by addressing what is wrong vis-à-vis political discourse and, in particular, political discourse in the United States. In general, civil discourse implies the reality of uncivil discourse, which Murray rightly fears is taking over the public space in the United States. Similarly, redemptive discourse suggests that something is in need of redemption; something is wrong and, theologically, this falls under the category of sin or missing the mark. In one sense, identifying what is wrong in our present discourse can lead one to imagine that if we "fix" this, we will be in good shape—the polis will be as it should. Yet, both notions—civil and redemptive discourse—highlight the perennial struggle in human life to live in community and society. That is, there is always a tendency toward uncivil discourse, and thus a democracy (or any polis) in every generation must create and foster civil discourse. Likewise, from a theological perspective, sin exists, in varying degrees, in human relations and communications. There is, in other words, no full redemption on this side of the veil.[4] However, we can experience redemption in the here and now, even though it is fragmentary.[5] After describing what is wrong with political communication, I identify the attributes of civil discourse, arguing that it can be understood as *just* speech. From this discussion, I move to address what I mean by redemptive discourse and how it more radically expresses the ethics of care *and* ethics of justice.

4. Brown, *Politics Out of History*, 15, addresses the questions and issues that arise in postmodernity when the notion of progress no longer makes sense vis-à-vis history. Indeed, she invokes Walter Benjamin, who sought to sever redemptive politics from progress. My use of these concepts—a civil and redemptive discourse—avoids any notion of the idea of progress, as if there is some future polis where there will be civil and redemptive discourse. Each generation has the responsibility to create and nurture civil and redemptive discourses.

5. See Pannenberg, *Theology and the Kingdom of God*.

Let me pause briefly to offer a couple of clarifications. When I bring up the notion of redemptive discourse in the contested area of politics and power, some likely consider it idealistic if not naïve. Moreover, when considering the realm of politics where one faces hard realities and difficult decisions (realpolitik) that often fall outside the routine notions of morality and ideals, the idea of redemptive discourse seems ill fitting. Surely, in politics, Machiavelli is a more apt guide than theology. To these charges let me first point out that there is a distinction between idealism, which can easily venture away from the practical and less savory realities of human life, and having ideals. Ideals are the cherished principles that are necessary for shaping our virtues, our relationships, our behaviors. It is hard to imagine life without ideals, even if we often fail to live up to them. Yet, if we entertain the possibility of life without ideals, we will stare into the abyss of a dystopic polis corrupted by despair and violence. Let me shift here to illustrations of ideals in the contested area of power politics. I mentioned Tutu, Mandela, and King,[6] and to this list we can add Rosa Parks, Emma Goldman, Medger Evers, and Eugene Debs as people who possessed and advocated for their ideals; they were hardly naïve idealists who did not deal with the realpolitik of their times. They faced considerable political obstacles and violence, all the while holding on to and living out their ideals. Moreover, their principles were part of the political power they sought to employ.[7] Redemptive discourse is an ideal in the face of the hard, routine realities of human frailties and failings, but it also takes into account the practical realities of politics as a contact sport, as well as the machinations of uncivil political discourse.

My second clarification involves the tendency in political life to focus on ideas, policies, and programs without much attention to *how* we talk about these things. To be sure, some rules guide speech in a democratic society, and the outer limits of political speech in a democratic society are addressed by laws or social expectations dealing with slander, libel, and hate speech. As a rule, however, we do not pay enough attention to public discourse; instead we pay more attention to ideas and policies. More accurately, if we are to be honest, we pay more attention to the spectacles of politics and

6. Brown, *Politics Out of History*, 25, addresses the interplay of principles and power in politics, mentioning both Martin Luther King Jr. and Gandhi. She writes that "these movements [e.g., Gandhi's campaign and the civil rights movement] also turned principle into an explicit and self-conscious form of power that worked by distinguishing itself in style, bearing, and tactics from the power and interests of the regime it decried." Brown is pointing to the idea that ideals have power, even in the presence of oppressive political contexts.

7. Ibid.

are more focused on political ends rather than means used to attain those ends.[8] I am not suggesting that we enact more laws about speech, but rather that we pay greater attention to the kind of discourse we use to engage in our contestations with others about public matters.[9] Our methods of communicating are as important as our political ideas, and sometimes methods can be divorced from democratic ideas and ideals. For example, ad hominem attacks, or what we call attack ads, are rife in political campaigns and on talk radio, especially during our interminable presidential campaigns. These communication strategies are considered effective in gaining votes. This *ends justifies the means* perspective illustrates how the democratic ideals associated with reasoned argumentation are eschewed for vitriolic name-calling, which adds a great deal of heat to serial political monologues, but no light. In short, the way we engage in public discourse has everything to do with the kind of polis we seek to create and sustain, and the prevalence of uncivil discourse promotes the barbarism of a totalitarian polis.

WHAT IS WRONG IN THE POLIS?

John Courtney Murray was concerned about the rise of uncivil discourse that could undermine the democratic polis. Since the 1960s, it has worsened, making his comments all the more prescient. Nolan McCarty, Keith Poole, and Howard Rosenthal, political scientists, extensively research and analyze the rise of political polarization in the United States, arguing that "we now live in an era where political elites literally hate each other and CEOs live on a different planet than their lowest-wage employees."[10] Their approach has been to identify "some causal pathways" to explain deepening and expanding political and economic polarization—polarization that represents the attenuation of the space of appearances in the polis.[11] Political polarization and the attending uncivil discourse, they argue, accompany deep and pervasive social and economic inequalities and conflicts. In a similar analysis, Marc Hetherington and Jonathan Weiler depict the

8. Any cursory examination of elections in the United States reveals the media's (and our own) fascination with flash rather than substance. See Boorstin, *The Image*.

9. Any good-enough parent (and any child psychologist) realizes that communication is as important as his/her behavior in responding to a child's assertions. A voice can "touch" a child, soothe him, affirm her, and so forth. Likewise parental speech—not just words—can wound. If we know it is important to attend to communication in families, then we should pay attention to communication in larger human configurations such as the polis.

10. McCarty et al., *Polarized America*, 191.

11. Ibid.

widening gulf between conservatives and liberals and the rise in authoritarian dispositions in the body politic. Between 1972 and 2004, they note, the "distance between ideological self-placement of the average Democrat and Republican . . . has increased dramatically."[12] The body politic is more divisive and less democratic.

From a different perspective, political philosopher Wendy Brown argues that we "live in the shadow and sometimes paralyzing disorientation of the historical and metaphysical losses" associated with the undermining of modernity's notions of progress, reason, free will, moral truth, and sovereignty.[13] This dizzying reality gives rise to "righteous moralism . . . in contemporary political discourse" and, correspondingly, anti-intellectualism.[14] Moralism is "a hegemonic form of political expression" that relies on discourses of exclusion to create what I call theopolitical enclaves of same-minded people who eschew critical thinking and who construct political opponents as demeaned Others. This is exacerbated by individuals listening to news outlets that only reinforce, instead of challenge, their prejudices and biases. For Brown, moralism and anti-intellectualism are symptoms of disavowed despair and anxiety[15] that come from the threat of the demise of one's cherished ideals. This disavowed despair and anxiety lurk beneath and fuel the agitated angst of political polarization and the accompanying polarized discourse, which, in turn, reveals a fragile and attenuated space of appearances in the body politic.

The present fractious state of political discourse in the United States has other possible political, economic, and social sources. It is important to identify underlying factors that fuel the particular hegemonic forms of political discourse in a specific era and society, yet I suggest that while uncivil discourse is rife today, precarious existential realities of being human can give rise to the totalitarian tendency in human life, the symptom of which is totalizing speech.[16] To be sure, unique conditions and factors are associated with particular locales of uncivil discourse, but the seed lies in all human beings, in all human attempts to form a polis. Indeed, I suggest that attempts to form utopian political communities are doomed from the start, because they fail to acknowledge how embedded this human tendency is in social relations, a tendency that can be mitigated but not erased. In

12. Hetherington and Weiler, *Authoritarianism and Polarization in American Politics*, 25.

13. Brown, *Politics Out of History*, 14.

14. Ibid., 15.

15. Ibid., 37.

16. H. Richard Niebuhr linked the notion of sin and idolatry to the totalitarian tendency in human life. See Niebuhr, *The Meaning of Revelation.*

other words, I am making an anthropological claim about human beings vis-à-vis the polis and political discourse—a claim I argue is represented in psychological, philosophical, and theological perspectives, though each uses a different language. Briefly discussing each perspective yields a picture of the totalitarian tendency and totalizing speech.

Let me begin with psychology and its rendering of this totalitarian tendency in human life. Psychoanalysts, starting with Freud,[17] believe that anxiety is a key emotion in human life, which shapes perception, personality, and behavior. In Freud's later work, he considered anxiety to be a signal of danger that initiates a defensive response.[18] At best, signal anxiety functions to help organize the psyche to prepare for action, but anxiety can also be disorganizing or psychologically disruptive. This is seen in cases of neurotic anxiety, which can paralyze a person, impeding social relations and the ability to function effectively. The neurotic's attribution of the sources of anxiety, or more accurately, danger is incorrect, indeed, illusory, indicating a distortion in perception as well as behavior. Yet, it is not simply neurotics who misattribute the source of anxiety and behave in destructive ways. Relatively healthy people can as well, and Freud's work on mass psychology points to how group anxiety can lead to an undifferentiated ego mass and negative or destructive group behavior.[19]

To carry this further, signal anxiety both alerts human beings and is transformed into more tolerable affects. Generally, human beings find most anxiety uncomfortable or disturbing, and thus are not aware or do not acknowledge anxiety vis-à-vis the source of danger. As Rollo May notes, anxiety is often joined to, if not transformed into, fear and hostility, which are, for most human beings, more tolerable emotions because they have a clear target, provide a sense of agency, and lead to actions.[20] When anxiety is changed into fear and hostility, four things occur. First, the internal and external sources of anxiety are obscured. That is, we misattribute the sources of anxiety. To return to Wendy Brown, moralism is a symptom of anxiety due to significant social changes that undermine cherished ideas (sovereignty, free will, progress) that we use to make sense of ourselves and reality.[21] Moralism

17. See May, *The Meaning of Anxiety*. There is a great deal written about anxiety in the area of psychoanalysis. It is not my aim to address the intricacies of these views. Instead, I am aiming toward outlining an existential view of the origins of the totalitarian tendency in human life. Moreover, while psychoanalytic literature tends to address anxiety, this does not mean other emotions are unimportant.

18. See Freud, "Inhibitions, Symptoms, and Anxiety."

19. See Freud, *Group Psychology and the Analysis of the Ego*.

20. May, *The Meaning of Anxiety*, 204–5.

21. Brown, *Politics Out of History*, 18–44.

and anti-intellectualism, which carry a streak of hostility, screen the sources of anxiety and locate danger in those individuals and groups believed to undermine the social order. For example, moralists angrily denounce gay marriage, arguing that it undermines the very foundations of society. They generally do not acknowledge their anxiety and fail to identify the source of anxiety associated with the systemic loss of their previously dominant worldview. Their fear and hostility, focused on gays and lesbians, prevents them from mourning. Second, and relatedly, unacknowledged signal anxiety transformed into fear and hostility has the effect of fostering anxiety in the target group.[22] Heterosexuals do not face public opprobrium, violence, and censure for expressing their affection in social settings. Hence, in public settings, heterosexuals are, generally speaking, not anxious. This is not the case for many LGBTQI individuals, though, to be sure, there are safe public places in many cities. LGBTQI individuals experience the anxiety that is, in psychoanalytic parlance, split-off and projected onto them from homophobic moralists. Third, in transforming anxiety into fear and hostility, human beings project responsibility for their internal distress onto others. In other words, we tend to see the Other as responsible and ourselves as innocent, which is, in psychoanalytic circles, the defense of splitting. To return to the example of the moralism of some Christians against gays and lesbians, these Christians claim to have the truth, which means they are righteous and innocent while their opponents are sinners—wholly responsible for social discord. Fourth, signal anxiety that is disclaimed and subsequently morphed into fear and hostility provides participants with the illusion of agency and control. I say "illusion" because an individual believes s/he is acting toward the right object in the right way at the right time when in fact, the individual misrecognizes the source of anxiety and eschews responsibility, and acts toward the wrong object with the wrong approach and at the wrong time.

This discussion about signal anxiety, how it can be altered, and its psychosocial dynamics is a preliminary step in depicting from a psychological perspective the totalitarian tendency in human life. Returning to Rollo May, he argues that heightened social-cultural anxiety gives rise to totalitarianism, which "is a cultural neurotic symptom of the need for community."[23] It is neurotic because the totalitarian tendency binds (in my view, transforms) some anxiety and provides individuals relief, all the while depending on the illusion of self-certainty.[24] It is also neurotic because of the misattribu-

22. Marris brings an analogous political-economic example of this. He notes that in the capitalist system, the lower classes bear the anxiety of uncertainty, which is placed or displaced on them by the upper classes. Marris, *The Politics of Uncertainty*.

23. May, *The Meaning of Anxiety*, 212.

24. Ibid., 12.

tion of the source of anxiety, the diminishment of self-reflective capacity, the projection of responsibility, the illusion of agency, and the poor level of differentiation.[25] May, while arguing this is a feature of human existence, locates the source of the present totalitarian tendency in "feelings of powerlessness and helplessness of the isolated, alienated individuals produced in a society in which competitive individualism has been the dominant goal."[26] Here we note that, for May, a function of the totalitarian tendency, in our current situation, is to provide a sense of collective belonging, which I call theopolitical enclaves that rely on totalizing speech to reinforce group self-certainty—same-mindedness. We could add here that this collective belonging accompanies a sense of group identity—an identity that is constructed in opposition to the feared and despised Other.

Writing a few decades later, psychoanalyst Christopher Bollas also takes up the notion of totalitarianism, depicting this in terms of what he calls the fascist state of mind,[27] to which he notes all human beings are susceptible. The fascist state of mind "is the presence of an ideology that maintains certainty through the operation of a specific mental mechanism aimed at eliminating all opposition."[28] Uncertainties, "doubts and counterviews are expelled, and the mind ceases to be complex, achieving simplicity," rejecting the polysemous reality of political symbols and communication. This is what Freud and Melanie Klein termed the collapse of the symbolic equation. This collapse brings about a "non-differentiation between the thing symbolized and the symbol."[29] Eschewing complexity depends on omnipotent thinking, which accompanies both the refusal to contain or metabolize anxiety and, correspondingly, the omnipotent construction of the Other as the absolute source of danger. A fascist state of mind, then, rejects not-knowing and embraces certainty, or what Freud called overdecisiveness. Overdecisiveness occurs when an individual "is too easily tempted into pushing aside thoughts which threaten to break into [the mind], and in exchange, one is left with a feeling of uncertainty which in the end one tries to keep down by over-decisiveness."[30] Certainty or overdecisiveness is integral to the psychology of the totalitarian tendency and its totalizing speech.

25. To believe that the source of danger is external when it is internal reflects a struggle of differentiation and is, according to Niebuhr, "more than an epistemological fallacy." For Niebuhr this is the foundation of idolatry. Niebuhr, *The Purpose of the Church and Its Ministry*, 43.

26. May, *The Meaning of Anxiety*, 212.

27. Bollas, *Being a Character*, 200–207.

28. Ibid., 200.

29. Segal, "Notes on Symbol Formation," 393.

30. Freud, "The Future of an Illusion," 21.

Relying on the work of Hannah Arendt,[31] Bollas argues that this fascist state of mind, whether in individuals or groups, claims total explanation.[32] Thus the "total explanation of the past, the total knowledge of the present, and the reliable prediction of the future" means individuals "cannot learn anything new, even if it is a question of something that has just come to pass."[33]

The totalitarian tendency or fascist state of mind, for Bollas and May, is part of the human condition,[34] yet this feature of being human need not be active or acted upon. When it is, the totalitarian tendency is revealed in totalizing speech, which is thoroughly uncivil and leads to the attenuation of the space of appearances. Totalizing speech has *the* answer, *the* truth, *the* explanation regarding the current situation. It is empty of ambiguity and uncertainty. Totalizing speech invites no discussion and it demands acceptance. I am saying that it is uncivil not because totalizing speech is necessarily vitriolic and polarizing—though it often is—but because it overtly or secretly rejects democratic dialogue and views the Other as a danger, which, more often than not, means the Other is not recognized and treated as a person. By contrast, civil discourse possesses some basic level of respect for the Other as person, inviting discussion, complexity, difference, cooperation, and compromise. The uncivil discourse of totalizing speech seeks same-minded disciples whose anger and outrage screen anxiety and despair that, in turn, accompany the refusal to mourn or let go and the occult desire to remake the world into their image.

It is easy to find examples of the totalitarian tendency and uncivil discourse amid the din of ad hominem discourse (more correctly, monologues) in a politically polarized United States. Whether from the political Left or Right, totalizing speech fills the airwaves and fiber optic cables. Fox News, MSNBC, Sean Hannity, Bill Maher, Ann Coulter, Keith Olbermann, Rachel Maddow, Rush Limbaugh, Bill O'Reilly, Glenn Beck, and Gordon Liddy are just some of the organizations and persons who engage in totalizing speech. These are more obvious illustrations of uncivil speech and, yes, the fascist state of mind. There are also subtle examples of totalizing speech. I recently listened to a prominent Southern Baptist leader speaking with

31. Arendt, *The Origins of Totalitarianism*, 470–72.

32. Bollas, *Being a Character*, 200.

33. Arendt, *The Origins of Totalitarianism* 470.

34. While I focus on totalizing speech vis-à-vis the polis, one can find this in other organizations, proving the point that it is a feature of human life. A cursory reading of the history of psychoanalysis reveals this totalitarian tendency as individuals held on to the certainty or orthodoxy of their version of psychoanalysis and the subsequent rejections of other analysts who differed (e.g., Adler, Ferenczi, Bowlby to name only a few). See Breger, *Freud: Darkness in the Midst of Vision*; Gay, *Freud: A Life for Our Time.*

a PBS commentator about the importance of civil discourse in the public sphere. The Southern Baptist leader appeared open, calm, rational, and interested in engaging those who held different views. What became apparent was that he entered the political arena, not with the aim of listening and learning from others, but with the goal of persuading others of his version of the Christian Truth. It *appeared* that he was open to other ideas, it *appeared* that he was willing to engage in dialogue, but in reality he was not.

The calm, ostensibly reasoned speech of this Baptist gentleman is seen in prominent political individuals such as Dick Cheney. Citizens are fooled into thinking that calmness and reason signal civil discourse. To be sure, both are part of civil discourse, but when this "civil discourse," accompanies self-certainty, total explanations, the truth, and a Manichean worldview, then we are moving away from the ideal of a democratic polis that depends on a diversity of perspectives. Whether totalizing speech appears as the rant of ad hominem attacks or the seemingly calm and reasoned speech of political operatives, there is a deep disavowed anxiety and an avowed hostility and disdain toward those who do not hold the same truth. In other words, to perceive the Other as not having the Truth can tend toward pity or indifference, which masks disrespect and hostility that contribute to alienation and political polarization. For instance, evangelical (religious or secular) self-righteous fervor—despite proclaiming care for the Other—covers a hostile denial of the Other's beliefs, desires, needs, and experiences. The barely concealed hostility of the fascist state of mind inevitably erupts into violence, in speech and action, undermining the polis by collapsing the space of appearances. As Pascal noted, human beings "never do evil so completely and cheerfully as when they do it from a religious conviction." We might add here political conviction as well.

The source of uncivil discourse or totalizing speech, from these psychological perspectives, resides not in a particular type of polis but in each individual, family, community, and organization. Using different language, theological perspectives highlight the inherent struggle of humanity vis-à-vis totalitarian conviction or, more broadly, totalitarian faith and its consequences for individuals, families, and societies. For example, idolatry or evil imagination, for H. Richard Niebuhr,[35] is a theological rendering of the totalitarian tendency in human affairs. Evil imagination "interprets every sorrow as due to the pride of others,"[36] whether that is evident in an individual or group.[37] People in the group consider themselves to be the center of the

35. Niebuhr, *The Meaning of Revelation.*

36. Ibid., 73.

37. Ibid., 74–75.

world, and because the group believes that it possesses the truth, it is closed to any criticism or correction from the outside.[38] In terms of knowledge, idolatry inherently involves the "confusion of the subject with the subject's object [which] is more than an epistemological fallacy."[39] In other words, the totalitarian tendency or idolatry involves confusing our representation of God for God. A contemporary of Niebuhr, Karl Barth, echoes this, writing, "We suppose that we know what we are saying when we say 'God.' We assign to Him the highest place in our world . . . we press ourselves into proximity with him . . . [but] secretly we ourselves are masters in this relationship . . . And so, when we set God upon the throne of the world we mean God ourselves . . . God Himself is not acknowledged as God and what is called 'God' is in fact Man."[40] This idolatry, according to Paul Tillich, involves making the relative and contingent universal, timeless, and absolute.[41]

Like the psychological perspective, idolatry entails the illusion that we not only possess the truth, but all the truth there is. This elevation of the relative and contingent to the absolute is exhibited in totalizing explanations, interpretations, and perspectives that resist or reject critique, correction, and difference. Totalizing explanations, for these theologians, are idolatrous and not simply a religious phenomenon. Put another way, it is not simply religious people who are susceptible to the seductive illusion of having all the truth there is. All human beings and groups can fall under the siren song of idolatry, resulting in the loss of empathy toward others and, at times, in violence.[42]

To account for the presence of this totalitarian tendency and obsessive purchase on the Truth, theologian Edward Farley argued that human beings often respond to existential vulnerability and its accompanying anxiety by absolutizing the relative and contingent.[43] That is, in an effort to "transform inescapable vulnerability into something contingent and man-

38. Niebuhr's rendering of idolatry in human life seems strikingly close to features of narcissism, but idolatry, while psychological, does not fall under the category of mental illness. Sane, mentally healthy persons can engage in idolatrous relations, which are evident in the destructive and alienating consequences of their behaviors. I add here that idolatry signifies a distortion of reason and the will, but not necessarily a diminishment of these capacities, as reflected in psychological perspectives on psychopathology. Niebuhr addressed this tendency when commenting on the beliefs and attitudes of Americans during World War II. See Niebuhr, "War as the Judgment of God"; and Niebuhr, "War as Crucifixion."

39. Niebuhr, *The Purpose of the Church and Its Ministry*, 43.

40. Carter, "Between W. E. B. Du Bois and Karl Barth," 92–93.

41. See Tillich, *Love, Power, and Justice.*

42. See Farley, *Divine Empathy*; Volf, *Exclusion and Embrace.*

43. Farley, *Good and Evil.*

ageable," human beings "refuse the structure and situation of their finitude" by absolutizing the relative and contingent.[44] This avoidance of existential vulnerability and its anxiety is secured by the unassailable belief (illusion) that we possess all the truth there is, which leads to alienation from God and all those who do not possess the truth. Yet, existential anxiety and fear continue to lurk beneath the absolutized object and totalizing speech, indicating that psychosocial energy must be ongoing to maintain the illusion of Truth. These emotions may, in part, be projected, denied, or transformed into hostility, but they are never absent. They must continually be kept at bay by totalizing narratives and speech.[45] Any critique or correction vis-à-vis the absolutized object and its narratives is met with righteous rage and hostility, because it is deemed to be a threat to the Truth. If there is no Truth, then vulnerability, fear, anxiety, and possibly despair await. The loss of the absolutized object (and associated narratives and rituals) is unthinkable, because it would expose the horror of vulnerability.

What can go wrong in human relations, whether in a marriage, family, or polis, are people falling into what theologians have called idolatry, evil imagination, the totalitarian tendency, absolutizing the relative and contingent. The totalitarian tendency reflects a bad faith, and by that I mean a faith that trusts only in one's own absolutized beliefs (and attending objects and narratives) and distrusts all Other persons and perspectives. It is bad because it leads to behaviors that alienate Others through varied forms of coercion and violence—either forcing people to adopt the Truth or finding ways to eliminate them, which represents the collapse of the space of appearances. Put another way, the bad faith of the totalitarian tendency in human life is seen in the lack of care for those who disagree, for those who have different truths; it is revealed whenever, in speech and action, opponents are not given their due (recognition as persons meriting respect). In the polis, idolatry takes the form of uncivil speech that attenuates the space of appearances.

John Courtney Murray viewed uncivil speech as barbaric because it did not follow reasonable laws or rules of argument. The use of the adjective "barbaric" suggests an almost atavistic aspect of human life and also seems to suggest human progress in history—progress that can be threatened by uncivil speech. Yet, from both a psychological and theological perspective uncivil speech reflects the human tendency part and parcel of every individual, society, and era. We all have barbarian genes, if you will. From a psychological perspective, uncivil speech is a symptom of a fascist state

44. Ibid., 132.

45. See Fingarette, *Self-Deception*.

of mind that overlooks or denies anxiety and fear by transforming them into hostility and self-certainty, rejecting other perspectives and persons that disagree or challenge cherished beliefs. Theologically, uncivil speech is rooted in idolatry, which deflects the anxiety of existential vulnerability by absolutizing the relative. In both perspectives, uncivil speech is totalizing. It accompanies a total interpretation and explanation of the present situation. It totalizes one's opponents as being completely wrong (bad, crazy, or evil), while those on one's own side are completely right (good, sane, innocent). Totalizing speech leads to polarization of the body politic, and this polarization is a symptom of the collapse of the space of appearances.

This Manichean stance, which reflects carelessness toward opponents and denies them due respect, does not simply avoid anxiety associated with existential vulnerability. To return to Rollo May, totalizing speech also functions to provide the solace of social connections. Put differently, uncivil speech functions to form a "polis" within a polis, or what I call theopolitical enclaves that provide members with, not only the illusory comfort of being absolutely convinced of their views, but also the pleasure and (false) security of being with *same-minded* others. Likewise, the uncivil speech of theopolitical enclaves is not aimed simply at reinforcing the intellectual boundaries between us and them; it is also aimed at using political power or, more accurately, force (also a source of pleasure and gratification) to remake society and its political realities into the group's own images and ideas. So, the totalitarian tendency reflected in uncivil speech is not democratic at all. Indeed, uncivil speech in a democracy rejects the fundamental premises of democratic life, which is the plurality of truths, opinions, and perspectives, and the necessity of compromise and cooperation. In short, when a democracy becomes increasingly polarized, the presence of uncivil speech functions to carve out theopolitical enclaves that are totalizing in their worldview, providing members with shared identity and sense of belonging. The proliferation of totalizing theopolitical enclaves reveals the attenuation of the spaces of appearances in the body politic, which becomes increasingly fragmented.

In my haste to depict the features and sources of uncivil speech, I neglected to offer concrete examples. I suspect most of us think that uncivil speech is hostile, vitriolic, boorish, mean, petty, and simplistic. To be sure, it often is, but, as I noted above, it can also be couched in reasonable tones, coming across as thoughtful, forthright, urbane, seemingly open to democratic ideals. Consider Newt Gingrich's book in which he writes,

> To put it plainly, America is facing an *existential threat*—and it comes from a movement that fundamentally *rejects* the

> traditional American conception of who we are. No longer, in the Left's view, are we the Americans of the frontier, the sturdy, independent farmers; no longer are we America the capitalist colossus serving as the *arsenal* of democracy; no longer are we the America that believes our liberty is an unalienable right that comes from God. All this, the *secular socialist* wants to deny—and is denying—in favor of a secular, bureaucratic society guided by government elites . . . Overall, the fundamental definition of what it means to be *American is being undermined and distorted* by the values, attitudes, and actions of the *secular-socialist machine.*[46]

Claiming to present a clear assessment of the state of the nation, Gingrich nevertheless uses emotionally evocative language to construct the social-political situation in terms of a zero-sum game between exceptionalist capitalism and secular socialism. His Manichean, simplistic worldview provides a total explanation and prediction that relies on depersonalizing language (e.g., the word "machine") vis-à-vis his opponents (apparently traitors). "Eventually one of these value systems," Gingrich writes, "will defeat and replace the other . . . If we lose this struggle, the America of our fathers and forefathers will be forever lost, giving way to a secular-socialist machine that will never relinquish power of its own accord."[47] The fear and anxiety, while screened by hostility toward those who would destroy his world, are rampant and disclaimed. There can be no compromise or cooperation between these "value" systems. There is nothing to learn from his enemies, who happen to be citizens.

More obvious examples of the hostility of totalizing speech are heard and seen from political pundits such as Ann Coulter, Rush Limbaugh, and Grover Norquist. Coulter has written extensively,[48] relying on a kind of combative totalizing discourse to sell books and gain popularity among right-wing conservatives. Indeed, her popularity, like that of Rush Limbaugh, is evidence not only of polarization, but of the uncivil speech that creates, maintains, and increases divisions between groups. For instance, she wrote, the "Democrats and the [liberal] media are generally fighting for the same thing: the total destruction of the United States of America."[49] She characterizes Democrats and liberals, who for her hold clearly inferior beliefs and values, as duplicitous, hypocritical, and bent on seeking domi-

46. Gingrich, *To Save America*, 6 (italics added).

47. Ibid., 10.

48. See Coulter, *Treason*; Coulter, *Godless*; Coulter, *Guilty*.

49. Coulter, *Guilty*, 20.

nation. In an earlier book, Coulter accuses liberals of treason, putatively documenting myriad treasonous acts during the Cold War.[50] In the same vein, Rush Limbaugh, in his books and radio shows, relies on metaphors that heighten anxiety and aggression, signifying a kind of simplism toward policies and people who hold views differing from his own. In a book written with Mark Levin, Limbaugh and Levin write that "liberals are also denying the president [George W. Bush] his judicial appointment power by blocking well-qualified appointments purely for political reasons . . . Let me tell you, folks, this is a subject in need of urgent attention. And this book provides the ammunition you need to defend your liberty."[51] Like Coulter, their speech reflects a Manichean total explanation, which is also evident in this comment of Grover Norquist, the head of Americans for Tax Reform: "The Democrats are the Lefties . . . They are not stupid, they are evil. Evil."[52] This total Manichean explanation functions to transform anxiety into aggression against despised Others. Their totalizing speech is unjust speech, because it denies what the Other is due—recognition and treatment as a person (basic respect). To be sure, these examples of the totalitarian tendency provide "benefits" such as solidifying the certainty of same-minded people and the pleasure of groupthink and identity. Negatively, totalizing speech undermines the polis's space of appearances.

Let me hurry to state that uncivil or totalizing speech is not simply a conservative issue. Those on the Left are also prone to use combative totalizing discourse. The opening chapter of David Coates's book *A Liberal Tool Kit*, is titled, "A Call to Arms."[53] Coates writes, "Creating that debate is not easy, however, because the structures generating and sustaining this conservative orthodoxy are already extensive and firmly in place . . . The wonderful thing about armies, however, is that they contain divisions."[54] While this book does promote guidelines for enhancing public discourse, the war metaphors suggest looming dangers that arise from powerful conservatives. Similarly, Matthew Kerbel[55] writes that Republicans and religious conservatives are enemies of democracy who must be defeated if democracy is to survive. And in another book, John Dean and Judith Warner devote two

50. See Coulter, *Treason.*

51. Limbaugh, "Introduction," in Levin, *Men in Black*, ix.

52. Waldman, *Being Right Is Not Enough*, 3.

53. Coates, *A Liberal Tool Kit.*

54. Ibid., 2.

55. Kerbel, *Get this Party Started.*

chapters to the looming loss of democracy and the Democratic Party's need to defeat Republicans.[56]

Whether progressive or conservative, Democrat or Republican, combative totalizing political discourses often masquerade as sophisticated and balanced political analyses of their opponents. Nevertheless, these ostensibly sophisticated discourses feature of zero-sum-game or Manichean thinking, simplism, total explanations, and hostility toward demeaned opponents. These discourses foster, in other words, an attenuation of the space of appearances: the space is restricted only to the same-minded. Uncivil discourse is not barbaric but rather a human tendency and strategy to escape facing one's existential fears and anxieties through totalizing speech and groupthink/identity. Today in the United States, the proliferation of uncivil speech, which accompanies pervasive political polarization, signifies the heightened presence of the totalitarian tendency, which can be understood psychologically as the fascist state of mind and theologically as idolatry.

CIVIL DISCOURSE

A great deal has been written about the importance of civil discourse for the health of democratic societies, and so I have narrowed the focus to feminist philosophers and care ethicists. My predilection toward these writers stems from their frank acknowledgment of the social-political challenges of a postmodern world; their interest in justice for marginalized and oppressed individuals and groups; their respect for diversity, particularity, and contextuality; their critical stance toward latent social, economic, and political systems and structures that distribute power and prestige to the socially and politically privileged; and their acknowledgment of the importance of respectful recognition of the alterity of human beings. In general, these writers highlight three principles of civil discourse in democratic societies, namely, equality, complementary reciprocity or reversibility, and universalism. These principles foster a space of appearances wherein diverse views are given voice and where compromise and cooperation are possible in contested political spaces. Stated differently, the presence of these principles reduces the presence of totalizing discourse.

The principle of equality vis-à-vis the political realm is often proclaimed but not clearly understood. Iris Marion Young helps clarify this principle stating that equality "refers not primarily to the distribution of social goods, though distributions are certainly entailed by social equality. It refers primarily to the full participation and inclusion of everyone in a society's major

56. Dean and Warner, *You Have the Power.*

institutions, and the socially supported substantive opportunity for all to develop and exercise their capacities and realize their choices."[57] She argues further that "a democratic public should provide mechanisms for effective recognition and representation of distinct voices and perspectives," especially of those "groups that are oppressed or disadvantaged."[58] This is the case because oppressed and marginalized groups within society are not recognized or treated as equal, which is evident not only in the presence of social disrespect but also in the lack of access to social, political, and economic resources, and the lack of full participation in social-political structures. For example, the Department of Justice investigation into the justice system in Ferguson, Missouri, found that the police and the municipal courts work hand in glove to fine and jail African Americans—the intersection of classism and racism.[59] Poor blacks are not recognized as equal citizens, and not only do they not have equal access to social-political institutions, but they are penalized unfairly by these institutions. This quiet oppression necessarily accompanies uncivil discourse that supports relations, systems, and structures that promote and sustain inequalities. Equality in a democratic society means that institutions and procedures exist that make it possible for citizens to have a voice, to have that voice heard, to act on their values and needs, and to participate in the social-political milieu as full citizens: it is what they are due. Equality means, then, that citizens are treated fairly by and have equal access to political and economic structures and systems: it is what they are due.

Benhabib echoes this by arguing for the principle of universal moral respect—egalitarian reciprocity—wherein we "recognize the right of all beings capable of speech and action to be participants in the moral conversation."[60] Civil discourse, then, "requires us to view each and every rational being as an individual [a person] with a concrete history, identity and affective-emotional constitution . . . Our relation to the other is governed by the norms of equity and complementary reciprocity: each is entitled to expect and to assume from the other forms of behavior through which the other feels recognized and confirmed as a concrete, individual being with specific needs, talents and capacities."[61] Both Young and Benhabib acknowledge that while the United States developed documents and institutions that establish formal legal equality, certain members (and groups) in society are in various

57. Young, *Justice and the Politics of Difference*, 173.

58. Ibid., 184.

59. Tuttle, "Predatory Government Burdens the Vulnerable."

60. Benhabib, *Situating the Self*, 29.

61. Ibid., 159.

ways excluded from having a voice and/or participating in society's major institutions (e.g., gays, lesbians, immigrants). More strongly, Arendt noted that refusals to grant equality "take on such terribly cruel forms."[62] These cruel forms emerge from the seeds of uncivil discourse embedded in social-political systems and structures that impoverish the space of appearances necessary for a healthy polis by failing to recognize and treat Others as persons. Thus, citizens must also take a critical stance toward societal institutions and practices that subtly or overtly marginalize or oppress people and consequently exclude their participation and mute their voices in the polis.

In a complex and diverse society, the idea of equality must take into account the reality of difference or alterity. Sevenhuijsen, arguing from the perspective of the ethics of care vis-à-vis citizenship, notes that democratic citizenship involves making value judgments, and these judgments "always take place at the intersection of equality and difference."[63] "Democratic judgments," she writes, "have to be capable of dealing with the radical alterity of human subjects, though recognizing their individuality and diversity, while at the same time conceiving of them as equals."[64] In political discourse the presence of competing values, desires, expectations, judgments, positions, and identities inevitably give rises to clashes and disagreements. Equality, as recognition of the person's right to participate in political conversations, necessarily includes respect for the integrity of each participant and respect for the differences inherent in their experiences, needs, and values. Diversity and alterity vis-à-vis a democratic polis rest on the principle of equality that undergirds social respect. The importance of respect, Arendt notes, is "not unlike the Aristotelean *philia politike*, [which] is a kind of 'friendship' without intimacy and without closeness; it is a regard for the person from the distance which the space of the world puts between us . . . Thus the modern loss of respect, or rather the conviction that respect is due only where we admire or esteem, constitutes a clear symptom of the increasing depersonalization of public and social life."[65] The depersonalization Arendt refers to reveals the presence of the totalitarian tendency, a tendency that fundamentally eschews respect, which is a key feature of the principle of equality. Positively stated, the principle of equality is inherent in civil discourse, which is just speech, giving what is due (equal regard or respect, equal access and participation) to members of society.

62. Arendt, *The Origins of Totalitarianism*, 54.

63. Sevenhuijsen, *Citizenship and the Ethics of Care*, 15.

64. Ibid.

65. Arendt, *The Human Condition*, 243.

Equal regard and respect do not imply agreement or acceptance of the Other's position. I may strongly dislike and disagree with a person's economic proposal to reduce taxes for the wealthy, though I believe that she has a right and obligation to participate in the conversation. Moreover, equal regard means, in speech and action, respecting the person qua person. Civil discourse, then, expresses both equal regard and respect, which makes possible the space of appearances in a pluralistic society.

One might raise questions about the limits of the principle of equality in civil discourse. In other words, should we allow the participation in societal discourse of neo-Nazi groups, al-Qaeda members, or criminals? The principle of equality suggests a very wide interpretation of participation, but the limits, in my view, are drawn in the presence or advocacy of harm or violence toward others, which is a symptom of the loss of the principle of equality and an attenuation or collapse of the space of appearances. Civil discourse cannot take place in the presence of violence, hatred, and excessive fear. Of course, one party may exhibit the principle of equality in the face of someone bent on domination, but that does not mean civil discourse takes place. This said, a democratic society must be able to contain, to some degree, individuals and groups whose communication reflects the hostility that attends the totalitarian tendency and denies principle of equality. Containment does not involve silencing these groups, but it does put clear limits on speech and action. For instance, hate speech, which is clearly shown to contribute to violence, would be considered outside the principle of equality vis-à-vis political discourse. Yet we would continue to recognize the individual who is involved in hate speech as a person.

This is an example of an extreme limit. Let me linger here to consider examples of the uncivil discourse of pundits like Bill Maher, Rush Limbaugh, and Ann Coulter. These popular, polarizing figures frequently show disrespect and, at times, hostility toward people who do not share their views. In those moments, their disrespect reveals a common problem in human relations, the inability or unwillingness to differentiate between the views a person holds and his/her personhood. I may not respect an individual's political stance, but that does not give me license to demonstrate disrespect toward the person. A democratic polis can and must contain a certain amount of uncivil speech, because many human beings will inevitably succumb to the pleasure of their own hatreds, fears, and self-righteousness. However, when uncivil discourse becomes the rule instead of the exception, then the health and vitality of a democratic polis is in question. Stated differently, an underlying premise of a democratic polis is equality, and when this is eclipsed in speech and action, we see the presence of the totalitarian tendency and the attenuation of the space of appearances.

A second feature of civil discourse is the exercise of reversible perspectives. Benhabib, building on Kant's and Arendt's notion of enlarged mentality, argues that "we view discourse as moral conversations in which we exercise reversibility of perspectives either by actually *listening* to all involved or by representing to ourselves imaginatively the many perspectives of those involved."[66] This is necessary because the "concrete other" cannot be known "in the absence of the *voice* of the other."[67] Put another way, when there is an absence of "engagement, confrontation, dialogue and even the 'struggle for recognition' in the Hegelian sense, we tend to constitute the otherness of the other by projection and fantasy or ignore it in indifference."[68] The presence of and listening to the concrete Other's speech ideally invites the diminishment of projection and the possibility of empathy. Benhabib is careful to distinguish reversibility from empathy, though she suggests they are partially related. I believe Benhabib implies that one need not empathize with the concrete Other (versus the amorphous, projection-ridden, generalized Other) to be able to understand her perspective.[69] For instance, in listening to someone who espouses keeping the federal minimum wage at its current level, I can understand the logic of that position and the values and principles that are part of the argument. My values, principles, and perspective are very different, and I arrive at a different place. Reversibility (and equality) is present, though not necessarily empathy.

Sevenhuijsen carries this further, arguing that recognition of differences vis-à-vis concrete Others is not sufficient for civil discourse in a pluralistic and complex society. She contends that a democratic society needs an ethic of care as a social practice: members of a democratic society need concrete practices of caring about and for "others with whom they share their 'being in the world.'"[70] Care as a social practice includes respectful recognition of differences and respectful, empathic listening to the Other's stories. Whether empathy is or is not present vis-à-vis reversible perspectives, it is clear that civil discourse requires some respect for and understanding of the Other's position. This said, I lean toward Sevenhuijsen's view. There must be some basic element of care in reversibility. I must, in civil discourse, care about the Other as person for me to garner respect and to do the work of understanding his/her position.

66. Benhabib, *Situating the Self*, 54 (italics added).

67. Ibid., 168 (italics original).

68. Ibid.

69. Benhabib, "The Generalized Other and the Concrete Other."

70. Sevenhuijsen, *Citizenship and the Ethics of Care*, 19.

Reversibility, as both Benhabib and Sevenhuijsen claim, requires listening to the Other. Neither author spends much time discussing the challenges of the practice or habit of listening, especially given the struggle to listen to others with whom we strongly disagree. Corradi-Fuimara believes that "unless we are ready, receptive—and also, possibly, vulnerable—the experience of listening appears to be impossible."[71] Whether we speak about reversibility, enlarged mentality, or the ethics of care, it appears that civil discourse will not occur unless the participants are ready and willing to be moved by the particular story of the Other. The labor of listening in the contentious political realm is based on the principles of equality and reversibility. By contrast, uncivil discourse is the presence of a series of disputatious monologues where there is a deliberate refusal to listen. Why listen when one has a total explanation, the truth? This refusal is accompanied by the intentional rejection of the principles of equality and reversibility. Uncivil discourse is unjust speech.

The third principle of civil discourse is universalism, which is a controversial and much-debated term. Fiona Robinson, for instance, points out that Kantian universalism highlights abstract reasoning and impartiality, as well as presumes autonomous actors and a generalized Other, all of which tend to deny or overlook particular contexts and differences.[72] She writes that "within Kantian and rights-based moral theory, social and political dimensions of moral problems are obfuscated and little or no reference is made to relationships—personal, social, and political—and structures—economic, social, and political."[73] Moreover, Kantian or liberal accounts of universalism claim that "human beings possess the powers of practical reasoning necessary for moral judgment regardless of whether they belong, now or in the future, to a common co-operative schema."[74] This impartial, transcendent Other, she rightly argues, is a fiction—a fiction that overlooks the particularity and diversity of contexts, as well as the reality of moral reasoning that supports coercion, violence, and exploitation. In brief, universalism, Robinson argues, "asks us to eradicate difference and to understand identity and community in terms of our shared humanity."[75] Instead of this type of universalism, she advocates for an ethic of care, which involves our ability "to see the other as a concrete, particular person who exists not as an 'other' in an absolute, objective sense, but as another whose uniqueness

71. Corradi Fiumara, *The Other Side of Language*, 191.

72. Robinson, *Globalizing Care*, 119–20.

73. Ibid., 53.

74. Ibid., 88.

75. Ibid., 75

and particularity emerges through her relations with others."[76] In terms of civil discourse, this perspective on universalism, Benhabib argues, requires participation of the concrete members of society, whereby "participation is not focused around belonging, oneness, and solidarity, but rather political agency and efficacy, namely the sense that we have a say in economic, political, and civic arrangements."[77] Both Robinson and Benhabib, while critical of universalism, possess a universal ideal of people recognizing other human beings as persons embedded in particular relationships and contexts.

Benhabib, relying on Habermas's communicative ethics and feminists' ethic of care, puts forth the idea of an interactive universalism or a historically self-conscious universalism[78]—a universalism that does not rely on some abstract, disembodied, decontextualized, generalized Other, but rather a concrete, rational individual with a particular history, identity and affective-emotional constitution.[79] She recognizes that not encountering and communicating with the concrete Other "can leave all our prejudices, misunderstandings, and hostilities in society, just as they are, hidden behind a veil."[80] Benhabib's interactive universalism involves conversations with concrete Others who hold different values. She relies on the principles of Habermas's communicative ethics to outline the parameters and principles of the communicative engagement among and between moral communities. Put differently, interactive universalism posits that there are distinctly different moral communities that can engage in conversations with others by following standards of communicative practices. Implicit here is the universal principle of engaging all Others in ongoing conversations and not simply those of our particular community.

Ideally, civil discourse, whether among people of a particular nation or between people of different countries, depends on equality, complementary reciprocity or reversibility, and universalism, which enable a diverse democratic society to handle tolerable levels of conflict, disagreement, and difference. Of course, there is a fairly large gap between what is, with regard to social and political alienation resulting from totalitarian speech, and what ought to be, with regard to equality, reciprocity, and respect. Young, Sevenhuijsen, Benhabib, and others (e.g., Maurice Hamington, Virginia Held, Nel Nodding, and Joan Tronto) derive their philosophical-political ideals against the background of oppression, violence, and marginalization. They

76. Ibid., 102.

77. Benhabib, *Situating the Self*, 81.

78. Ibid., 30, 165.

79. Benhabib, "The Generalized Other and the Concrete Other," 81.

80. Benhabib, *Situating the Self*, 168.

are, in short, not naïve about human greed, parochialism, and narcissism, which is why they advocate a critical analysis of the social political situation, identifying structures, practices, and narratives that operate to privilege one group, at the same time marginalizing, oppressing, and dehumanizing another group(s). Nevertheless, while they address the principles necessary for civil discourse, they do not, in my view, consider questions regarding how one attends to the presence of uncivil speech and what is needed to repair the harm done to the polis by unjust speech. What invites the return of the space of appearances? For this reason, I suggest the Christian traditions of care offer some ideas that can build on the principles outlined above—ideas that fall under the heading of redemptive discourse.

REDEMPTIVE DISCOURSE AS JUST AND CARING SPEECH

There are moments in the life of a democratic polis when civil discourse, while desired and needed, is not enough. These are instances in the history of the polis when political turmoil and change are embroiled in tendrils of fear and hatred, giving rise to fascist states of mind, totalizing speech, and violent and demeaning behaviors that shrink the space of appearances. In the United States, we note this in the late nineteenth century and into the early twentieth, when women were agitating for the right to vote and others were pushing for justice vis-à-vis exploited workers. More recently, many people living today observed the violence and hatred aimed at African Americans who pushed for civil rights during the 1950s and 1960s. In South Africa, it is seen in the decades of turbulence resulting from policies and laws associated with apartheid and brutal police crackdowns on black South Africans. To be sure, these are moments when the presence of the principles of civil speech were sorely needed, but a much more radical stance was exhibited by courageous persons such as Susan B. Anthony, Elizabeth Cady Stanton, Eugene Debs, Emma Goldman, Martin Luther King Jr., Rosa Parks, Fanny Lou Hamer, Desmond Tutu, and Nelson Mandela. Of course, these women and men exhibited the principles of civil discourse, but I contend they went beyond that to a redemptive discourse.

In general, redemptive discourse is just and caring speech, giving the Other what the person is due qua person and the offer of genuine care for the Other's experiences and needs regardless of the presence of uncivil speech and behavior. This offer of care in redemptive discourse includes the *possibility* of the work of forgiveness and reconciliation when hostility, conflict, and alienation are present in the polis. At its base, redemptive discourse includes the acknowledgment of the reality and consequences of human finitude (e.g., sin, alienation, the totalitarian tendency) while also acknowledging the reality of grace that *invites the realistic possibility* of social repair and the restoration of the polis's space of appearances. Put differently, redemptive discourse is prophetic speech in that it transgresses and subverts political speech that is totalizing and political behavior that seeks domination and marginalization. The cultivation of redemptive discourse is *an individual and ecclesial pastoral-political attitude, discipline, and response to a society in crisis and conflict.* Redemptive discourse is the leaven that contributes to a polis with a broad and deep space of appearances that embodies care and hope for its members. To explicate this term further, I discuss three biblical ideas: *imago dei*, *kenosis* (self-emptying), and the kingdom of God. These concepts outline contours of redemptive discourse in the midst of a polarized society. To illustrate this, I make use of Martin Luther King Jr. as an example (among many other individuals and communities in the civil rights movement) of someone who did the hard work involved in redemptive discourse—work enlivened and supported by the grace of God incarnated in familial and communal relationships of mutual support.

The idea that human beings are created in the image and likeness of God is found at the very beginning of the Hebrew Bible (Gen 1:26–28). Since biblical scholars have extensively explored the meanings associated with image and likeness of God,[81] my aim is not to provide an exegesis of this concept. Instead, my goal is to view this metaphor through the prism of theological and philosophical perspectives that emphasize the ontological singularity of individual human beings and the concomitant values of equality, dignity, and freedom.[82] That is, redemptive discourse embodies and expresses the existential claim that my political comrades and opponents are unique, valued, and inviolable.

To begin, it is important to address two questions that emerge from the notion of *imago dei*: what does it mean to be created in the image of God, and what does it mean to have a likeness with regard to God? The Judeo-Christian traditions portray God as (a) mystery, beyond our ability to apprehend God as God, (b) inviolable, (c) singular, (d) worthy of adoration—that is worthy in Godself, and (e) founding relationships (as Creator, in covenant, and so on). In terms of *imago dei*, as human beings, our likeness to God means that we experience ourselves as mystery—known and beyond knowing—beyond our abilities to assign categories that definitively

81. See, Middleton, "Created in the Image of a Violent God," 341–55; Miller, "In the 'Image' and 'Likeness' of God," 289–304.

82. See, Farley, *Divine Empathy*; Levinas, *Otherwise Than Being*; Macmurray, *Persons in Relation*; Min, *The Solidarity of Others in a Divided World*; Mounier, *Personalism*.

capture who we are.[83] This clearly undercuts totalizing discourse that claims complete knowledge of the Other. Human beings are also inviolable, sacred, unique, and valuable in relation to the Creator and each other. That is, we exist and have our being in relation to and for others, which is an anthropological perspective rooted in the concept of the Trinity[84] and in the notion of divine empathy.[85] As Dussel writes, "A person . . . is born from someone, not from something . . . [and] anterior to all other anteriority is the responsibility for the weak one."[86] The absolute singularity or uniqueness of a human being in relation to Others is also seen in Levinas's phenomenology of the Other (transcendence in the face of the Other) where singularity is founded in relation.[87] These philosophers and theologians affirm that the absolute uniqueness of individual human beings is grounded in relation, whether that is understood in terms of other human beings or in relation to God. The absolute uniqueness and inviolability of the Other, in my view, is a central feature of the notion of *imago dei*, which in turn founds redemptive discourse.

Of course, the phrase "image and likeness" does not denote identity with God. While we are unique, inviolable (with inherent dignity as persons), and valued, we know that human beings are bound by existential limitations. These limits evoke anxiety, which may give rise to human motivations and actions that entail violence and cruelty present in totalizing speech and action. Theologically, speech and action that contribute to alienation (attenuation of the space of appearances) are regarded as sin, highlighting the reality that human beings often handle the anxiety of separation and existential limitations by victimizing, demeaning, and depersonalizing each other.[88] Nevertheless, despite the reality of sin, the notion of *imago dei* signifies an ontological reality—a reality that cannot be destroyed by the efforts of human beings to deny, harm or destroy other human beings. Stated positively, in everyday life, *imago dei* is lived out and partially realized whenever we recognize and treat Others as souls—unique, inviolable, valued, responsive human beings—as-ends-in-themselves-as-persons. Existential limitations, in other words, may obscure but cannot eliminate the ontological reality of persons' singularity and, hence, likeness to God.

83. See Zizioulas, *Communion as Otherness.*

84. See LaCugna, *God for Us.*

85. Farley, *Divine Empathy.*

86. Dussel, *A Philosophy of Liberation*, 18–19.

87. Levinas, *Totality and Infinity.*

88. See Farley, *Good and Evil.*

We can further understand the notion of *imago dei* vis-à-vis redemptive discourse by returning to the philosophical perspective of John Macmurray and the psychoanalytic notion of omnipotent thinking. Recall from chapter 2 that Macmurray argued that human beings have the capacity to recognize and intentionally treat another human being as a person—a unique, inviolable, valued, agentic subject—personalization. Personalization is, for Macmurray, both a matter of fact and a matter of intention.[89] It is a matter of fact in that while we ideally experience the Other's personhood as a matter of fact, we are unconsciously, omnipotently constructing him/her as a person. This is a paradox.[90] In the moment of recognizing the Other as a person, I experience the Other's personhood as a matter of fact, which is linked to my omnipotent construction of him/her as a person. In other words, the paradox is that I intend to recognize the Other as a person, though the Other qua person is experienced as a matter of fact—a fact that I create through my omnipotent construction. This construction necessarily accompanies respect and reverence[91] for the Other, as well as an intention to understand him/her.

The idea that we can intentionally and omnipotently construct other human beings as persons is confirmed by the shadow side of human life. Just as we can construct through speech and behavior the Other as a person, so too we can omnipotently construct the Other as something less than a person. Macmurray wrote that "whenever one person treats another as an instrument for his use, or as an object for his enjoyment, he denies in practice the other's essential nature as a person."[92] In those instances, the individual consciously or unconsciously intends to construct the Other primarily as an object to be used and, secondarily, at best, as a person. In these moments, which usually attend forms of exploitation or neglect, there is no respect or reverence for the Other and, hence, no understanding. To return to the idea of *imago dei*, we could say, positively, that we participate in God's creation whenever we omnipotently construct and treat the Other as a person—a unique, inviolable human being.

89. Macmurray, *Persons in Relation*, 92–105.

90. The paradox is that in my omnipotent construction of the Other as person, s/he remains outside my control. The very construction of the Other as a person means that there is a gap or space for the Other to appear in his/her own unique way.

91. Woodruff argues that reverence is "the capacity to be in awe of whatever we believe lies outside our control—God, truth, justice, nature, even death." I would include the Other as person, who remains outside of my control and is beyond my knowledge to fully understand. See Woodruff, *Reverence*, 3.

92. Macmurray, *Conditions of Freedom*, 71–72.

Redemptive discourse is founded on this understanding of *imago dei*. The Other who is proximate or distant in the dialogue is *first and foremost a person*—a unique, inviolable, responsive subject—possessing a soul. The Other as person is neither constructed nor treated as a means or object. Even the Other as opponent or enemy is constructed and treated as a person in speech and action. More concretely, this means treating the Other not merely with respect, which is essential to civil discourse, but with reverence, which is foundational for redemptive discourse. To revere the Other does not mean one agrees or accepts his/her views. To revere one's opponents also does not imply the absence of vigorous political resistance. However, it does suggest that in disagreement and conflict the Other is seen and cared for as an absolutely unique creation of God. Creating and treating the Other as a person and revering the Other are partially redemptive, because it liberates us from the bondage of superior-inferior dynamics and the compulsion to maintain superiority by constructing Others as inferior, which is present in totalizing discourse. When speech and behavior embody justice and care for the Other in the midst of incivility, there is an invitation to repair, an invitation to reestablish the space of appearances.

Redemptive discourse, at its core, possesses the belief that all human beings are created in the image and likeness of God. This belief undergirds speech and actions that cocreate the Other as person, which necessarily accompanies just and caring actions. By contrast, in totalizing speech and action the Other is not recognized and treated as a person who merits justice or care. Instead, in the fascist state of mind, the Other is a threat to be controlled, changed, or eliminated. A genuine belief that the Other is created in the image and likeness of God subverts this totalitarian tendency, which is present in uncivil discourse. Of course, it is not simply a matter of possessing a belief. It is also a matter of living out this belief in just and caring speech and action, which is exceedingly difficult in a polis marred by uncivil discourse and polarization. The temptation in human life is to be seduced by the pleasure of self-certain righteousness, avoiding the more difficult discipline of revering Others who oppose us.

Let me move from this abstraction to a concrete example. As a child, Martin Luther King Jr. experienced the daily humiliations of the totalizing speech and actions of racism. Racism is embodied in speech and action that is unjust in that through this speech and action the Other is not given his/her due as a person; and racism is care-less because of indifference toward the existential needs of the Other. Understandably, given the totalitarianism and terrorism of racism, King felt hatred toward whites, though he was admonished by his parents and religious community that it was his Christian duty to love white people, which, as his father demonstrated, did not mean submitting to their hatred.[93] Admittedly this was very difficult to do, yet as King went to college and graduate school, and traveled to India, he became more convinced about the morality and effectiveness of nonviolence as a method of protest. Steeped in the biblical tradition, King grounded this method in theology—a theology that proclaimed that all human beings are sons and daughters of God, meriting respect and reverence. For King, this was no facile theological belief to which he assented but that he did not live out. Time and time again, King sought in speech and action to treat those who attacked him (physically and verbally) with justice and care. This was not some softheaded, sentimental, idealistic belief and approach. King worked hard to refuse succumbing to the seductive pleasure of hate and the attending Manichean simplism of totalizing speech. Instead, he had the grace, courage, and soul strength—derived from God and community—to live out this belief of seeing and treating all human beings as created in the image of God. Put another way, the redemptive discourse spoken by King and many other African Americans carried a political power that invited cooperation, expanding the space of appearances that had otherwise been marred by white supremacist uncivil communication and behavior.

King's story reveals the challenges of holding to this belief in a social milieu of racist hatred and hostility. And if we are honest with ourselves, we would admit that this is even difficult to do when the political and social stakes are not as high and when we are faced with people who simply differ with our cherished values and aims. So, how do we create psychic and relational space to welcome the Other as *imago dei* when there is hatred and hostility or when there is merely strong disagreement? Henri Nouwen wrote, "Someone who is filled with ideas, concepts, opinions and convictions cannot be a good host. There is no inner space to listen, no openness to discover the gift of the other. It is not difficult to see how those who 'know it all' can kill a conversation and prevent an interchange of ideas. Poverty of the mind as a spiritual attitude is a growing willingness to recognize the incomprehensibility of the mystery of life."[94] This poverty of mind or soul, revealed in redemptive discourse, requires self-emptying, a *kenosis*—setting aside cherished ideas, values, aims, and motivations to create a space for the recognition and treatment of the Other as person. *Kenosis*, a Greek term, which means "self-emptying," is found in Phil 2:7; "Jesus Christ who, though he was in the form of God, did not regard equality with God as something to be exploited, but emptied himself, taking the form of a slave, being born in human likeness." My interpretation is that self-emptying did

93. King, *The Autobiography of Martin Luther King, Jr.*, 7–10.

94. Nouwen, *Reaching Out*, 74.

not mean Jesus gave up his identity, values, beliefs, role, or mission. It is rather setting to the side one's own convictions, ideas, and so forth in order to recognize, understand, and be moved by the Other as person. Put another way, *kenosis* is the difficult discipline of clearing the psychic room to make space for and welcome the Other in reverence, and this psychic room is related to the space of appearances of the polis. The fruits of a kenotic discipline are humility and hospitality, which are key to redemptive discourse and its aims of inviting, revering, respecting, and understanding the Other. This is redemptive because it seeks to overcome alienation by inviting the possibility of real meetings between persons in the midst of disagreement. Let me stress that the discipline of *kenosis* vis-à-vis redemptive discourse does not imply agreement, consensus, or the absence of conflict. Rather, it is a foundational pastoral political attitude and discipline that involves, before all else, setting to the side any beliefs, thoughts, or feelings that impede one from recognizing and treating the Other as a person created in the image and likeness of God. *Kenosis*, then, is necessary for just and caring speech.

I think there must be an ongoing self-emptying process and discipline for redemptive discourse to be possible, especially in conditions of intense societal conflict that tempt us to retreat to our theopolitical fortresses so that we might reinforce our grip on the Truth while lobbing ideological grenades at our opponents. This self-emptying requires self-confrontation and accountability. Like King, we have to face and contain our hatreds, fears, resentments, and desires or even lust for self-righteousness. By taking accountability, we have the opportunity to set our "demons" aside so that we do not act on them but instead act on our belief that the Other is created in the image and likeness of God. It is a discipline precisely because we have to do this again and again, because we will always be tempted to proclaim a total explanation of the Other. Redemptive discourse depends on this discipline of *kenosis*, and it is God's grace that gives us the courage to confront our own sins, failings, and pettiness so that we can cocreate, in speech and action, our opponents as sons and daughters of God.

King certainly had many opportunities to exercise this discipline of self-emptying through self-confrontation and accountability. While in Chicago, King was booed by young black persons and "went home that night with an ugly feeling."[95] I interpret this to mean he was aggrieved and starting to feel self-righteous—the seeds of the totalitarian impulse. Yet, King began to reflect on what happened. "I finally came to myself," he writes, "and I could not for the life of me have less patience and understanding for those

95. King, *The Autobiography of Martin Luther King, Jr.*, 302.

young people."[96] Yet, King, while not understanding them, created a space where he revered them and sought to understand their positions. During this time, King and many others were marching in Chicago. "Some people who had been brutalized in Selma and who were present at the Capitol ceremonies in Montgomery," he notes, "led the marchers in the suburbs of Chicago amid the rain of rocks and bottles, among burning automobiles, to the thunder of jeering thousands, many of them waving Nazi flags."[97] To able to retain a nonviolent stance in the midst of this level of hostility and hatred requires tremendous courage, discipline, and grace, which, in turn, require containing one's own impulse to participate in unjust and uncaring speech and action. There were also times when King also tried this nonviolent (just and caring speech) toward people in his own group.

Implicit in this discussion of *imago dei* and *kenosis* is the metaphor kingdom of God. This phrase, a political metaphor, appears numerous times in the Synoptic Gospels and points to a realm where people will abide with God and with each other in harmony, peace, and justice. Citizenship in this kingdom overturns typical human notions of participation and inclusion. For instance, Matt 5:3, 10 name poverty of spirit and pursuit of righteousness as criteria for citizenship. Later, in Matt 25:34–36, care of the vulnerable manifests the inbreaking of the kingdom. The kingdom of God also appears to upend common notions of power and authority. In Matt 18:1–5 and Matt 19:23 (see also Mark 10:25 and Luke 19:25) we note that humility and the absence of acquisitiveness and accumulation of wealth (instead of bravado and riches) are features of citizenship in this realm. In this kingdom, the first shall be last and the last shall be first (Luke 13:30). Another important feature of this metaphor, especially in the Gospel of Luke, is that it points to a present experience of a future reality.

Theologians such as Pannenberg,[98] Moltmann,[99] and Volf[100] argue that the kingdom of God is not divorced from the present but rather reaches into the present, though realized in fragmentary ways. God's care and justice, for instance, reach into the present political milieu whenever and wherever human beings act in cooperation with God's grace—grace that restores and affirms experiences of being a-person-with-other-persons in speech and action. The kingdom of God is partially realized whenever Others are recognized and treated as brothers and sisters, created in the image and likeness

96. Ibid.

97. Ibid., 305.

98. Pannenberg, *Theology and the Kingdom of God.*

99. Moltmann, *The Coming of God.*

100. Volf, *Exclusion and Embrace.*

of God. It is seen in moments of reverence, justice, and care even when all three are rejected. Here I am thinking of the words of forgiveness Jesus utters to his torturers (see Luke 23:24), words that reveal reverence, care, and transcendent justice.

This political metaphor parallels Macmurray's notion of mutual-personal relations vis-à-vis community or polis. Remember, for Macmurray, the experience and dignity of being a person are realized and maintained in community and society, where members omnipotently construct, recognize, and treat each other as persons. "Personality," Macmurray writes, "is mutual in its very being . . . The self only exists in the communion of selves."[101] Community founds personhood. In theological terms, this community of real meetings signifies the inbreaking of the kingdom of God and God's being, wherein people live in just and caring relations that give rise to harmony and peace. The inbreaking of the polis of God accompanies practices of redemptive discourse, wherein recognition and treatment of Others serve as invitations to real meetings (I–Thou relations, not I–It relations) in the polis. An I–Thou attitude, if you will, fosters redemptive discourse even in the midst of conflict and disagreement. The Other as opponent is never an "it," a means, an obstacle, an inferior object. The Other is always a citizen of the kingdom of God, because s/he is created in the image and likeness of God. Conflict and disagreements do not revoke someone's citizenship in this kingdom. Redemptive discourse, then, has as its foundation the realization that the Other is, like me, a citizen of God's kingdom, even when we are at odds. This belief finds its concrete expression of *kenosis*, whereby one labors to set aside (not to get rid of) cherished beliefs and values that would impede one from recognizing and treating the Other as a citizen of God's creation.

Of course, the kingdom of God is only partially realized, if at all, on this side of the veil. This means that there are moments of alienation, hostility, and misrecognition. Redemptive discourse vis-à-vis the notion of the kingdom of God requires the realization that I may have contributed to alienation, and therefore my response is to seek forgiveness. Confession and forgiveness are necessary features of redemptive discourse precisely because we fail, sometimes often, and human relationships need strategies of repair, which are completely lacking in totalizing discourse.

Redemptive discourse, in contrast to totalizing discourse, does not construct the situation into a zero-sum game; it does not create the Other as an It, an obstacle to overcome, a foe to be defeated, an inferior Other to be colonized. Instead, redemptive discourse involves the recognition

101. Macmurray, *Persons in Relation*, 78.

and treatment of the Other as a singular, inviolable human being—a fellow citizen in the kingdom of God. Respect, reverence for, and the intention to understand the Other are aspects of recognizing and treating the Other as a person. All of this requires a kenotic discipline of setting to the side our political agendas and expectations so that in the foreground of meeting the Other, we value and practice recognizing and treating the Other as a person created in the image and likeness of God. Since redemption is not fully experienced in this life, active participation in discourse that is partially redemptive necessitates our willingness to confess our failures and to risk forgiveness for the sake of returning to the practice of recognizing and treating the Other as a unique, inviolable creation of God. It is forgiveness, as Desmond Tutu argues, that engenders hope for the restoration of a polis marred by alienation.[102] Forgiveness is the invitation to do the work of restoring the space of appearances of a polis, and when this invitation is accepted, there is a partial, present realization of the polis of God.

These three concepts are the founding principles of redemptive discourse and together reveal a radical hope. In totalizing discourse, hope is framed in terms of victory over one's opponents, which may include eliminating, converting, colonizing, or subduing them. The hope of redemptive discourse is to join the Other, to engage in a dialogue of vigorous difference among brothers and sisters. This hope is radical, because at its roots is trust that, even in the midst of darkness, alienation, and division, the grace and ground of persons-in-relation cannot be destroyed. This is not a naïve view. It is a view forged in Martin Luther King Jr.'s (and others') struggle against the injustices of racism. His trust in God and God's creation is evident in the hope he expressed in the face of numerous death threats—a trust and hope reflected in his last speech to the sanitation workers of Memphis. King's civil and redemptive discourse was neither sentimental nor naïve. On the contrary, his just and caring speech reflects Christian realism because he acknowledged and experienced the realities of sin, conflict, and alienation; he recognized and experienced the threat of hatred and division, but he did not succumb to the despair of the violence and hostility of totalizing discourse. Rather, he stood committed to recognize and engage Others as persons and in the process to foster communities and a society of care.

CONCLUSION

As a society and as Christian communities living in a polarized society, we need to pay more attention to our speech. In a deeply fractured society like

102. Tutu, *No Future without Forgiveness.*

ours, civil discourse frequently devolves into monologues, self-righteous rants that only further alienate citizens from one another. Yet, as I have argued in this chapter, it is not simply the return of civil discourse that is needed, though that would surely be a welcome relief from simplistic, hostile political discourse. We need the kind of redemptive discourse that rejects the facile pleasures of self-certain total explanations and opts for the belief in and practice of just and caring speech in the face of hostility and hatred. To be sure, as Martin Luther King Jr.'s life shows, this is no easy task, and it is not the singular achievement of one person. It requires communities of faith and leaders who are willing to do the work that invites hope, that invites social repair, that summons the return of the space of appearances so that a polis can survive and thrive.

5

CARE AND THE U.S. EMPIRE

Systemic Violence, Idolatry, and the Corruption of Care

For surely what is seen in history is not a universal, independent source and goal of existence, not impartial justice, not infinite mercy, but particularity, finiteness, opinions that pass, caprice, arbitrariness, accident, brutality, wrong on the throne and right on the scaffold.[1]

Woe to him who builds his house by unrighteousness,
and his upper rooms by injustice. (Jer 22:13)

We are an attractive empire . . . Afghanistan and other troubled lands today cry out for the sort of enlightened foreign administration once provided by self-confident Englishmen in jodhpurs and pith helmets.[2]

These [American values] are God-given values. These aren't United States-created values. We will export death and violence to the four corners of the earth in defense of our great nation.[3]

1. Niebuhr, *The Meaning of Revelation*, 40.
2. Johnson, *Sorrows of Empire*, 70.
3. George W. Bush, quoted in Ryn, *America the Virtuous*, 7

OUR GREAT SACRAMENT IS celebrated every fall, and on this Thanksgiving Day Americans feast on the myth of their origins—a seemingly benign story of the roots of the U.S. Empire. American Indians and English colonizers sat down together and shared a meal, a scene of peace and tranquility. It is a constructed screen "memory," as are many other U.S. myths, that hides the ruthless and relentless expropriation of lands and a trail of broken treaties by colonizers from the British Empire; these myths obscure the long history of brutality and violence toward aboriginal peoples in North America and the cruel exploitation of native Africans. It is certainly true that all empires take lands and conquer people, but it is both tragic and ironic that the seeds of the United States "empire of democracy" were sown from the tree of the British Empire—seeds that landed and sprouted from the soil of stolen lands.

It may be puzzling that a book on a pastoral political theology would first take issue with the U.S. Empire. The choice is deliberate and has four explanations. First, the roots of the U.S. Empire, as I indicated above, were present long before the birth of the nation. The sense of entitlement coupled with arrogance and expansionist desires—whether for economic and/or religious freedom rationales—were part of the earliest settlements, the crossing of the Appalachian Mountains, the push toward the northwest, the appropriation of the southwest, and the colonization of lands outside U.S. continental borders. Entitlement, arrogance, and expansionism are also evident in our meddling with other economies with the sole aim of retaining economic hegemony.[4] I begin here, first, because empire is part of our cultural-psychic DNA, and a political pastoral theology means facing the consequences—past and present—of a long legacy of injustices and acts of stunning carelessness in our march toward empire. Second, given that empire is part of our psychic DNA, the spreading tendrils of the U.S. Empire provide the remaining subjects of this book. In other words, the expansionism of empire is not unrelated to the expansionism evident in the U.S. style of neoliberal capitalism, which seeks to colonize (privatize) sectors previously public—schools, prisons, and so forth. Third, I begin with empire because most Americans, as Tocqueville[5] observed, wear rose-colored glasses when it comes to seeing themselves or facing their sins. Indeed, Reinhold Niebuhr observed that Americans tend to see themselves as "tutors of mankind in its pilgrimage to perfection."[6] Even when faced with the fact that the U.S. is an empire, politicians either deny it or claim we are a benevolent superpower

4. See Fullbright, *The Arrogance of Power*; Klein, *Shock Doctrine.*

5. Tocqueville, *Democracy in America*, 700–703.

6. In Bacevich, *American Empire*, 54.

and that the world needs an American Empire. These beliefs overlook or deny the injustice and carelessness required to become an empire and to maintain hegemony.

I suspect that some readers will quickly question this, pointing to the good done by the United States in its history. I have no quarrel with this view, at least in part. The U.S. has done and continues to do good: America has aided peoples encountering natural disasters—helping victims of the 2015 Nepal earthquake and victims of the 2004 Indian Ocean tsunami—and takes in about seventy thousand refugees a year. That said, the good that is done should not be used to deflect attention from the sins. Moreover and more importantly, claiming that the U.S. has done a great deal of good in the world seems to be an ends-justifies-the-means argument and an argument made by the victor. A similar argument defends the bombings of Hiroshima and Nagasaki as unfortunate but necessary because they ended World War II. Apparently, horrific war crimes can be overlooked or justified as long as one blames the victims (the Japanese started it) and finds some good that results (the end of the war). In either case, there is a profound deafness toward the cries of victims. As H. Richard Niebuhr noted in two articles during the Second World War, even if there is a just war, combatants are not innocent.[7]

Other readers may point out that empires, in their quest for land and wealth, do indeed kill, maim, and threaten. Yet, like historian Niall Ferguson,[8] who is British and an Americanophile, these critics claim that you have to break a few eggs to make an empire omelet. More directly, empires, despite their sins, provide necessary global security and stability. This point of view seems to suggest that without empires the world would be a violent, chaotic, impoverished arena. It is also strikingly similar to the ends-justifies-the-means argument, with the good in this case being global security and stability. One might ask the Aztecs, Incas, and numerous other indigenous peoples, as well as Africans, how they felt about the security and stability offered at the hands of British, French, and Spanish empires. Or we might ask the victims of the two world wars, which were fought by imperial powers, how they benefited from enhanced security and stability of these powers. Or we might consider the current empire's attempt to ensure stability and security in the Middle East. Usually the people who opt for the benefits of security and stability of empire sit comfortably writing books in their air-conditioned offices instead of facing the sharp end of the empire's spear. Indeed, these arguments are often made from the safety of the metropole,

7. See H. R. Niebuhr, "War as the Judgment of God"; H. R. Niebuhr, "War as Crucifixion."

8. See Ferguson, *Colossus*.

far from the fringes of the empire where force, coercion, and violence are used to maintain stability. Finally, this argument lacks imagination: for does stability and security result only from the presence of a superpower? This argument also overlooks the instability and insecurity that empires create in their bid for security and stability—an inherent contradiction and a factor in the downfall of all empires.

The fourth reason for beginning with the U.S. Empire has two parts. Empires are by their very nature violent, especially, as Julian Go notes,[9] when they are in decline. The United States, while still hugely powerful, has been on the decline since its heyday after World War II. Empires in decline attempt to maintain power and control, even as both slip from their fingers despite the uptick in violence. Note President Obama's "pivot" to Asia, as China grows in economic and military strength.[10] This pivot does not simply direct our economic attention to Asia but repositions military forces and resources to counter China's rise. Even as the U.S. Empire holds on to power as past declining empires have, the U.S. Empire also confronts the reality of global warming and the instability that will come with declining global resources. Consider a Pentagon report "asserting decisively that climate change poses an immediate threat to national security, with increased risks from terrorism, infectious disease, global poverty and food shortages. It also predicted the rising demand for military disaster responses as extreme weather creates more global humanitarian crises."[11] In this report, the War Department[12] "lays out a road map to show how the military will adapt to rising sea levels, more violent storms and widespread droughts. The Defense Department will begin by integrating plans for climate change risks across all of its operations, from war games and strategic military planning situations to rethinking the movement of supplies." One could argue that it would be irresponsible for the War Department not to have contingency plans. My point is that the plans are for maintaining security and stability benefiting the United States as empire. The decline of the U.S. Empire and the numerous problems of global warming, I argue, will be a dangerous mix and will lead to increased violence and hence to increased carelessness and injustice. For these reasons I begin this chapter with a political pastoral theological analysis of the U.S. Empire.

9. Go, *Patterns of Empire*, 174–86.

10. Drysdale, "America's Pivot to Asia and Asian Akrasia."

11. Davenport, "Pentagon Signals Security Risks of Climate Change."

12. I note here that the Department of Defense was previously referred to as the War Department. The previous name is clearer and more apt when we consider the long history of American aggression, as well as the proposed present and future aggression aimed at securing and maintaining its position as sole superpower.

To begin, it is important to define what is meant by empire, especially since the United States does not fit the traditional parameters of this term, and because the attributes of empire have changed during the last century. This definition of *empire* accompanies a brief overview of the roots of the U.S. Empire: how it adapted to changing political and economic circumstances, and the changing discourses and narratives it used to justify expansionistic policies. From there I will turn to the forms of systemic violence used to build and maintain empire. More particularly, I argue that the systemic violence of the U.S. Empire is better conceptualized as diverse forms of violations, dependent on official, dominant narratives and rituals of superiority, exceptionalism, and innocence. These violations and their accompanying official narratives are integral to establishing, maintaining, and legitimating the U.S. Empire, while at the same time undermining control and stability.[13] I contend further that the U.S. Empire, like any empire, is inherently undemocratic in its actions toward other nations, though this is masked by its rhetoric of concern and, in the case of the U.S., the rhetoric of advancing democracy. Another way of depicting this is to say that empires distort and corrupt the space of appearances between nations, and in a "democratic" empire this will eventually corrode and corrupt its own public-political space. The forms of violence corrupt the space of appearances and accompany acts of carelessness and injustice, especially toward subordinate states and peoples. I conclude with several suggestions aimed at (1) prophetically confronting the realities and consequences of empire and (2) restoring and furthering care, justice, and the space of appearances in churches, synagogues, mosques and small communities.

I am compelled to offer several clarifications before embarking. We are told that dealing with the complicated and harsh realities of politics, and especially foreign relations, requires hardheaded, if not coldhearted, practical leaders who consider care and justice to be expedient. It is Machiavelli, not the Dalai Lama, who is needed to respond to the complexities of foreign relations. This seems self-evident to many, including to Reinhold Niebuhr, who described his approach to political realities as Christian realism, which takes seriously sin and selfishness.[14] Thus, Niebuhr argued that when we apply the concept of justice to a nation's foreign policies and relations, we need to recognize that a nation may have to participate in evil to provide security and stability—an argument that parallels Niall Ferguson's. Niebuhr, for instance, argued against those who sought to avoid war with the Axis

13. For a discussion of the contradictions of empire and how violence increases instability see Johnson, *Blowback*.

14. Niebuhr, *Love and Justice*, 42–43.

powers, even though he said the U.S. did not face an existential threat.[15] This argument seemed so compelling then and still does now, and it is especially so when we hear on the news about terrorism. But this point of view is often expressed by those who benefit from the use of force. Empires in particular always make the case for an existential threat as they march to expand their control and power. Christian realists such as Niebuhr supported the U.S. Empire, though, to his credit, criticized the hubris and exceptionalism of the U.S.

Relatedly, political pragmatists, during periods of peace, are comfortable using the notion of justice as the nation seeks to work cooperatively with others. In the midst of crises, however, justice is at best a secondary aim, and at worst so distorted that it becomes unrecognizable or meaningless.[16] My point here is that the notion of justice is still used as an interpretive frame and that even if it is distorted, we do not simply get rid of it for the sake of an "ideal" of pure exploitation and dominance. No, in an Orwellian fashion, we use the notion of justice to cover what is inherently unjust, if not criminal. Regardless, the notion of justice is a relevant term for assessing political actions, whether one is a Christian realist or political pragmatist. Machiavelli may be prince of realpolitik, but the claims of justice are no less demanding even when they are ignored or distorted.

Of course, I have not yet mentioned the notion of care, which on its face seems almost silly to our erstwhile political pragmatists. They might settle on the notion of justice when considering political affairs, but the idea of care seems absurd—something relegated to social workers and not nations. But here too we note that nations do express, in limited ways, care for their neighbors and others. Indeed, this can become part of a national narrative, much like in the United States. The notion of care is also expressed in the United Nations Charter, and we see this every year as nations respond to various crises, accepting refugees, sending aid and experts to disaster sites. But why do this? We could save money and resources by letting countries fend for themselves. There would be less stress and struggle if Germany had closed its borders to refugees fleeing the Gulf wars. A more calculated or realist response as to why we care is that we do this to keep our brand name,

15. Ibid., 200–205.

16. Consider U.S. policy toward Iraq in the 1990s. Madeleine Albright, the U.S. secretary of state at the time, was queried by a reporter about the effects of the policy that placed onerous sanctions on Iraq. The reporter indicated that independent agencies had estimated that between 300,000 and 500,000 Iraqi children had died as a result of the embargo. He asked: Was the price of their deaths worth it? Albright responded affirmatively. No doubt she believed the policies were just, but that can be done only if "justice" becomes warped. See Zinn, *A People's History of the United States*, 659.

to improve our image, to gain leverage, but this would overlook the very real sentiments of care expressed by citizens, politicians, and aid workers. If this is so, then the notion of care must become a critical hermeneutical lens in any examination of a nation's foreign and domestic policies and programs. Indeed, as chapter 2 asserted, the concept and practice of care are crucial as we deal with a world with more people and fewer resources.

DEFINING EMPIRE AND THE EMERGENCE OF THE U.S. EMPIRE

The debate about whether the U.S. is an empire or imperialistic has waxed and waned over the last 150 years.[17] Frederick Douglass,[18] Mark Twain,[19] William James,[20] Eugene Debs,[21] Emma Goldman,[22] Henry Wallace,[23]and others publicly decried acts of U.S. imperialism in the nineteenth and twentieth centuries, while people such as Catherine Beecher, Harriet Beecher Stowe,[24] and Senator Albert J. Beveridge[25] wrapped U.S. imperialistic expansionism under the cloaks of helping savages, U.S. entitlement (e.g., Manifest Destiny and the Monroe Doctrine), and Christianizing or civilizing natives. Much of this discourse died down or shifted after the two world wars fought by dying colonial powers. However, shortly after World War II a number of writers[26] warned that Cold War rhetoric, American arrogance, and the typical American reluctance to see ourselves as imperialistic shielded the general public from the reality that many U.S. political, economic, and military policies aimed at establishing and maintaining U.S. hegemony throughout the world. With the waning of colonial, imperial powers, a new form of empire was emerging. Then, with the fall of the Soviet Union, the discussion of U.S. hegemony or status as an empire became more popular and acceptable in many circles. Conservatives like Dinesh D'Souza, Charles Krauthammer,

17. For a discussion on the history of U.S. anti-imperialism, see Tyrrell and Sexton, *Empire's Twin*.

18. In Zinn and Amove, *Voices of a People's History of the United States*, 159.

19. Ibid., 248–50.

20. Zinn, *A People's History of the United States*, 314.

21. Freeberg, *Democracy's Prisoner*.

22. Zinn and Amove, *Voices of a People's History of the United States*, 270–72.

23. Stone and Kuznick, *The Untold History of the United States*, 138.

24. Kaplan, *The Anarchy of Empire in the Making of U.S. Culture*, 29–32.

25. Johnson, *Sorrows of Empire*, 43.

26. See Alstyne, *The Rising American Empire*; Fish, *The Path of Empire*; Herring, *From Colony to Superpower*; Johnson, *Blowback*; Perkins, *Denial of Empire*.

and Max Boot enthusiastically embraced the idea of a U.S. Empire. "We are," Boot wrote, "an attractive empire . . . Afghanistan and other troubled lands today cry out for the sort of enlightened foreign administration once provided by self-confident Englishmen in jodhpurs and pith helmets."[27] Democrats, less bombastic, either pointed to how the U.S. was a reluctant, if not benevolent, empire or superpower, differing from previous colonial empires of the past, or simply denied that the U.S. was an empire.[28] There were, of course, progressive voices—barely audible—that warned of blowback[29] or that narrated the crimes of empire.[30] And certainly many citizens, if not most, outright deny the U.S. was or is an empire. Indeed, perhaps the most notable and consistent deniers are U.S. presidents, including Barack Obama.[31] "Officially, to be sure," Niall Ferguson wrote, "the United States remains an empire in denial."[32]

In this cacophony of past and present voices, various definitions and attributes of empire surface. Even those who deny the U.S. is an empire possess some notion of empire—a notion that aids in their denial. And when we consider the political and economic changes in the nineteenth and twentieth centuries that shaped powerful nations, we see that the forms of empire shifted, which means the definition shifts as well. A traditional definition, which hearkens back to imperialistic powers of the seventeenth, eighteenth, and nineteenth centuries, refers to empire as "the formal political control of one state over another's external and internal policy."[33] The obvious reference here is to colonialism, which the U.S. actively pursued in the late nineteenth century and in the early twentieth century with the acquisition of Cuba, Puerto Rico, the Philippines, Hawaii, and so forth. This conventional definition of *empire*, however, overlooks the violent expansionism of the United States in the eighteenth and nineteenth centuries through wars (e.g., the Mexican War and the Spanish-American War), ethnic cleansings (e.g., the Trail of Tears), and territorial and economic expropriations.[34] Historian Paul Kennedy remarked, "From the time the first settlers arrived in Virginia from England and started moving westward,

27. Johnson, *Sorrows of Empire*, 70.

28. See Bender, "The New Rome"; Go, *Patterns of Empire*; Rieff, "Liberal Imperialism."

29. See Bacevich, *American Empire*; Johnson, *Blowback*.

30. Boggs, *Crimes of Empire*; Chomsky, *Imperial Ambitions*; Kinzer, *Overthrow*.

31. See Go, *Patterns of Empire*, 243.

32. Ferguson, *Colossus*, 9.

33. Lundestad, *The American "Empire,"* 37.

34. For a list of land purchases, see Ferguson, *Colossus*, 40.

this was an imperial nation."[35] So when we consider the expansion of the United States in what became a continental nation, the process of expansion does not conform to conventional notions of empire building because the affected territories were not sovereign nations when they came under U.S. control. That said, indigenous peoples were considered to be sovereign and were under the control of the U.S. government. A conventional definition of *empire* also glosses over political ideas and policies, such as the Monroe Doctrine and the notion of Manifest Destiny, that "legitimized" U.S. territorial, economic, and political interventions in Central and South America; none of this involved *formal* political acquisition of lands or direct control of governments.[36]

Clearly, the formal definition applies to one period of U.S. history (even there it screens other forms of empire), but it is not sufficient to grasp significant Western political and economic changes of the twentieth century. Seeking a broader definition, Lundestad argues that an empire like the U.S. is "a hierarchical system of political relationships with one power clearly being much stronger than any other."[37] Similarly, Julian Go defines "empire as a sociopolitical formation wherein a central political authority (a king, a metropole, or imperial state) exercises unequal influence and power over the political processes of a subordinate society, peoples, or space."[38] The power that is used to gain client states or to gain influence over other nations is not merely political but rather an amalgam of economic and military power. Both Go and Lundestad contend that empires and hegemons need not have direct,[39] formal political control. More particularly, Go,

35. In Stone and Kuznick, *The Untold History of the United States*, xv.

36. Saying that the U.S. did not take formal control over lands means that it did not rule, but through political, economic, and military coercion U.S. companies (e.g., United Fruit Company) were able to acquire "legally" huge tracts of land for private corporations.

37. Lundestad, *The American "Empire,"* 37.

38. Go, *Patterns of Empire*, 7.

39. Julian Go noted that a nation may be an empire without being a hegemon. By hegemon, he meant processes associated with ideological, cultural, and economic domination. In particular, he argued that "a hegemon is a state that enjoys relative preponderance over the world economy." For decades the U.S. has been a hegemon, though it has clearly been on the decline since the 1970s. While the U.S. has and will continue to lose its hegemonic status, this does not mean it will no longer continue imperialistic policies and practices. Indeed, as Go has extensively depicted, empires and hegemons that are in decline engage in more imperialistic, military types of violence. Go, *Patterns of Empire*, 8, 169–70.

Herring,[40] and Ferguson[41] argue that after World War II the United States became more of an informal empire preferring indirect rule—exercising influence and political and economic control over societies and client states that were not colonies. Go notes, the "imperial state keeps these nominally independent territories in line or compels them to meet its interests, but does not declare sovereignty over them."[42] Naturally, informal rule did not mean the absence of military force. Informal empires, Go points out, use more military force to maintain control, especially as they decline.[43]

Julian Go makes an important distinction between formal and informal empires vis-à-vis imperialism. He argues that "Empires are involved in *imperialism*, which is the process by which they are established, extended, and maintained. They often have *imperial policies*, which are official and stated plans and practices by which power is exercised."[44] The United States is, from Go's perspective, an informal empire that has imperialistic policies, which include devising strategies and deploying tactics to maintain and extend economic and political influence over client states. The economic and political influence is supported by military power. Evidence of this is the approximately 725 known American military bases in over thirty-eight foreign countries and over 254,000 military personnel in 153 countries.[45] While the U.S. is not an occupying force in these countries, the presence of these military bases and the use of regional "proconsuls"[46] and economic power[47] to alter the policies and actions of foreign countries are all signifiers of the presence of an American Empire.

For a nation to become an empire requires, at the very least, the majority of its people to support the economic, military, and political aims, policies, and actions necessary for expansionism and dominance. And support is developed and maintained by narratives and discourse that undergird an ideology of expansionism and dominance. I call this empire or imperial discourse, which has deep roots in U.S. history and is represented in private and public communications. In a letter to James Monroe (1801), the newly appointed ambassador to France, Thomas Jefferson, wrote of his

40. Herring, *From Colony to Superpower*, 538–94.
41. Fergusson, *Colossus*, 61–104.
42. Go, *Patterns of Empire*, 11 (italics original).
43. Ibid., 174–86.
44. Ibid., 7.
45. Johnson, *Sorrows of Empire*, 154.
46. See Chomsky, *Hegemony or Survival*; Bacevich, *American Empire*.
47. See Young, "Imperial Language."

plans to acquire New Orleans and other lands.[48] A few years later, Jefferson's expansionist aims were manifested in a letter to James Madison. Jefferson (1809) mused about expanding the U.S. to the north and the south (Canada, Florida, and Cuba). And what better nation to obtain territory than an "empire of liberty"? He wrote, "we should have such an empire for liberty as she has never surveyed since the creation: & I am persuaded no constitution was ever before so well calculated as ours for extensive empire & self government."[49] Having recently severed the chains of their colonial masters, Jefferson and others (e.g., James Madison, James Monroe, and Andrew Jackson) advocated expansion of U.S. territories; they clothed expansionist aims in idealistic rhetoric: over time expansionist rhetoric has included terms such as "empire of liberty," the notion of protecting American Indians, and the rationale of guarding national security.[50] For instance, less than a decade after Jefferson's letter, Secretary of War John C. Calhoun "inaugurated the policy of removing 'Indians' to the ninety-fifth line of longitude, a policy that became law in 1825."[51] A concrete manifestation of expansionism in the form of ethnic cleansing took place in 1818, when Andrew Jackson invaded Florida to subdue rebellious Seminole tribes with the ostensible aim of protecting U.S. interests. Clearly there was no liberty for these and other indigenous peoples.

Expansionistic or imperial discourse continued to be part of the American story throughout the nineteenth century. The question was how expansionism would be justified. One idea, which hearkened back to Jefferson, emerged during the 1820s and continues in our century: the idea of the U.S. as a protector of the liberty of other nations. The Monroe Doctrine (1823) embodied this idea, which helped justify numerous economic and military interventions in South America and the Caribbean in the nineteenth and twentieth centuries. Just a short step away from the idea of the U.S. as protector of the liberty of nations throughout the Americas was the idea of Manifest Destiny. The U.S., because of its putative unique status in history and the world, was destined to expand to the Pacific Ocean. This idea later gave rise to policies that sanctioned violence and the ruthless expropriation of land from American Indians and Mexicans. Of course the stories told about this expansion were couched in the idealistic fictions of protecting peoples, bringing order to the chaotic West, and providing

48. See the page about the Louisiana Purchase on the Monticello website: https://www.monticello.org/site/jefferson/louisiana-purchase/.

49. Library of Congress, Letter from Thomas Jefferson to James Madison, April 27, 1809.

50. Chomsky, *Imperial Ambitions*.

51. Ferguson, *Colossus*, 36.

government and education to the uncivilized Indians. The grandiose visions of Jefferson's empire of liberty, the stories proclaiming the U.S. the benevolent defender against Western European colonialism (enshrined in the Monroe Doctrine), and the idea of Manifest Destiny all served to justify forms of expansionism (i.e., the expansion of land, political power, or economic influence). In addition, these ideas were part of the expansionist trajectory that extended into the Pacific (with the acquisition of Hawaii and the Philippines) and deep into Asia (e.g., China). Secretary of State John Hay, for instance, issued the Open Door Notes, which dealt with the recognition of Chinese territorial integrity, but, more important, established the American right to the same expansionist aims and economic privileges that imperialistic European countries had.[52]

What is interesting in the discourse and stories of U.S. expansionism in the nineteenth century is the inclusion of Christian stories and ideas in what otherwise were political secular aims (i.e., democracy, freedom). During the nineteenth century, secular ideas of democracy and freedom were generally subordinate to the idea of using Christianity to bring civilization to ignorant native peoples. Examining popular novels, magazines, and tracts, Kaplan notes the numerous links among imperialism, Christian discourse, and domesticity during the nineteenth century.[53] For instance, Catherine Beecher, writing during the mid-nineteenth century, believed that the mission of the United States was to exhibit "to the world the beneficent influences of Christianity, when carried into every social, civil, and political institution."[54] Catherine's sister, Harriet Beecher Stowe, wrote, "Ere long colonies from these prosperous and Christian communities would go forth to shine as lights of the world, in all the now darkened nations. Thus, the Christian family and Christian neighborhood would become the grand ministry as they were designed to be, in training our whole race for heaven."[55] This domestic and feminized evangelical zeal found a different voice in the political realm. Senator Beveridge of Indiana, for example, believed that the United States had a "duty to bring Christianity and civilization to 'savage and senile peoples.'"[56] Many men and women believed in the need and duty to Christianize (civilize) "others." Stories associated with Christianity were, therefore, joined to and supported by stories of bringing freedom and democracy to the uncivilized. Together, these stories and associated political

52. Herring, *From Colony to Superpower*, 331–34.

53. Kaplan, *The Anarchy of Empire.*

54. Ibid., 29.

55. Ibid., 32.

56. Johnson, *Sorrows of Empire*, 43.

rhetoric gave social legitimacy to and support for foreign interventions and, by and large, were accepted by most Americans,[57] which served to cloak the violence of expansion.

During the twentieth century, a recognizable shift occurred from blatant Christian-political discourse that frequently supported imperial ambitions to the sacralization of the secular ideals of democracy, freedom, and capitalism (later free-market economies). In other words, explicit Christian discourse faded, in part, and was replaced by the implicit and, at times, explicit view that freedom, democracy, and free markets are God-given, sacred, inviolable, eternal, natural, and, hence, universal. For example, Johnson contended that the height of intellectual justification for American power could be found in Woodrow Wilson's "hyperidealistic, sentimental, and ahistorical idea that what should be sought was a world democracy based on the American example and led by the United States."[58] Woodrow Wilson's evangelical zeal for democracy was undoubtedly consonant with his Protestant evangelical roots and easily fit the cognitive schemas of most Americans, who were Protestant. Ronald Reagan continued this legacy, saying, "I have always believed that this anointed land was set apart in an uncommon way, that a divine plan placed this great continent here between two oceans to be found by people from every corner of the earth who have a special love of faith and freedom."[59] Reagan merely echoed Wilson's belief in the U.S.'s global mission to democratize the world and bring about the "ultimate peace of the world."[60] Similarly, Bill Clinton viewed the end of the Cold War as "the fullness of time" and the U.S. as an "indispensable nation" in helping the world toward democracy, peace, and economic prosperity.[61] Like his predecessors, Clinton linked economic expansion to political freedom, though the rules of the marketplace and the new freedoms would, not surprisingly, be used to the advantage of the U.S. Even more recently, the triumphalism of George W. Bush's administration and his moral justification for military interventions in the Middle East and elsewhere are simply extensions of democratic evangelism and the transcendence of free market fundamentalism.[62] While decidedly secular, this imperial discourse

57. There were, of course, noted exceptions of dissent from the majority's desire for expansionism. See Tyrrell and Sexton, *Empire's Twin*.

58. Johnson, *Sorrows of Empire*, 51.

59. Lundestad, *The American "Empire,"* 17.

60. Johnson, *Sorrows of Empire*, 47–48.

61. Bacevich, *American Empire*, 1.

62. See Ryn, *American the Virtuous*; West, *Democracy Matters*.

has strands of religious evangelism, which fits well the cognitive maps of many Americans.

This theopolitical discourse and the concomitant stories surrounding American expansionism have been and continue to be supported by religious-mythic narratives[63] that proclaim America's special role in the world and in history. These grand narratives—often intertwined with Christian meanings—are used by politicians, the media, and many citizens to give meaning, purpose, and understanding to expansionist foreign policies and actions, as well as to silence or marginalize dissenting views. Of course, sacralization of secular ideals and the background presence of Christian beliefs are often difficult to tease apart. For example, Reagan, in his farewell speech, said, "We meant to change a nation, and instead, we changed a world. Democracy, the profoundly good, is also the profoundly productive. But in my mind it was a tall, proud city built on rocks stronger than oceans, windswept, God-blessed, and teeming with people of all kinds living in harmony and peace; a city with free ports that hummed with commerce and creativity."[64] Bill Clinton's "indispensable nation" and, more recently, George W. Bush's assertions of America's "God-given values" are further illustrations of the mixed discourse in the process of making sacred the ideas of American-style democracy, freedom, and market economics.[65] All of this makes it difficult to see and be accountable for the policies and actions of injustice and carelessness "necessary" to achieve hegemony.

It is important to point out that supporters of U.S. Empire have included isolationists, liberal expansionists, and realpolitik expansionists/imperialists. Moreover, voices of dissent and criticism have emerged, but the track record reveals that expansionist voices have been dominant and hugely successful. Indeed, in most any history book one finds very little about those who have actively denounced U.S. imperialism (people such as Mark Twain and W. E. B. Du Bois) or stories and perspectives of defeated peoples. The absence of these biographies and stories suggests that active attempts have been made to marginalize criticism and dissent.

In brief, expansionists and imperial discourse have carried and continue to carry the day. All of this is to say that even though we can acknowledge the fact that while citizens possess diverse motivations with regard

63. The beliefs and values associated with the special role of the United States in history are not simply linked to narratives or speeches. Civil rituals (e.g., press conferences, inaugurals, congressional sessions, the Fourth of July), cultural rites (e.g., sports events), and social entertainment (e.g., movies) are other means by which values and beliefs associated with American expansionism are internalized and maintained.

64. This speech is readily available on numerous websites.

65. Ryn, *America the Virtuous*, 7.

to their political lives, critical masses of people have supported, tacitly or overtly, expansionist policies and actions that moved the U.S. to superpower status. I would add here that political, economic, and military leaders almost certainly possess greater motivation to pursue expansionism policies and actions, though they could not continue to do so without the tacit or overt support of the citizenry. The point here is that while there may not be, strictly speaking, a collective mind, there are shared, dominant stories that organize experience and shape motivations such that citizens accept, in varying degrees, expansionist or imperial aims, policies, and actions. This suggests that a critical mass of citizens, who vote, tends to rely on what I call empire narratives, which are prevalent in the culture and used to justify U.S. expansionism.

FORMS OF EMPIRE'S VIOLATIONS: CARELESSNESS AND INJUSTICE

The discourse supporting the U.S. Empire's expansionism both reveals and conceals the forms of violence used to become an empire. The prosecution of wars or the varied ethnic cleansings in the continental United States cannot be entirely denied or hidden, but, through an Orwellian kind of discourse, they clearly can be made to look as if they were just, necessary, and noble. Perhaps we use cherished stories and ideas not simply to deny our baser motives but also to shield ourselves from the horrors of the mountains of injustices and chasms of carelessness that formed as we sought to become an empire. As Samuel Huntington observes, "The West won the world not by the superiority of its ideas or values or religion but rather by its superiority in applying organized violence."[66] Organized violence vis-à-vis the U.S. Empire comprises systemic[67] violence or varied interrelated forms of violation. I prefer the notion of violation because it means to interrupt, break, disturb, profane, traduce, infringe, transgress, and offend individuals, families, cultures, and societies.[68] Another way of saying this is that forms of

66. Huntington, *Who Are We?*, 51.

67. By "systemic," I mean an organized and interrelated set of political, economic, and military narratives, policies, and practices aimed at establishing, legitimating, and maintaining an empire and hegemon.

68. In this chapter, I focus on systemic violence and its consequences vis-à-vis peoples of other countries. Some U.S. citizens, however, are also harmed by imperialist policies and actions. Martin Luther King Jr. recognized the connection between military spending, war, and poverty at home, as well as the disproportionate representation of the lower classes among soldiers. King said, "A nation that continues year after year to spend more money on military defense than on programs of social uplift is

violation represent an eclipse or distortion of an ethic of care and an ethic of justice.

To understand the systemic violence of the U.S. Empire, I briefly depict five interrelated forms of violations, namely, territorial, physical, ethnic or cultural-psychic, economic, and political. These types of violations occur through a combination of direct military actions, covert military and paramilitary operations by U.S. personnel or those trained by the U.S., as well as through intrusive, coercive economic and political policies and programs that destabilize cultures and societies for the sake of exploitation, expropriation, and control. Moreover, all violations are justified by official, dominant narratives and discourses of U.S. exceptionalism, superiority, and innocence. Finally, all these violations reveal pervasive injustice and carelessness, traits that bring about the attenuation or collapse of the space of appearances between the United States Empire and peoples of other nations experiencing the brunt of these violations.

Before proceeding, it is important to point out that the notions of violation and violence may imply passive victims who have little power. To be sure, there are many victims of U.S. aggression and coercion, but they were hardly passive.[69] American Indians resisted encroachments on their territories; Filipinos, Cubans, and Hawaiians struggled against U.S. colonialism. There were frequent outbreaks of resistance in the Caribbean and Central America, which triggered the U.S. sending in the Marines.[70] In the face of significant force, people of other countries have found creative overt and subtle ways to resist imperial policies and actions. Thus, the notion of violations accompanies forms of resistance, though I will not depict these because our main focus is on the injustice and carelessness of the U.S. Empire.

Territorial violations were integral to the birth of the American colonies and later became part of the U.S. march to the Pacific Ocean and beyond. While one could argue that not all territorial expansionism took place as a result of military aggression (e.g., the Louisiana Purchase), it is painfully clear that securing and maintaining these new territories required military and paramilitary forces working in concert with political policies that marginalized, oppressed, and sanctioned the killing or removal of indigenous people—all of this revealed, not simply gross injustices wrapped in the rhetoric of entitlement, racial superiority, and the gift of white civilization, but also mendacity and carelessness. Military violence, though, was but one

approaching spiritual death" (quoted in Zinn and Amove, *Voices of a People's History of the United States*, 426). Also, Martin Luther King Jr. believed that our spiritual anemia was and is the result of our profligate military spending and imperialist policies.

69. See Hardt and Negri, *Commonwealth*, 67–71.

70. See Butler, *War Is a Racket*; Petras and Veltmeyer, *Power and Resistance*.

violation of indigenous people and their territory. Political arrangements in the form of treaties (over three hundred) were made with various American Indian tribes and all these treaties were violated by the U.S.—more injustice and carelessness.[71] Moreover, political policies such as the ethnic cleansings that took place in Florida, in southern states, and in western territories could not have been implemented without the military and the support of white citizens and the larger public in general. This imperialistic territorial expansion did not end with the acquisition of the western shores of the U.S. At the end of the nineteenth century, the U.S. acquired Cuba and the Philippines after the Spanish-American War, shattering the hopes of Cubans and Filipinos who had been fighting their previous colonial master.[72] The U.S., through military and political force, garnered lands and resources in cases where formal annexation did not occur. For example, by forcing the Cuban government to adopt the Platt Amendment, the U.S. was able to "purchase" over "1,900,000 acres of land for about 20 cents an acre," and by 1909, U.S. companies, including Bethlehem Steel, controlled "at least 80% of the export of Cuba's minerals."[73] The same kind of territorial violation occurred in countries not under our direct political control (e.g., Guatemala, Nicaragua, El Salvador, Honduras, and Brazil).

Physical violations or harm naturally occurred when the U.S. reaped more territory, but they also happened whenever the U.S. sought to exercise political and economic control of states. Of course physical (and psychological) harm resulted from different forms of military violence, and the list here is depressingly long,[74] from killings of American Indians in the eighteenth and nineteenth centuries to more recent use of drones and covert operations to violate the territorial sovereignty of various countries (e.g., Pakistan), all the while killing and wounding men, women, and children.[75] Once the U.S. became a colonial power, the U.S. killed and tortured thousands of Filipinos and Cubans after the Spanish-American War.[76] Not counting the numerous wars in which the U.S. has been involved, military operations by U.S. forces or forces trained by the U.S. during the twentieth century in Central America have resulted in hundreds of thousands of deaths. Indeed, Boggs argues that "a rather conservative accounting of civilians killed by the

71. See Welch, *After Empire.*

72. Zinn, *A People's History of the United States*, 299–320.

73. Ibid., 310.

74. See Boggs, *Crimes of Empire*; Turse, *Kill Anything That Moves*; Vidal, *Perpetual War for Perpetual Peace.*

75. See Scahill, *Dirty Wars.* Scahill's book details the numerous covert and overt violent interventions taken by the U.S. before and after 9/11.

76. Zinn, *A People's History of the United States*, 314–17.

U.S. military since 1945 would number in the vicinity of eight million."[77] This figure does not include those wounded and maimed, which a conservative estimate would put at three times the number killed. Moreover, Boggs's figure does not include indirect deaths—deaths that resulted from the repressive actions of dictators actively supported (if not installed) by the U.S. or from U.S. economic interventions. Indirect or noncombat physical harm also occurs as a result of military and political stratagems that enforce U.S.-led economic sanctions. For example, it is estimated that over five hundred thousand Iraqi children died as a consequence of economic sanctions after the first Iraq War.[78]

What becomes clear from any cursory reading of the history of the American Empire is that interlacing formal and informal territorial violations result in transgressions of bodies as well as ecological systems.[79] Yet, the physical harm that results from imperialist policies and actions has nearly always accompanied devastating psychic-cultural violations. Lear, for instance, chronicled the cultural devastation of the Crow and Sioux peoples.[80] Removed from their lands and denied their cultural rituals and languages, these indigenous peoples suffered not just physically but also psychologically; this suffering affected future generations. Further west, the Hawaiian people and their culture were almost wiped out as a result of being "non-violently" taken over by U.S. businessmen and politicians who engineered a regime change.[81] Poignant accounts of the cultural and psychological violations that accompany colonial or formal rule are represented in the works of Fanon[82] and Nandy.[83] While writing from their own cultural locations that reflected French and British colonialism, both are applicable to the imperialistic policies of the U.S.

As I indicated above, the U.S. gradually shed or politically incorporated territories (e.g., Hawaii, Puerto Rico, Guam), becoming a more informal empire. Informal empires continue to use military violence, but not necessarily with the aim of establishing colonial governments and direct political control. Instead, violence or the threat of violence is used in concert with

77. Boggs, *Crimes of Empire*, 52.

78. See Crossette, "Iraq Sanctions Kill Children."

79. The near-complete extermination of the buffalo; the use of defoliants in the Vietnam war; the use of uranium-tipped ammunition, of mines, of fire bombings, and of hydrogen explosions are just a few examples of ecological violations that resulted from the imperialist policies and actions of the U.S. government.

80. Lear, *Radical Hope*.

81. Kinzer, *Overthrow*.

82. Fanon, *The Wretched of the Earth*.

83. Nandy, *The Intimate Enemy*.

economic interventions that give advantage to U.S. corporations. These economic violations, which often accompany military threat or violence, also result in cultural and social harms. Two-time Medal of Honor winner Major General Smedley Butler noted this relationship while reflecting on his long career. He wrote that, during his thirty-three years in the Marine Corps, "I spent most of my time as a high class muscle-man for big business, for Wall Street and for bankers . . . I helped in the raping of half a dozen Central American republics for the benefit of Wall Street."[84] More recently, Granada, Panama, Iraq Wars I and II, and numerous other military operations contributed to expanding or maintaining U.S. economic hegemony. In addition, as Naomi Klein has detailed in her book *Shock Doctrine*, the U.S. has been covertly involved in violating other countries' economic laws, policies, and programs through nonmilitary, covert interventions that destabilize these societies. For instance, U.S. academics, the CIA, and other government officials played a central role in Augusto Pinochet's orchestration of a coup that resulted in devastating social and economic upheavals in Chile. This was an engineered crisis, Klein convincingly argues, aimed at forcing through economic laws and policies that favored U.S.-style capitalism and U.S. corporations.[85] Klein thoroughly details U.S. exploitation of economic crises in Bolivia, Poland, South Africa, Russia, and other countries, led by U.S. economists and government officials, all aimed at extending U.S. economic power. As John Gray notes, the "American government has never observed the rule of non-interference in economic life."[86] The economic violations have had and continue to have devastating impacts on people's bodies and minds, seen in increased poverty.

The final type of violation that has cultural and psychological negative effects is political violations. By political violations, I am referring to two strategies. The first is the use of covert violence and threats to destabilize sovereign governments and to replace them with state officials loyal to U.S. interests, though not to U.S. constitutional values (i.e., democratic freedom,

84. Zinn and Amove, *Voices of a People's History of the United States*, 252.

85. The intersection of colonialism and capitalism, along with its violent expropriation of land and capital from colonized countries was explicated by Rosa Luxemburg in the early twentieth century. See, Hudis and Anderson, *The Rosa Luxemburg Reader*, 53–70. The United States followed this pattern, though Klein's work shows how the capitalistic methods of exploitation vis-à-vis other countries shifted during the period we call postcolonial. I add here, as mentioned above, that the decline of overseas markets tagged for privatization and expropriation meant that U.S. capitalists shifted their attention to their own country and toward how to privatize previously public spaces, utilities, and so forth. See, LaMothe, "The Colonizing Realities of Neoliberal Capitalism," 23–40.

86. Gray, *False Dawn*, 104.

justice, equality). In an engineered coup by the CIA, Iran's popular prime minister Mohammed Mossedeq, who had nationalized the oil industry, was replaced by Mohammed Reza Pahlavi, leading to over two decades of vicious totalitarianism.[87] Shortly thereafter, the U.S., used mercenaries trained by the CIA, to overthrew Guatemala's democratically elected leader, Jacobo Arbenz, ushering in decades of violence leading to as many as three hundred thousand deaths.[88] We can add to this list the U.S.-supported coup of Chile's democratically elected president Salvador Allende.[89] These are only three of the numerous nations whose political sovereignty was undermined by U.S. covert interventions.[90] The second type of political violation is manifested in U.S. foreign policies that actively support and help keep in place dictators who serve the interests of the U.S. A partial list includes the following: the Dominican Republic's Tiburcio Carías Andino, Nicaraguan presidents Adolfo Diaz and Anastasio Somoza Garcia, Cuba's Fulgencio Batiste, Iraq's Saddam Hussein, South Korean presidents Syngman Rhee and Park, and Egypt's president Hosni Mubarak. Supporting and helping to install dictators not only violates the political sovereignty of particular nations, but it leads to other violations that result in physical, psychological, economic, and social harms, especially with regard to the client state's people. The numbers of dead and maimed following the coups in Guatemala and Chile, as well as the dictatorships in Cuba, Nicaragua, and El Salvador, are overwhelming. Moreover, these countries continue to struggle with pervasive poverty, which is largely a legacy of an empire's meddling, which continues today.[91]

These forms of empire violations have in common the eclipse or distortion of an ethic of care and an ethic of justice, which accompanies the loss or attenuation of the space of appearances. Each form of violation, I argue, requires a misrecognition or nonrecognition of Others, which, in turn, attends a corruption or absence of care and justice. Consider, for example, the territorial expansion that began with the colonies. American Indians were represented as savages, as less than whites, as less than human, making it "justifiable" to take their land and kill or remove them. Whenever individuals and groups represent Others as less than persons, one can be sure that the actions that follow have nothing to do with care of these Others, and *justice* will be a hollow term, fit only to screen the filth of violations. Indeed,

87. Ferguson, *The War of the World*, 639.

88. Zinn, *A People's History of the United States*, 439.

89. Ibid., 554.

90. Kinzer, *Overthrow*.

91. See Danner, *Stripping Bare the Body*; Scahill, *Dirty Wars*.

these types of misrecognition are occasions for justifying violence, exploitation, oppression, and marginalization. Similarly, to take their lands at the very least means they were not given their due. To kill or forcibly remove persons from their ancestral homes necessarily means they were not cared for or about. Someone might protest and say that they were given lands (as if it was white Europeans' land to give), even if they were forcibly removed from other parts of the country. Is that not some form of care, some type of justice? First, as I mentioned above, the U.S. made over three hundred treaties with American Indian groups, and all of them were broken—hardly an estimable track of care and justice. Second, it is strange reasoning to say one is giving a people their due (as in land) when the land was not one's own to begin with.

I suspect that all empires emerge and are sustained by diverse forms of injustice and carelessness vis-à-vis other peoples. Yet it is not that the U.S. Empire is indifferent to the notions of justice and care, but when it comes to Othered peoples, these terms are relative or fluid. By this, I mean it depends on whether other nations are deemed to be obstacles to empire, client states (supporters of empire), or weaker states worth exploiting. On the path to empire and its decline, human beings and their governments have the ability to rationalize, deny, and prettify horrible acts of injustice and psychopathic carelessness while advocating for justice and care for their own citizens or the citizens of client states.

Yet this is not the whole story regarding the carelessness and injustice of empire. The exploitation of other peoples and nations is for the sake of enriching the metropole while also reinforcing its political, economic, and military power. The United States has reaped enormous material benefits on its way to becoming a superpower, which means that its citizens benefit as well. Or so it would seem. Violations, in other words, are not simply directed at other peoples. They also occur within the empire, especially to the least of these. Trillions of dollars are spent on the military and security industrial complexes for the sake of maintaining hegemony. This means that not enough money is directed toward alleviating poverty within the United States, let alone within other countries. This is an indirect violation, which impacts in very real and concrete ways the poor and working classes. As Mahatma Gandhi remarked that "poverty is the worst form of violence." Later, Martin Luther King Jr., probably echoing Gandhi, came to believe that war is the enemy of the poor, which he experienced firsthand when President Johnson directed funds to the war machine and rather than to the so-called war on poverty.[92] But it is not just war, but a war-dependent

92. King, *The Autobiography of Martin Luther King, Jr.*, 337.

society and economy. As I noted above, during the last twenty years, the U.S. Empire has spent trillions of dollars in "defense" and security—money not spent to address poverty at home (or abroad). In his style of prophetic speech, King preached, "And I come by here to say that America too is going to hell if she doesn't use her wealth. If America does not use her vast resources of wealth to end poverty and make possible for all God's children to have the basic necessities of life, she too will go to hell."[93] Poverty is the result of various forms of violations supported by carelessness and deliberate amnesia about justice. In the United States many citizens are distracted by the drumbeat of empire, which proclaims exceptionalism and enemy fear. The distractions enable the violence of poverty to flourish.

What Martin Luther King Jr. did not point out in his critique of the use of wealth on military spending is that the vast wealth of United States is largely the result of its expansionist policies and its attempts to maintain economic hegemony. The way that the U.S. maintained its wealth is analogous to the way early settlers took American Indian lands before giving only some land back. So, to be sure, it would be ideal to spend money to help impoverished citizens, but much of this wealth was expropriated. Also, we need to acknowledge that the vast military and security expenditures do enrich citizens. The military and national security complexes employ hundreds of thousands of people, who in turn spend money in their communities supporting other businesses. If we were to reduce these expenditures so that we could provide better education and housing to the poor (and help the poor of other countries), many people would lose their jobs, one could argue. There is little hope that more funds will be directed toward the poor and lower classes, because empires are focused on maintaining power and wealth, which means that some portion of their citizens will be sacrificed as the acceptable cost of doing the empire's business. I brief, marginalized and poor citizenry are objects of neither care, nor justice, even as other citizens enjoy the nation's vast wealth, largely derived from imperial hegemony.

In summary, when we consider the United States as an empire or superpower, it is necessary to explore the varied means by which it has arisen and how it maintains its power and wealth. I have suggested that it is better to consider the diverse forms of violations rather than the more restrictive concept of violence, because the term "violence" can facilitate our overlooking forms of carelessness and injustice. Not all of the U.S. Empire's actions are clearly violent, in the sense of causing bodily harm, death, and destruction of physical resources. Yet, the various forms of violations reveal the

93. Ibid., 354.

subtle forms of oppression and marginalization that take their toll on the bodies and psyches of other peoples and poor citizens of this nation.

RESPONDING TO EMPIRE: CREATING COMMUNITIES OF CARE AND JUSTICE

The rise of the U.S. Empire has not been without its critics,[94] though it becomes painfully obvious that critics and resisters were not even speed bumps on the way to its superpower status. Of course in some instances protests became rife, as during the Vietnam War, and politicians had to retreat; but these and other instances are minor setbacks that hardly altered the trajectory of the U.S. Empire. This is not a counsel for despair, but rather a sobering and tragic reality that should undermine any fantasy that individual and collective action will necessarily stop the march of empire. Given this, a radical hope in the face of empire is not contingent on success, though even small successes are worth noting and celebrating. Put another way, resistance is not dependent on winning an argument, convincing political officials, and transforming society. Instead, actions that manifest radical hope are dependent on the grace of incarnating God's care and justice in the face of carelessness and injustice. It is about incarnating, if only in fragmentary ways, a polis of God where the space of appearances reveals mutual recognition and the realization of the common good. This radical hope is not another form of anti-imperialist discourse and resistance, but rather it is an *alterimperialism* or an *alterempire*.

In their edited work, Ian Tyrrell and Jay Sexton note that the imperial and anti-imperial discourses are intertwined in U.S. history, each type reinforcing and influencing the other type.[95] One could argue that each player is using the grammar of imperialism and that even the anti-imperialist is simply reinforcing the reality of the imperium. In an analogous discussion, Michael Hardt and Antonio Negri describe modernity and antimodernity discourses, which they argue restrict the options for responding and narrows our understanding of what is taking place. They then offer new terminology—"altermodernity," a term with connections to alterglobalization.[96]

94. For a discussion on the intersectionality of imperial and anti-imperial discourses, see Tyrrell and Sexton, *Empire's Twin*.

95. Ibid.

96. Hardt and Negri, *Commonwealth*, 102–7. They are arguing that terms like *antimodernity* and *antiglobalization* do not capture the complexity of the discourse. For example, many people are not antiglobalization, but rather against the globalization that is confined to U.S. neoliberal economics. I am not using the term *alterimperialism* to suggest that there is greater nuance in positions, such as some people are who want

Hardt and Negri seek to break out of binary discourse with the aim of offering an alternative—a different grammar and way of being in the world.[97]

In a similar way, I offer a term, *alterempire*, that shifts the discourse enough to consider an alternative that does not depend on the grammar of the imperium. The notion of *alterimperialism* or *alterempire* has a couple advantages. First, it is not confined to the straitjacket of the rules and meanings of imperial—anti-imperial discourses. More specifically, I will address the change of grammar by considering the life and ministry of Jesus.[98] This is particularly apt, because Jesus's ministry took place in a place subjugated by the Roman Empire. Second and relatedly, anti-imperialism simply implies that one opposes imperial policies and practices. The problem often is the lack of clarity with regard to what one is for, or with regard to what vision is being offered. Alterimperialism suggests that there is something other than imperialism. There is a reality, a way of being in the world, that is radically different—a radically different alternative. Again, I rely on Jesus's life and ministry—a radical life and ministry later hijacked by theologians who argue for state-sanctioned violence (e.g., consider Augustine's just war), which ends up tacitly or overtly supporting empire's expansionism and forms of violence.

What then is this alternative? I begin by turning to another time and another empire. The Roman Empire was the superpower of its day, controlling huge areas of Europe, North Africa, and the Middle East. Insurrections and acts of resistance were occasional and ruthlessly put down by Roman legions. As Richard Horsely notes, "the initial Roman conquest of new peoples often entailed devastation of the countryside, burning villages, pillage of towns, and the slaughter and enslavement of the populace."[99] After surveying the gruesome aftermath of a Roman invasion, Polybius, a Roman historian, said, "It seems to me that they do this for the sake of terror."[100] Once a people was conquered, the Romans used various forms of public torture and sanctioned executions of resistors and insurrectionists—real and imagined—to terrorize the populace and, in so doing, to keep the populace fearful; thus the empire thwarted the possibility of resistance and rebellion.

---

to retain superpower status and eschew imperial policies. Rather, it refers to Other than imperialism.

97. Ibid., 119–28.

98. Months after writing this chapter I came across Mark Taylor's book *The Executed God.* He addresses the language of Paul in light of the language of the Roman Empire. Taylor argues that Paul was hoping to build *altercommunities*—communities that resisted the empire (221–43).

99. Horsley, *Jesus and Empire*, 23.

100. Ibid., 27.

These public spectacles of force and coercion (one of which was crucifixion) displayed for all to see Rome's imperial power.[101]

The Roman Empire, like all other empires, sought to extend and maintain its power over conquered peoples, creating "a culture in which the ruled are constantly tempted to fight their rulers within the psychological limits set by the latter."[102] The imperial elites set the limits of discourse (e.g., anti-imperialism, anti-Roman, anti-colonialism). This binary relation locks the imperialists and anti-imperialists in a vicious circle of violence and counter-violence. I suggest that Jesus's ministry exemplifies an alternative to this binary relation. By and large, Jesus ministers in the midst of empire but is not overly concerned with engaging empire—at least directly. To have done so would have meant being caught in the violent dance. This does not suggest he ignored it or was deaf and blind to the effects of empire. Rather, he lived, preached, and ministered in an alternative way of being in the polis.

Jesus, then, was not an anti-imperialist in any meaningful sense of that term, though we can understand his ministry as *alterimperialistic*. For instance, Horsely notes that Jesus's answer to the question of what is due to Caesar was not a waffling on the subject, but a form of resistance in the face of religious and imperial totalities.[103] This resistance is not derived from an anti-imperial stance but out of a vision that has nothing to do with imperialism or the imperial/anti-imperial binary. Further, Jesus's decision to go to Jerusalem, Hendricks contends, was political, taking his alternative message into the heart of both religious and imperial power.[104] Of course, this alternative message brought him to the attention of imperial authorities, and it is safe to say that while Jesus was not "rebelling" against Rome, his alternative must have been viewed as a threat to the status quo of the imperium. Jesus's public torture and death were state sanctioned and a political imperial practice of terrorizing subjugated peoples.[105] Jesus's response to torture is yet another display of *alterempire*. He forgives his tormentors and executioners. One interpretation of Jesus's remark that his tormentors do not know what they are doing (Luke 23:34) is they are captive and blind to the ways of empire. It is hard to imagine Jesus's forgiveness being replicated by those who advocate empire.

Let me say more about *alterempire* and the ministry of Jesus. While Jesus grew up in a world where Roman imperialism was daily fare, his

101. Horsley, *Jesus and the Power*, 180–85.

102. Nandy, *The Intimate Enemy*, 3.

103. Horsley, *Jesus and Empire*, 98.

104. See Hendricks, *The Universe Bends toward Justice*.

105. See Crossan, *Jesus*; Crossan, *God and Empire*.

ministry, his way of being in the world, was not based in opposition to empire. In other words, Jesus's public actions were not anti-imperialistic, but they were *alterimperialistic* in the sense that Jesus offered an alternative, and this alternative is represented by the term *kingdom of God*. The kingdom of God is not in opposition to the imperium, at least in the direct sense. Rather, it is an alternative polis that has nothing to do with imperial practices. Indeed, imperial policies and practices are inconceivable in a kingdom based on love, compassion, care, mercy, justice, and forgiveness. To return to Jesus, Hendricks argues that the principles of Jesus's politics were "justice (*mishpat*—'the establishment of fair, equitable, and harmonious relationships in society'), righteousness (*sadiqah*—'behavior that faithfully fulfills the responsibilities of relationship both with God and humanity'), and steadfast love (*hesed*)."[106] From another angle, Crossan writes that the "Christian Bible presents the radicality of a just and nonviolent God repeatedly and relentlessly confronting the normalcy of an unjust and violent civilization."[107] The gospels tell the story of God's unyielding care for those who suffer, and this care was incarnated in the life and ministry of Jesus. Jesus's solidarity with the poor, healing the sick, preaching forgiveness, and commanding compassion and love revealed the possibility of inclusion. His ministry embodies an ordering of society around care, mercy, and compassion—virtues that are alternative to empire's force, violence, control, hubris, and greed. In other words, Jesus's public ministry was political because it reflected the polis of God, the power of caring cooperation, and conflicted with and undermined the fundamental principles of imperial force, coercion, privilege, and prestige.

The principles of love, justice, and care are integral features of Jesus's methods—methods founded on an alternative polis. Jesus's living out and demonstrating compassion and love represented just relations found in the kingdom of God. The kingdom of God is not and cannot be a political totality precisely because love, compassion, mercy, and forgiveness are for all people, without distinction.[108] Care and justice, in this polis, are due everyone and all, as citizens, participate in the space of appearances. By contrast, imperial Rome, like other empires, recognized and differentiated between citizen and subjugated peoples, indicating that care, justice, and space of appearances are conditional and rooted in the forces of the imperium. There are no such distinctions in the kingdom of God. So, while Jesus was not a political activist or anti-imperialist, his ministry and what he represented

106. Hendricks, *The Universe Bends toward Justice*, 207–8.

107. Crossan, *God and Empire*, 94.

108. Ibid., 116–18.

contrasted with and was seen to threaten the political order of empire. In my view, his *alterempire* ministry did not directly confront or resist the Roman Empire, yet this alternative way of being in the world undermined the very ground of the imperium.

I add here that Jesus's ministry was not based on defining success by resistance to the machinations of empire. Indeed, his *alterempire* ministry was aimed at compassionate caring (e.g., healing, feeding), justice, mercy, and forgiveness. The cross, from the perspective of both empire and anti-imperialist, is a total failure in the sense that the subjugated was defeated by the violence of empire. Thus, Jesus's execution is a success for the empire in that because of it the empire retains power and privilege. Jesus, however, is not trapped by the grammar of terror and violence and, instead, offers a radical alternative—caring for the perpetrators of empire through mercy and forgiveness. Note here that the grammar of forgiveness and mercy is not in direct opposition to empire, though there is no collusion with empire. This grammar of care is *alterempire*, and in its lived expression is simply other than empire—an "other" alternative that is not dependent on empire's grammar or way of being in the world. By contrast, anti-imperial stances depend on the empire in the sense that anti-imperial stances resist and aim to overcome the empire; inasmuch as resistance depends on the presence of something to resist, any reflection on successful resistance also reflects on the status of the empire. Whether the Roman Empire changes, however, is not the aim and hope of *alterempire* and this is reflected in it not being dependent on empire. Rather, hope is based on living a life of care and justice in relation to all Others.

Of course establishing *alterempire* is easier said than done. When we turn to Acts, this becomes evident. The first Christian communities struggled to live out the principles of radical care and justice. They were *alterempire* by virtue of living out these principles, as well as through the practice of welcoming others and sharing property in common. Relations were not based in power, privilege, and prestige, but on care for others (members and nonmembers) and living a life in common.[109] One may point to the failures of these early Christian communities as deriving from the prevalence of human sin vis-à-vis living in community. While I agree, another explanation of the "failure" of *alterempire* communities is the prevalence, even dominance, of empire principles and values in society. Communities, more often than not, survive and thrive when they reflect the values and principles of the larger society. When a community's principles are radically different from those of the larger society, the struggle to survive and thrive is exceed-

109. Boer, *In the Vale of Tears*, 112–22.

ingly challenging. The gravitational pull is to adopt the more pervasive and dominant grammar of the society. This is a reason for these early failures.

Current counterexamples prove my point. Christianity, and in particular Christian communities in the United States, has had a long tradition of success, which is not to applaud them. To be sure, there are failures in community living and failures of some Christian communities to survive, but, by and large, Christianity has been successful because it has adopted or colluded with the values of the U.S. Empire and attending patriotism—many communities of faith have drunk deeply from the troughs of American exceptionalism. There are, of course, peace churches (e.g., the Quakers), but these are a tiny minority. If a first-century Christian community were to be formed today, it would be labeled naïve or, worse, communist—a code word used by supporters of neoliberal capitalism and U.S. superpower status. And I suspect that if a Christian leader (and community) were to offer compassion, forgiveness, and mercy to the Taliban s/he would be seen as un-American (which, in one sense, would be true). All of this is to say that *alterempire* vis-à-vis the life and ministry of Jesus is exceedingly challenging to live out, individually and communally, in a nation dominated by the values of empire.

Despite this challenge, some church communities work to live out what I am calling *alterempire*. These are transgressive communities where liturgy and public action express compassionate nonviolence, mercy, and forgiveness. The liturgical life of these faith communities nurtures and is closely aligned with internal and external or public actions of compassionate nonviolence. To the degree that community members believe in and live out compassionate nonviolence, they become a sacrament of *alterempire* and, as an alternative, critique and defy the injustice and carelessness of an empire's violence. Put another way, compassionate nonviolent resistance is founded on the recognition and treatment of Others as persons, which is already an invitation for opponents to cooperate in creating a space of appearances where seeking the common good for all people becomes the task at hand. These are communities of inclusion, communities in which all people are seen as created in the image and likeness of God.

Alterempire communities' care, justice, and compassionate non-violent resistance are necessarily transgressive. *Alterempire* communities critique—whether by word or action or simply their way of being in the world—established canons of American exceptionalism and innocence. They protest the American Empire's accepted forms of violations. They resist the public's desire for self-righteous vengeance when other people resist and critique the United States. They are transgressive because they reveal the sins and failures of the empire, debunking the soporific public narratives that overlook, deny, or rationalize injustices and carelessness.

This depiction may seem idealistic, but we have seen communities of compassionate nonviolence in U.S. history. Quaker communities were some of the first faith groups to actively resist slavery—a careless and unjust practice of empire. More recently, African American faith communities during the civil rights movement held to the principles of care, love, compassion, and nonviolence. During the 1980s, faith communities involved in the sanctuary movement resisted and defied U.S. imperial policies by welcoming "illegal" immigrants from El Salvador and Nicaragua.

If we were to speak to anyone from these communities, I suspect we would hear that trying to live up to and out of the principle of compassionate nonviolence was (and is) very difficult. It is difficult simply because of normal human failings. It is increasingly difficult when one is faced with the aggression of the state and the public, which Martin Luther King Jr. and others encountered daily. The seductions of empire's grammar of violence and self-righteousness are always present and prevalent, tempting people to construct opponents as demeaned Others. Similarly, members of *alterempire* communities may fall into despair or a sense of futility and may lack motivation to do their work of compassionate nonviolence, especially when facing tremendous odds and experiencing little if any success. Yet, we also see in these *alterempire* communities a resilience and persistence despite "failures," despite the seemingly unmovable juggernaut of empire's carelessness and injustice. King and many African Americans sought justice for themselves and others despite the resistance from the government and society. Their daily and weekly commitment, practice, and support were required to live out compassionate nonviolent resistance in community and in the empire's public square.

I add here that *alterempire* communities are not simply compassionate to those who suffer the violations of empire abroad and at home. Care and justice also are offered to those who advocate for policies and programs that expand and maintain the U.S. Empire. Compassion, I believe, is and will be necessary during the inevitable painful decline of the U.S. Empire. Of course, this does not mean that resistance, protest, and critique are absent. One can be empathic and compassionate toward opponents while stating clearly the injustices and carelessness of U.S. government officials and citizens who support imperial policies and practices.

It is important to stress that forms of resistance and the transgressive features of *alterempire* communities do not imply that these communities are dependent on the U.S. ceasing its imperial practices. For instance, imagine if the U.S. suddenly decided to cease being an empire, dismantling its vast military and seeking cooperation among equal nations. If these things happened, some might suggest that the community's reason to exist would cease, that the reason for an anti-imperialist's resistance would also cease. *Alterempire* Christian communities' way of being in the world is determined by the values and virtues of care and justice. And it is their very way of being in the world that is transgressive in a society that accepts and lives out imperialism. Thus, protests, and acts of resistance that emerge from these communities are secondary to their way of being in the world. If the U.S. Empire would cease being an empire, the communities would continue to try to create, foster, and maintain relations of care and justice. A similar point to stress is that these *alterempire* communities are not dependent on whether they are successful at moving political officials or altering imperial policies. It is not that these goals are unimportant. Consider, for instance, King's concern and hope to change the imperial policies of the U.S. government via-a-vis Vietnam. Success, instead, is determined by the degree to which these communities live out care and justice vis-à-vis their members and all others.

When considering *alterempire* it might be easy to dismiss it as politically naïve, idealistic, and impractical. Certainly, it is tempting to agree, but it is tempting precisely because of the prevalence of imperial discourse and narratives that define and construct the world in terms of the logic and grammar of force, coercion, prestige (exceptionalism), and privilege. From the perspective of this logic, the *alterempire* of Jesus's ministry is impractical, then and now. Yet, *alterempire* is not captive to an imperial/anti-imperial discourse and worldview. We can acknowledge and accept that to the imperium *alterempire* is impractical, but for those who seek to live by the grammar and logic of compassionate care and justice for all, *alterempire* is not an issue of practicality or impracticality. Living out *alterempire* is an issue of whether we care, whether we seek justice for all.

CONCLUSION

Rejecting the facile notion of human progress in history, H. Richard Niebuhr remarked, "For surely what is seen in history is not a universal, absolute, independent source and goal of existence, not impartial justice nor infinite mercy, but particularity, finiteness, opinions that pass, caprice, arbitrariness, accident, brutality, wrong on the throne and right on the scaffold."[110] This is all very abstract, and most people might readily agree that history is littered with injustices and brutal forms of carelessness. Yet closer to home, many

110. H. R. Niebuhr, *The Meaning of Revelation*, 40.

Americans who bask in the rays of American exceptionalism, vigorously resist this view, overlooking the long wake of carelessness and injustice that results from the pursuit of imperial policies and practices at home and abroad. Both Reinhold and Richard Niebuhr recognized that Americans are myopic when it comes to our faults. Indeed, Reinhold Niebuhr stated forcefully that "The gospel cannot be preached with truth and power if it does not challenge the pretensions and pride, not only of individuals, but of nations, cultures, civilizations, economic and political systems."[111] Perhaps, as Americans, our pride and pretentions are the scales that blind us to the consequences of our violence toward others; our pride and prententions allow us to continue avoiding not only the terrible horrors but also appropriate emotions of guilt and shame. In our blindness, we refuse the painful revelation of our political misdeeds, and this refusal of revelation consequently means the refusal of God's grace to mourn, to ask for forgiveness, to change.

In saying this, I am also aware that in the darkness of empire radical hope flickers in *alterempire* communities. I viewed these communities in terms of the grammar of the life and ministry of Jesus Christ, but *alterempire* communities can emerge from other religious, as well as humanist, traditions. An *alterempire* community is a polis of care, justice, and inclusion, a community that transgresses the being of empire.

111. R. Niebuhr, *Love and Justice*, 97.

6

THE RISE OF A MARKET POLIS

Neoliberal Capitalism and the Distortion of Care

Marx insisted that the aim of capitalist society is not to enrich human needs and capabilities, but rather to augment value. Capitalism . . . has one over-riding goal: to accumulate value for its own sake.[1]

What I'm saying to you this morning is that communism forgets that life is individual. Capitalism forgets that life is social, and the kingdom of brotherhood is found neither in the thesis of communism nor the antithesis of capitalism but in a higher synthesis. It is found in a higher synthesis.[2]

Religion has become an empty shell; it has been transformed into a self-help device for increasing one's powers for success. God becomes a partner in business.[3]

If I look at the world today it seems to me that the most powerful religion of all—much more powerful than Christianity, Judaism, Islam, and so

1. Hudis, *Marx's Concept*, 176.

2. The Southern Christian Leadership Conference Presidential Address by Martin Luther King Jr., 16 August 1967.

3. Erich Fromm, quoted in Carrette and King, *Selling Spirituality*, 24.

> on—is the people who worship money . . . The banks are bigger than cathedrals, the headquarters of the multinational companies are bigger than mosques or the synagogues. Every hour on the news we have business news—every hour—it is a sort of hymn to capitalism.[4]

> For Rousseau capitalism "bound new fetters in the poor, and gave new powers to the rich . . . fixed forever the laws of property and inequality; converted clever usurpation into an inalienable right and for the sake of the few ambitious men, subjected all mankind to perpetual labour, servitude and misery."[5]

> It seems to me axiomatic that expansionary, competitive, and exploitative logic of capitalist accumulation in the context of the nation-state system must . . . be destabilizing and that capitalism . . . is and will for the foreseeable future remain the greatest threat to world peace.[6]

THE WAITING ROOM WAS nearly empty when I went out to greet Dolores early Wednesday evening. She was a petite young woman wearing jeans, a red flannel shirt, and sneakers. Despite her polite smile and firm handshake, an underlying weariness emanated from her. As we sat down, I learned that Dolores was thirty years old with two children and a loving husband, Dave. Several weeks ago, Dolores struggled to get out of bed to wake her children. She felt exhausted, even after sleeping for seven hours. Dave told her to go back to sleep; he would get the kids ready for her parents to pick up. "I just couldn't get motivated, but I did make it to work," she said flatly. Feelings of exhaustion continued, and Dave encouraged her to see a physician, though they both worried about how they were going to pay for it. After several tests, Dolores and Dave sat across from the doctor, who told them the tests were negative and that she may be suffering from depression. The best method of treatment, her doctor said, is therapy and medication. Dave encouraged her to go, with the assurance that they would find a way to cover the expenses.

4. Tony Benn, quoted in Carrette and King, *Selling Spirituality*, 23.
5. Eagleton, *Why Marx Was Right*, 199.
6. Ellen Meiksins Woods, quoted in ibid., 200.

That evening, Dolores told me that her family had grown up on the wrong side of the tracks. Her father worked at a factory but drank a lot of the money away until he sobered up when she was seventeen. "He wasn't a mean drunk. He was just mostly absent," she said. Her mother understandably worried a great deal about making it financially, though Dolores, looking out the window, remarked that her mother was simply a worrier. Even now that her parents were in better financial shape, her mother fretted over many things.

After high school, Dolores went to work in the same factory as her father, only to find out four years later that the plant was being moved to another country. She quickly found another job at a national chain store, though it was at lower pay and without benefits. Almost a decade later, she was still working for less than she had earned at the factory. The good news, she smiled, was this is where she met her husband. They married and, with both of them working sixty or more hours a week, they were able to buy a "fixer-upper," which still needed a lot of work. Two children quickly followed and their lives were consumed with work, parenting, and the house.

The roots of her depression, Dolores believed, were biological and developmental. After hearing the news from the doctor, Dolores began wondering if her depression was genetic. "You know I think my dad drank because he was depressed and I know my mom's mother was a depressed woman, though they would not have called it that back then." Dolores went on to consider whether the struggles of her parents, when she was growing up, were also sources of her depression. "It was not a happy household," she explained.

Dolores's story is not uncommon and her understanding of the roots of her depression is common enough in Western cultures. Biology and childhood are, of course, not insignificant etiological factors in mental suffering, but Dolores's story reminded me of James Baldwin and Frantz Fanon. James Baldwin writes that while in New Jersey, "I first contracted some dread, chronic disease, the unfailing symptom of which is a kind of blind fever, a pounding in the skull and fire in the bowels."[7] The disease was systemic racism, and Baldwin knew that some people succumbed to it. His father, Baldwin remarked, "was defeated long before he died because, at the bottom of his heart, he really believed what white people said about him."[8] The source of Baldwin's and other African Americans' mental anguish and depression was and is the pervasive reality of racism. From the other side of the world, Frantz Fanon, an Algerian psychoanalyst, wrote, "I must help

7. Baldwin, *Notes of a Native Son*, 94.

8. Baldwin, *The Fire Next Time*, 4.

my patient to '*consciousnessize*' his unconscious, to no longer be tempted by a hallucinatory lactification, but also to act along the lines of a change in social structure . . . My objective will be to enable him to *choose* an action with respect to the real source of the conflict."[9] Fanon's patients were people who had lived under the brutal yoke of French colonizers. He believed that the source of the neurotic suffering of Algerian citizens was due to the oppressive realities of the colonizers. If patients believed the source of their suffering was biology or childhood, they would not only mystify the real sources and collude with colonizers but also would not be able to direct their actions toward the real source. While Dolores's depression was not rooted in racism or imperial colonization, it was inextricably linked to the oppressive realities of living in a polis dominated by the social imaginary of neoliberal capitalism.

Capitalism has been of interest to some pastoral theologians largely because of its relation to suffering, exploitation, and classism.[10] Generally speaking, the focus is on how capitalism is implicated in various forms of struggles and suffering, such as domestic violence, racism, and depression. My focus is different. I examine neoliberal capitalism at a more macro level, depicting how it molds citizens' subjectivities, organizes social relations, and undermines the polis by way of corrupting care and justice; this corruption, in turn, contributes to various maladies of the soul. I begin by providing a brief overview of neoliberal capitalism, its attributes, and its rise in becoming the grand narrative that organizes society—market society. The argument here is that neoliberal capitalism is not merely an economic symbol system for organizing economic transactions. Rather, it is a complex, highly adaptable social and political symbol system with meanings, beliefs, values, and expectations that dominates the polis and shapes subjectivities, socially shared perceptions, and behaviors. The next section deals with the ways neoliberal capitalism and its disciplinary regimes undermine care and justice, eclipse the common good and distorts the polis's space of appearances. The third section provides evidence of soul suffering—individual and collective—that arises when a society becomes a market society. The final section briefly considers ways citizens and faith communities can

9. Fanon, *Black Skin, White Masks*, 80 (italics original).

10. See Poling, *Render unto God*; Smith, *The Relational Self*; Rogers-Vaughn, "Powers and Principalities." I wish to note that religious institutions and groups have also been critical of capitalism and its effects on society. The Lutheran World Federation, the World Council of Churches; see Rieger, *Opting for the Margins*, 124–25. Of course, there are also conservative religious groups and institutions that tout capitalism (e.g., the Acton Institute; see also MacDonald, *Thieves in the Temple*).

respond toward the "real source of the conflict" by creating *altercapitalist* communities.

A few brief remarks are necessary before beginning. First, it is fitting to bring a critical pastoral political perspective to the issue of capitalism after a chapter on U.S. imperialism and violence. The handmaiden of U.S. expansionism was and is capitalism.[11] Like all imperial powers, the U.S. metropole derived its wealth largely from exploitation of other peoples, and myriad forms of economic exploitation reveal a profound distortion of both care and justice. My second comment concerns the relation between a macro critical analysis and the suffering of individuals, like Dolores. It is easy to get caught up in a macro analysis and lose sight of the concrete suffering of individuals. So I will return to Dolores and her family at different points in this chapter. This said, it is not just individuals and families who suffer from a market society. Communities suffer as well, though other communities, including religious, reap and tout the benefits of capitalism.[12] Third, I recognize that a critique of neoliberal capitalism has been taken up by many authors, usually running the length of a book, not a mere chapter. This chapter is a more modest and introductory analysis of a very complex social, political, and economic reality—one that I intend to show undermines the kind of care and justice necessary for a vibrant polis that deliberately seeks the common good for all members. Related to this is the question of why a pastoral theologian, having studied capitalism for over ten years and who is far from being an expert in economics, has the temerity to critique neoliberal capitalism. My response is that while I make no claim to be an expert in economics, I, like millions of others, live in a market society. Simply living in a market society breeds familiarity with neoliberal capitalism and its effects—positive and mostly negative. Dolores, for instance, may not be an economist or a business leader, but, like colonized persons, she *knows* that the system is rigged against her and others like her. As William Easterly points out, "experts" often refuse to hear or take heed from non-experts who have important knowledge of their own situation.[13] Dolores and my fellow pastoral theologians who are critical of capitalism have intimate knowledge of a system. My other response is that even if a pastoral theologian is not an expert in politics or economics, s/he is obliged to understand and critique the varied sources of individual, communal, and societal suffering (and flourishing), which requires delving into other human science disciplines. As I will point out below, the physical, psychological, and soul maladies

11. See Butler, *War Is a Racket*; Klein, *Shock Doctrine*.

12. See MacDonald, *Thieves in the Temple*.

13. Easterly, *The Tyranny of Experts*.

that result from neoliberal capitalism are maddeningly pervasive, thus demanding a critical, caring analysis and response. Finally, this chapter is only a preliminary foray into this wildly dense and complicated subject; more work and more conversations need to take place if we are to find ways to reform a market society so that care, justice, and the common good are applicable to all.

NEOLIBERAL CAPITALISM AND THE RISE OF A MARKET SOCIETY

Before addressing the complexities of neoliberal capitalism and its rise, it is necessary to offer a few brief remarks on capitalism itself. Capitalism, in general, is a complex semiotic system or social imaginary[14] comprising ideas, narratives, treatises, rituals, and other practices that order relationships and institutions vis-à-vis financial exchange. In moving toward a definition, we immediately discover that there is no single definition or type of capitalism. There are instead various kinds of capitalism and, even within these various types there is often no clear consensus on a definition. There is, for instance, classical capitalism,[15] laissez-faire capitalism, supercapitalism,[16] neoliberal capitalism,[17] state-corporate capitalism,[18] state-run capitalism (e.g., present in China), and democratic capitalism,[19] and there are differences even within these specific forms. Complexity and contestation will not deter me from attempting to provide a brief sketch of capitalism and, more particularly, of neoliberal capitalism and its salient attributes.

14. The term "social imaginary" is taken from Charles Taylor's work, *Modern Social Imaginary*. The concept suggests that capitalism is a human construction, which then means a rejection of any idea that capitalism is natural, inevitable, or ontological.

15. For example, the works of Adam Smith and David Ricardo, which are discussed in Mann, *Disassembly Required*; Wolff and Resnick, *Contending Economic Theories*.

16. Reich, *Supercapitalism*.

17. See Harvey, *A Brief History of Neoliberalism*; Wolff and Resnick, *Economics*. Neoliberal capitalism, at times, falls under the heading of late capitalism. The adjective "late" seems to suggest that we are either in the midst of the most recent form of capitalism or that this is the final stage of capitalism wherein it collapses under its own contradictions. I prefer the term "neoliberal capitalism" because it points to the underlying ideology of the most recent edition of capitalism. Moreover, while Marx revealed the contradictions of capitalism, the proponents of capitalism have proven to be remarkably resilient in insuring capitalism survives. A recent example of this is Robert Reich's book, *Saving Capitalism*.

18. Duménil, and Lévy, *The Crisis of Neoliberalism*.

19. Wolff, *Democracy at Work*.

Since neoliberal capitalism has its roots in classical capitalism, it is important to offer a short description of capitalism before discussing neoliberal capitalism's rise as a dominant social imaginary. The fathers of classical capitalism were two British subjects, Adam Smith (1723–1790) and David Ricardo (1772–1823). They and others were highly influential in laying the groundwork for the philosophical and legal principles of capitalism, as well as its relation to the state. Briefly, classical capitalism is an intricate economic symbol system that outlines the dynamics and ends of financial exchanges within and between societies, as well as how the financial system is related to the state. More particularly, this semiotic system is "organized . . . around the institution of property and the production of commodities,"[20] which is determined by a "rational" calculus of cost and price—commodification of goods and services—and the market law of supply and demand.[21] The aims and values of capitalism are productivity and profit or the accumulation of capital for the purposes of reinvestment, market expansion, and greater profits. Profit, then, is the central value, motive, and telos that largely determines "rational" decisions vis-à-vis expanding production; seeking larger market shares; and setting wages, hiring, benefits, expenditures, and so forth. Labor and wages, for instance, are inextricably linked to and ostensibly determined by material production, services, supply and demand, and, naturally, the overarching aim of securing profit.[22] Surplus labor and value are integral to the overall profit, which is kept by those who are owners or shareholders of the business. In addition, the means of production in

20. Bell, *The Cultural Contradictions of Capitalism*, 14. The "institution of property" cannot exist without laws and mechanisms of enforcement that are provided by the state. Laissez-faire and neoliberal capitalists incessantly argue for deregulation or for the state to remove itself from "interfering" in the market. As Anita Chari notes, this obfuscates the state's role in regulating markets by suggesting the "market" and the state are two completely different entities when, in fact, the market could not exist without the state. Indeed, pointing to the Krippner's research, she writes that "neoliberal politicians and elites pursue policies that obscure the state's role in regulating markets, allowing them to govern the economy at a remove while avoiding political responsibility for economic policies and outcomes" (Chari, *A Political Economy of the Senses*, 30).

21. I have placed the term "rational" in quotes to suggest the underlying illusion that the so-called market or those involved in the market make rational, objective decisions. Any casual observer of the rises and falls of the stock market notes the presence of greed, fear, hubris, anxiety, and anger, which all play a large role in making "rational" decisions, which Alan Greenspan only realized after the financial collapse of 2008. [King, "Greenspan: Crisis prompted re-examination of economic beliefs."] I would add here that the notion of "rational" vis-à-vis capitalism is a kind of rationalism that is associated with the advancement of each individual's self-interest. It is instrumental and individualistic. This is decidedly different from a rationalism associated with making decisions with regard to the interests and needs of others.

22. Wolff and Resnick, *Contending Economic Theories*, 39.

classical capitalism are privately owned, whether by an individual, a family, or stockholders. (More precisely, socially constructed legal entities called corporations have stockholders.) In terms of the relation between consumers and producers, Adam Smith touted the "invisible hand" of the market whereby each individual "rationally" maximizes self-interest in a milieu wherein supply will equal demand, increasing the wealth of producers and shareholders while providing goods and services to consumers.[23] Each subject, then, is self-referential, maximizing his/her self-interest, which, it is believed, will lead to an overall "good" for the society. This "good" is understood primarily in terms of wealth, which is measured by what we call the GDP (Gross Domestic Product).

In classical capitalism, the state and the economic system are differentiated with the state possessing the power to regulate capital, though this relation can be obscured. While the market may function as an invisible hand (a metaphor suggesting autonomy between economics and the state), the state, in classical and laissez-faire capitalism, still retains power and control. Indeed, the invisible hand is inextricably linked to and dependent on the arm of the state. For instance, in laissez-faire capitalism, the state is seen as restricting its own power by not interfering with so-called market forces. Of course, this does not mean the state does not continue to use its power, even in situations of deregulation, which actually is another form of regulation. The very creation and sustenance of classical capitalism, then, depends both on the state creating legal fictions such as corporations, as well as on the use of the police and military to ensure security and stability of national and international commercial exchanges, property rights, and so forth.

Adam Smith could not have envisioned the rise to dominance of the market's so-called invisible hand in Western societies. The proliferation of capitalism had its roots not simply in the rational ethics of liberal Protestantism[24] and the eclipse of a grand narrative[25] but also in the Western imperialism and industrialization of the nineteenth and twentieth centuries.[26] As the United States and other colonial powers used military force and economic coercion to seek greater territory and markets, capitalism became the lingua franca of Western politicians and business leaders.[27] Even the

23. Hendricks, *The Universe Bends toward Justice*, 152, points out that John Maynard Keynes dismantled this claim, indicating that "supply cannot be counted on to create its own demand."

24. See Weber, *The Protestant Ethic and the Spirit of Capitalism.*

25. See Lyotard, *The Postmodern Condition.*

26. See Stone and Kuznick, *The Untold History of the United States*; Zinn, *A People's History of the United States.*

27. See Petras and Veltmeyer. *Power and Resistance.*

decline of colonialism in the mid-twentieth century would not stem the expansionist aims of capitalism. For instance, before the end of World War II, the United States organized a financial conference (in Bretton Woods, New Hampshire) that was instrumental in creating international financial institutions (e.g., the World Bank and the International Monetary Fund [IMF]) that were created to stabilize the international markets; this stability, in turn, ensured the supremacy of capitalism and largely benefited the United States and its European client states.[28] This expansion of capitalism did not remain confined to the creation of global financial institutions. Klein, for instance, painstakingly details the collusion of U.S. government leaders and economic experts from the Chicago School to destabilize governments and economies (for example, in Chile, Argentina, and Brazil) during the latter half of the last century in an effort to install capitalistic systems that favored U.S. and European interests.[29] The creation of international economic institutions and the economic colonization of other countries accompanied an evangelical zeal for establishing "free" markets through deregulation and economic treaties.[30] The history of the expansion of capitalism in the United States and elsewhere reveals that the hidden hand of the market was often a not-so-hidden fist that depended on the arm of the state.[31]

Yet, long before World War II ended, the seeds of neoliberal capitalism were sown: they sprouted after the war and flowered after the late 1970s. Pierre Dardot and Christian Laval point out that the "creation of the Mont Pelerin Society in 1947 is often incorrectly cited as marking the birth of neoliberal capitalism. In fact, the founding moment of neoliberal capitalism came earlier: it was the Walter Lippmann Colloquium," which was held in 1938.[32] Of course, the colloquium and its attending economic theories were decades in the making and largely a response to the trends toward "policies of redistribution, social security, planning, regulation and protection that had developed since the end of the nineteenth century."[33] These policies,

28. For a history of capitalism in the twentieth century, see Jones, *Masters of the Universe*.

29. Klein, *Shock Doctrine*; see also Reich, *Supercapitalism*, 44–47.

30. In his book *Economics as Religion*, Robert Nelson provides an interesting history of the proponents of capitalism in the late nineteenth and early twentieth centuries and their religious fervor in preaching the good news of capitalism. It is interesting that this accompanied, as Jean Lyotard noted in *The Postmodern Condition*, a growing decline of a religious grand narrative for ordering social life.

31. See Major General Smedley Butler, in Zinn and Amove, *Voices of a People's History of the United States*, 252.

32. Dardot and Laval, *The New Way of the World*, 49.

33. Ibid.

in fact, were first favored because of the crushing and extensive economic injustices citizens experienced as a result of unrestrained capitalism. The attendees of the Lippmann Colloquium reacted against these social-economic trends and, in particular, Keynesian economic policies—policies aimed at greater regulation of the markets and redistribution through tax reforms with the aim of limiting the inevitable boom-bust cycles associated with classical capitalism.[34]

World War II interrupted the momentum of neoliberal proponents, but also gave them greater motivation to see their plans succeed. Political philosopher Friedrich Hayek and his compatriot Ludwig von Mises knew of the devastation wrought by totalitarian economies in Eastern Europe and they worried about the social democratic economies of Western Europe. These men and others were instrumental in establishing the Mont Pelerin Society.[35] This group included such luminaries as Milton Friedman, whose Chicago School played a central role in destabilizing various nations in the attempt to establish neoliberal capitalism during the 1970s and 1980s. The catalyst, however, for the flowering of neoliberal capitalism and the meteoric rise of its proponents to positions of power and influence in the United States was the economic crisis of the 1970s in the United States and Britain.[36] Through the creation of think tanks,[37] popular publications,[38] schools of business, and the IMF,[39] and by attaining government positions, neoliberal capitalists and their ideas took hold. The election of U.S. president Ronald Reagan is usually cited as the beginning of neoliberal economic policies, but Jimmy Carter, who inherited the economic crisis from Gerald Ford, instituted a series of deregulatory policies and appointed Paul Volcker as chairman of the Federal Reserve.[40] Nevertheless, the Reagan administration rapidly extended neoliberal policies. As Anita Chari points out, "In the 1970s and 1980s, neoliberalism in the Euro-American context was associated with a set of policies known as the Washington consensus, which carried out policies of fiscal austerity, privatization, and pro-corporate policies through institutions such as the World Bank, IMF, and Federal Reserve."[41]

34. See Wolff and Resnick, *Contending Economic Theories*, 320–35.

35. Harvey, *A Brief History of Neoliberalism*, 20.

36. Harvey argues that the power and influence of neoliberal ideas came to fruition in the 1970s / '80s with the proliferation of conservative think tanks, as well as the elections of Margaret Thatcher and Ronald Reagan.

37. See Jones, *Masters of the Universe*, 134–79.

38. Hayek, *Road to Serfdom*; Friedman, *Capitalism and Freedom*.

39. See Mann, *Disassembly Required*, 141.

40. Jones, *Masters of the Universe*, 248–53.

41. Chari, *A Political Economy of the Senses*, 27.

Neoliberal capitalists such as Friedman reinterpreted or reframed some of Adam Smith's and David Ricardo's beliefs, overlooking some of their warnings about corporate powers and the role of the state in regulating the market. While disregarding some warnings of classical capitalists, neoliberal capitalists kept the premise (more accurately, the dogma[42]) that "the hidden hand of the market was the best device for mobilizing even the basest of human instincts such as gluttony, greed, and the desire for wealth and power *for the benefit of all.*"[43] For a neoliberal economist, the strong belief in the hidden hand of the market included the rejection of Keynesian types of government interventions to regulate financial institutions. Neoliberal capitalists publicly decry state regulation, arguing that the market should be independent of the state if it is to flourish. Anita Chari, relying on Krippner's research, writes that "neoliberal politicians and elites pursue policies that obscure the state's role in regulating markets, allowing them to govern the economy at a remove while avoiding political responsibility for economic policies and outcomes."[44] The state is very much involved in expanding and maintaining the practices, ideology, and policies associated with neoliberal capitalism.

Although no clear consensus exists about which attributes characterize neoliberal capitalism, I nevertheless identify ten central features of this social imaginary, namely, the following: (1) human well-being, understood almost exclusively in economic terms, is best achieved by providing entrepreneurial freedoms so that individual actors (including corporations) can act out of their "rational" self-interests;[45] (2) social goods will be maximized by expanding the reach and frequency of market transactions;[46] (3) anything and anyone can be commodified;[47] (4) the state is not to intervene to control markets or restrict the reach of commodification; (5) the state functions to ensure private property rights and deregulation so there can be free markets and free trade; (6) where markets do not exist, entrepreneurs and the state work together to privatize and deregulate (to privatize public education, prisons, health care, and the like);[48] (7) corporations are to inform the state as to the laws that will enhance profit and market expansion; (8) greed

42. See Brown, *Undoing the Demos*, 67.

43. Harvey, *A Brief History of Neoliberalism*, 20 (italics added).

44. Chari, *A Political Economy of the Senses*, 30.

45. Implicit here is that individuals are largely responsible for their economic failures and success, which is a core tenet of neoliberalism.

46. Rieger, *No Rising Tide*, 15.

47. See Sandel, *What Money Can't Buy*.

48. The market, in other words, becomes the organizing principle of the state and not citizenship and the common good.

benefits society;[49] (9) "market freedoms are natural and political restraints on markets are artificial";[50] (10) individual citizens are to be entrepreneurs in a competitive state—*homines oeconomici.*[51] *Homo oeconomicus* is a "hypermobile, entrepreneurial neoliberal subject who must assume the burden of risk that the state no longer shoulders."[52] "Capitalism," Terry Eagleton writes, "wants men and women to be infinitely pliable and adaptable."[53]

Let me linger for a moment on this last feature. Foucault, in his 1978–79 lectures, argued that the neoliberal market society means that the individual enters the market "being for himself his own capital, his own producer, the source of his earnings."[54] This new *homo oeconomicus* is formed and maintained by the disciplinary regimes of the state, media, and market. What is important to note is that the state, Wendy Brown argues, is "subordinated to the market, govern[s] for the market, and gain[s] and lose[s] legitimacy according to the market's vicissitudes." As a result, citizens lose their "orientation to the public and toward values enshrined by, say, constitutions."[55] Brown notes further, "No longer are citizens *most importantly* constituent elements of sovereignty, members of publics, or even bearers of rights. Rather, as human capital, they may contribute to or be a drag on economic growth; they may be invested in or divested from depending on their potential for GDP enhancement."[56] Neoliberal capitalism with its fetishizing individualism leads to what Brown calls responsibilization, which is "forcing the subject to become a responsible self-investor and self-provider."[57] At the same time, "subjects are constructed as labor or labor power, as commodities or creatures of exchange, as consumers, clients, entrepreneurs, or self-investing human capital."[58] The subject, then, as "human capital . . . is at once in charge of itself, responsible for itself, and yet a potentially dispensable element of the whole."[59] Thomas Lemke makes a similar claim, arguing that citizens "are expected to cope with social risks and insecurities, to measure

49. See Duménil and Lévy, *The Crisis of Neoliberalism*; Couldry, *Why Voice Matters;* Harvey, *The Enigma of Capital and the Crisis of Capitalism.*

50. Gray, *False Dawn*, 17.

51. See Chari, *A Political Economy of the Senses*, 28; Dardot and Laval, *The Crisis of Neoliberalism*, 104, 255.

52. Chari, *A Political Economy of the Senses*, 9.

53. Eagleton, *After Theory*, 118.

54. Foucault, *The Birth of Biopolitics*, 225–26.

55. Brown, *Undoing the Demos*, 108–9.

56. Ibid., 110 (italics original).

57. Ibid., 84.

58. Ibid., 83.

59. Ibid., 110.

and calculate them, taking precautions for themselves and their families. In this perspective, it is entrepreneurial action, rational risk management, and individual responsibility that accounts for social success or failure."[60] Jennifer Silva's research on the working class illustrates both Brown's and Lemke's claims about neoliberalism's *homo oeconomicus* and responsibilization. Finding it difficult to obtain a college education, incurring large debts, and being limited to low-wage jobs, working-class men and women blame themselves, believing they alone are responsible for their economic woes.[61] There is "the constant threat of unemployment and poverty, and anxiety about the future," which heightens fear and "stimulates a consciousness of economic risks and uncertainties that accompany the socially expected entrepreneurship."[62] At the same time, the poor and people in the lower working classes feel marginalized and powerless with regard to their role in the public sphere (as *homo politicus*), which only further enhances and emboldens neoliberal capitalists' political and economic power by hiding the real source of the suffering of the poor and lower laboring classes.[63] Dolores, for instance, began counseling because she was depressed, not realizing the major source of her depression could be attributed to the market society and its attending depoliticized space—attenuation and distortion of the space of appearances.[64]

The proliferation of the notion of entrepreneurial selves has been aided by new technologies. Steven Hill describes the myriad of Internet-based companies. He remarks that the

> sharing economy is turning out to be a giant loophole that allows more businesses to dump their regularly employed (W-2) workers and more easily hire a lot more freelancers and independent contractors (1099 workers), cutting their labor costs by 30 percent because they don't provide any safety net for these workers (health care, Social Security, Medicare, unemployment and injured workers compensation, retirement or paid sick leave and vacations and more). One new economy booster clarified employers' new strategy: "Companies today want a workforce they can switch on and off as needed"—like one can turn off a television. If the employer-employee relationship used to be

60. Lemke, "The Risks of Security," 65.

61. Silva, *Coming Up Short*. See also Illouz, who discusses Freud's understanding of emotions and their relation to class hierarchies (*Cold Intimacies*, 72–73).

62. Lemke, "The Risks of Security," 68.

63. See Marris, *The Politics of Uncertainty*.

64. For more on the relation between capitalism and depression, see Rogers-Vaughn, "Blessed are those who mourn"; Cvetkovich, *Depression*.

> a sort of marriage, today it is becoming a series of one-night stands.[65]

The good news, for neoliberal capitalists, is that Internet platforms can help us monetize our home, garage, driveway, tools, even our free time. In an extreme economy, everyone becomes an independent contractor, everyone is an individual entrepreneur, which means social benefits are drastically reduced but profits for corporations soar. The individual worker is left to fend for herself, unless, of course, she is a corporate leader.

The market society's *homo oeconomicus* has also made its way into churches and theological renderings of Scripture, resulting in churches serving as yet another disciplinary regime of the neoliberal society. The prosperity gospel advocates, for instance, are not ignorant of human suffering, and they have their own perspectives on theodicy. That is, capitalistic-touting theologians and pastors take note of the suffering of many people within society and interpret this suffering in two basic ways. First, religious leaders such as Joel Osteen subtly or overtly condemn people in poverty.[66] This condition is, from their perspective, something that poor people have brought on themselves (i.e., from lacking motivation, responsibility, enthusiasm, and discipline), and poor people are believed to be drags on the economy. According to their capitalistic-theological logic, poverty is the absence of God's blessing; this implies that individuals who are poor have sinned. Consider Reverend A. R. Bernard, who proclaims that "There is no way you can equate God with poverty."[67] Similarly, Reverend Creflo Dollar states that "Having no increase renders you useless to the kingdom of God."[68] The prosperity gospel is a clear example of theology that relies on neoliberal capitalist assumptions about individuals who are not entrepreneurs and so who have no value vis-à-vis the community. This is a powerful message to congregants in the sense of motivating them to be of "value" to God and to justify their pursuit of wealth (greed).

A second way for capitalistic religious leaders and theologians to make sense of poverty and suffering vis-à-vis capitalism is to retreat to the age-old Christian maxim take up your cross. Michael Novak is perhaps the best known advocate for this theological position. In one of his books,[69] Novak includes a chapter on a theology of economics, which finds further support in his later book, *A Theology of the Corporation*. In these books, Novak believes

65. Karlin, "Runaway Capitalism Is Crushing American Workers."

66. See Ehrenreich, "On Turning Poverty into an American Crime."

67. Quoted in Macdonald, *Thieves in the Temple*, 4.

68. Quoted in ibid., 5.

69. Novak, *The Spirit of Democratic Capitalism*.

Christians are to accept the world as it is and not pine for a kingdom of God on earth. As an apologist for neoliberal capitalism, he says, "If God so willed his beloved Son to suffer, why would He spare us."[70] What he is referring to are people who are suffering economically—failed entrepreneurs. Capitalism, in Novak's view, provides great wealth, and there will always be winners and losers. Losers need to accept the reality of capitalism and accept their suffering. Novak's comment not only exemplifies the underlying sadistic nature of his kind of God—a cruel god fitted to be the deity of capitalism's hidden fist—but also communicates clearly that the poor who suffer are to take up their cross meekly. Moreover, the metamessage in his theological worldview is to accept uncritically the notion of *homo oeconomicus* and the attending theologically distorted view that all economic suffering comes from God and, therefore, suffering must be accepted. Another metamessage is the justification of his and other persons' wealth or acquisitiveness. One can be assured that Novak and other theological devotees of neoliberal capitalism have said this from the comfort of their expensive homes, sheltered from the laments of those on the receiving end of both the slap of the hidden hand and the punch from the hidden fist of the Market.[71] More to the point, these religious leaders, their theologies, and their churches function as yet one more disciplinary regime in the construction of *homo oeconomicus*.

What is evident in these theologically distorted views of Christianity is the reversal of Max Weber's account of the role Christianity vis-à-vis and the rise of capitalism.[72] Weber argued that Protestant religious values were instrumental in facilitating the emergence of capitalism, while at the same time serving to restrain its acquisitiveness. In this scenario, Christianity still held the reins, subordinating capitalism to Judeo-Christian anthropology. In a neoliberal capitalist society, *homo oeconomicus* reigns, and many Christians and theologies serve, justify, and evangelize for their new master.

In summary, neoliberal capitalism with its attending anthropological claims and its views of the role of the state has become the dominant social imaginary for organizing social relations in public-political and religious life. As Georg Lukács presciently noted, "Capitalism has created a form for the state and a system of law corresponding to its needs and harmonizing with its own structure."[73] This market society with its disciplinary regimes is similarly bent on producing economic subjects—entrepreneurial

70. Novak, *Toward a Theology of the Corporation*, 341.

71. "Market" is capitalized here to emphasize its "transcendent" (or fetishized) features in a neoliberal capitalistic society.

72. Weber, *The Protestant Ethic and the Spirit of Capitalism.*

73. Lukács, *History and Class Consciousness*, 95.

individualists who are acquisitive, commodifiers, and responsible for their financial success and failures. Once produced, market subjects or *homines oeconomici* support and re-create the neoliberal state and capitalist economy. The rise of neoliberal capitalism and the *homo oeconomicus* in the United States reveals a truly Hobbesian society.

NEOLIBERAL CAPITALISM'S DISTORTION OF CARE AND JUSTICE

Aristotle believed "that any polis which is truly so-called . . . must devote itself to the end of encouraging goodness . . . such as will make the members of a polis good and just."[74] He goes on to say that if citizens "were associated in nothing further than matters of exchange and alliance, they would have failed to reach the stage of a polis."[75] The very notion of *homo oeconomicus* was inimical to Aristotle's view of the polis, considering such a creature as unnatural.[76] Indeed, Aristotle recognized that "involvement with the exchange for profit can easily incite the desire for wealth for its own sake,"[77] which would conflict with and undermine his notions of common good and the good life. Moreover, privileging economic relations contradicts the aim of the polis, which is to cultivate the virtues, not vices such as greed and acquisitiveness. In a similar vein, Martin Hengel argues that "Jesus attacks mammon with utmost severity where it has captured men's heart, because this gives it demonic character by which it blinds men's hearts to God's will—in concrete terms, to their neighbor's needs."[78] Bruce Longenecker, Kelly Liebengood, and other religious scholars contend that a key theme in Christian Scriptures is the warning that economic exchanges may end up promoting greed and neglecting the needs of the poor.[79] Long before capitalism, ages before there were modern critics of capitalism, Aristotle and early Christian authors recognized the dangers that economic exchanges posed for society, whether that was understood in terms of undermining virtues, faith, or the polis itself. Stated positively, they realized that for interpersonal relations to flourish, economic exchanges must remain subordinate to the recognition and treatment of others as persons.

74 Barker, ed., *The Politics of Aristotle*, 119.

75. Ibid.

76. Brown, *Undoing the Demos*, 91.

77. Ibid., 90.

78. In Capper, "Jesus, Virtuoso Religion, and the Community of Goods," 71.

79. See Longenecker and Liebengood, *Engaging Economics*.

Wariness about economic relations also accompanied the emergence of capitalism in the late eighteenth century, even by proponents such as Adam Smith. Pierre Dardot and Christian Laval point out that in the nineteenth century, French sociologist Auguste Comte argued that the major defect of economic liberalism "stemmed from the impossibility of erecting a viable social order on essentially a negative theory."[80] Of course, Karl Marx and Friedrich Engels are perhaps the best known nineteenth-century critics of capitalism and its excesses.[81] Yet it was not just critics who worried about the excesses of this system. John Maynard Keynes was concerned about the boom and bust cycles, which he believed could be managed by state regulations, and, recently, Robert Reich notes the dangers of poorly regulated markets.[82] In this section, I take a different tack from typical criticisms of capitalism by arguing that neoliberal capitalism undermines interpersonal caring relations—relations that are foundational for a just and thriving polis. To do this, I first highlight some of the central criticisms of capitalism, which pave the way for understanding not only how care is corrupted, but also why we cannot build a viable social order on an essentially negative theory that lauds acquisitiveness and greed.

Alienation is a consistent term used in connection to Marxist critiques of capitalism. Karl Marx, Anita Chari notes, believed that labor is central to human life and "is a form of self-production."[83] Ideally, a human being, through labor, produces an object, and the object is an objectification of the creator's consciousness.[84] In the activity of labor, a human being also produces himself or herself as a subject. Perhaps, the easiest illustration of this is art. The sculptor produces an object that is an expression of his or her subjectivity and in turn the labor itself produces the subject as an artist. In capitalism, Marx contends, labor is alienated because it is commodified.[85] The object is "is made into an alienable, sellable thing, produced only in order to be sold. The laborer himself . . . becomes a commodity."[86] In alienation, the relationship between the worker and the product is inverted. The "worker comes to the product

80. Dardot and Laval, *The New Way of the World*, 58.

81. Wolff and Resnick, *Contending Economic Theories*, 133–251.

82. See Wolff and Resnick, 39–41. John Maynard Keynes developed his economic theory based on the dangers of unregulated capitalism. See Wolff and Resnick, *Contending Economic Theories*, 18–21, 123. A recent critic of current excesses of capitalism, Robert Reich, also wishes to preserve capitalism. See Robert Reich's book *Saving Capitalism*.

83. Chari, *A Political Economy of the Senses*, 97.

84. Ibid.

85. Ibid., 98.

86. Ibid.

of labor as if it is an alien object that has power over her, rather than as an objectification of her own self-conscious activity. Through this inversion, the world of things comes to dominate the world of humans."[87] In a similar vein, Wendy Brown depicts the alienating feature of capitalism in terms of the self. Instead of being a "creature of power and interest," the worker "become(s) capital to be invested . . . As human capital, the subject is at once in charge of itself, responsible for itself, and yet a potentially disposable element of the whole."[88] Like any commodified object, once it loses its use and economic value vis-à-vis profit, the laborer and the product become disposable. Here I am reminded of Arthur Miller's play *Death of a Salesman*, where Willy Loman is fired because he no longer produces profit for the company. As an alienable object, he is easily eliminated.

Coming from another angle, Wendy Brown notes that Marx sought "to forge an analytic link between economy and psyche, between the mode of production and *habitus*."[89] And this *habitus* is a life that "is alienated, stratified, and controlled by alien power, the consciousness also suffers these effects."[90] The source of this alienation, in part, is the commodification of labor, which is "purchased, wielded, and exploited by capital."[91] Paradoxically, "commodification is itself achieved through alienation . . . Alienation [, in other words,] is not merely an effect but the condition of the production of the commodity."[92] In a market society, commodification is rife, and this means pervasive objectification, which leads to psychological and social alienation. Georg Lukács recognized that "Capital and with it every form in which the national economy objectifies itself is, according to Marx, 'not a thing but a social relation between persons mediated through things.'"[93] In Buber's terms, the social relations of a market society are I-It relations.[94] Even Wilhelm Röpke, a proponent of a form of neoliberal capitalism, recognized the dangers of the dominance of capitalism in organizing society. He wrote that capitalism, when left to itself, "is dangerous and untenable because it reduces human beings to an utterly unnatural existence" of alienated or I-It relations.[95] I-It relations are pervasive when citizens "accept the

87. Ibid.

88. Brown, *Undoing the Demos*, 110.

89. Brown, *Politics Out of History*, 74.

90. Ibid., 78.

91. Ibid., 72.

92. Ibid., 75.

93. Lukács, *History and Class Consciousness*, 49.

94. Buber, *I and Thou*.

95. Dardot and Laval. *The New Way of the World*, 98

market situation . . . and incorporate the need to calculate their individual interest if they do not want to lose out in the 'game' and, still more, if they want to enhance their personal capital."[96]

Marx's view of alienation is primarily aimed at manufacturing and its material production, but alienation applies to service industry workers and what Hardt and Negri call immaterial production.[97] Arlie Hochschild, for instance, depicts how capitalism has led to the commercialization of feeling, wherein "feelings take on the properties of a resource. But it is not a resource to be used for the purposes of art, as in drama, or for the purposes of self-discovery, as in therapy . . . It is a resource to be used to make money."[98] Airline workers and other service industry workers, for instance, are coached into expressing positive feelings for the sake of greater profits. Their emotional life is objectified and commodified and thus becomes something alien, which, in turn, reflects a social alienation: one is empathic for the sake of obtaining a sale, and the personhood of the buyer is at best secondary. Eva Illouz takes this further, arguing that emotional capitalism "is a culture in which emotional and economic discourses and practices mutually shape each other."[99] The concept of emotional intelligence, she notes, is used to "classify productive and non-productive workers,"[100] which represents a troubling illustration of a kind of alienation Marx did not describe. That is, one's emotional subjectivity, instead of being viewed in terms of self-fulfillment, love, community, or the common good, becomes aimed at productivity, which means it too is commodified.

Gérard Duménil and Dominique Lévy emphasize that "neoliberalism is indeed the bearer of a process of general commodification of social relations."[101] Alienation vis-à-vis consciousness or subjectivity is inseparable from social relations. *Homo oeconomicus* engages in social relations, which are framed in terms of commodification that leads to social alienation. The alienated subject is by definition in an alienated relation to others. In a market society, we are all prostitutes. Our bodies are commodified. We have to sell ourselves. We ask if our relationships are productive. Do these relationships add quantifiable value to our lives? Michael Sandel provides numerous examples where people use their bodies or the bodies of others

96. Ibid., 170.
97. Hardt and Negri, *Commonwealth*, 132–33.
98. Hochschild, *The Managed Heart*, 55.
99. Illouz, *Cold Intimacies*, 5.
100. Ibid., 65.
101. In Dardot and Laval, *The New Way of the World*, 9.

for advertisements, having babies, body parts, etc.[102] The individual who uses his body to advertise for a company is commodifying his body and, in turn, the company paying for the advertisement does so as well. In public, he becomes a spectacle—an object of advertising. Examples such as this one illustrate the extent of alienation vis-à-vis the self and social relations.

Social relations and alienation are also evident in the relations between employers and employees. Employers calculate labor costs in relation to productivity and profits. Innumerable examples exist of companies "downsizing" in order to increase profits. Owners calculate the costs associated with each worker in relation to the upmost aim of garnering profits, deciding that units of labor must be reduced to secure greater profits for the shareholders. The worker, like the product, is measurable. Her value can be calculated precisely. The logic of the market dictates this commodifying calculation and concomitant alienation. To return to Arthur Miller's play *Death of a Salesman*, Willy Loman begs his boss to keep him on the company payroll. Willy pleads, invoking his long loyalty to the company. Yet, as Wendy Brown notes above, in a market society where individuals and relations are commodified, people, in terms of market logic, are disposable when they fail to produce, when they fail to contribute to corporate profits. The *personal* loyalty Willy is pleading for does not exist in a market society. Loyalty (and trust) itself is commodified. Loyalty is measured in terms of how one contributes to the bottom line, and hence Willy, who is not producing, is not loyal or, if loyal, is completely ineffective in fulfilling his duties and thus loyalty is not due him. Personal loyalty in a market society has no meaning. According to market logic, Willy must be fired or, in modern parlance, downsized.

Reification is a closely related term to *alienation* and helpful in depicting the kind of rationality associated with capitalism. Georg Lukács's[103] depiction of reification is, perhaps, the best-known version, though certainly contested.[104] Reification, for Lukács, "requires that a society should learn to satisfy all its needs in terms of commodity exchange."[105] The process of reification, Anita Chari notes, "refers to the very process of becoming material and 'thingly' in its etymology."[106] When this process dominates a society, the society becomes ill, so to speak, and, in Aristotle's framework, unnatural. For Lukács, reification "becomes the central social pathology of capitalist

102. Sandel, *What Money Can't Buy*, 180–87.

103. Lukács, *History and Class Consciousness*, 83–109.

104. Chari, *A Political Economy of the Senses*, 121–28.

105. Lukács, *History and Class Consciousness*, 91.

106. Ibid., 5.

society."[107] This social pathology is manifested in the reality that the "social relation is consummated in the relation of a thing, of money, to itself."[108]

The reification of the social relation accompanies a reified consciousness or what Lukács called a reified mind.[109] Turning to the works of Max Weber, Lukács points to the cognitive capacities of a reified mind, namely, rational calculation.[110] This has also been called "technical reason (Marcuse), means-end rationality (Habermas), or instrumental rationality (Weber)."[111] In this kind of reasoning, the individual calculates the economic value and use of other individuals, social relations, and objects. As Wendy Brown puts it, in a market society calculative reason becomes the "governing rationality extending a specific formulation of economic values, practices, and metrics to every dimension of human life."[112] Economist Gary Becker wrote a book, *The Economic Approach to Human Behavior*, that exemplifies the dominance of instrumental or calculative rationality.[113] In this book, Becker "rejects the old-fashioned notion that economics is 'the study of the allocation of material goods.'"[114] Instead, he advocates for a kind of economic, calculative approach to all aspects of life. "I have come to the position that the economic approach is a comprehensive one that is applicable to human behavior."[115] Becker's apotheosis for an economic approach to human behavior illustrates the dominance of instrumental rationality and the ubiquitous presence of Lukács's reified mind or consciousness.

Whether termed technical reason, means-end rationality, or instrumental rationality, it is clear that this human capacity was present long before capitalism emerges. We can understand this further by returning to the work of John Macmurray. Macmurray argues that calculative or instrumental reason falls under the heading of object knowing, which is nascent in early childhood and a necessary form of knowing itself. For Macmurray, object knowledge is prior to and necessary for personal knowing—recognizing the other as an immeasurably valued, unique, inviolable, and responsive subject.[116] Objective knowing, which is not about facts or truth, refers

107. Chari, *A Political Economy of the Senses*, 5.

108. Lukács, *History and Class Consciousness*, 94.

109. Ibid., 93.

110. Ibid., 95–96.

111. Brown, *States of Injury*, 33.

112. Brown, *Undoing the Demos*, 30.

113. Becker, *The Economic Approach to Human Behavior*.

114. Sandel, *What Money Can't Buy*, 49.

115. Ibid.

116. See chapter 2 for an elaboration on this.

to the capacity to locate and identify an object among other objects, and this is the foundation for the eventual capacity for recognition of the Other as a person. In chapter 2 I argued that personal knowing is foundational for a viable polis. Given this, how are we then to understand the reified mind or the dangers of the proliferation of instrumental rationality vis-à-vis a market society? Recall that Aristotle warns that economic exchange can be unnatural when separated from the needs of the household; and if it is the main way citizens engage each other, then there will not yet be a polis. *It is not that instrumental rationality or objectification is unnatural, but that it is unnatural when it becomes the dominant way of thinking and relating.* Macmurray's formulations help here. While object knowing is necessary, it must be subordinate to personal knowing if there are to be, to use Buber's terms, I–Thou relations.[117] As Comte noted, you cannot build a society on a negative theory, and object knowing or calculative reason is negative, by which I mean it is devoid of the personal. This said, there are certainly times when personal knowing *is subordinate* to object knowing, but, for Macmurray, these moments are only ethical if it can be clearly shown that it is for the sake of aiding an individual, family, or community and that they are time limited. A physician, for instance, when diagnosing, objectifies the patient, using calculative reasoning to diagnose the problem. This is deemed ethical if it aids the patient and it is limited in time. That is, the physician does not continue to objectify the patient when it is no longer necessary to do so. What is problematic about a market society is that object knowing predominates in the form of calculative reason vis-à-vis individuals and social relations. The Other is no longer immeasurably valuable and unique; rather s/he is measurable in terms of economic value and use value. Alienation and reification, in light of this perspective, mean impersonal or depersonalized relations (I–It relations), and such relations, in turn, accompany subjective alienation.

This does not mean that in a market society all social relations are necessarily objectified, impersonal, or depersonalized. Rather, it means that personal knowing is subordinate to object knowing. I purchase food at the grocery and I recognize the cashier as a person, yet in the grocery this personal recognition is subordinated and the commercialized role is foregrounded. I am not particularly interested in the cashier's needs and experiences, nor is he interested in mine. What is in the foreground are the objectified roles. Robert's stockbroker seems like a nice man and they exchange pleasantries. However, the interaction is economic. Robert and the stockbroker are not interested in each other as persons, at least not in

117. See Buber, *I and Thou.*

the sense of friendship or comradeship. The relationship is founded on economic exchange and lasts only as long as the reciprocal economic contract is fulfilled. The personal is subordinate to the object, the economic rationality. In both instances, there is no *personal* loyalty or trust. Rather, trust and loyalty are constructed in contractual and conditional terms. To be sure, as Macmurray recognizes, every society has these types of relations, but they cannot be the foundation of a society or the polis. Yet, in a market society, these relations are dominant.

Of course there are worse examples, relations characterized by an absence of personal knowledge in economic exchanges and the practice of calculative rationality. Richard Posner has suggested, for example, that markets be used "to allocate . . . adoptions."[118] Economist Gary Becker would like this. Babies are commodities and the market should dictate exchange. In this cold, reptilian logic, babies are not persons but commodities subject to market laws. Sandel offers another egregious case where personal knowing is absent while acquisitive, calculative reason is dominant. A Walmart employee died while working, and Walmart received three hundred thousand dollars because it had taken out insurance policies on some of its workers. A spokesperson for Walmart rejected the idea that the company profited from the death of this worker. "We had considerable investment in these employees," the spokesperson said.[119] The insurance is for a cog in the machine rather than for the person. In other words, the insurance was not used to benefit any person, but the corporation (unless one holds the illusion that corporations are persons). The worker's family did not receive any compensation. In this instance, there was no loyalty to the employee and his family. Loyalty was framed only in terms of how the employee provides economically for the welfare of Walmart.

Of course, market relations existed long before capitalism (e.g., slavery as a horrific example of calculative reason and depersonalization), but in a market society where everyone is expected to be an entrepreneur, personal knowing takes a backseat to instrumental rationality. *Homo oeconomicus* calculates, quantifies, and measures his/her exchanges in the public realm, perhaps reserving personalization—where object knowing is subordinate to personal knowing—for family members and friends. Economist Gary Becker's approach to social living wins out in a market society, and in the process, loyalty and trust become completely conditional—a market faith, which is no faith at all.[120]

118. Sandel, *What Money Can't Buy*, 95.

119. Ibid., 131–32.

120. In his book *Faith on Earth*, H. Richard Niebuhr viewed faith (existential and

We might all agree that the instrumental rationality of a market society is unethical or horrible when it results in acts of depersonalization. We might cringe not only when we read about entrepreneurs who charge outrageous prices for food, water, and shelter after a natural disaster, but also when we read the reptilian logic of economists, like Thomas Sowell and Jeff Jacoby, who dispassionately argue that this is not gouging, greedy, or unjust. Rather, it is "how goods and services get allocated in a free society."[121] But when it comes to everyday kind of market relations, it may appear that society functions pretty well, even if personal knowing is subordinate to object knowing. I can still be polite and respectful to the cashier without being personal. I don't have to know the person who cuts my hair, fixes my car, or cashes my checks. To some degree, this is true. A society can continue to function, which is obvious given the last forty years in the U.S. Yet, when neoliberal capitalism becomes the dominant social imaginary for constructing social relations and subjectivity, then, according to numerous critics, social and subjective alienation and reification abound, which is not healthy for a polis. If money and profit are the dominant aims of society, it cannot flourish, though it may survive. A society, then, may continue to function, but at what costs? More to the point, I want to argue that the alienation, reification, and calculative reason of a neoliberal capitalist society are symptoms of a deeper social malady and that is the corruption of care. A society where care is corrupted is, to follow Aristotle, hardly worthy of the name of polis. Instead, it is one step removed from a dystopia, a Hobbesian society of individual entrepreneurs competing to survive and where the notion of the common good devolves into what is good for me. Moreover, what is good for me is profit. It is not a society in which each cares for all the others and no one for him;[122] rather it is a society where each cares for himself and for no others.

This is a large claim, and I have to first explain what I mean by the corruption of care, and second, provide evidence, which I reserve for the next section. Recall that in chapter 2 I argued that care of other human beings is foundational for a polis to flourish and that this care depends on the

religious) in terms of three interrelated dialectical pairs, namely, belief-disbelief, trust-distrust, and loyalty-disloyalty. While I do not elaborate on this above, economic faith is completely conditioned and supported by instrumental reasoning. In economic faith, loyalty and trust are framed in terms of market values and expectation such as efficiency, market expansion, and profit. This "exchange" faith precedes capitalism. When it becomes the dominant way of organizing social relations, the polis cannot thrive because personal faith and its unconditional and unconditioned elements are absent.

121. Sandel, *Justice*, 4–5.

122. Macmurray, *Reason and Emotion*, 159.

recognition and treatment of other human beings as persons—unique, inviolable, valued (immeasurable), and responsive subjects. This personal care refers to activities or practices aimed at meeting individuals' and families' vital biological needs, developing or maintaining "their basic capabilities, and avoiding or alleviating unnecessary or unwanted pain and suffering, so that they can survive, develop, and function in society."[123] Care, I argued further, is not simply aimed at individuals' survival and flourishing, but also families' and communities'—those social entities from which the individual emerges and on which s/he depends. There is, ideally speaking, an unconditional element in the care of persons. The good enough parent, for whom the child is a person of immeasurable value, does not make caring actions conditional, and reason is not merely calculative. The parent's loyalty is unconditioned care. The Good Samaritan recognized the man in the ditch as a person (made in the *imago dei*), first and foremost, and second used calculative reason to assess wounds and devise caring interventions. He no doubt felt obliged to bind the injured man's wounds and provide necessary funds for his recovery. There were no conditions on his care.

In a competitive society, in a society of entrepreneurs, care at its best is corrupted and worse, absent. To survive in a neoliberal capitalist society, individuals must find ways to compete for scarce resources. As indicated above, reification and alienation mean that the individual objectifies himself and others. He calculates, measuring his value as a commodity. If we were to say that *homo oeconomicus* cares, it is care about acquisition, about objects of use and measurable value. The entrepreneur cares about profit and market expansion. The notion of caring for the common good in a market society is eschewed or rationalized as trickle-down economics. Economists like Thomas Sowell do not care (or care little) that people are suffering and dying. They care about the market "laws." Even if they acknowledge that persons are dying and suffering, this is not care at all because these individuals are being sacrificed on the altar of neoliberal capitalism. If care is present, in the sense of addressing human needs, it is completely conditional and monetized, as we can imagine in Gary Becker's proposal. The neoliberal capitalistic Samaritan would want to know what is to be gained by caring for the man. How will it profit me, he might query, as he calculates his labor costs and the costs of housing and medical care. As an entrepreneur, he cannot be bothered to recognize the man in the ditch as a person, which would oblige him to care regardless, would compel him to regard the ontological obligation to care that comes from recognizing the Other as a person. Personhood is immaterial or at least subordinate to the question of profit.

123. Engster, *The Heart of Justice*, 28.

A reader from a market-oriented society might interpret this parable very differently, saying that the Samaritan in the end profited because he would gain the immeasurable gift of eternal life, proving again the economic exchange theory of salvation and the corruption of care. Or, more crudely, the Samaritan was a fool for forgoing profit, much like a "foolish" grocery store owner who gives away bottled water to people after a hurricane.

A reader might fire back and point out that there are business owners who care about their employees. She might note that regular citizens and businesspeople alike respond with care during a natural disaster, by refusing to raise prices. The generosity of Bill and Melinda Gates is used as another illustration of care for people in desperate need of medical resources. I do not claim that in a society dominated by neoliberal capitalism care is absent or in all instances corrupted. When genuine care appears in the marketplace, it is not because of the neoliberal capitalist social imaginary. Instead, care appears because the individual is making use of another (humanist, religious) social imaginary to guide caring decisions and actions. The business owner who agonizes over having to let go some workers, not because the company needs to make greater profits, but in order for the company to survive, is contending with opposing social imaginaries. One social imaginary tells him that these people are persons who have families and friends. It is a social imaginary founded on personalization that gives rise to the logic of empathic knowing necessary for caring actions. The other social imaginary is founded on commodification that supports instrumental or calculative reasoning—a sociopathic kind of thinking. When a neoliberal capitalist social imaginary dominates, care is corrupted by the power of market reasoning, which elides any semblance of *imago dei*. In the end, the business owner succumbs to the seemingly inevitable logic of the marketplace, firing her employees. Jung Sung called this the cruel mystique of the market, where the needs of persons are subordinate to the needs of the market.[124] In this instance, the owner's care means little or nothing to workers who must struggle to find work to care for themselves and their families.

Let me take this a bit further. Max Weber argued that capitalism promotes a spirit or attitude of acquisitiveness.[125] Acquisitiveness, Weber argues, "is an attitude toward material goods which is so well suited to that system [capitalism] . . . that there can today no longer be any question of a necessary connection" between capitalism and the promotion of an acquisitive attitude.[126] If we were going to ask what is the "virtue" (attitude

124. Sung, *Desire, Market, and Religion*, 17.

125. Weber, *The Protestant Ethic and the Spirit of Capitalism*, 56.

126. Ibid., 172.

and habit) that fuels neoliberal capitalism, it is acquisitiveness or, more accurately, greed. To be sure, in terms of the euphemisms used by market evangelicals, this would be called making a profit or charging what the market will bear. Profits and market expansion vis-à-vis capitalism are without limits, or the limits are imposed by market laws, which are pretty loose. Consider entrepreneur Martin Shkreli, "who acquired the anti-malarial and anti-parasitical drug Daraprim—used primarily to treat children and AIDS patients—and jacked up the price from $13.50 per pill to $750 per pill . . . 5,500 percent increase."[127] Shkreli is not an anomaly in a society where neoliberal capitalism holds sway; he is merely an icon or paradigmatic figure of the market. He is what a neoliberal capitalist society produces and what keeps it going. Like the fictional character Gordon Gekko, Shkreli and his board believe that greed is good; charge what the market will bear, even if that means people who cannot afford the drug or who have no insurance will suffer and die.[128] Operating out of the market logic, like Sowell does, there is no shame or guilt about price gouging because one is simply obeying the "transcendent" rules of the market.[129] Acquisitiveness and greed are inimical to care. Greed ignores or denies the ontological obligation to care for persons and thus there can be no shame or guilt because one has not violated an obligation; *homo oeconomicus* is free of shame and guilt, unless, of course, he fails to produce. No one could possibly argue that Shkreli and his business associates care about people suffering from AIDS. Neoliberal capitalism, then, deforms ontological care into care for and about oneself and attending material objects, which is the result of and results in social alienation and, in the end, self-alienation. In short, neoliberal capitalism, as a semiotic system that promotes acquisitiveness and greed, is incapable of nurturing caring relations.

The presence of depersonalization and carelessness is necessarily accompanied by injustice and a corresponding attenuation of the space of appearances. In a market society, the notion of justice itself becomes commodified in the sense that justice is framed in terms of economic contractual obligations. For economist Thomas Sowell, raising the prices of food, water,

127. Pitt, "A Corrupt CEO Busted?"

128. Perhaps Mr. Shkreli believes that insurance companies and the government will pay the tab, calculating that individuals will still get the medication. First of all, insurance companies, according to market logic, will have to spread the costs by raising premiums. They have to make a profit as well. This means that individuals may not be able to afford insurance or will have to make other sacrifices to make ends meet. The government, while not making a profit, will have to deal with the rise in costs by raising taxes or cutting funding to other programs. In short, Mr. Shkreli's price gouging has nothing to do with the common good and everything to do with his own "good."

129. See Nelson, *Economics as Religion*.

and shelter in the aftermath of a natural disaster is completely justified, even if the cruel realities of the market mean that many people will not receive what they are due vis-à-vis their survival. Luckily, though, the market will receive its due. There may be some partial outrage at Shkreli's 5000 percent price increase on a needed drug, but according to market logic it is completely just, even when people who need the medication are unable to afford it. The disciplinary logic of neoliberal capitalism frames justice in terms of commodification and contractual, conditional relations that are determined by market values and expectations; this reframing of justice undermines and deforms traditional notions of justice. Put another way, in a market society, the fundamental question is, what is due the market? To be sure, the notion of justice is professed in a market society, but what is operative is an Orwellian justice. There is no outrage when Willy Loman is fired. From a market perspective he got what he was due. And we are not surprised when the Willy Lomans of a market society begin to entertain suicide, calculating their deaths in terms of costs (life insurance money that will come to loved ones) and debts (a dead man is no longer a burden). Depression and suicide, in this instance, are expressions of misdirected outrage at the injustice of the market's logic of justice. Here I recall Dolores, whose depression was linked to the underlying powerless of not being given her due by the polis.

Neoliberal capitalism's corruption of care and justice is further noted in the attenuation of the space of appearances. When workers are constructed in terms of market rules, when citizens are deemed to be entrepreneurs, the political and public space they inhabit is emptied of personal recognition. That is, individuals in a public-political space dominated by a neoliberal capitalist social imaginary are not permitted to appear in all of their uniqueness and immeasurability. The public-political space is not ultimately for them, but rather they are in service and in debt to the market. If they appear, they do so as entrepreneurs who are beholden to the gods of the market, the hidden hands. The rise of the neoliberal capitalist social imaginary signifies a return to a kind of feudalism wherein the "subjects" appear not as persons—immeasurable, valued, unique subjects—but as beings in service to the overlords of the market.[130]

130. This is a strong claim, especially when most citizens acknowledge that we live in a democracy. Clearly, many citizens hold democratic ideals, but the reality is that the United States functions as a plutocratic/oligarchic-democracy. This may seem oxymoronic, but it is not. See Couldry, *Why Voice Matters*. We have democratic beliefs, practices, and political institutions, yet large corporations, which are hierarchical and non-democratic, and the wealthy hold a tremendous amount of political power on both sides of the political spectrum. See Gasparino, *Bought and Paid For*; Stiglitz, *The Great Divide*; Wolin, *Democracy Incorporated*. Groups such as the American Legislative Council, which represents the interests of large corporations, have, for decades,

I close this section by returning to Dolores. Dolores and her husband are hard workers. Their employer pays them a little more than minimum wage and they are given a few meager benefits. The company is hugely profitable and the family that owns it is immensely wealthy. According to neoliberal capitalist logic, the wealth is rightly or justly acquired, even if it is the result of "legal" expropriation. They say that they care for their employees and perhaps at some level they do, but this care is corrupted by a logic that workers are paid what the market will bear. If workers believe their labor is worth more, they, as individual entrepreneurs, can leave and work for another company, so market evangelicals say. The company, in truth, does not care for their employees, except to the extent that they are healthy enough to do their jobs for low wages and few benefits. And if perchance they die on the job, the insurance will help the company hire and train another cog. What is clear is that the company's family owners and corporate leaders care more about profits, which means expropriating money from the workers through lower wages and fewer benefits. Companies, like the one Dolores works for, are only "forced" to offer higher wages and more benefits when skilled labor is scarce and they seek to enhance employee loyalty so that they can reduce costs of training—loyalty in this instance is again monetized and instrumental. Dolores's suffering is largely rooted in the carelessness of a capitalist company and a society that relies principally on calculative or instrumental reason while subordinating or ignoring personal knowing and its accompanying ontological obligation to care. There is little chance that the ghosts of Christmas will change the acquisitive and greedy practices

---

worked behind the scenes to influence and create legislation at state and national levels—outside the scrutiny of the American public. This kind of practice is endemic. Lisa Dugan's intriguing book called *The Twilight of Equality* examines the numerous covert ways wealthy Republican and Democrat neoliberals have used social issues to screen political moves to privatize public sectors such as public education. Echoing Dugan's analysis, Nobel Prize winner in economics Joseph Stiglitz expressed concern that huge economic disparities, which have been growing in the last three decades, threaten democracy. What is clear is that plutocrats and oligarchs in a neoliberal economy are not interested in the common good or democracy. Understandably, because they operate out of neoliberal capitalistic values and principles, they are interested in expanding their control of political-economic space to achieve what is "good" for them—greater wealth and political power. This results in the nondemocratic use of political institutions to lure politicians to find more ways to privatize public sectors. Corporate interests wish to reduce public (not corporate) entitlements and to reduce or eliminate government bureaucracies that administer social programs. These corporate actors want to expand profits through redistribution upward. They want to undermine unions and shrink regulatory agencies. Put another way, in a market society run by corporate actors, the space for regular citizens to take part in genuine democratic processes attenuates, though the illusion of democracy remains.

of corporate leaders and market evangelicals enough so that they have the empathy to care and the motivation to provide persons what they are due.

EVIDENCE OF NEOLIBERAL CAPITALISM'S CONTRIBUTIONS TO SUFFERING IN THE POLIS

Before delving into the social and psychological evidence for the kinds of cruelty and carelessness that attends a society dominated by the social imaginary of capitalism, I briefly return to how the beliefs of neoliberal capitalism have come to infect some Christian communities and their leaders, resulting in theological distortions that embody and support the undermining of care in the larger society. Indeed, some churches have become disciplinary regimes that support a neoliberal kingdom that has little to do with the kingdom of God preached by Jesus. This momentary detour is important because not only does it demonstrate the semiotic flexibility of capitalism,[131] but it also reveals how Christians, who actually possess an anthropological antidote for neoliberal capitalism, are implicated in and contribute to the corruption of care and justice in a market society.

Various theologians have focused on how capitalism's ethos has altered and distorted Christian theology, which is reflected in aberrations vis-à-vis liturgy, evangelization, morality, and community. As Joerg Rieger notes, for "many mainline Christians, Christianity and capitalism appear to be referring to the same reality . . . The God who empowers people appears to empower them to become capitalists."[132] For Rieger, capitalism threatens to undermine Christianity itself by thoroughly distorting its fundamental precepts of love, compassion, and moral sacrifice in meeting the needs of others.[133] Another theologian, Jung Sung,[134] convincingly shows how belief in the market economy (e.g., infinite progress and profit) encourages

131. Other writers have noted that capitalism as it is lauded in the United States has become a religion or, at the very least, has taken on religious dimensions, which make it easily transportable to religious believers. See Nelson, *Economics as Religion*; Frank, *One Market under God*. It is a heresy to question capitalism, and people who do so are not called witches or burned at the stake, but they are pilloried with epithets of communist, socialist, or what have you. The defenders of the "faith" are high priests, and the daily liturgy is played out on Wall Street and in the moment-to-moment spectacle of the ups and downs of the market. Transcendence is observed in the notion of the hidden hand of the market, which functions to mystify anyone who dares pull back the Ozian curtain. See Rieger, *No Rising Tide*, 69–72.

132. Rieger, *No Rising Tide*, 106.

133. Ibid., 127.

134. Sung, *Desire, Market, and Religion*.

the mimetic desire of appropriation, which echoes Weber's[135] notion of the spirit of acquisitiveness. We see this happening with the rise of the prosperity gospel movement, wherein religious leaders proclaim that achieving financial wealth and job promotions are signs of God's blessings. Macdonald provides numerous examples of Christian leaders and churches that link God with money and poverty with the lack of God's grace.[136] Moreover, economically savvy church leaders adopt a corporate, consumerist style of organizing their churches and entice members by focusing on meeting their individual interests and desires.[137] Jerry Falwell believed "they would be wise to look at business for a prediction of future innovation,"[138] which then means the church serves as yet another social institution functioning as a capitalistic disciplinary regime.

Similarly, Ehrenreich demonstrates the prevalence of the prosperity gospel perspective seen in the discourse of popular religious motivators, such as Joel Osteen. Osteen gives an illustration of using one's imagination to obtain a premier parking spot or a table at a crowded restaurant and then thanking God when this occurs.[139] Here we note the absence of meeting any genuine need. In a further example of the collusion of capitalistic ethos and Christianity, Osteen advises listeners to be enthusiastic at work because "employers prefer employees who are excited about working at their companies." For those who are not excited, "You won't be blessed, with that kind of attitude. God wants you to give it everything you've got."[140] The maxim, "be a good worker so God will bless you," is the favorite theological mantra for religious neoliberal capitalists. The cheerleaders of the prosperity gospel movement, like Osteen, collude with capitalism's acquisitiveness and they collapse God's blessing with the pursuit and achievement of one's desires. These leaders and their disciples exemplify the emergence of acritical sub-

135. See Weber, *The Protestant Ethic and the Spirit of Capitalism.*

136. MacDonald, *Thieves in the Temple*. See also Sung, *Desire, Market, and Religion*, 43.

137. MacDonald, *Thieves in the Temple*, 29–88. To be sure, there are instances of churches and church organizations that critique and resist capitalism. The Lutheran World Federation in 2003 released a statement highly critical of capitalism, which was followed by another from the World Alliance of Reformed Churches. See Rieger, *No Rising Tide*, 124–29. Recently Pope Francis released an encyclical (*Evangelii Gaudium*) that, in line with previous church documents (e.g., Leo XIII's, *Rerum Novarum* and *Economic Justice for All* from the United States Conference of Catholic Bishops), is critical of capitalism. These are glimmers of hope in the face of the dominance of capitalism as a social imaginary that is corrupting Christianity.

138. In Wolin, *Democracy Incorporated*, 124.

139. Ehrenreich, *Bright-Sided*, 127.

140. Quoted in ibid., 145.

jects who enthusiastically embrace the ethos of capitalism, confusing acquisitiveness for virtue and desire for need. They consider financial success as a signifier of God's blessing and poverty as God's absence. This said, does the distortion of Christianity by the prosperity gospel movement contribute to carelessness or malice?

As I indicated above, the prosperity gospel advocates are not ignorant of human suffering, and they have their own perspectives on theodicy. That is, capitalistic theologians take note of the suffering of many people within society and interpret this suffering on the basis of neoliberal beliefs. Together these beliefs and their interpretation of the problem of evil promote cruelty and carelessness vis-à-vis persons suffering financially. Religious leaders like Osteen subtly or overtly condemn people in poverty. This condition is, from their perspective, something that poor people have brought on themselves (e.g., by lacking motivation, enthusiasm, discipline): this theology mirrors neoliberal beliefs. As Paul Dumouchel writes, "Since evil never occurs without reason, and no one has wronged them, it seems more probable that the poverty they suffer comes either from a moral failing, or from a form of incompetency that makes them unfit for the market system."[141] Above I noted both Reverend A. R. Bernard's proclamation that "There is no way you can equate God with poverty"[142] and Reverend Creflo Dollar's comment that "Having no increase renders you useless to the kingdom of God."[143] These are classic examples of neoliberalism's blaming the victim, as well as gross misrepresentations of Judeo-Christian Scripture.[144] Moreover, they represent a distorted view of care. Indeed, these beliefs foster carelessness toward people in lower economic classes, and Christians who are in the lower classes may internalize these "religious" beliefs, blaming themselves for their sins in not fulfilling God's desire for them to be successful entrepreneurs.

Theological depictions that blame the poor or basically tell them to suck it up without complaint are illustrations not only of distorted theologies, but, worse, disciplinary regimes that promote the absence of empathy and compassion, or we could say the cruel mystique of the market wherein the needs of persons are subordinate to the needs of the Market.[145] Michael

141. Dumouchel, *The Barren Sacrifice*, 138. See also Karlin, "Banishing the Poor."

142. MacDonald, *Thieves in the Temple*, 4.

143. Ibid., 5.

144. See Longenecker and Kelly, eds., *Engaging Economics*. These and other Scripture scholars highlight the strong and consistent condemnation of greed and the dangers of mammon in Scripture and early church texts.

145. Sung, *Market, Desire, and Religion*, 17.

Novak[146] and prosperity gospel evangelizers reveal a kind of cruel carelessness toward the poor and lower classes. They wrap the dominant social imaginary of capitalism in the cloak of Christianity and, in so doing, hide (mystify) the hidden fist of a market society—a fist evident in individual and collective indifference and carelessness toward the poor. Instead of promoting Christian virtues, they want the church to function as yet another disciplinary regime for neoliberal capitalism.

Perhaps it is not surprising that in a society dominated by a neoliberal capitalistic ethos that some Christians and their communities find themselves captive to its logic, consequently distorting traditional Christian notions of care and justice. This suggests, then, that many Christians are complicit in the cruelty of the market. Here I shift to consider the fallout of a society dominated by a neoliberal capitalistic social imaginary. Since the rise of a neoliberal economy, the ranks of the poor and working classes, as well as the exploitation of economically depressed communities, have risen. A 2010 University of Michigan study found that the poverty rate had increased to 15.1 percent of the population and that childhood poverty had risen to 22 percent.[147] The rise is due in part to financial legislation that redistributes financial wealth upwards and also to the corresponding demonization and criminalization of people who are poor.[148] The poor are socially constructed as economically useless or as drags on the economy.[149] Many of us are familiar with the propaganda of politicians like Ronald Reagan, who lamented about so-called welfare queens; he and others constructed the poor as corrupt manipulators of financially secure citizens' largesse.[150] This, of course, is a clever and ironic distraction from the monstrous financial legal and illegal corruption of the kings and queens of Wall Street and its devastating effects on the lives of many citizens. Further evidence

146. Novak, *Toward a Theology of the Corporation*; Novak, *The Spirit of Democratic Capitalism*, 134.

147. See University of Michigan, "Poverty in the United States: Frequently Asked Questions."

148. See Giroux, *Disposable Youth*, 163–64.

149. Jennifer Silva, *Coming Up Short*, depicts the challenges of working-class young people in adapting to the effects of neoliberal capitalism. From her interviews, she noted that most of these working-class youth have internalized neoliberal beliefs about success being achieved by one's will and behavior. These young men and women blame themselves for not being successful financially, and this reveals how they have internalized the cruelty of the market. Many also have negative beliefs about the poor, which again illustrates the acritical internalization of neoliberal capitalism's beliefs.

150. Now many politicians say the poor do not have enough opportunities to make their way out of poverty. Republicans and Democrats alike want to make it a bit easier for them to be entrepreneurs. See Wacquant, *Punishing the Poor*.

of cruelty vis-à-vis poorer classes is seen in (1) the federal government's cutting food stamps, (2) some states' refusing to expand Medicaid for the poor, (3) attempts to eliminate or reduce workers' compensation, and (4) states' adopting so-called right-to-work legislation aimed at weakening or eliminating the power of unions. Cruelty and carelessness are evident in the silence about the suffering of poor children and the growing food insecurity that plays havoc with their psyches and bodies.[151] In a similar way, Peter Marris argues that the wealthier segments of the population have resources to provide physical and psychological security while poorer citizens bear the brunt of economic anxieties.[152] More obvious illustrations of cruelty are depicted by Christopher Hedges and Joseph Sacco.[153] Recall that they describe the devastation of communities and peoples in what they call economic sacrifice zones, which are kept hidden from the eyes of the larger public by the corporate media. In these sacrifice zones, people have higher poverty rates, physical and mental illness rates, and death rates. That most Americans have no idea that these zones exist has to do with societal carelessness and the corporate media's aim to keep these sacrifice zones out of the news. According to neoliberal logic, people in the sacrifice zones are responsible for causing their own problems and for finding their own solutions.

The undermining of care is linked to the overall decline of social capital in the larger society. Sociologist Robert Putnam provides a great deal of evidence of the decline of what he calls social capital in the United States over the last four decades.[154] In other words, social and community engagement and care for fellow citizens have declined—a decline that Putnam does not attribute to the rise of neoliberal capitalism. Yet, a more recent study has shown how neoliberal capitalism has deeply and negatively impacted the social capital of working-class people. Jennifer Silva details how working-class people have adopted neoliberal beliefs, such as individualism, self-reliance, and the pursuit of one's own interests, blaming themselves for any failures at achieving better financial status while overlooking larger systemic forces that quietly undermine their ability to succeed.[155] These self-attacks accompany greater disconnections from family and attenuation of other religious and social-communal ties. These fraying ties contribute to experiences of alienation and helplessness. Such alienation and helplessness also manifest in the larger society, including within church communities. The precipitous

151. See Giroux, *Disposable Youth.*

152. Marris, *The Politics of Uncertainty.*

153. Hedges and Sacco, *Days of Destruction, Days of Revolt.*

154. See Putnam, *Bowling Alone*; Putnam, *Our Kids.*

155. Silva, *Coming up Short.*

decline in social capital corresponds to the rise in depression, anxiety, and alienation during the last four decades.[156]

Silva and others[157] argue that capitalism negatively shapes subjectivity in profound ways. In particular, a market society produces mobile selves, able to move with the flow of capital, able to pursue employment wherever it is, not weighed down by familial and communal obligations and traditions. As Silva notes, "the only way to survive in such a competitive and bewildering labor market is to become highly elastic and unencumbered by other obligations—including their own families."[158] As individuals become mobile selves, they understandably become more susceptible to loneliness: they raise questions such as, who will care for and about me? And who will I care for?

But neoliberal capitalism does not increase simply suffering associated with loneliness. Ann Cvetkovich explores the way capitalism produces depression,[159] which is related to both a higher level of economic insecurity (including food insecurity) and feelings of helplessness among lower classes.[160] Economists too have identified the psychosocial and material impacts of rampant capitalism. Jerry Mander lists numerous studies that point to rising violence, anxiety, depression, and suicide in the United States,[161] which he attributes to the dominance of neoliberal capitalism. Citing studies from Jean Twenge, a psychologist, Mander notes that levels of anxiety (and depression) are very high when compared to levels found forty to fifty years ago.[162] Further, Nobel Prize–winning economist Joseph Stiglitz charts the rise of economic insecurity and anxiety among many lower-class people as corporate capitalism has come to rule society.[163] While many socioeconomic factors can contribute to psychological suffering, these writers and

156. I am not suggesting that there are no other factors involved in the rise of depression and anxiety. I am arguing that a market society with its beliefs in individual entrepreneurs who are responsible for their economic successes and failures is the significant variable in the rise of depression and anxiety.

157. See Cushman, *Constructing the Self, Constructing America*; Deleuze and Guittari, *Anti-Oedipus*; Dufour, *The Art of Shrinking Heads.*

158. Cushman, *Constructing the Self, Constructing America*, 31.

159. Cvetkovich, *Depression.* See also Rogers-Vaughn, "Blessed Are Those Who Mourn."

160. See Ehrenreich, *Bright-Sided.*

161. Mander, *The Capitalism Papers*, 226–34; see also Hendricks, *The Universe Bends toward Justice*, 174–77.

162. Ibid., 234.

163. Stiglitz, *The Price of Inequality.*

others identify the rise of neoliberal capitalism as a significant source of material and psychological suffering.

Other writers have examined capitalism and its negative impact on subjectivity. Gilles Deleuze and Felix Guittari argue that capitalism contributes to the construction of a schizophrenic self, disconnected from others and reality. A social environment characterized by neoliberal capitalism leads to the proliferation of alienated selves unable to form life-enhancing relationships of trust and fidelity.[164] In a similar vein, Dany-Robert Dufour contends that neoliberal capitalism and the dominance of commodifying rationality lead to a psychotic self—a self not in touch with reality and preoccupied by desires and fantasies—an alienated subject, lonely and alone in a crowded world of entrepreneurs on the make and take.[165] These authors are depicting the consequences of the demise of an interpersonal, existential care—a demise resulting from the dominance of the conditional, objectifying relations of neoliberal capitalism. As Dufour argues, neoliberal capitalism "wishes to replace this doubly determined subject with an *acritical* subject with, insofar as that is possible, *psychotic tendencies*. This is, in other words, a subject who can be plunged into anything, a floating subject, always receptive to commodity flows and communication flows, and permanently in search of commodities to consume."[166] One might call this an isolated and empty self, available to exploit others and to be exploited. In either case, whether the self is schizophrenic or psychotic, such a self cannot be expected to be adept at caring for the self or others.

While I find Deleuze's, Guittari's, and Dufour's views on how capitalism produces schizophrenic selves or subjects with psychotic tendencies to be compelling, I believe capitalism, in producing acquisitive entrepreneurs, fosters sociopathic tendencies. Consider Michael Novak, capitalism's evangelical theologian, who strikes me as neither schizophrenic nor psychotic. That said, there is a terrible cruelty or sociopathy in his and others' dismissal of the poor. The same can be said for those who disregard, blame, or victimize members of the lower classes. The sociopathic tendency is represented in the cruel logic behind firing employees so that the company can obtain greater profits; this logic demonstrates a genuine carelessness for workers as persons and cares more about profits. Business owners who subscribe to neoliberal capitalist beliefs can be caring men and women, but when the neoliberal capitalistic ethos has been internalized and is used to make the

164. Deleuze and Guittari, *Anti-Oedipus*.

165. Dufour, *The Art of Shrinking Heads*.

166. Ibid., 93 (italics original).

"hard" decisions, we see the presence of the sociopathic tendency in human life—a tendency devoid of care and deaf to justice.

PASTORAL RESPONSES IN A MARKET SOCIETY: FOSTERING ALTERCAPITALIST COMMUNITIES

The evidence of neoliberal capitalism's dominance as society's social imaginary, as well as evidence for its attending undermining of care and justice can seem overwhelming, especially when we see efforts at critique attacked or ignored by mainstream media and politicians. How are we to respond to this Hobbesian reality? How can we foster more caring social relations? Can we find ways to reinvigorate social justice and reestablish the common good? As Peter McLaren asks, "Can we organize our social, cultural, and economic life differently so as to transcend the exploitation that capital affords us?"[167]

These are difficult questions to answer, and, in truth, there are no definitive answers. This said, I would like to offer briefly some general ideas. Let me begin by saying that I am not sanguine about the possibility of changing the market society or about the view that capitalism will collapse from its own contradictions, as Marx and others suggest. Capitalism as a semiotic system has proven incredibly adaptable and resilient.[168] Instead, I believe we need to start small, and by that I mean with the local church, the *ecclesia*, which ideally functions as a ground of care and justice. I say this despite declining social capital and waning mainline denominations. Given our situation, we should be less concerned about the decline and more concerned about fostering communities of care and justice, even if they are smaller. We might gain confidence in the fact that small Christian communities have survived and thrived during dark times and that they have served as leaven in societies. What I wish to promote are communities that are not only *alterimperialist*, but also *altercapitalist*.[169] This does not in any way suggest that small Christian (or other religious and humanist) communities retreat from the world, though in history some Christian communities have. Rather, I want to claim that *altercapitalist* communities engage in caring and just relations within community and the larger local community and society. The

167. McLaren, *Pedagogy of Insurrection*, 32.

168. For a historical overview of capitalism and its resiliency see Jones, *Masters of the Universe*; Wolff and Resnick, *Contending Economic Theories*. For a current attempt to save capitalism see Reich, *Saving Capitalism*.

169. I will continue with the notion of *altercapitalist* communities in the next chapter.

altercapitalist community is witness to the larger market society of caring relations and justice vis-à-vis the common good. And as a witness, it is also functioning as a prophetic community, critiquing and calling into question the market society's commodification of life, hyperindividualism, rampant entrepreneurial competitiveness, blind acquisitiveness, and indifference to the poor.

Altercapitalist communities are not engaged in or captive to anticapitalism discourse, because they operate out of different language games and "disciplinary regimes." As a small polis, the *ecclesia* promotes, through liturgy, preaching, retreats, classes, and stories, the standard Christian virtues of faith, hope, and love—virtues necessary for care and justice. Indeed, the very notions of care, justice, and the common good are tied to these virtues so that the notions do not become distorted by the values associated with the market society (i.e., with the commodification of care). Living as an *altercapitalist* community necessarily includes being deliberate about nurturing interpersonal relations and fostering a critical reflective stance toward the larger society so that community members and leaders are not co-opted by the hegemonic discourse associated with the values and expectations of the market. An *altercapitalist* community serves, then, as a countercultural entity by developing subjects with capacities for a type of critical thinking connected to caring virtues and for the kind of social relations that are personal.

By adhering to the logic of love and care, an *altercapitalist* community is not engaged in or captive to the market logic. The community is not anticapitalist in the sense of engaging in an economic debate that adheres to the discourse of market values and beliefs. Instead, an *altercapitalist* community provides an alternative to the discourse of the market and an alternative to organizing social relation.

The primary frameworks for pastoral analysis and discussion in these *altercapitalist* communities would be care and justice. How do we, as a community, care for our members and for those in our local community? What are the real and pressing needs (not simply desires) of our members and those of the local community—what are they due? What humane methods will ensure their needs are met? How is our community organized (what is our polity?) so that the community reflects or embodies the principles of care and justice? Is our polity shaped by the common good vis-à-vis the community and the larger society? Is the notion of the common good framed in terms of needs associated with human beings' (and other creatures') survival and flourishing? How do we, as a moral and pastoral community, respond—guided by care and justice—to social and political structures, including individuals and groups, that promote economic, political, and social injustice and carelessness? The answers to these questions depend on the particular realities of each community's situation, as well as its traditions with regard to polity, liturgy, and charisms.

Naturally, these communities and their members will have to participate in the market society. Churches pay staff members, take out loans to purchase equipment, and pay utilities; some churches have investments. Yet, the community is deliberate and reflective about engagement in a market society. For example, perhaps a loan is taken from a community bank that is engaged in helping the town or city. Or perhaps a church with some investments may focus on socially responsible companies and how to use these investments to care for members and for the larger community. The *altercapitalist* community may also decide to decline to invest, because members do not wish to tacitly or overtly give support to corporations—in this sense the community would be leaning toward being anticapitalist. There is wide latitude in how an *altercapitalist* community can express care and justice.

I end this chapter by describing the Christian community I had in mind when writing this all too brief section. It is a small Christian community with all the typical problems human beings have living and working together. Most members are deeply involved in the life of the community and its ministries to the larger community. These ministries involve care for church members (e.g., meeting the needs of the homebound) and social justice vis-à-vis the local residents. Its liturgies are preceded by conversations, hugs, expressions of concern, and laughter. The leadership engages members to consider various local economic and political issues that impact people of the city. In other words, the community's leaders help cultivate a moral and caring discourse vis-à-vis community members and city residents. This church does not seem interested in trying to change society or to adapt to a neoliberal culture. They are not anticapitalist per se, but they do offer an alternative to the larger market society. With all their typical challenges of living a life in common, this is an *altercapitalist* polis that struggles to live by an ethics of care and an ethics of justice.

7

CLASS, CLASSISM, AND CLASS CONFLICT

Distortions of Care and Justice in the Polis

Through the tax code, there has been class warfare waged, and my class has won.[1]

It sometimes happens in a people amongst which various opinions prevail that the balance of the several parties is lost and one of them obtains an irresistible preponderance, overpowers all obstacles, harasses its opponents, and appropriates all the resources of society to its own purposes. The vanquished citizens despair of success and they conceal their dissatisfaction in silence and in general apathy. The nation seems to be governed by a single principle, and the prevailing party assumes the credit for having restored peace and unanimity to the country. But this apparent unanimity is merely a cloak to alarming dissensions and perpetual opposition.[2]

We need to fight against rising inequality, but we also need first and foremost to understand the causes of capitalist exploitation and immiseration.[3]

1. Bradford, "Warren Buffett: 'My Class Has Won' And 'It's Been A Rout.'"
2. De Tocqueville, *Democracy in America*, 206.
3. McLaren, *Pedagogy of Insurrection*, 61.

LATELY, THERE IS A good deal of talk in the media about the rise of income inequality in the United States; the talk begs the question, are critics of income inequality seeking income equality? This is doubtful. Instead, center-left Democrats want to raise the minimum (or living) wage to help move people out of poverty, while concerned Republicans resist efforts to mandate hikes in the minimum wage. (Republicans say, let the invisible hand of the market determine wages.) Instead they want to make it easier for people to become entrepreneurs. The concern over income inequality and the proposed solutions obscure, if they do not mystify, the reality of class and class conflict in the United States. Of course Americans are brought up to believe that we are equal and that even if class stratification exists, with hard work one can ascend the class ladder. When confronted with the reality of class, many citizens believe that it does not really matter. We exclaim proudly that we are not like Downton Abbey of old Europe with its strict delineations between classes, though the reality is quite different. Social economic mobility and income inequality have worsened over the last four decades in the U.S., while social mobility in Europe is higher.[4] And people from all classes tend to hold the neoliberal belief that individuals are responsible for their own material success and failure, even when the game is rigged to advantage the wealthy.[5] These beliefs along with a focus on income inequality screen or mystify the underlying reality of class, classism, and class conflict/warfare that accompanies capitalism and, more particularly, the vagaries of a neoliberal market society.

In this chapter I explore the notions of class, classism, and class conflict from the perspective of care and justice. This chapter naturally flows from and builds on the preceding discussion regarding neoliberal capitalism and how it undermines care and justice in the polis. Indeed, what is evident in the rise of neoliberal capitalism and the concomitant decline of more fiscally regulated Keynesian-style capitalism is sharper class divisions and steeper inequalities. The proliferation of luxury skyboxes, the presence of poor doors, the emergence of gated communities are physical and geographic signifiers of clear class divisions. Perhaps one could say we are simply better and more clearly sorted according to economic class, though class divisions accompany any form of capitalism, as Marx noted.[6] What I argue is that class, classism, and class conflict reflect distortions of care and justice in the polis, which are especially prevalent in a neoliberal market

4. See Sandel, *What Money Can't Buy*; Panousi et al., "Rising Inequality."

5. Hooks, *Where We Stand*, 45. See also Silva, *Coming Up Short*, for a sociological depiction of working-class beliefs vis-à-vis lack of material success.

6. Hudis, *Marx's Concept*, 26–33.

society where class divisions and conflict, while often denied or overlooked, are more readily apparent. I begin by addressing what is meant by class, classism, and class conflict or struggle. Here I claim that a neoliberal market society creates *homo oeconomicus*, who is not simply a social animal, but a class animal. He is born into a class, internalizes a class ethos,[7] and, as an agent in a market society, reproduces class. Before moving to a discussion about how class and classism represent the undermining of care and justice, I briefly discuss class in terms of Scripture and the interrelated theological notions of *imago dei* and kingdom of God. This provides the theological lens through which I consider problems of care and justice given a market society's construction and ongoing support of class and classism. This reality is perhaps most clearly seen in how the poor are depicted or socially constructed (and treated[8]) and their near exclusion from the polis's space of appearances. I conclude with a brief discussion about *altercapitalist* communities—communities that eschew class and classism as a way of organizing social relations.

CLASS, CLASSISM, AND CLASS CONFLICT

Richard Wolff and Stephen Resnick point out that "since ancient Greece, class has been used for groups of people according to the wealth and property they own."[9] Another traditional understanding of class "refers not to ownership of wealth or income but to power."[10] Not surprisingly, the ruling class almost always comes from the propertied class or the class of haves, and hence they are the primary operators of the space of appearances in the polis. Even when there is or is a coup by the have-nots, the new ruling class appropriates wealth and property. We note these depictions of class in Scripture and read that King David came from modest origins, yet came to be a part of the ruling, propertied, and wealthy elite of his society. Class, then, seems to have been around for millennia, preceding capitalism and leading many people, perhaps, to believe, incorrectly, that it is as natural way of organizing a society.

Karl Marx rejected any notion that class was natural to society. He argued that previous revolutionary attempts, which stemmed from class conflict, failed "to understand the importance of the organization of surplus

7. For a depiction of class ethos, see Fussell, *Class*.

8. See Soss et al., *Disciplining the Poor*.

9. Wolff and Resnick, *Contending Economic Theories*, 153.

10. Ibid.

labor in reinforcing societies' inequalities."[11] This meant that revolutions that emerged out of class conflict inevitably reproduced class, though often in different forms. For example, after the Russian revolution, the new Soviet state "abolished" private property, though in reality the state was the property owner that benefited from the surplus labor of its citizens. Put differently, the Soviet state was involved in a form of capitalism "because the defining principle of social organization is the reduction of human labour to ever-more abstract forms of value-creating labour," which the state controlled.[12] State functionaries and other government officers were the top political-economic class, simply reproducing class both in terms of political power and wealth. This class determined and "owned" the polis's space of appearances in the Soviet Union.

Marx conceptualized class, then, not in terms of "wealth and power distribution but rather to processes of producing and distributing surpluses in society."[13] That is, people are sorted by class "according to their participation in the production and/or distribution of surplus labor."[14] Wolff and Resnick contend that "Marx's focus on class in surplus terms sharply differentiates him from the neoclassical economists who are generally disinterested in class,[15] deny that a surplus exists, and place emphasis on individuals and market interactions."[16] Marx focused on and "developed a class theory because class in his time was—as it largely remains today—an overlooked, undertheorized, and often repressed dimension of modern capitalist society."[17]

There is a great deal more I want to say about class before turning to classism, but to understand Marx's view I need to pause and explain, if only briefly, his complex view on the origins of class and how it is reproduced in capitalist societies. In particular, it is helpful to explain his ideas of labor power, labor time, and surplus labor vis-à-vis value. Marx was in agreement with David Ricardo—an early nineteenth-century economist—that labor is the source of value,[18] but Marx did "not agree that value expresses the actual

11. Ibid., 154.

12. See Hudis, *Marx's Concept*, 17.

13. Wolff and Resnick, *Contending Economic Theories*, 154

14. Wolff and Resnick, *Economics: Marxian versus Neoclassical*, 145.

15. One might wonder if their disinterest was/is because they are part of the upper classes and thus have an unconscious motivation to avoid critiques.

16. Wolff and Resnick, *Contending Economic Theories*, 28.

17. Ibid., 29.

18. Value is not identical to material wealth. Value "is wealth computed in monetary term." See Hudis, *Marx's Concept*, 6.

number of hours of labour performed by the worker."[19] Value, Marx argued, is both imaginary, in the sense that human beings come up with what is valued and to what amount, and expressive of a social relationship, one based on exchange. He believed that in a capitalist society "social relations become governed by the drive to augment value, irrespective of humanity's actual needs and capacities."[20] Value, it should be pointed out, is not identical to material wealth; instead, "it is wealth computed in monetary terms."[21]

In disagreeing with Ricardo, Marx arrived at the conclusion that value "is determined by the average amount of necessary labour-time needed to create" a commodity.[22] To understand this further, let's return to the notion of labor. As Marxist scholar Peter Hudis remarks, Adam Smith and David Ricardo viewed labor "as a *thing* or commodity that could be bought or sold, instead as the expression of social relations that take on the form of things"—not persons."[23] Labor power, for Marx, refers to laborers who sell their ability to work—labor in this sense is a commodity because it is exchanged for money.[24] So, labor power is the agency, skills, and time necessary to produce a commodity, and this labor, which is objectified or reified, is the source of value. In Marx's view, it is more complicated than this. Consider, for instance, an individual who works one hour of labor time to produce a commodity, while another worker producing the same commodity does so in ten minutes. In terms of labor time, this means that the fifty extra minutes produce no value. Marx argued that competition to produce a commodity in the least amount of time influenced the value. In addition, value is further "determined by the *average* amount of *necessary* labour-time needed to create" a commodity.[25] In terms of the example, value is largely determined, not by the time it takes to produce the object, but "the minimum time it could possibly be produced in."[26] Put another way, "labour-time does not create value; instead, the *social average of necessary* labour-time creates value."[27] Richard Wolff and Stephen Resnick illustrate this using the unit value of a chair.

19 Ibid., 96.

20. Ibid., 5–6.

21. Ibid., 5.

22. Ibid., 97.

23. Ibid., 155 (italics original).

24. Wolff and Resnick, *Contending Economic Theories*, 168. This idea that one's labor is a commodity also reflects Marx's view about alienation, which was discussed in chapter 6.

25. Hudis, *Marx's Concept*, 97 (italics original).

26. Ibid.

27. Ibid., 158.

> In a competitive market, the unit value of a chair—its market value—is the average of the different labor times required by each industrial capitalist to produce its chairs. Like any average, some capitalist firms produce below the average, some above, and some even produce at the average. In other words, productive efficiencies as measured by these respective labor times differ across enterprises within the chair industry. The socially necessary labor attached to a chair is in fact the computed average of all these individual labor times.[28]

Labor time, then, is actually a bit more complicated than the minimum time to produce the commodity.

To add another wrinkle, a part of the labor time needed to produce a commodity comprises what some economists call necessary labor, which refers to the goods and services the laborer consumes in order to survive.[29] Since laborers tend to work longer than needed to supply their own needs, this "extra labor is what Marx called surplus labor."[30] To use a simple illustration, let's imagine that Karen works five days a week, producing widgets. She sells her labor power to the company and receives a wage. Her wages are used to purchase commodities she needs to survive, yet she works longer and produces more widgets than is reflected in her wages, which is surplus labor, and this surplus labor has value appropriated by the owner. This can be understood in another way. "By purchasing labour-power," Hudis notes, "the capitalist can compel the labourers to create value greater than the value of their labour-power or means of subsistence."[31] This increased value is surplus value that appends to the capitalist.

To return to the idea of class, capitalism produces and is dependent on classes. Basically, those who sell their labor power are called direct laborers, who make up what we might initially call the working classes or, more broadly, the laboring classes. Those who own the means of material production, who purchase labor power, and who "own" surplus labor and concomitant surplus value are the capitalist class. This bifurcation, though, is much more complicated, especially given modern society. First of all, capitalist and working classes overlook those who are not involved in material production. Michael Hardt and Antonio Negri argue "that our understanding of labor cannot be limited to waged labor but must refer to human creative capacities in all their generality. The poor . . . are thus not excluded from this

28. Wolff and Resnick, *Contending Economic Theories*, 186.

29. Hudis, *Marx's Concept*, 152.

30. Ibid.

31. Ibid., 162.

conception of class but central to it."[32] The poor, the unwaged, the homeless, and the unemployed, while not taking direct part in material production, still participate in society or social production "even when they do not have a waged position."[33] Indeed, they argue that "it has never been true . . . that the poor and the unemployed do nothing. The strategies of survival themselves often require extraordinary resourcefulness and creativity."[34] Another complicating factor involves those who are workers though not involved in material production. Hardt and Negri point out, "In the final decades of the twentieth century, industrial labor lost its hegemony and in its stead emerged 'immaterial labor,' that is immaterial labor that creates immaterial products, such as knowledge, information, communication, a relationship, or an emotional response."[35] The decline of material labor and the predominance "of immaterial labor tends to transform the organization of production from linear relationships of the assembly line to the innumerable and indeterminate relationships of distributed networks."[36] In other words, "information, communication, and cooperation become the norms of production, and the network becomes its dominant form of organization."[37] So, for Hardt and Negri, there is a shift in how labor and surplus value are understood. They state that "exploitation under the hegemony of immaterial labor is no longer primarily the expropriation of value measured by individual or collective labor time but rather the capture of value that is produced by cooperative labor."[38] In terms of class, then, this means that the notion of "working class" is more complicated and varied than Marx's conceptualization. However, while the notions of surplus labor and surplus value have changed, they still apply in the sense that laborers do not have control of their surplus labor or value. Material and immaterial laborers still sell their labor time, and the owners continue to garner the surplus labor and surplus value.

One might say that all of this sounds fair. The owners of material and immaterial labor have purchased the equipment, space, and so forth for the work to take place. They have to recoup these costs. Fair enough, but Marx's point is that the workers have no say, no agency with regard to how their surplus labor is used—a further sign of alienation. And, just as important, the aim of the capitalist class is not to recover the costs, but to reap as much

32. Hardt and Negri, *Multitude*, 105.

33. Ibid., 131.

34. Ibid.

35. Ibid., 108.

36. Ibid., 113.

37. Ibid.

38. Ibid.

profit as possible and those profits are directly related to surplus labor and surplus value that have been expropriated. Thus, the owners control the property, which is part of material wealth, and they have ownership of the profits—profits that, while legally theirs, are directly related to the labor surplus of the workers. This is especially pernicious in a neoliberal capitalist society, where expropriation of surplus value or profit is excessive, as compared to Keynesian economics, and creates incredible economic and political inequalities that are, of course, legal, but what is legal is not always fair or just.[39]

We can see from this perspective of class that class struggle or conflict is seemingly inevitable. An overly generalized view of this struggle is that one side fights to reduce surplus value, while the other side fights to increase it.[40] Wolff and Resnick note that people of different classes take part in this struggle. "A union of productive laborers," they write, "that presses for higher wages is a class struggle. Management pressing productive workers to accept compulsory overtime is a class struggle. The fight between two groups of representatives in Congress over a law that would raise the legal minimum wage is a class struggle."[41] This struggle, I should emphasize, is not merely between better wages and lower profits. Andrew Sayer writes that class matters to us, not only because of the differences in material and economic security, but also because "it affects our access to things, relationships, experiences and practices which we have reason to value, and hence our chances of living a fulfilling life."[42] He goes on to say that class "struggles are not merely for power and status but about how we live,"[43] which indicates problems in being recognized and participating in the polis's space of appearances. Consider class differences in access to the following: health care, competent legal representation, education, healthy food, transportation, and housing.[44] Class struggle is seen in the geography of cities where economic apartheid exists. Economic apartheid means that people of higher or more powerful economic and political classes have greater access to nutritious foods, health care, clean air and water, and the like.[45] As a result,

39. See Piketty, *Capital in the Twenty-First Century*; Mander, *The Capitalism Papers*; Stiglitz, *The Price of Inequality*.

40. Wolff and Resnick, *Contending Economic Theories*, 181.

41. Ibid., 181.

42. Sayer, *The Moral Significance of Class*, 1.

43. Ibid., 3.

44. See Putnam, *Our Kids*, for a sociological analysis of the problems associated with rising income equality vis-à-vis the lives of the lower class during the last forty years.

45. Berkman and Epstein, "Beyond Health Care."

they are more likely to have resources to meet needs for flourishing and they live longer. They benefit from the mystification of class struggle. To be sure, the struggle is not as overt as actual verbal or physical conflict, but it is manifest when the wealthy form gated communities "protected" by private police forces, when they persuade politicians to enact legislation that benefits the upper classes (such as legislation about who enters and operates in the polis's space of appearances), when they construct skyboxes and poor doors to avoid contact with the proles, and when they send their children to private elite schools far from the deteriorating schools of the inner city. And while class solidarity has been undermined by various political and economic realities of neoliberalism, class struggle is, in a market society, clearly present, though often mystified.[46] Perhaps the class struggle is not apparent because, as Warren Buffett remarked, the upper classes have won.

The notion of class struggle naturally moves toward the reality of the intersection of class, economics, and politics. Hardt and Negri rightly affirm that class (and class struggle) is a political concept.[47] Put another way, while capitalism reproduces class and class conflict, capitalism and class are also deeply embedded in and dependent on the political realm. Legislatures enact laws that have to do with the creation of corporations and financial products. Laws, not nature, legitimate capitalist possession of surplus labor. The privatization of health care, prisons, and education are all dependent on legislatures passing laws and crafting policies that make this possible. The decline of the labor unions, which has occurred for a number of reasons, is due in part to legislation that seeks to undermine them, which reveals class struggle in the realm of politics. There is no invisible hand or, more accurately, fist of the market. The "invisible hand" depends on the arm of the government for its very existence and for its reach into public sectors. Moreover, it is a mistake simply to consider politicians and the political systems significant players in class conflict. The political realm is suffused with the capitalist class, which possesses tremendous financial resources and hence political power vested in nongovernmental organizations (e.g., think tanks, lobby groups, and so forth). This means that the laboring classes, especially with the decline of unions, are significantly disadvantaged in the realm of politics vis-à-vis class struggles. In terms of the space of appearances, it is the capitalist class that largely operates in this space, while the poor and working classes remain on the political and economic fringes.

Class and class struggle, then, are inextricably yoked to the political and to political power. The ruling elite, then, make up a class, much like the

46. Sayer, *The Moral Significance of Class*, 80.

47. Hardt and Negri, *Multitude*, 104.

ruling elite in Aristotle's and King David's societies. In a neoliberal market society, however, the ruling class and government institutions are intertwined with the capitalist class. While legislators may not be of the capitalist class, they often serve their interests. The American Legislative Exchange Council includes business leaders from various corporations who have worked at state and national levels to create legislation that reduces regulations on corporations, and to create regulations that undermine unions. In short, their aim in the class struggle is to use political leaders and systems to increase their share of surplus value, furthering not only class division but class struggle.

To be sure, class can be understood in terms of wealth, power, surplus labor, and access to resources. Yet, class has also been understood in terms of group ethos and what people share in common. In other words, people tend to sort themselves into groups sharing similar social, political, and economic beliefs, which in turn often means possessing similar socioeconomic status and mores. For instance, Rauschenbusch considered class as "a body of men who are similar in their work, their duties and privileges, their manner of life and enjoyment, [such] that a common interest, common conception of life, and common moral ideals are developed and connect individuals."[48] Roland Boer calls this the subjective dimensions of class consciousness that includes a "complex web of cultural assumptions, modes of speech, social codes, world outlook and religion."[49] Paul Fussell, in an incisive and biting way, illustrates this in his depiction of the idioms, habits, and styles of working-, middle-, and upper-class people.[50] "Today, however, a class as a group that shares an ethos is less clear than perhaps it was during the height of the power and presence of labor unions. This said, the waning of "class solidarity and the absence of mobilization in no way imply class [or class struggle] is disappearing."[51] Indeed, in their recent work Hardt and Negri, recognizing the steep economic and political equalities and the fading of clear class distinctions, argue for the notion of the multitude—those who are exploited by the 1 percent.[52] The multitude includes those who are excluded from wage labor—the unemployed, the poor, and the homeless.[53] The multitude comprises "innumerable elements that remain different, one from the other,

48. Quoted in Estey, "Protesting Classes through Protestant Glasses," 131.

49. See Boer, *Marxist Criticism of the Hebrew Bible*, 98.

50. See Fussell, *Class*.

51. See Sayer, *The Moral Significance of Class*, 80.

52. See Hardt and Negri, *Multitude*.

53. Ibid., 129.

and yet communicate, collaborate, and act in common."[54] A recent example of the action of the multitude vis-à-vis class and class struggle is the protest against Wall Street—Occupy Wall Street—that included individuals from various laboring classes.

Even when lacking clear solidarity and ethos, class and class struggle frequently accompany negative and positive valuations that fall under the heading of "classism," which has affinities to racism.[55] Andrew Sayer notes that "racism is a necessary condition for the production of 'race,' but 'classism' is not necessary for the production of class."[56] What Sayer is arguing here is that racism produces the notion of race, but classism does not produce class. It is capitalism that creates and depends on class. Classism, however, often attends class, especially when economic and political inequalities are great. This is understandable because class and classism emerge in relation to the distribution of surplus value. People from the upper classes "feel obliged to justify their differences,"[57] though, as Sayer argues, class (and classism) lacks moral justification.[58] Individuals—capitalists (and political elites who support them)—who obtain the surplus value can begin to hold the illusion that because they hold the value (and power), they are more socially valuable and superior to those who do not (lower classes).[59] The poor and unemployed, classism holds, are of lesser value—a drain on the economy because they do not contribute to the creation of surplus value. Classism, then, comprises a valuation of inferiority and superiority based on position in a class hierarchy. Upper classes, in classism, deem themselves to be superior while considering the lower classes to be inferior. Like racism,[60] classism entails the double recognition that one group of individuals is superior while Others are inferior, and like racism, classism has very real consequences. For instance, the construction of a poor-door entrance to a building so that wealthy persons do not have to encounter lower-class

54. Ibid., 140.

55. The primary focus here is on classism and class. That said, classism, from Sayer's perspective, cannot be separated from racism and sexism, or from ethnicity and gender orientation. Sayer, *The Moral Significance of Class*, 90–92. See also Goldberg, *The Threat of Race*; Johnson, *Race, Religion, and Resilience*.

56. Sayer, *The Moral Significance of Class*, 94.

57. Ibid., 4.

58. Ibid.

59. Ibid., vii.

60. I note here that class and race are intertwined in the United States. African American representation in the capitalist class is tiny. Moreover, African Americans were hit the hardest during the great recession. See http://www.pewresearch.org/fact-tank/2014/12/12/racial-wealth-gaps-great-recession/. See also Johnson, *Race, Religion, and Resilience*.

people reveals the presence of classism and not simply class.[61] But more pernicious consequences of classism are seen in the neglect and simultaneous disciplining of the poor.[62] The poor and their communities are marginalized, experiencing the material and psychological effects of exclusion from or lack of access to resources such as education, health care, healthy food, transportation, adequate housing, and a clean environment; and this exclusion accompanies beliefs that the poor are inferior citizens in need of discipline. As Sayer points out, "The suffering of the unemployed derives from denial of income and lack of recognition, and lack of access to the means to remedy it,"[63] which, again, signals problems of the polis's space of appearances—a space constructed in terms of class and classism.

One might argue that it is class and not classism that results in members of the so-called lower classes having less access to resources for survival and flourishing. Yet classism entails a psychology that leans toward conflict *and* neglect, a psychology embedded in economic and political structures that marginalize and oppress members of the lower classes. In terms of class conflict, it is not only that there is a struggle over surplus value and access to various public goods. Class conflict is almost always interlaced with classism, because of the elite's negative valuation and perception of lower classes. To be sure, the disdain toward the lower classes can accompany a similar disdain of the upper classes, though often without any real consequences, since the political-economic elites have access to political, social, and economic goods and services. A cultural example of a psychology of classism and its relation to class conflict is seen in a recent cover of the *American Spectator* (June 2014), a conservative magazine. The illustration depicts a bespectacled and paunchy rich man being led to the guillotine and an official raising a bloody copy of Thomas Piketty's book *Capital in the 21st Century*. Near him is a guillotine with a bloody blade; many other wealthy people had likely already been guillotined. Implicit is that Piketty's book, which provides extensive evidence of huge economic disparities, is the apparent justification for violence toward the wealthy.[64] This is a violent cultural fantasy with echoes of the brutality of the French Revolution. It is a fantasy of class struggle, where the rich are innocent and the envious poor are guilty of vicious and unjust violence. In other words, the lower classes are depicted as brutal, lacking in humanity and justice vis-à-vis the wealthy. In my view, the fantasy represents classism and its attending power, though

61. Babin, "New York Skyscraper's Separate 'Poor Door' Called a Disgrace."

62. See Soss et al., *Disciplining the Poor*.

63. Sayer, *The Moral Significance of Class*, 61–62.

64. Piketty, *Capital in the Twenty-First Century*.

in an interesting way. The demeaned and deprived lower classes now have power, but they continue to be constructed as lower because they are using this power for revenge rather than justice. The message is, they are not worthy to govern. They are a mob. The upper-class "gentleman" is depicted as meek and innocent. What remains the same here is that the lower class remains lower, even if they have power. The wealthy remain superior in their innocence, denying or overlooking the subtle and overt "legal" violence perpetrated on the poorer classes by the expropriation of surplus value and limited access to the social, political, and economic resources needed for flourishing.

CLASS AND CLASSISM: SIGNIFIERS OF DISTORTIONS IN CARE AND JUSTICE

Before addressing class and classism in terms of care and justice, I wish to turn to Scripture. I do so for two reasons. First, class vis-à-vis rich and poor, the politically powerful and the politically helpless, is evident in Hebrew and Christian Scriptures, where one gets a chance to see how class is depicted by various writers. Second, Christian Scripture, in particular, has a trajectory toward critiquing the inevitable problems of care and justice that arise out of class. Moreover, in Christian Scripture, the notion of class has no meaning in light of the notion of the kingdom of God. Indeed, I suggest that there is a latent anthropological nugget of wisdom in Christian Scriptures regarding class. After this brief excursus, I turn to a depiction of the problems of class and classism in terms of care and justice.

Scripture scholar Carolyn Osiek contends, "There is no single position maintained in Hebrew scripture regarding rich and poor. Yet, certain definite patterns emerge."[65] The poor, she continues, "are the objects of God's special attention, because they are abused by the powerful."[66] In turning to prophetic literature, she notes that prophetic diatribes are aimed at the rich, whom the prophets blame "for the social abuses that are destroying the covenant community."[67] These prophetic diatribes identify the sources of the suffering of the poor and they introduce a subversive element by having an all-powerful God siding not with the wealthy but with the poor, widows,

65. Osiek, *Rich and Poor in the Shepherd of Hermas*, 15. Osiek also is quick to point out that "distribution of resources was dependent much more on power relations than on the market."

66. Ibid., 16.

67. Ibid., 19.

and orphans. Their hope is not in the political, wealthy elite[68] who write the stories and conduct rituals that support the logic of their cherished positions, but in a God who hears the laments of the oppressed. The covenant, in other words, does not condone alienating or marginalizing the poor, widows, and orphans. They too are part of the community of faith. Of course, Osiek also notes there are times when Hebrew Scripture acknowledges that wealth is a sign of God's blessing, which often becomes a scriptural defense of the prosperity gospel folk. Nevertheless, she points out many more references where "God champions the cause of the poor."[69]

To complicate this further, Michael Walzer notes that in Hebrew scriptures God establishes a political class, and the culmination of this is the monarchy.[70] It would seem, then, that God supports the class of the political elites, yet Walzer finds this too simplistic. He notes that the prophets arrive with the birth of the monarchy, establishing a conflict between political power and the admonitions of God. Prophecy, Walzer writes, "is also at war with politics itself—not only when politics is a form of self-aggrandizement but also when it is a form of self-reliance and self-help."[71] Granted, not all prophets spoke truth to the politically powerful,[72] and some were closely allied with the monarchy. Nevertheless, a trajectory of prophetic admonitions emerges against the political class who have strayed from the covenant, resulting in harm to society, not only with regard to survival of the community but also with regard to the diminishment of life-enhancing ways of being in the world. Isaiah, for instance, proclaims that "The Lord rises to argue his case; / he stands to judge the peoples. / The Lord enters into judgment / with the elders and princes of his people: / It is you who have devoured the vineyard; / the spoil of the poor is in your houses" (3:13–14). Not only does the vineyard represent the common good of food needed for survival; it also represents a good that is life-enhancing vis-à-vis individuals and the group.

In his survey of the Hebrew Bible, Obery Hendricks echoes the passage in Isaiah regarding class struggles. According to Hendricks, three distinct commands make up the core of the Hebrew Bible tradition: "(1) to lessen, if not fully eliminate, the economic class differences that already existed; (2) to guard against the further development of economic class differences in

68. Oakes, "Methodological Issues," 11, notes that unlike in modern times, during the time of Jesus the "distribution of resources was dependent much more on power relations than the market."

69. Osiek, *Rich and Poor in the Shepherd of Hermas*, 19.

70. Walzer, *In God's Shadow*.

71. Ibid., 67.

72. Ibid., 76–78.

society; and (3) to protect the poor and vulnerable against exploitation by the rich and powerful."[73] Hendricks contends further that "the early attempts by the Hebrews to develop an egalitarian social system did not express their hatred of Egypt's brutal class hierarchy, nor can it be dismissed as merely a function of a primitive political economy"[74] Instead, he says the "Hebrews' egalitarian social organization was an expression of their understanding of how God required them to live in the world as the reciprocal, covenantal duty their freedom from bondage placed upon them."[75] These commands, which are the basis of an economic egalitarian society, are, for Hendricks, the ground out of which Jesus's message is shaped.

Turning to the Christian Scriptures, Stephen Barton, surveying Matthew, Mark, Luke, and Acts, argues that "Jesus' teaching . . . represents a *challenge to the ordering of things, persons, and patterns of exchange* represented by 'the Pharisees,' in favor of a different ordering, one expressive of the new economy of salvation understood as 'good news to the poor.'"[76] Indeed, the gospel, he adds, "*radicalizes, intensifies, confounds, and disrupts* dominant notions of what really counts and how to attain it"—a new economy.[77] This said, Brian Capper points out that Jesus did not condemn wealth outright. Indeed, Jesus, Capper notes, "was supported on his own preaching tours by the patronage of women of means."[78] Yet, "Jesus demanded that those with wealth generously assist the destitute and undernourished."[79] Shifting to Acts, Capper argues that the economic pattern "based on a common purse into which large donations were received from wealthy patrons . . . bore the stamp of Jesus' authority and practice."[80] Carrying this further, Aaron Kuecker writes that "Luke describes a community of unconditional availability in which relationships with group members are privileged over relationships to personal possessions."[81] "One of the primary effects of this transformation," he continues, "is a radically reoriented economic praxis that privileges the 'other' over the self in economic exchange."[82] What these authors are pointing to is that the ministry of Jesus and the early church

73. Hendricks, *The Universe Bends toward Justice*, 132.

74. Ibid., 135.

75. Ibid.

76. Barton, "Money Matters," 51 (italics original).

77. Ibid., 57 (italics original).

78. Capper, "Jesus, Virtuoso Religion, and the Community Goods," 73.

79. Ibid.

80. Ibid., 77.

81. Kuecker, "The Spirit and the 'Other,' Satan and 'Self,'" 84.

82. Ibid., 82.

represent a movement toward a society structured and dominated by relations of mutual respect and forms of distribution and exchange that mitigate class, classism, and class conflict.

As if to problematize these views, Roland Boer trenchantly wonders about the "relevance of class for interpreting biblical texts," especially when one considers that the texts "are products of that small fraction of the ruling class known as scribes."[83] Doesn't the ruling class produce stories and rituals that secure their positions of power and privilege? Steeped in Marxist theories, Boer claims that biblical texts, despite being written by the ruling elite, "tend to reveal the contradictions of ruling class ideology." Indeed, the scribes, he continues, "preserve the mechanisms of rebellion"—no doubt unwittingly.[84] Turning to Ernst Bloch, Boer states that the "Bible is also the church's bad conscience: it has the uncanny knack of undermining any position one might want to take."[85] In other words, the Bible subverts those interpretations of the Bible that function to secure privilege and power for political and wealthy classes. Two current examples of where bad conscience should be present come from the prosperity gospel, where blessing and favor are framed in terms of the production of wealth. Consider Reverend A. R. Bernard, who proclaimed, "There is no way you can equate God with poverty."[86] Similarly, Reverend Creflo Dollar stated that "Having no increase renders you useless to the kingdom of God."[87] These pastors use the Scripture to secure and justify economic privilege, confusing emancipation and freedom with wealth. Overlooked is the subversive scriptural seed of God born in a manger, not in a palace, to poor parents. Denied are the trajectory of economic justice and a reordering of covenantal relationships around recognizing and responding to the needs and flourishing of the least of these.

In another work, Boer discusses the position of Ernst Bloch in greater depth. Bloch, unlike other Marxists who are critical of myth as ideology, argues for greater nuance.[88] To be sure myth can be used to retain class privileges, but it can also "possess an emancipatory-utopian dimension."[89]

83. Boer, *Marxist Criticism of the Hebrew Bible*, 12.

84. Ibid., 13.

85. Boer, *In the Vale of Tears*, 164.

86. MacDonald, *Thieves in the Temple*, 4.

87. Ibid., 5.

88. Boer, *Criticism of Heaven*. While Boer clearly admires Bloch, he is also critical, arguing that Bloch "moves too quickly from repression to emancipation and would have done well to tarry with the negative somewhat longer" (27). There are also other shortcomings Boer identifies.

89. Ibid., 27.

Indeed, Bloch posits that there is indeed an "anti-ruling class, anti-powerful, anti-wealth" thread in Scripture.[90] Two figures loom large in Bloch's view of the Bible as subversive—Moses and Jesus. Moses led his people from the chains of Egypt, establishing a religion of opposition, resistance, and rebellion.[91] Of course, it is important to point out that Moses's rebellion and subsequent liberation were followed by the killing and displacement of people in Palestine.[92] Jesus is also a revolutionary figure for Bloch, who focuses "on Jesus's 'downward attraction', towards the poor, and his 'upward rebellion against above,' against the powerful."[93] Bloch is not alone in considering Jesus to be subversive vis-à-vis the reigning powers. John Dominic Crossan,[94] James Cone,[95] Gustav Gutiérrez,[96] Richard Horsely,[97] Jeorg Rieger,[98] and Jurgen Moltmann[99] are some recent theologians and Scripture scholars who elevate the subversive features of Jesus's ministry vis-à-vis the wealthy and politically powerful classes who exploit the vulnerable, whether in relation to the Roman Empire, the wealthy class, or the politically privileged class.

In this discussion of class and Scripture, one might come away thinking that class conflict seems to be a part of every society and that scriptural moral admonitions are attempts to motivate the wealthier classes to be more charitable, to care about the needs for survival and flourishing of all people. This view might further suggest that scriptural writers did not seem to question whatever the current market and political structures were at the time.[100] Didn't Jesus say, "Render unto Caesar. . ."? I think, however, there is something intriguing and latent in the threads of critiques regarding the wealthy and political classes. As I noted above, class is not a natural category. It is not endemic to nature, and thus class, while rife, is not something that is inevitable in all communities or societies. Similarly, capitalism, which creates and depends on class, is not natural, implying that other systems of

90. Quoted in Boer, *Marxist Criticism of the Hebrew Bible*, 189.

91. Boer, *Criticism of Heaven*, 38.

92. Boer, *Marxist Criticism of the Hebrew Bible*, 66.

93. Boer, *Criticism of Heaven*, 45.

94. Crossan, *Jesus: A Revolutionary Biography*; Crossan, *God and Empire*.

95. Cone, *The Cross and the Lynching Tree*.

96. Gutiérrez, *A Theology of Liberation*.

97. Horsley, *Jesus and Empire*; Horsley, *Jesus and the Power*.

98. Rieger, *Christ and Empire*; Rieger, "Why Class Matters in Religious Studies and Theology."

99. Moltmann, *The Gospel of Liberation*.

100. For an intriguing interpretation of Jesus (as presented in the Gospels) and in the letters of Paul vis-à-vis politics, economics, and empire see Taylor, *The Executed God*, 203–59.

exchange cannot only be imagined, but also created.[101] When class does emerge, as Scripture writers seem to note, typical and expectable societal problems arise. The upper political and economic classes typically and inevitably exploit the lower classes. Is it possible, then, that these admonitions point to a basic anthropological problem that accompanies the emergence of class, whether that is based on politics or neoliberal capitalism? Are there two or more competing anthropological views, wherein one is incompatible with class and classism while the other is not? One view suggests that class is a reality of society, and occasional moral admonitions are necessary to remind people to care for those of lesser means. Another view is that whenever classes emerge in society, classism and class struggle are bound to be present, reflecting a society dependent on and rife with exploitation and marginalization. Put differently, the presence of class signals problems in fulfilling the covenant and is antithetical to the notion of the kingdom of God. Class, in this anthropological perspective, distorts the polis's space of appearances and disrupts living a life in common with others. More specifically, I want to argue that the emergence of class and classism inevitably accompanies distortions of care, which then give rise to and accompany various kinds of injustice. Distortions in care and justice represent falling short of the kind of polis wherein all citizens, as daughters and sons of God, share in their obligation to recognize and meet the survival and flourishing needs of others. The kingdom of God is, in part, among us whenever we see the absence of class and classism and the presence of care and justice.

Recall that genuine human care is contingent on the recognition and treatment of individuals as persons—absolutely unique, immeasurably valued, inviolable, responsive/agentic subjects. Theologically, this is understood in terms of the notion *imago dei* and implies an infinite obligation to recognize and respond to the needs of Others so that everyone can live a life in common and share in the common good. This personal recognition, which is a form of knowledge, contains, but subordinates, object knowing. Those caring situations wherein personal knowing *is subordinate* to object knowing are ethical if this state of affairs is time-limited and clearly aimed at meeting the needs of the individual or family. For instance, the physician who is treating the trauma patient objectifies the patient in order to heal. Once these actions have been completed and the patient's needs are met, object knowing should return to being subordinate to personal knowing. I also argued that the basis of a good enough family, community, and society is contingent on care and reparative rituals that restore care whenever it is breached. Class, understood in terms of capitalism and, in particular,

101. See, Hudis, *Marx's Concept.*

neoliberal capitalism, fundamentally distorts caring relations in several ways. First, the conditions for the emergence of class are based on the expropriation of surplus labor from the laboring classes. This means that workers are commodified or conceptualized in quantitative ways, which, in turn, means that object knowing reigns and personal knowing is, at best, in the background. As Peter Hudis notes, "Capitalists treat human beings as objects insofar as capital remains the defining principle of social organization."[102] Workers, then, are seen, constructed, and understood in terms of how they can contribute to the profits of the company. They are valued in relation to profit. Object knowing (commodification) and instrumental rationality, in other words, are in the foreground and attend the capitalist motivation to expropriate surplus labor/value for profit. The needs of the company (and the capitalist class), then, are primary, and the needs of the workers are subordinate to the company's survival and profit. Care for the workers, then, is conditional; that is, care is measurably based on the degree to which workers function to secure greater profits. When workers do not "care" for the goals of the company (i.e., when they are not producing profit) the company is not motivated to care for them. Impersonal or depersonalizing knowledge subsumes these relations, undermining any possibility of genuine care.

Recently, a person was fretting about her company's process of downsizing. Over several months, with little warning, security staff would come up to one or more technicians and watch them pack up their belongings before escorting them out of the building. After three months, more than a third of the workers were fired. In this case, we can assume that many, if not all, of the workers were productive, but the decline in the market for the company's products resulted in leaders cutting the workforce. The company CEO and his managerial class had to come up with ways for the company to survive and eke out some profit for the year. This is the logic of the market where the needs of workers are completely subordinate to the needs of the corporation. The insensitivity, the carelessness, the inhumanity of treating people like objects to be tossed aside is justified by and pervasive in a market society.

This does not mean that those associated with the capitalist class are necessarily indifferent or callous to the needs of laborers or the poor. A business owner could feel emotional pain and sadness in "having" to fire workers so that the company will survive. The workers, to him, are persons, and he knows their families. The sadness and helplessness means that he cares and that he knows they will struggle to meet the needs of their families without jobs. Yet, the cruel logic of the market demands its sacrifices,

102. Hudis, *Marx's Concept*, 143.

and while we may take comfort in knowing there are those in the capitalist class who care, it does little good for the workers who are currently without work, sacrificed on the altar of capitalism. It appears that all must bow to the ineluctable power of the market and its logic.

There is another facet to this, which can be brought to the surface by turning to Charles Dickens. No doubt we are all familiar with Scrooge, a miserly, insensitive and inhuman capitalist who, like all good capitalists, "accumulate[s] value for its own sake."[103] It is, overall, a cheery and hopeful tale with the awakening of Scrooge's conscience after visits from the ghosts of Christmas past, present, and future and the subsequent care he extends to his worker, Bob Cratchit, and his family. Prior to those spectral visits, Scrooge, blinded by his acquisitiveness, is unwilling to truly recognize his secretary as a person. This means concretely that Bob Cratchit's personal and family needs were overlooked or denied. Scrooge simply treated Bob as an object who performed duties for minimal pay, maximizing Scrooge's profits. Lower-class Bob Cratchit is an affable and forgiving man, seemingly resigned to his lot in life and grateful he has a job even if it is not enough to meet the needs of his family. After the spirits visit Scrooge, readers are comforted that Scrooge wakes up a changed man, and to the readers' delight, four things are overlooked regarding class, capitalism, and care. First, the generous care that Scrooge comes to display is largely based on a lifetime of exploitation, which undermined his secretary's ability to care for himself and his family. Scrooge's moral conversion, in other words, is to be praised, but the underlying realities of capitalism and class that distort care remain untouched. It is as if the master becomes kindly to the slave, making sure the slave's needs are met, yet the institution of slavery that distorts care and denies justice continues. A second issue is Bob Cratchit's dependence on Scrooge's upper-class kindness to meet basic needs for survival. After Scrooge's conversion, this relationship has not changed, except for the fact that Bob Crachit will gratefully accept Scrooge's help in securing care for his son. We might raise questions about the forced dependency of one class on the *chance* moral awakening and largesse of the wealthier classes to meet needs of survival and flourishing. Why should the Bob Cratchits of the world be forced to be dependent on a class of people who have "legally" expropriated their surplus labor? Is there any *consistent* (versus occasional and anecdotal) evidence of moral awakenings of the upper classes vis-à-vis caring about the poor and working classes?[104]

103. Ibid., 176.

104. I recall a story on National Public Radio about a well-known restaurant owner who was quite pleased with himself for raising his workers' pay to $15 an hour. He was held up as an example of a conscientious busines man, and he deserves some praise.

Third and relatedly, why does Dickens make Bob Cratchit into a benign, forgiving, meek person who seems content to accept his lot, including the possible death of his son due to his inability to pay for treatment? Bob Cratchit seems to accept, if not excuse, Scrooge's cruel indifference and carelessness. There is no moral outrage that comes from Bob Cratchit in being treated as an object and in being denied access to the resources to care for his family. This character is what the capitalist class desires (acceptance, meekness, obsequious dependence, and obedience), lower-class persons deferentially accepting the scraps of food they prepared and the table they built. Finally, Scrooge is the natural apotheosis of the capitalist within capitalism: a human being who cares more for his material wealth than for other humans. Nothing and no apparent human need or anguish can dislodge his motivation to secure more profit. Only the prospect of *his* eternal damnation moves Scrooge to share his wealth. We see here that Christianity—a semiotic system that challenges the fundamental assertions and ends of capitalism—functions as moral suasion of care. In a market society, all that is left to address the distortions of care vis-à-vis class is seemingly moral exhortation, leaving again intact the underlying class dynamics and expropriation of value from lower classes. The story, in other words, leaves us with only moral persuasion as a tool to move people of Scrooge's class. Any cursory glance of history reveals just how effective moral persuasion is vis-à-vis moving those ensconced in the upper classes to care. Capitalism and class remain, leaving any alternative hidden behind the delighted praises of one greedy man's conversion.

Care is also distorted in a neoliberal market society by virtue of the overemphasis on personal responsibility vis-à-vis wealth. Each citizen, as an entrepreneur, is responsible for his/her own success and failure. This is related to the notion that each individual's material and immaterial labor are commodified, which means responsibility, instead of being constructed in terms of care for others, is quantified or calculated in terms of material wealth. To return to what Wendy Brown notes about neoliberal capitalism fetishizing individualism, she argues that it leads to responsibilization, which is "forcing the subject to become a responsible self-investor and self-provider."[105] This view is inimical to care in general and problematic in terms of both care and class. Recall first that care for others implies that human beings are interdependent and are responsible for recognizing and responding

---

That said, in the interview the owner related that he owned several homes and had other expensive items. This gentleman and the interviewer did not see that he had been expropriating his workers' surplus value for years, enriching himself at the expense of meeting their needs.

105. Hudis, *Marx's Concept*, 84.

to the needs of others and not simply for themselves. Responsibility is not simply individual; it is fundamentally social, something Scrooge learned toward the end of his life. Moreover, responsibility should not be reduced to monetary calculation and individualism. In other words, in a neoliberal economy, Bob Cratchit is solely responsible for his economic situation. The fact that he struggles to support his family is his fault and not his employer's responsibility or the fault of a system rigged against him. In terms of class, in a neoliberal society, the Scrooges of the world are not responsible for the economic "failures" of the lower classes. Thus, there is no obligation to care about the Cratchits of the world, because they are obliged to care and be responsible for themselves.

Of course care and responsibility are also about economics. Bob Cratchit needed money to pay for food, housing, and health care for his son. But care and responsibility in the polis are much more than what can be quantified. If Scrooge had simply sent money to his secretary, something would be missing in his care. Scrooge's responsibility toward Bob Cratchit would ideally accompany empathy and affection, his desire to join and get to know the members of the family, all of which would accompany financial resources given for the family to survive and thrive. Even better, Scrooge's care and responsibility might extend to ending his expropriation of surplus labor and, instead, considering Bob Cratchit's view on how surplus labor should be justly allotted. Responsibility to care for others, then, includes diverse aspects of care aimed at survival and human flourishing. And this responsibility, as Scripture repeatedly affirms, means caring for all members of society and not simply oneself or one's own class and is not simply or solely understood in term of economics.

A market society dominated by a neoliberal ethos, then, emphasizes that each individual is responsible to care about his/her own economic success, and both care and responsibility may extend to Others only to the degree that Others aid in achieving one's individual aims vis-à-vis wealth. In other words, a market society is a Hobbsean society wherein each is, first and foremost, responsible for caring about his/her own (financial) well-being, which tends to lead not only to social alienation but also to tenuous and contractual social cooperation vis-à-vis class. Individuals, then, cooperate with those of the same class to advance their aims, and individuals in different classes to form contractual cooperation. From another angle, the capitalist classes can band together to secure more wealth and political power, which they do, while the lower classes can band together to try to limit expropriation of their surplus labor. Class conflict, then, can include cooperative care within opposing groups, yet care in this context is corrupted by recognizing the Other as enemy (so that I am not responsible to care), by individualizing responsibility (so that my responsibility is to my own class), and by reducing and restricting care and human needs to economics.

For some readers, this picture may be too stark. Surely, we see daily occurrences of people from different classes caring for Others in unconditional or noninstrumental ways. A middle-class man volunteers at the homeless shelter, a restaurant owner feeds a homeless person, wealthy patrons help people in an inner-city school obtain computer equipment, a politician writes legislation that proposes health care for all, an unemployed man helps a well-off elderly woman into her car. I agree that many acts of unconditional care take place, even in a neoliberal market society, across significant class divisions. My point is that in a market society, the production of class, classism, and class conflict undermines and corrupts social care, which does not mean that care in its unconditional form is entirely absent. Indeed, unconditional forms of care necessarily occur in families wherein good enough parents care in innumerable ways to meet their children's needs for survival and flourishing. However, this kind of caring, which is necessary for founding families and communities, takes place against the backdrop of a neoliberal market society that has numerous disciplinary regimes that counter (and socially undermine) that kind of care.

Another seemingly inevitable feature of class is classism, which further illustrates the corruption of care in a market polis. When perception of Others is captive to superiority-inferiority valuations, it inevitably shapes caring motivations and behaviors. At one end of the continuum is the person who by virtue of upper-class status perceives laborers and the unemployed to be inferior and then feels no compunction or obligation to care. The inferior, unemployed Other—often deemed to be lazy and responsible for his/her condition—is considered to be of little worth in a market society.[106] The valuation of inferiority means she does not merit care, but she merits discipline.[107] Of course, those of the "inferior" class can also construct the "superior" Other as not meriting their own care and concern. The laborer may sneer in disdain at the upper-class individual, reciprocating the lack of obligation to care in a society imbued with classism and class conflict.

We may note that people in the upper classes, while believing they are superior, give to various charities that aid the poor and working classes. This might lead one to argue that classism does not interfere with care—and that claim is partially correct. Whenever superior-inferior valuations exist, care, when it is present, is distorted. Consider the presence of classism and racism

106. See Wacquant, *Punishing the Poor.*

107. See Soss et al., *Disciplining the Poor.*

in the care offered Malcolm X and his family by white government officials and institutions.[108] Before Malcolm X's father had been murdered, the Little family was not only economically lower-class, they were also black. In terms of classism and racism, which were intertwined,[109] they were deemed inferior by race and class. Malcolm X recalled that in 1934 the family began to deteriorate psychologically.[110] Prior to this, they took solace in their resilience and not having to depend on the state for support or what was called "relief." Yet, the realities of the Depression, racism, and his mother's struggle to find work led them to having to accept food from the government, which was stamped "Not to be Sold."[111] We note that Malcolm X and his family felt pride in not receiving government help, which suggests that while they were on the low rung of a class hierarchy, they were not the lowest. To be dependent on the government was seen as humiliating, indicating an inferior social-economic status that, I would argue, was promulgated by the disciplinary regimes associated with capitalism and classism. Care is provided, but it is corrupt, not only because it inherently communicates inferiority to those who are desperate, but also because it involves the misrecognition of other needs, such as psychosocial needs for genuine respect and dignity. Moreover, care is often minimal because the ruling and economic elite held and hold "the idea that welfare should not be accessible or generous enough to offer an attractive alternative to the worst jobs in the formal economy."[112] Malcolm X, for instance, found these experiences of receiving care from white state officials to be humiliating and that they fostered a greater sense of psychological and social alienation.

This vignette exemplifies the problems of care vis-à-vis persons who are constructed as inferior in a market society dominated by a racialized neoliberal ethos.[113] The poor, homeless, and unemployed are constructed as inferior in all kinds of ways, even as the state has programs to meet some of their needs for survival (but not for their flourishing).[114] They are deemed to be inferior because they are seen as irresponsible, lazy, and dependent. These Others are deemed to have less worth and, if there is any doubt about this, consider that social programs that help the poor are usually the first to be considered in budget cuts. The U.S. spends over $700 billion for the

108. X, *The Autobiography of Malcolm X.*

109. See Johnson, *Race, Religion, and Resilience.*

110. X, *The Autobiography of Malcolm X*, 14.

111. Ibid.

112. See Soss et al., *Disciplining the Poor*, 112.

113. See Johnson, *Race, Religion and Resilience.*

114. See Soss et al., *Disciplining the Poor.*

military (and this amount does not include billions for the intelligence services), while less than $368 billion go toward all the social programs to help struggling families.[115] This also extends to other spending priorities. "In 1980," Soss, Fording and Schram note, "the United States spent 58% more on AFDC [Aid to Families with Dependent Children] than on jails and prisons; by 1995, U.S. spending on jails and prisons exceeded investments in AFDC (132 percent greater) as well as Food Stamps (69 percent greater)."[116] In a neoliberal capitalistic society, those who "merit" respect, attention, and social-political support are those of the upper classes. These classes merit participation in public-political spaces of appearances. The poorer classes, by contrast, are deemed to be "undisciplined and irresponsible; their work ethic is underdeveloped."[117] The "poor can achieve full citizenship" or participate in the polis's space of appearances by submitting to the disciplinary regimes of a market society.[118] In short, care for the poor is distorted by a neoliberal ethos that aims to discipline them while at the same time undermining the resources necessary for care.

It is important to say more about the distortion of care vis-à-vis class and what Joe Soss, Richard Fording, and Sanford Schram call neoliberal paternalism. The political and economic elites are involved in paternalist governance of the poor, because it is believed that the "poor lack the competence needed to manage their own affairs."[119] The logical result is that the state "must step in as a disciplinary authority."[120] This has led to "greater surveillance and documentation of poor people's behavior, closer measurements to evaluate and incentivize performance."[121] The goal of paternalist neoliberal governance "is to transform the poor into subjects who, under conditions of apparent autonomy, choose to act in ways that comply with market imperatives and political authorities."[122] Under the guise of care, the "poor" (the

115. *Federal Safety Net*, http://federalsafetynet.com/welfare-budget.html/.

116. Soss et al., *Disciplining the Poor*, 103. One could argue that spending more on prisons does not seem to benefit the upper classes, but the rise in spending for prisons corresponds to the rise of neoliberal capitalism wherein the government works with corporations in privatizing public sectors such as prisons. Soss et al. note that "between 1982 and 1997 state correctional spending grew 383 percent," much of which went to private corporations.

117. Ibid., 81.

118. Ibid.

119. Ibid., 25.

120. Ibid. It is important to stress that these authors depict the various ways neoliberalism has been intertwined with racial coding, disproportionally impacting African Americans.

121. Ibid., 27.

122. Ibid., 28.

lower classes) are deemed unable to care for themselves or even to know well enough their own needs.[123] This wholesale objectification necessarily distorts and undermines care because the Other is objectified and denied adult agency. Moreover, the "poor" are constructed as inferior citizens who must be disciplined to perform in a market economy. So, we might ask, are "poor" people cared for in a paternalistic polis? Are the numbers of poor decreasing? We know that in a neoliberal society the percentage of poor people is increasing. Do poor people have a correspondingly greater access to health care, education, healthy food, and decent housing? There is no evidence that poor people have greater access to resources needed for survival and flourishing. Perhaps one of the most despicable examples of a distortion of care with regard to poor people by neoliberal, paternalistic political and economic elites is the political exploitation of the poor to further the aims of neoliberal capitalism. As Soss, Fording, and Schram write, "Poverty governance was reconfigured as part of a much broader political campaign . . . to de-regulate industries, cut taxes, shift risks onto private actors, and weaken social protections for the middle class."[124] Neoliberal capitalism also exploits the poor by privatizing welfare programs, and privatization results in fewer resources for the poor and greater profits for companies.[125] In the march to becoming a market society, the poorer classes become objectified and politically and economically disciplined and exploited, which reveals in stark terms the distortion and undermining of care.

I decided to address the notion of care and class first, instead of justice, not only because care is a central category in political pastoral theology, but also because class and justice are commonly paired. Indeed, the issue of justice is usually in the foreground; care is left aside or in the distant background. If the notion of care is foregrounded, though, then justice is not far behind when one considers the examples above. Scrooge's carelessness, for example, is also an issue of justice because Bob Cratchit and his family are not getting what they are due with regard to their survival and flourishing. Moreover, Scrooge's carelessness is wedded to his unjust expropriation of Bob Cratchit's surplus labor—an expropriation legitimated by a capitalistic system unjust at its core. So, in this and other examples, we note that care and justice are two sides of the same coin.

As in my discussion on class and care above, I am not arguing that justice is absent in a market society where class and class conflict are present.

123. This kind of paternalism is also reflected in Easterly's book, *The Tyranny of Experts*.

124. Soss et al., *Disciplining the Poor*, 19.

125. Ibid., 176–202.

Rather, I contend that justice is fundamentally misshapen whenever class and classism are present in society. Of course, the capitalist class would argue that disparities associated with class are just, because it is entirely legal to secure profit by expropriating surplus labor. From a capitalist perspective, the laborer is receiving a just wage in accordance with market rules; never mind the fact that she struggles to meet the needs of family members. Well, the capitalist counters, if a laborer feels she is being treated unfairly with regard to wages and benefits, then she is free to market her skills and labor elsewhere. But it is difficult to move when one has few resources. True to neoliberal capitalistic logic, a capitalist might suggest that nations and individuals need to start somewhere, and, with a bit of hard work anyone can enjoy economic success. The issue of justice, then, is captive to and supportive of the logic of the market. What is due so-called lower-class individuals, families, and communities is, at best, secondary to what is due to the market. This is one way the notion of justice becomes misshapen.

The view that justice is related to the rules of the market can also be accepted by the working classes. Indeed, the disciplinary regimes of the market and the state can instill neoliberal capitalist beliefs, leaving workers to blame[126] themselves for not obtaining what they are due or simply accepting the state of affairs, which means in both cases the notion of justice is either completely overlooked or distorted. Bob Cratchit is clearly a good illustration of the kind of worker who does not conceptualize his situation in terms of justice. To be sure, he wishes to be paid more and to have better working conditions, yet he is dependent on Scrooge's generosity, implying that Scrooge's wealth is justly obtained. (In terms of market logic it is.) Indeed, Bob is gracious to his boss as if to accept the reality of the market and Scrooge's greed. Bob cannot see that he (and his family) is being exploited. It is not simply unjust that Bob is unable to make enough money to adequately care for his children's needs for survival and flourishing; it is unjust that his boss is expropriating Bob's surplus labor for Scrooge's coffers. Yet, the market and its disciplinary regimes tend to obscure or mystify economic injustice.

Class conflict is a symptom of a fundamental flaw vis-à-vis justice in a market society. Class conflict emerges as a result of expropriating surplus labor. The capitalist class seeks to increase this surplus to gain more profit, while the laboring classes seek to reduce it to obtain more wages/benefits. This is all part of the rules of the game, if you will. But, it is unjust at the outset to expropriate surplus labor, even if the capitalistic system, supported by legislation, deems it to be fair. The worker's labor produces a product

126. See Silva, *Coming Up Short*.

that is sold for profit. Some of the cost of the product is due to the materials and equipment used in making it and the cost associated with paying the laborer enough to live. The worker's surplus labor is "owned" by the factory owners. Imagine that a worker who agreed to pay the owner the costs (plus 10 percent) associated with the equipment and material, while being able to keep costs associated with her necessary and surplus labor. As she is walking home, the worker is forced by the owner to hand over the surplus labor. We would call this stealing, but in a market society it is deemed licit. As "Marx insisted[,] . . . the aim of the capitalist society is not to enrich human needs and capabilities, but rather to augment value. Capitalism is an abstract form of domination that has one over-riding goal: to accumulate value for its own sake."[127] Dickens's tale is in part a story that reveals the excesses of capitalism while mystifying its unjust core. The problem is not simply or solely Scrooge and his unjust treatment of Bob Cratchit. The problem is that individual excess has been called into question without also calling into question the very system that gives rise to greed, acquisitiveness, and systemic exploitation. The problem is that Bob Cratchit (and perhaps Dickens himself) is unable or unwilling to face his unjust dependency on the largesse of a man who has unjustly expropriated Cratchit's surplus labor, putting himself and his family at risk. Perhaps the ghosts should have visited Bob Cratchit as well, awakening him to the exploitation of his boss and the system that legalizes it.

It seems odd to say that a system is just when large numbers of people struggle to have enough to ensure that they themselves and those they love survive and flourish. Indeed, I argue that a market society dominated by a neoliberal ethos that deepens class inequalities fundamentally undermines and distorts both care and justice. While we may take for granted the system and its rules justifying its existence and mystifying its excesses, the realities of class, classism, and class struggle continue and they continue to be part of society's misshapen care and justice.

ALTERCAPITALIST COMMUNITIES: NO NEED FOR CLASS

In the book of Acts, we learn that the early believers gathered and "no one claimed private ownership of any possessions, but everything they owned was held in common . . . There was not a needy person among them, for as many as owned lands or houses sold them and brought the proceeds of what was sold. They laid it at the apostles' feet and it was distributed to each as any

127. Hudis, *Marx's Concept*, 176.

had need."[128] These early believers were trying to form a community based on principles derived from their understanding of the ministry of Jesus. One principle was likely that of caring for the poor. Another principle may have been reflected in Paul's letter to the Galatians wherein he expresses concern about differences vis-à-vis class, which violates the theological tenet that we are all children of God. Paul writes "There is no longer Jew or Greek, there is no longer slave or free, there is no longer male and female; for all are one in Christ Jesus."[129] Paul's pairings are telling; there are no divisions according to ethnicity, economics/class, and politics/class. It is not that slaves and the privileged free are equal; rather these distinctions have no meaning in a Christian community that seeks to embody in part the kingdom of God.

Of course we know that the community in Acts had trouble from the very beginning, and perhaps many would see this experiment as a naïve, though noble, failure. The pragmatists may have won the day, deciding that it was not realistic to press wealthier folks to hand over all of their wealth. The pragmatists, I suspect, were likely people of wealth. The grand experiment failed, yet these principles endured, though they became spiritualized and, if I may, liturgized. In liturgy, we celebrate that we all are children of God—not separated by class and ethnicity—and our prayers of petition include God's care for the poor. But who could blame us for spiritualizing and liturgizing these principles when living out these principles in the real world is simply too hard and every utopian community seems destined to fail.

Perhaps we need to understand why communities such as these fail. One could point to Ananais and Sapphira, who kept back some of the proceeds from the sale of a piece of property.[130] Death seems a tad harsh for wanting to keep a portion of the proceeds for oneself and one's spouse, yet we get the point that there will be people of means who find it untenable to hand over everything. Greed, pride, and other deadly sins also make living in a classless community very difficult. Yet individual sin is not the only obstacle or even the most important. The early Christian community was attempting to live out an ethos that contradicted the way that the larger society organized relations. Consider also the reality of living in the Roman Empire where distinctions and hierarchies functioned to maintain social and political dominance. The Roman ruling class worked with the local ruling class to maintain order and to secure power and privilege for the political and economic elites. It is very difficult to be countercultural when people have internalized the values and beliefs associated with political

128. Acts 4:32–35.

129. Gal 3:28.

130. Acts 5:1–5.

and economic classes. This is especially true today given the dominance of neoliberal capitalism's in U.S. society with its disciplinary regimes promoting individual responsibility, acquisitiveness, and greed. As I stated above, the disciplinary regimes not only foster citizens' internalization of the neoliberal ethos as the unquestioned reality but also discipline those who attempt to criticize it.

Even with these obstacles, there are echoes of the early Christian community in many faith communities today. The only special parking is for people with disabilities. Everyone else shares a common parking lot, unlike corporate headquarters. There is no special seating section for those of higher social-economic classes. While there are skyboxes in arenas (a secular liturgical setting), there are none in churches. There are no distinctions with regard to those coming to Communion (at least with regard to class), and no one obtains a better or larger piece of the bread or a better vintage of wine. Of course, class may be present in that a faith community may be located within or near an upper- or lower-class part of the city, but the church does not function as a country club. A person from a lower-class part of the city may attend and join. Entry is by way of baptism rather than how much income one has or how much power one wields.

My point here is that remnants of the early Christian community of Acts live on even though we do not have congregations that require turning over one's wealth so that it could be distributed to members who are in need. These remnants can serve as a basis for developing an *altercapitalist ecclesia* where responsibility is understood in terms of how each person cares for Others, where each person is concerned about what is due Others. An *altercaiptalist* church makes no distinctions in its membership vis-à-vis class, yet it is not blind to class in its solidarity with the poor both inside and outside the community. This solidarity, which necessarily includes proximity to, connection with, and learning from those who are poor, can take myriad forms (food banks, health care clinics, housing, job training, childcare, elder care), depending on the needs found in the congregation and neighborhood.

Many churches, synagogues, and mosques do these things, but this is not enough. An *altercapitalist ecclesia* can educate its members and Others about the origins of class and income inequalities. This education can include taking a critical, prophetic stance toward the larger society and political-economic systems implicated in fostering class, classism, and class struggles, and so in undermining care and justice in the polis. Advocating for a living wage, demanding redistribution of wealth so that the people of lower classes can meet their needs for survival and flourishing, protesting the privatization of public sectors (e.g., dismantling the prison profit system that marginalizes and oppresses people of color and those in lower classes), promoting health care for all people, and advocating easier access to good education among the lower classes are just some ways an *altercapitalist* community can play a prophetic role.

It may be clear that an *altercapitalist* community in this society will continue to have classes within the church. I am not sure that it is reasonable or possible to eliminate the reality of class in a society dominated by neoliberal capitalism. I also believe that requiring people to hand over all that they have to church leaders is a recipe for the creation of a cult or other problems, which have been seen throughout history.[131] Those who seek to bring the kingdom of God to earth by building utopian communities are doomed to fail, because they overlook the reality of human finitude and sin. Instead, I believe we must look for ways to acknowledge our failings and shortcomings, while also seeking to live out the principles of care, compassion, and justice with people within the faith community and those outside. An *altercapitalist ecclesia*, in other words, primarily organizes social relations in terms of mutual care and justice, instead of in terms of economic exchange and class. There may be classes in the community and in the community's ministry to the wider community, but these are in the background or, better, subordinate to the principles of compassion, hospitality, mercy, and inclusion. Put differently, what is in the foreground vis-à-vis organizing social relations is the tenet of *imago dei*, a tenet that renders class mute and moot in relation to the in-breaking of the kingdom of God. This tenet places on us an infinite demand, one that we often fail to meet. Because of finitude and sin we fail to recognize and respond to the needs of those in our community and in society for survival and flourishing.

CONCLUSION

In my imagination, the early Christian community in Acts was made up of a critical mass of people who had seen and experienced the political and economic divisions and consequences associated with the Roman Empire and the local political and economic elites. Perhaps they saw the suffering of the poor and questioned a kind of society wherein the needs of the poor

131. I should point out there are successful examples of people living together who share their goods in common. Religious and monastic communities have a long tradition whereby members share incomes to meet the needs of all members. Entry into these (clearly *altercapitalist*) communities requires years of formation and vows that go beyond the typical baptismal vows. These communities also have rules of governance that mitigate cult-like leaders. Having said this, I do not see these communities as models for churches because of the depth and breadth of commitment to this way of life.

to survive and flourish were neglected. Maybe they knew at some level that a society that creates and sustains classes inevitably fosters exclusion, alienation, and suffering, all of which would be inimical to what they were told about the kingdom of God. These early Christians may have thought that the answers to their questions could be found in the ministry of a man who did not come from the economic and political elites—a man who preached about the kingdom of God where there are no classes, where there are no categories of poor and rich. They offered an *alterclass* community where members gathered to care for one another's needs. Yes, they failed, at least with regard to perpetuating this kind of community. But they succeeded in imagining a community that did not depend on or reproduce class. They succeeded by envisioning a type of community where all members are responsible to care for others, to seek justice for all, a community where care and justice not rooted in legal systems that favor the wealthy and political elite.

Yes, this is pure eisegesis on my part, but a political pastoral theology also includes a critical and constructive imagination toward a society and its political-economic systems that create and sustain conditions where people of the lower classes have limited access to a public space of appearances, to good education, to health care, to healthy food, and the like A political pastoral theology engages not simply in the prophetic moral suasion of those in the upper classes but also in prophetically critiquing the very economic and political systems that create the so-called upper classes. This critique includes considering ways to develop types of *altercapitalist* communities, and envisioning political and economic systems that do not create and sustain class, classism, and class struggle.

8

POLITICAL PASTORAL THEOLOGY

Other Pressing Matters

The call to care for a person is simultaneously a call to care for the world.[1]

The most basic purpose of poverty governance is not to end poverty; it is to secure, in politically viable ways, the cooperation and contributions of weakly integrated populations.[2]

The previous three chapters have focused on critiquing macro systems, relying on the concepts of care and justice, as well as briefly considering responses that can counter systems that diminish the polis and its people. One goal of these chapters was to demonstrate how a political pastoral theological perspective can be used to critique systems that obstruct or inhibit meeting the survival and flourishing needs of individuals and communities. The underlying premise is that persons survive, develop, and thrive in good enough caring communities and societies wherein individuals are recognized and treated as persons—persons who participate in the polis's space of appearances—and where, ideally, everyone cares for each other. Care, then, as a hermeneutical lens, serves as both a framework for critique and a vision that points to new possibilities vis-à-vis social, politi-

1. Graham, *Care of Persons, Care of Worlds*, 14.

2. Soss et al., *Disciplining the Poor*, 1.

cal, and economic institutions, policies, and programs that seek to address the survival and flourishing needs of those within (and outside) the polis.

The importance and utility of this perspective can be seen by addressing other pressing matters in the polis where people are "othered" and so left on the margins of the polis's space of appearances and likewise limited in the needed resources for meeting their needs for survival and flourishing. These other matters are manifold, and in this chapter I briefly identify five pressing issues that certainly require more extensive critical attention and examination. I have selected these issues because they impact large sections of the polis (and in one instance citizens of the world); but more important, they disproportionately impact people of color and people in the lower classes, in particular, the poor—persons who are politically, socially, and economically disenfranchised, operating on the margins of the polis's space of appearances.[3] I begin with the issue of global warming, in part because it clearly points to the interrelation between care of the polis and care of the earth. Moreover, the issue and realities of climate change reveal that we must care not only about our own polis, but also for those around the world. In ways we have not seen before in history, care must be both global and local, because we share the same earth, breathe the same air, depend on the same oceans. I then move to discuss health care, education, the penal system, and finally the politics of exclusion.

Before taking up these other pressing matters, let me offer a few clarifications. First, it is obvious that these topics are contested and deeply complex. Indeed, each warrants a book-length analysis. So, why am I skimming the surface? The obvious answer has to do with limitations of space and time related to writing a book. This answer might lead to another question: why write about these issues at all? One answer is that due to present and future sufferings of untold numbers of human beings, these issues need greater attention and analysis through the lenses of care and justice. Another response is that I wish to invite more conversations about these issues among colleagues from all theological disciplines. A second clarification is that the topics of the last three chapters, namely empire, neoliberal capitalism, and class, are integrally related to each of the issues of this chapter to varying degrees. In other words, as I indicated in the previous chapters, I see that the expansionist policies and actions of the United Sates are supported by and inextricably related to capitalism and class struggle. Similarly, empire and capitalism cannot be separated from our headlong drive toward the disasters related to global warming. In addition, neoliberal capitalism's

3. Rob Nixon uses the term "remaindered humans," and Annu Jalais uses "dispensable peoples" to refer to groups precariously poised on the fringes of the polis. In Taylor, *The Executed God*, 168.

compulsive privatization of public sectors, fetishizing profit, and dizzying commodification of life clearly impact education, the judicial system (e.g., the privatization of prisons and the expanding prison population), health care costs, and what I call the politics of exclusion (e.g., voter suppression laws). These other matters, then, I view as an extension of the analyses presented in the previous chapters.

CLIMATE CHANGE: ATTRIBUTES AND CONSEQUENCES

Climate change has been in the news for the last forty years, though public attention has waxed and waned. In a recent poll conducted by Yale and Utah State Universities, 99 percent of counties in the United States believe in global warming.[4] In another poll, Davenport and Connelly note "that 83 percent of Americans, including 61 percent of Republicans and 86 percent of independents,[5] say that if nothing is done to reduce emissions, global warming will be a very or somewhat serious problem in the future."[6] Changing trends in public opinion seem to follow the acceptance of climate change among the world's scientists (an acceptance rate of 97 percent) and 18 leading scientific organizations.[7] Climate change deniers[8] have been marginalized because of the overwhelming scientific research and growing public opinion about the reality of global warming. One might wonder why, with this consensus, there have not been more changes to reduce greenhouse gas emissions.

This growing acceptance of global warming does not mean there is political consensus about how to address it, what the consequences of climate change are, and what the major contributing factors are. To be sure, some of these debates are less about science and more about political-economic winners and losers. For instance, in eastern Kentucky and West Virginia, coal-producing areas of the country, global warming often has been denied and, when that does not work, people deny that warming is due to fossil

4. Holthaus, "Poll."

5. These statistics naturally vary and can be broken down according to political beliefs. See Klein, *This Changes Everything*, 35–38.

6. Davenport and Connelly, "Most Republicans Say They Back Climate Change, Poll Finds."

7. National Aeronautics and Space Administration, "Scientific Consensus."

8. Many who previously denied climate change have shifted tactics. They admit the earth is warming but deny human beings are responsible for it.

fuels.[9] Understandably, people are anxious about their livelihoods—in the short term—which certainly motivates them to rely on their beliefs, however mistaken, rather than on research. To explain systemic, political inertia or resistance to evidence of climate change and actions to address it, Larry Bell[10] and Naomi Klein[11] argue that attachment to neoliberal capitalism's way of organizing societies is largely to blame. Those who most benefit from capitalism do not want to sacrifice wealth, privilege, and power to make the necessary political and economic changes to slow or avert global warming. "We have not done the things necessary to lower carbon emissions," Klein writes, "because those things fundamentally conflict with deregulated capitalism, the reigning ideology for the entire period we have been struggling to find a way out of this crisis."[12] Further, she contends that the actions that would benefit the majority "are extremely threatening to an elite minority that has a stranglehold over our economy, our political process, and most media outlets."[13] Inertia also can be explained by our individual choices that implicate us in increasing CO_2 emissions. To be sure, political and economic elites have shown little leadership in making necessary changes and, therefore, bear a good load of the responsibility, but those of us who enjoy economic privileges in the West are complicit as well.

Political and social inertia, then, reflect the lack of consensus regarding the sources of climate change and what to do about it, despite the consensus of the reality of climate change. The lack of political consensus does not imply that the scientific data are ambiguous. For instance, the Intergovernmental Panel on Climate Change—a group of independent scientific experts from countries all over the world—concludes that human activities have warmed our planet.[14] The human activities the report refers to are those that heighten CO_2 emissions, as well as other greenhouse gases,[15] which are implicated in the warming of the planet. Gernot Wagner and Martin

9. Holthaus, "Poll."

10. Bell, *Climate of Corruption.*

11. Klein, *This Changes Everything.*

12. Ibid., 18.

13. Ibid.

14. National Aeronautics and Space Administration, "A Blanket around Earth"; Intergovernmental Panel on Climate Change, *Climate Change 2007*, 2.

15. Wagner and Weitzman, *Climate Shock*, 45 point out that hydrofluorocarbons (HFCs) are "10,000 times as potent as carbon dioxide when it comes to global warming." So the Montreal Protocol that banned gases (chlorofluorocarbons—CFS) that were harming the ozone layer led to the production of HFCs. The ozone layer is expected to be healed by 2050, but we continue to use HFCs, though in smaller emission numbers than CO_2.

Weitzman note that current carbon dioxide levels are at 400 parts per million (ppm) and the last time they were that high was over three million years ago during the Pliocene Era when "sea levels were up to 20 meters higher and camels lived in Canada."[16] Like Gernot Wagner and Martin Weitzman, a NASA study confirms that atmospheric CO_2 has increased since the Industrial Revolution.[17]

Wagner and Weitzman point out further that the International Energy Agency (IEA) estimated that "the world is currently on track to increase total greenhouse gas concentrations to around 700 ppm by 2100."[18] These increases are almost entirely due to human activities.[19] As Christian Parenti notes, the "11 warmest years on record (since 1850) have occurred in the past 13 years. The five warmest years to date are 2005, 1998, 2002, 2003, 2007."[20] Unfortunately, high "levels of carbon dioxide remain in the atmosphere for centuries and millennia. Getting them down is extremely difficult"[21]—even if there was a consensus about what to do. The momentum for increased warming of the planet appears inevitable.[22]

Given this, what are the potential foreseeable consequences linked to global warming? Of course, there are all kinds of questions and debates about the consequences of global warming, but one very conservative group takes climate change very seriously and has for some years. Coral Davenport writes that the "Pentagon . . . released a report asserting decisively that climate change poses an immediate threat to national security, with increased risks from terrorism, infectious disease, global poverty and food shortages. It also predicted rising demand for military disaster responses as extreme weather creates more global humanitarian crises."[23] In this report, the Defense Department "lays out a road map to show how the military will adapt to rising sea levels, more violent storms and widespread droughts. The Defense Department will begin by integrating plans for climate change risks

16. Ibid., 10.

17. National Aeronautics and Space Administration, "Climate Change: How Do We Know?"

18. Wagner and Weitzman. *Climate Shock*, 31.

19. Two interesting facts that Wagner and Weitzman point out follow: First, the effects of greenhouse gases had been discovered in the nineteenth century (ibid., 35). The second interesting fact is that King Edward I "established the first air pollution commission in 1285. In 1306, he made it illegal to burn coal," though the law was soon vacated (ibid., 21).

20. Parenti, *The Tropic of Chaos*, 6.

21. Ibid., 40.

22. Volland, "Global Temperature Records in Close Agreement."

23. Davenport, "Pentagon Signals Security Risks of Climate Change."

across all of its operations, from war games and strategic military planning situations to a rethinking of the movement of supplies."[24]

The Pentagon report is based on scientific predictions, though as Wagner and Weitzman point out, predictions can be wrong, both in terms of actual effect or extent of harm.[25] This said, let me identify some possible consequences that will impact the lives of millions of people. While there is no clear data about the actual rise in temperature, it is clear, however, that temperatures are rising and will continue to do so. With a rise in temperature, there is a corresponding increase in melting ice sheets. Recently, NASA scientists predicted that the ten-thousand-year-old Larsen B Ice Shelf will melt by 2020.[26] The ice shelf has shrunk from 4,445 square miles in 1995 to 618 square miles. Glaciers are melting not only at the poles but throughout the world. This will inevitably lead to higher sea levels, though it is not clear exactly how high they will rise. Wagner and Weitzman write that the melting of "Greenland and the West Antarctic ice sheets alone already raise sea levels by up to one centimeter each decade. If the Greenland ice sheet fully melted, sea levels would rise 7 meters (23 feet). Full melting of the West Antarctic ice sheet would add another 3.3 meters (11 feet)."[27] This said, current predictions indicate that with current levels of global warming the sea levels will rise three feet by the end of this century. This may not seem like a great deal, but it is. Coastal cities will experience significant flooding, if not become uninhabitable, which, in turn, will cause huge migrations of people and loss of arable land for agricultural production. Indeed, some places are already experiencing significant problems due to rising sea levels.[28]

Let's remain with the oceans and the climate. The oceans have functioned as CO_2 storage containers, but with increasing CO_2 emissions the oceans will become more acidic, with devastating effects on coral reefs[29] (already happening) and fish populations.[30] Changes in ocean temperature will also increase the intensity and breadth of storms, or what are called extreme weather events, which have resulted and will result in destruction of property and lives.[31] Not only will these storms affect coastal regions (e.g., through flooding), but they will also impact other areas by virtue of changes

24. Ibid.
25. Wagner and Weitzman, *Climate Shock*, 23—26.
26. Imam, "NASA: 10,000-Year-Old Antarctic Ice Shelf."
27. Wagner and Weitzman, *Climate Shock*, 56–57.
28. See Lewis, ""Disaster after Disaster Hits Marshall Islands."
29. See Union of Concerned Scientists, "Early Warning Signs."
30. See D News, "Climate Change Has Raised Ocean Acidity."
31. See Union of Concerned Scientists, "Global Warming Impacts."

in weather patterns that will affect places far from the coast. Some areas may get excessive amounts of rainfall, while other areas will become more arid, experiencing what is called desertification.[32] Extreme weather events will no longer be anomalies that happen every one hundred years. As Governor Andrew Cuomo remarked to President Obama, "We have a 100-year flood every two years."[33] And for those areas of the continent that will become drier for long periods of time, there will be concurrent losses in agriculture and diminishing water supplies in some areas, resulting in enormous economic losses.[34] Flooding, drought, and massive storm damage likely will result in migration of economically desperate people to less stricken areas. Saskia Sassen points out that 6.5 million people in Bangladesh have already been displaced by climate change and rising sea levels.[35] Also, Mozambique has had to resettle its climate-displaced population, though with other attending environmental, social and economic difficulties.[36] Migrations will and do result when places become uninhabitable or unable to sustain life for large numbers of people. With the movement of peoples come untold losses and sufferings.

Most of us who have not yet been directly impacted by the effects of global warming have observed, from a distance, the human suffering that results from massive storms such as Hurricane Sandy, Typhoon Haiyan (killing six thousand) or Typhoon Bopha (displacing 1.8 million). These natural disasters, which are in part linked to global warming are intertwined with economic and political systems and structures, which frequently exacerbate human suffering. Saskia Sassen remarks that "we face shrinking economies in much of the world, escalating destructions of the biosphere all over the globe, and the reemergence of extreme forms of poverty and brutalization."[37] She argues that "predatory 'formations,' a mix of elites and systemic capacities with finance as a key enabler" are increasingly involved in brutal expulsions from what she calls life spaces, which can be homes, habitable areas of cities, and so forth.[38] Parenti likewise argues that there is a "collision of political, economic, and environmental disasters," which he

32. See U.N.E.S.C.O., Ecological Sciences for Sustainable Development; http://www.unesco.org/mab/doc/ekocd/chapter4.html.

33. In Wagner and Weitzman, *Climate Shock*, 2.

34. Union of Concerned Scientists, "Causes of Drought."

35. Sassen, *Expulsions*, 62.

36. Ibid., 63.

37. Ibid., 12.

38. Ibid., 13.

calls the catastrophic convergence.[39] This does not necessarily mean that some human beings are taking advantage of other persons' vulnerabilities, as in the case of economic exploitation such as price gouging.[40] To be sure, this does happen, but Parenti and Sassen are identifying and describing systemic networks of power that provide security for the privileged while brutally expelling the less privileged from life spaces. Stated differently, the real impacts of global warming, in partnership with "Global North's use and abuse of the Global South," destabilize some societies and nation-states.[41] And instability leads to greater insecurity, violence, and oppression as people scramble to survive—something the Pentagon report clearly notes. Parenti writes:

> Between the Tropic of Capricorn and the Tropic of Cancer lies what I call the *Tropic of Chaos*, a belt of economically and politically battered postcolonial states girding the planet's mid-latitudes. In this band, around the tropics, climate change is beginning to hit hard. The societies in this belt are also heavily dependent on agriculture and fishing, thus very vulnerable to shifts in weather patterns. This region was also on the front lines of the Cold War and of neoliberal economic restructuring. As a result, in this belt we find clustered most of the failed or semi-failed states of the developing world.[42]

Parenti and Sassen are highlighting the reality that catastrophes of global warming are exacerbated by political and economic systems (e.g., neoliberal capitalism) that rely on violence, oppression, and marginalization to secure privileges for the few. In short, we cannot adequately address the consequences of global warming without also taking into account the political and economic networks or systems of power that add to the catastrophic effects of global warming.

Rising temperatures, melting glaciers, rising ocean levels, more acidic oceans, desertification, flooding, extreme weather events, loss of habitable locales, and loss of arable lands are some of the ongoing and predicted consequences of global warming—consequences accompanied by tremendous human suffering. I cannot leave this topic without also acknowledging the principal sources for both global warming and human suffering that Parenti, Klein, and Sassen identify—the Global North and invasive neoliberal

39. Parenti, *The Tropic of Chaos*, 7.
40. See Sandel, *Justice*, 4.
41. Ibid., 8.
42. Ibid., 9.

capitalism.[43] To be sure, those of us in the Global North contribute to global warming in numerous ways. I drive to work. My wife and I fly to Vancouver to take a cruise to Alaska. I fly to conferences. I live in a temperature-controlled home that requires electrical energy—burning fossil fuels. Of course, we can all find ways to reduce our carbon footprint, yet when it comes to global warming, I am reminded of the phrase, "all have sinned." While I appreciate the focus on how we can all work together to mitigate global warming, this can be a distraction from critiquing and changing more systemic culprits in global warming and human suffering. Naomi Klein's compelling book depicts numerous examples of how state-corporate capitalism contributes to global warming and actively impedes local and national efforts to reduce carbon emissions and other greenhouse gases. Hedges and Sacco also identify sacrifice zones throughout the United States where people and their lands are devastated by exploitive corporations that receive the blessings of political and business leaders. For instance, they describe Welch, West Virginia, which was exploited by coal mining companies that left polluted waterways, toxic coal dams, devastated landscapes, and pervasive negative health effects.[44] Parenti also argues that neoliberal capitalism, which has been forcefully expanded throughout the world over the last five decades, has led to unstable and dependent governments in the Global South, as well as a great deal of violence and brutality.[45] These authors contend that neoliberal capitalism or state-corporate capitalism—as an economic and political system with networks of political, social, and economic power—is largely to blame for the ongoing contribution to global warming and its consequences. This system also actively blocks necessary changes that would benefit the common good of all people and not merely the Global North.

Contrary voices, such as Wagner and Wietzman, differ. They argue that "it's capitalism with all of its innovative and entrepreneurial powers that is our only hope of steering clear of the looming climate shock."[46] According to them, all we need to do is to give the invisible hand of the market free rein to reduce carbon emissions through carbon taxing, leaving neoliberal

43. Hardt and Negri discuss in their book *Empire* the networks of power related to empire and capitalism with the United States as the linchpin. They do not discuss global warming, but clearly their depiction of modern empire reveals the entrenched networks of power that ignore the common good and that are sources of oppression, alienation, and marginalization for millions of people.

44. Hedges and Sacco. *Days of Destruction, Days of Revolt*, 115–75.

45. Parenti, *The Tropic of Chaos*.

46. Wagner and Weitzman. *Climate Shock*, 151.

capitalism uncriticized and the economic-political system unchanged.[47] This view is naïve in the extreme and ahistorical, not only because it overlooks the history and nature of capitalism, but also because it eschews innumerable examples of political-economic elites—past and present—serving as obstacles to reducing carbon emissions and at the same time exploiting people and the earth. While we can agree that an entrepreneurial spirit, energy, and innovation seem to accompany capitalism,[48] nevertheless capitalism focuses on short-term profits, expansion of profits, and privatization; it also tends to foster greed, hubris, and lust for political and economic power. Moreover, Wagner and Weitzman clearly avoid the following problem in their book: retaining an unchanged economic system that has been responsible for huge increases in greenhouse gases with few contributions to reductions, overlooks the critical notion of the common good—a notion that does not inform neoliberal capitalism.

In summary, clear consensus exists among climate scientists that the earth is warming primarily due to human activities implicated in the rise of greenhouse gases. While science provides evidence for warming, it is more difficult to predict with accuracy the consequences of climate change. Some areas of the world may experience some short-term benefits, but many scientists predict extreme weather patterns, flooding, and desertification. These predictions are based on what is taking place today across the planet. Natural disasters and the increase of uninhabitable land will create huge economic costs and lead to the migration of millions of people. These changes will create instability and insecurity within and between nations and will likely be accompanied by violence and brutality, especially toward vulnerable populations. Again, these predictions are also linked to what is already happening in many countries today—countries that are already encountering the effects of climate change.

Given the realities and consequences of climate change, we know now more than perhaps ever before that care of the polis includes care of the earth, both locally and globally. Moreover, the care of persons is inextricably yoked to care for the earth and its climate. The discussion above also tells us that we must be even more vigilant with regard to care and justice in the

47. Ibid., 151. They reduce Naomi Klein's extensive analysis to one phrase; tax the rich, which is not even close to what Klein argues in her recent book on climate change.

48. Wagner and Weitzman, *Climate Shock*, make an error in logic when they associate creativity and innovation with capitalism, as if capitalism is the condition for creativity and innovation. Human beings are creative and innovative, and it is not a fact that capitalism in and of itself fosters creativity and innovation. Moreover, they fail to ask whether capitalism stifles innovation and creativity, especially when we consider those who do not benefit from it.

years ahead. By this I mean several things. First, to be forewarned is to be forearmed. That is, we are already seeing that individuals and communities are suffering as a result of the effects of global warming. In addition, we know that institutions and systems exacerbate human suffering by exploiting vulnerable populations. *Altercapitalist* and *alterempire* faith communities can through critique, education, and protest, spiritually defy regimes and systems that contribute to global warming and so exploit vulnerable populations locally and internationally.[49] Living as an altercapitalist, aliterempire community may include assisting climate refugees, whether from one's own polis or from other nations. Faith communities, in short, must take up the task of caring for the earth and for its citizens. This is an ethical demand—a categorical imperative—that derives, not from the theological belief that humans have dominion over the earth (which has clearly proven to be an illusion), but rather from the biblical notion of stewardship of the earth, which involves hearing and responding to the groans of the earth and its inhabitants (including from our fellow creatures in the animal kingdom) who suffer from the consequences of climate change. The biblical practice of stewardship places ethical and spiritual demands on our shoulders, including that we attend critically to and take action to influence local, national, and international matters that either negatively or positively impact climate change. A question that emerges from this existential-ethical demand is whether we can enshrine this in our state and national constitutions, making it a part of our institutions, legislation, policies, and so forth.

HEALTH CARE

Most of us think of health care in terms of having access to medical professionals and institutions. Of course this is an important feature, but health care also covers access to and education about healthy foods, clean water and air, adequate public facilities for walking and other forms of exercise (e.g., sidewalks, parks, and pools), and adequate, safe housing. People who suffer from food insecurity, who do not have access to and cannot afford healthy foods, who live near polluting factories, who are exposed to polluted water, and who live in crowded inadequate housing far from public parks will suffer from more physical and mental illnesses, while having less access to medical care.[50] Health care, then, involves much of life in the polis and it is clear that classism and racism negatively impact individuals and

49. See Myers, *Spiritual Defiance.*

50. See American Psychological Association, "Ethnic and Racial Minorities."

communities in each of these areas.[51] For example, asthma, hypertension, diabetes, obesity, heart disease, cancer, mental illness, and a host of other maladies disproportionally affect persons in the lower classes and people of color.[52]

To narrow the focus to medical care, the passage of the Affordable Care Act (ACA) has increased the number of people who now have insurance, and in some states Medicaid enrollment has expanded. On its face this is good news and, one could argue, a step in the right direction of providing universal access to health care. Let's examine this with greater scrutiny, because it overlooks systemic, philosophical, and theological problem with how health care is understood in the United States. First of all the number of uninsured dropped to fewer than 32 million in 2014 as a result of the ACA. Yet, this number remains high because people who do not qualify for Medicaid said they could not afford health care insurance even with assistance from the government.[53] Moreover, it is estimated that over 32 million people who have health care insurance are underinsured, leaving them exposed to crushing medical expenses.[54] Indeed, Dan Mangan writes that over two million Americans file for bankruptcy due to their inability to pay their medical bills, and approximately 56 million persons between the ages of nineteen and sixty-four will struggle to pay their medical bills.[55] I have personally come across this reality with some frequency over the years, listening to young and old alike who are stressed because they are not only underinsured but struggling to pay for needed medical procedures and medicines.

For those of us who are fortunate to have good health insurance coverage, our medical health care is some of the best in the world. Still, for those who are not insured or who are underinsured, claims about the quality of health care ring hollow. Consider David Squires's detailed comparison of U.S. health care with twelve other industrialized nations. Studies repeatedly show that while the U.S. significantly outspends other industrialized nations on health care; the leading health indicators rank the U.S. near the bottom.[56]

51. See Alder and Newman, "Socioeconomic Disparities in Health." See also the website called *The Effects of Poverty on Health*, and especially the webpage there called "The Relationship between Poverty and Health": http://theeffectsofpovertyonhealth.weebly.com/relationship-between-poverty-and-health.html/.

52. See Center for Disease Control and Prevention, "Health, United States, 2015—Poverty."

53. See Kaiser Family Foundation, "Key Facts about the Uninsured Population."

54. See Shoen et al., "America's Underinsured."

55. Mangan, "Medical Bills Are the Biggest Cause of U.S. Bankruptcies."

56. Squires, "The U.S. Health System in Perspective."

Indeed, when compared to nations around the world, the U.S. is 37th for overall health care system performance.[57] So while the ACA has helped, there are underlying systemic problems with health care in the U.S.

The fundamental problem in health care is the economic system that undergirds it. For decades the U.S. medical system has been privatized and any talk of single-payer systems or government-run health care for all people triggers a media and political storm. Capitalism is sacrosanct, and everything else is categorized as socialism or negatively compared to other nations that have health care for all. The rise of neoliberal capitalism in the 1970s has only exacerbated this trend, which means 32 million uninsured citizens and 56 million underinsured people are simply out of luck. A capitalistic-run medical system is problematic for several reasons. First and foremost, it is unseemly at best to profit from people's misery and vulnerability, especially when we consider that it is extremely difficult to "shop around for the best deal" when you are in need of health care. Also, even people who are not in need of immediate care and who can shop around are often not in the position of having enough knowledge about the "product" to make an informed decision. Nevertheless, even if people are well-informed, making a profit is unseemly and, worse, theologically unethical. Can we imagine the Good Samaritan returning to make the injured man not only pay for his care but to increase the Samaritan's profit margin? This is not to say that medical care providers should not be well compensated for their work, but to seek making a profit from people needing medical care violates the very principle of the notion of care (and justice) from either a philosophical or theological perspective.[58] Acts of caring for people in need are ideally motivated by a desire to aid the person who is suffering, like the Good Samaritan. This does not mean that a secondary motive to be compensated is not present, but compensation is not equivalent to the motivation for profit.

In the U.S. health care system, the pursuit of profit is a more systemic issue than discrete acts of care by nurses and doctors. A nurse caring for the patient at the bedside may manifest a motivation to care and has no thought of profiting. A surgeon likewise seeks to provide care for the very same patient. So it may appear that capitalism and its profit motive does not interfere with direct care, and that would be partly correct. However, the ethos of capitalism, with its fetishizing profit, inevitably corrupts care by putting pressure on medical staff and organizations to pursue profits by finding ways to cut costs and raise prices. One might counter that there are

57. Hill, "Not-For Profit vs. Profit Health Care."

58. Andre and Velasquez, "A Healthy Bottom Line."

not-for-profit health care companies, yet these companies garner significant profits[59] (consider also CEO salaries at these not-for profit companies[60]), and they also operate out of the capitalistic system and its values (profit, market expansion). If profit is the focus, then care is secondary, which does not *necessarily* mean that patients are not adequately cared for by individual nurses and doctors. Rather, the larger system is geared toward profit, so instead of three patients per nurse, it is more profitable to assign five or six patients, which raises risk factors vis-à-vis patient care. And of course, there are all kinds of stories about patients being prematurely discharged from hospitals because their staying would be economically ill-advised.[61] Moreover, any system that excludes 32 million citizens (not counting undocumented persons) and places financial burdens and stresses on more than 56 million others is fundamentally flawed, precisely because it impairs the health of citizens. And this flaw is the capitalistic ethos.

As I noted in chapter 6, the ethos of the capitalistic system does not fit well with the philosophical (or humanistic) and theological values associated with care. First, no notion of care is part of the capitalistic framework, and if it does appear, it is imported and becomes commodified—as in the case of the health care system. This said, existential and theological renderings of care resist commodification and monetary exchange. A hospital emergency room, for instance, cannot turn away a patient who cannot pay for the services. It is inconceivable for most people to have someone who is in desperate need of medical care be refused because she has no money to pay for the services and products. Of course, the hospital will do what it can to recoup lost revenue, but it would be shocking to most people to have a health care system that is run strictly by capitalistic rules of profit and exchange. If it were, the person would be refused care because she could not pay for the service. In a capitalistic system, if you do not have the funds to purchase the product, then you do not get it. Medicare and Medicaid are programs that at least point to the principle of care such that those who cannot afford to pay for medical care should still receive it. We as a society have accepted the idea that people in need of medical care who do not have the resources to pay for it should still get care, yet we are chained to an economic system that resists and undermines this value. So we have taken the square peg of capitalism and forcibly jammed it into a round hole of health care.

59. Hill, "Not-For Profit vs. Profit Health Care."

60. Landen, "Another Year of Pay Hikes for Non-Profit Hospital CEOs."

61. A quick Internet search on the reasons for and consequences of hospitals' premature discharging of patients yields hundreds of websites—many of which deal with malpractice.

This leads to a related issue concerning language and the use of language to construct a particular reality that corrupts care. Numerous articles on health care use terms such as *products* and *consumers*. Hospitals and pharmaceutical companies, for instance, offer an array of products and commodified services that are available for consumers to choose. This language corrupts the existential reality of persons in need of care. Individuals seeking care are patients who are not purchasing products but rather seeking caregivers to diagnose and treat them. There is a vast difference between going in to explore the various TV products at an electronics store and going to a doctor because one ill. I can choose to buy this or that TV or not to buy a TV, and the negative consequences of not doing so are nonexistent. This can also be seen in terms of my having greater agency. I am clearly not vulnerable, because I do not need a TV to meet my survival or flourishing needs. This is not the case for most people who need medical care. They are vulnerable because of their physical and mental distress. Their anxiety and illness can easily cloud reason and agency. Of course one could decide not to purchase the "product" at the doctor's office, but the consequences might be serious. The person who needs medical care is a patient who is vulnerable; s/he is not a consumer! Moreover, diagnosis and treatment are not products; they are part of the process of caring for an individual in need.

By way of a counter illustration, a friend who was vacationing in France fell down a flight of stairs. After being treated in the emergency room at a French hospital, he asked the doctor how much he owed the hospital. The doctor was taken aback and replied that there was no charge. She went on to say that the French people believe that everyone deserves health care and that through taxes the government is able to provide it. My friend was relieved, not simply because he did not have to pay, but also because he was not going to have to deal with tons of paperwork and bureaucracy from his insurance company in the U.S. In this French hospital the profit motive was completely absent and the health care professionals were able to focus their attention on caring for people in need of treatment.[62]

Medical care in the U.S. will continue to fail to meet needs of many people as long as it is tethered to a capitalistic system—a system that undermines care and justice. Untethering is not likely to happen anytime

62. We have all heard capitalists say that these government-run operations are not efficient precisely because there is no profit motive that would make the system become more efficient. Any cursory review of the soaring health care costs in the U.S. and of the profits and high salaries of health care executives would pour cold water on the capitalists' heated claim. As I indicated above, the fact that the U.S. significantly outspends Western countries (such as France) and continues to have 32 million people without insurance and 56 million underinsured people reveals that a capitalistically run system does not work efficiently.

soon because of the number of profit and not-for-profit companies that are currently dependent on the capitalistic system for their operations. In the meantime, medical bankruptcies should be abolished. People who cannot afford medical care or who are underinsured should be aided by the government via expanding Medicaid and Medicare; such expansion would require increasing taxes, including on corporations.[63] The government can also provide incentives for cooperative health care organizations, which eschew making profits while seeking to provide lower costs for their members. Finally, health care should be a human right and made part of the Bill of Rights. This would not necessarily eliminate inequities, but we would at least have it as a goal to work toward. Moreover, if health care were considered a human right, then citizens, especially the 32 million who do not have health care, might rise up and demand it. Finally, as I stated at the outset of this section, health care is broader than medical access. People should have adequate access to healthy foods, education about dietary needs, clean water, adequate housing, and safe places to exercise. All of this would require local, state, and national governments to work to make these possible for those who are excluded because of income and skin color. *Alterempire* and *altercapitalist* communities of faith can find ways to join this process and to defy legislation that impedes these goals. At the same time, these communities may work together to find ways to help provide healthy food, clean water, and the like.[64]

EDUCATION

While in previous centuries education was largely for children of the political and economic elite, contemporary democratic and industrialized nations recognize that the education of all its citizens is vital for both democracy and the economy. To care for the polis requires caring about the education of the next generation. To care about education is to raise myriad questions about the methods and aims (cultural, technological, or what have you) of education vis-à-vis children's survival and flourishing needs.

63. Individuals and corporations tell political leaders and local communities that if you raise taxes, corporations will move to other countries that are more favorable. This threat can be countered by sanctions levied against those companies that want to do business in the U.S. but maintain their headquarters offshore to protect their profits. We need to remember that during the years of a Keynesian-run economy higher taxes provided the government funds to complete massive infrastructure projects, which, in turn, aided the economy and the common good.

64. I know of ten faith communities in my city that coordinate with local farmers to provide fresh vegetables and fruit to people in poorer sections of the city.

In the United States education is a deeply complex and contested topic accompanied by issues and questions such as social class, race, religion, what subjects and content are being taught, testing, teacher qualifications, and, of course, funding. The complexity of this and other issues in this chapter means that my treatment of this topic will be cursory. Yet, I treat it because it is a topic not often addressed by pastoral theologians and rarely by political theologians. The premise that undergirds my discussion of education is that all citizens share responsibility to care for the next generations' education, not simply for the sake of the survival and flourishing of individuals, but for the polis itself. With this premise in mind, I consider care and education in light of privatization, class and race, discipline, and the politics of nationalism. I conclude with a few thoughts about restoring care vis-à-vis quality education for all children.

The privatization of education and state defunding of higher education has followed the rise of neoliberal capitalism.[65] This rise runs parallel to the decline in the notion of public education, which is viewed in increasingly negative ways. A 2011 Gallup poll showed public confidence in K-12 education falling to 29 percent. In 1973 it had been 58 percent.[66] There are many reasons for this drop, not the least of which is the successful bashing of public schools and teachers by Democrat and Republican neoliberals and, correspondingly, their laudatory promotion of charter schools. Jesse Hagopian notes that President Obama's secretary of education, Arne Duncan, doggedly pushed "for charter schools—schools publicly funded by taxpayers, yet run privately, outside the control of local school boards—and merit pay schemes where teachers are paid according to student test scores."[67] The constant drumbeat about the glories of charter schools is clearly false hype. Hagopian cites "a massive study by Stanford University, looking at data covering 70 percent of all charter school students nationally, found that bad charter schools outnumber good ones by a ratio of roughly 2 to 1—and an astonishing 83 percent of charter schools were either no better, or worse than, traditional public schools."[68] This study pours cold water on claims that charter schools and other schemes of privatization will save or are saving American education for its youth.

It is not just that charter schools are not measuring up to their hype. There are other inherent problems with privatization. The notion of public

65. Giroux, *Dangerous Thinking*, 128–32. For a more detailed analysis, see Lippman, "Neoliberal Education Restructuring."

66. Williams, "Perceptions of Public Schools."

67. Hagopian, "Schooling Arne Duncan."

68. Ibid.

education is part of the polis's responsibility for caring for its youth. By *polis*, I am referring to the state and its people. Local and state school boards ideally represent the voters' obligation to care about the education of the youth. Yet, as noted above, private schools are not accountable to local or state school boards. Of course they must comply with state and national regulations and standards, but they escape ties to local elected officials. To be sure, they are responsible to the parents whose children attend the school, and parents likely feel concerned about the individual charter school their children attend. This said, in a polis, all citizens are obliged to care for children's education. Moreover, educators and institutions are obliged to fulfill their duties vis-à-vis the polis's care for the educational needs of its children. Privatization removes education from the public realm, loosening the accountability ties between the people and the education of children, as well as the responsibility of state and national political institutions. The problem with private education is analogous to the problem with profit-driven health care. On its face, it is unseemly to seek to profit from children's need for education.[69] While schools have always been concerned about budgets, introducing the idea of profit tends to add a variable that corrupts the idea of public education. Do we want to frame education in terms of turning out good products when we talk about graduation rates? Are students consumers? Are we to profit from students' education? And what does it mean to secure profits in relation to poor students? Does profiting from students come at the expense of students and their parents or the government, or both? How does the notion of profit impact educational programs? Would decisions be made to cut arts education since it negatively impacts the bottom line? Worse, private schools with their language of profit, products, and so forth function as one more disciplinary regime aimed at producing entrepreneurial individuals,[70] more fitted to what Charles Derber and Yale Magrass call a militarized economy than to a democratic polis.[71]

Another perennial problem is that not all children have the same or even close to the same opportunities for education, which means issues of class[72] and race[73] continue to operate in the educational system in decidedly negative ways. This problem did not arise with neoliberalism and

69. See Derber and Magrass, *Bully Nation*, 142–45.

70. This is the case for schools that educate children in the benefits of capitalism, but not for schools in poorer sections of the city that tend to mirror lockdown facilities. See Giroux, *Dangerous Thinking*, 114–16.

71. Derber and Magrass, *Bully Nation*, 103–12.

72. Garland, "When Class Becomes More Important."

73. Orfield, "Race and Schools."

privatization, but it is exacerbated by them.[74] Consider top educator Arne Duncan's turnaround plan, which called for closing five thousand schools, something he had done in Chicago with very negative results for students' education and local communities.[75] Add to this the struggles of poor children and children of color "whose labor is unneeded, who are locked out of the commodity market, and who often inhabit the impoverished and soul-crushing margins of society."[76] These children, Henry Giroux writes, are subject "to harsh disciplinary controls" and schools that "neither educate nor provide even minimal training for the workplace. Instead, they simply mimic traditional lockdown institutions."[77] Indeed, schools over the last twenty years have increasingly partnered with police and private security firms to enforce discipline—a responsibility once held by teachers and school administrators.[78] Disciplinary education often involves zero-tolerance policies (policies that lead to more suspensions and expulsions), which disproportionately impact poor students of color. Indeed, the American Civil Liberties Union (ACLU) has documented widespread disparities in the court system's treatment of black youths.[79] Researcher Russell Skiba outlines the abject failure of zero tolerance programs.[80] These programs do not reduce school problems; they create even more problems, through expulsions and suspensions, for students who most need help.

Many of us might imagine that the involvement of law enforcement and the judicial system in students' education occurs in high school, but Giroux points to examples of young children being arrested, handcuffed, and shackled.[81] We might also imagine that the use of law enforcement means the infractions are serious. Giroux indicates that the "Chicago School System in 2003 had over 8000 students arrested, often for trivial infractions such as pushing, tardiness, and using spitballs."[82] He also notes the Denver school system had "a 71% increase in the number of student referrals to law enforcement, many for non-violent behavior."[83] One could only imagine the outrage of parents and politicians if these children were white middle-class

74. Giroux, *Zombie Politics,* 114.

75. Ibid.

76. Ibid., 113.

77. Ibid., 113, 114.

78. Ibid., 135.

79. American Civil Liberties Union, "Racial Disparities in Sentencing."

80. Skiba, "The Failure of Zero Tolerance," 27–33.

81. Giroux, *Zombie Politics and Culture in the Age of Casino Capitalism,* 125–26.

82. Ibid., 127.

83. Ibid.

students. Of course, we can acknowledge that caring for children requires some discipline, but zero-tolerance policies and the use of law enforcement distorts the notion of both education and discipline by divorcing it from care rooted in the recognition and treatment of children as persons—unique, inviolable, immeasurably valued, responsive subjects. Can students learn very well when they are under stress from excessive discipline, surveillance, food insecurity, and poor facilities?

One other problem with education emerges out of and is corrupted by the legacy of U.S. exceptionalism and imperialism, and what I call the politics of nationalism. Giroux describes a case where in "2014 the newly elected conservative Jefferson County[, Colorado] school board called for revamping the curriculum for the district's Advanced Placement history courses on the grounds that they were teaching acts of civil disobedience, which they labeled as unpatriotic."[84] The school board proposed a revised curriculum "that would 'promote citizenship, patriotism, essentials of the free-market system, respect for authority and respect for individual rights.'"[85] It is clear that the school board is threatened by education that calls into question the glories and exceptionalism of the United States as a capitalistic hegemon. Citizenship, in their worldview, involves uncritical and unthinking obedience to patriotic authority—a nationalistic way of organizing a polis. As Giroux points out, critical thinking is itself deemed to be a threat to the nationalistic order. What is taught is the dogma of American exceptionalism, patriotism, and capitalism. Critical thinking, social justice, the common good, social responsibility, and civil disobedience—features necessary for a vital democratic polis—are set aside and demeaned. Remarkably, the Texas Republican party in 2012 included the following in its party platform: "We oppose teaching Higher order Thinking Skills [because they] have the purpose of challenging students' fixed beliefs and undermining parental control."[86] These fixed beliefs are not simply religious (e.g., creationism); they include a jingoistic (racially coded) patriotism and unquestioning acceptance of capitalism. This approach to education, Henry Giroux rightly argues, leads to an age of uncritical thinking, authoritarianism, and the eclipse of compassion.

From the perspective of care, the politics of nationalism is not really concerned for individual students' education. To care for children means helping them to think for themselves, which involves cultivating

84. Giroux, *Dangerous Thinking*, 14.

85. Ibid., 15.

86. Ibid., 14.

imagination and critical thinking.[87] A good enough parent wants his/her child to eventually grow up and use higher order critical thinking skills to make decisions. This is at times challenging because children will critique and may even thoughtfully reject the parents' cherished beliefs and values. Parents who want their children to slavishly adopt their beliefs and values signify a significant problem in differentiation, but more important, distort care by trying to keep children from making their own decisions. A society that undermines critical thinking and the teaching of civil disobedience is concerned foremost with forcing or coercing children to adopt their narrow vision of society. This is a distorted view of care because it dismisses difference, individuality, freedom, intellectual exploration, and creativity. Moreover, it equates care and education with the adoption of the dogma of American exceptionalism and patriotism. For those children and adults who resist, care will be eclipsed by hostility, harsh discipline, public shaming, and rejection.

Education is essential to the survival and flourishing of children. Children need to learn to survive in the polis, but it is just as important to learn to flourish. Teaching survival and flourishing does not involve simply introducing children to arts education, but also inviting children to imagine and teaching them to think critically about issues political, economic, and social. This is what it means to care for children. This does not mean that children are not introduced to the social and cultural mores, but because their future is the future of the polis, they must learn to think critically about what they are being taught. They will be the ones who will eventually lead the polis, and they will not be equipped to do so if they are unable to think critically, if they are unable to imagine a polis different from the one they were born into. Yet to educate the next generation is a public good that is labor intensive and costly. For this reason, education should not be held captive to the ethos of capitalism. The education of children should not serve the market; the market should serve the children. Moreover, children of lower classes and children of color should not be sacrificed on the altars of militarism and empire, or what we euphemistically call security and freedom. The trillions of dollars spent on the military, wars, and the alphabet soup of private and governmental surveillance and intelligence organizations means there is less money available for education, especially for the education of children who are being deprived of it due to their class and race. Herein lies the seed of the fall of the empire. A nation most interested in its extension of political

87. Derber and Magrass, *Bully Nation*, 140–42, point out that there is a two-tiered education system based on class. Members of the upper class are encouraged to imagine and think creatively (not critically), while the underclasses are policed and supervised.

and economic power will neglect its children, and in this process of expansion and neglect, the polis will not flourish.

In the twentieth and twenty-first centuries, most citizens would agree that education is critical. All children should have access to and opportunities for K-12 and higher education. Like health care, quality education should be enshrined in the Bill of Rights. Children have a right to a quality education, regardless of their social class, gender, ethnicity, or color. And citizens likewise have a responsibility to provide this. We also need to reframe education not only in terms of social justice, but also in terms of care—a care that involves a critical imagination.[88] We know that good enough parents care deeply about their children's education, whether they make five hundred thousand, fifty thousand, or five thousand dollars. It is this care that obliges parents to help their children obtain an education that enables them to meet their survival and flourishing needs, as well as the survival and flourishing needs of others in the polis and beyond. And it is the responsibility of all citizens to care for the next generation.

THE JUDICIAL SYSTEM

With the rise of neoliberal capitalism in the late 1970s, the educational system was not the only public good that was aggressively privatized. The penal system was also being privatized, which, not surprisingly, was accompanied by increasing prison populations.[89] Penal profits extend to people on parole and undocumented persons. Consider that in 1980, under two million people were in the judicial system (prison, jail, probation, and parole), with around two hundred thousand in prison. While the overall numbers of people in the penal system has declined *slightly* since 2009, it is still just under 7 million with over 2.3 million in prison and jail.[90] From 1970 to 2005, the prison population grew by 700 percent.[91] Per capita, the United States leads other nations in incarcerating citizens. Not even a totalitarian capitalistic state like China can compare to the U.S. rate of incarceration. This unprecedented rise accompanied the corporatization of the judicial system.

The penal system is generally not much of a concern to corporate media outlets unless it is titillated by the arrest of a celebrity or politician. Otherwise, most of the people caught up in this system generally do not rate the public's care or concern. Out of sight of the polis, out of mind. "Why

88. See Giroux, *Dangerous Thinking*.

89. Gottschalk, *Caught*, 25–78.

90. See United States Department of Justice, "Key Statistic."

91. Hedges, "The Prison State of America."

should we care? These people deserve what they get," someone might reply. "Crime in my part of the city is down, so why should we change anything?" Caring might truly begin if Christians start upholding the biblical injunction to care for the least of these (including people in prison) and taking time to understand the problems associated with the current penal system. More particularly, the polis's judicial system reflects troubling issues associated with the polis itself and, in this case, the prevalence of cruelty,[92] public indifference, and rank injustice[93] are symptoms of a polis in which care is undermined and justice is emptied of meaning.

To echo my comments about the privatization of health care, it is unseemly to profit from persons' suffering, and it is even more indecorous to exploit people who have few rights, no voice, and few resources. Chris Hedges reports that "Corrections Corporation of America, the largest owner of for-profit prisons and immigration detention facilities in the country, had revenues of $1.7 billion in 2013 and profits of $300 million."[94] How are these profits made? Gabrielle Canon's research reveals that private prison companies shift sick and older prisoners to federally operated prisons, thus increasing their profits by reducing medical costs while increasing costs to the state.[95] Prisons also become places where companies have a pool of "free" labor. "The wages paid to prisoners for labor inside prisons," Hedges notes, "have remained stagnant and in real terms have declined over the past three decades. In New Jersey a prisoner made $1.20 for eight hours of work—yes, eight hours of work—in 1980 and today makes $1.30 for a day's labor." Prisoners in private prisons make as little as 17 cents an hour.[96] The motivation for profit also means that private companies will find ways to increase the prison population[97] (through "tough" sentencing laws, confinement of undocumented immigrants, and cutting programs that reduce recidivism), charge higher fees to the government, reduce costly programs, and find ways to exploit the labor of prisoners. All of this is accomplished in

92. All kinds of cruelty go on in prisons. See Taylor, *The Executed God*, 101–10. It is easier to engage in cruel practices when prisoners are demeaned by the wider public and when prisons remain out of the public spotlight and thus are not held accountable.

93. While I do not address a number of problems with the judicial system, I do note here that in most cities people from the lower classes and people of color are not provided with competent legal representation, which often leads to extended prison sentences and fines. CNN reported that in Chicago less than 1 percent of persons arrested on the south side of the city were provided legal representation. Flores, "In Chicago."

94. Hedges, "The Prison State of America."

95. Gabrielle, "Here's the Latest Evidence."

96. Hedges, "The Prison State of America."

97. Alexander, *The New Jim Crow*, 219.

collusion with political leaders who wrongly believe that private companies are more economically efficient. Hedges discovered that "for-profit prison corporations spent an estimated $45 million over a recent 10-year period for lobbying."[98] We can be sure that the $45 million was not aimed at lobbying for improvements in health care or education for prisoners. But we should not place the entire blame for cruelty and exploitation on prison corporations. Political leaders, under the guise of "get tough" policies, support legislation and programs that directly or indirectly line corporate coffers. James Gilligan and his colleagues researched some of the few prison programs that provided college education to prisoners. Their research showed that over a period of thirty years, these programs had a 1 percent rate for recidivism compared to the typical 65 percent rate.[99] This is extraordinary. After the research was publicized, several state legislatures and the U.S. Congress decided to cut funding for these programs, arguing that prisoners should not receive these benefits, and uncovering the truth that the U.S. acts as a punishing state.[100] Gilligan considered these to be irrational and self-defeating policies,[101] but they are rational if one recognizes that eliminating education programs from prisons ensured that private prison companies would have a more secure supply of "product" (i.e., more prisoners) to exploit. The cruelty embedded in these decisions is stunning.

It is not simply that we have created a punishing state;[102] the punishing state is wedded to corporate cruelty and public amnesia. Many of us think that when a person who commits a crime and serves a sentence, justice is achieved. Ignore for the moment the extrajudicial punishments (e.g., solitary confinement, prison guards use of beatings, rape, and other cruelties) and corporate exploitation of prisoners serving time, and turn attention to what happens after men and women are released. Persons who have served their sentences find it very difficult to find work because most businesses require background checks or that forms be filled out that ask applicants if they have a criminal record. As Michelle Alexander notes, "Nearly every state allows private employers to discriminate on the basis of past criminal conviction."[103] This discrimination also extends to housing, making it very difficult for persons who have served their time to find an adequate

98. Ibid.

99. Gilligan, *Why Some Politicians Are More Dangerous Than Others*, 90–91.

100. See Gottschalk, *Caught*, 98–116.

101. Ibid., 92.

102. Giroux, *Dangerous Thinking*, 48–61.

103. Alexander, *The New Jim Crow*, 146.

place to live.[104] Those ex-prisoners who are fortunate enough to obtain a job quickly discover that fees are owed to various agencies. Alexander reports that some of these pre- and postconviction fees result in the garnishment of wages, adding yet another punishing obstacle to an ex-prisoner's societal reintegration.[105] These obstacles add to the high recidivism rate and reveal an indifferent and cruel society hell-bent on punishment.

In discussing the judicial and penal systems, we cannot avoid the fact that the punishing state disproportionately impacts people of color and the poor. I recall hearing someone say that if you want to commit a crime, go to Wall Street. Even if you get caught (and that is a big if given that only one person has been convicted vis-à-vis the 2008 Wall Street meltdown), the prison sentence will be light and the prison upscale. The comment reveals issues of class and race. Michelle Alexander describes in detail how the collapse of Jim Crow laws and regulations gave way to laws that negatively affected African Americans (and Hispanics), ushering in the New Jim Crow era when African Americans (and poor Hispanics) were disproportionately affected.[106] These "get tough" laws led to mass incarceration, which Mark Taylor argues represents "a racialized state formation that entails mass exposure of racially-marked groups to premature death."[107] Citing other sources, Taylor points out that nearly 70 percent of prison populations are people of color.[108] Taylor, Alexander, and others have detailed the ways discrimination exists at every stage of the criminal justice process.[109] Alexander also describes how punishment follows one's release from prison through legal obstacles to getting a job, finding housing, paying postconfinement fees, and so forth.

When persons are publicly demeaned, when they remain out of the public eye, when they are sequestered behind physical and legal walls, when they face numerous political and economic obstacles, their voices are not heard, or if they are heard, they are quickly dismissed. Without recognition and without a voice, persons of color and persons in the lower classes become easy targets for political and economic exploitation, while the public forgets them. In the criminal justice system, care is minimal, at best—not simply because the justice system is rife with injustices, but because it is divorced from care. When the public seeks to forget or malign seven million

104. Ibid., 141–44.

105. Ibid., 150–52.

106. Ibid., 96–97.

107. Taylor, *The Executed God*, 90.

108. Ibid., 91.

109. Ibid., 95.

of its citizens, it is also saying that they do not merit care, especially if care has anything to do with the survival and flourishing needs of prisoners and ex-felons. A polis necessarily establishes a system of justice wherein some people who commit crimes face the consequences such as prison. Yet, a good enough polis does not bifurcate care and justice. Instead, a polis's judicial system weds justice with care, which is seen in offering programs for education (GED courses, college courses), in establishing fair housing laws, in removing pre- and postconviction fees for those who cannot afford them, in providing drug and alcohol rehabilitation programs, in restoring voting rights, and in proffering reentry programs. Care, as I have noted in previous chapters, is often difficult and labor-intensive. Some people need more help than others, and people who for various reasons are swept up into the judicial system require more, so that they may return to life in the polis.[110]

THE POLITICS OF EXCLUSION

I wish to end this chapter and this book by addressing a perennial pressing matter. A cursory glance at world history in general and U.S. history in particular reveals the human tendency to secure political and economic power for oneself and one's group while at the same time excluding or marginalizing other citizens of the polis. Readers might push back and say that in the course of two-hundred-plus years the U.S. has expanded the vote to nonpropertied white men, black men, and (last) women. Readers might also point to the expansion of rights that resulted from the civil rights movement and from the work of LGBTQI activists. These achievements are to be applauded, but we must recognize that they came about as a result of tremendous sacrifices and decades of struggle. Moreover, these political gains neither point to nor prove the notion of inevitable political progress, and they do not undermine the claim that human beings tend to secure power for their own group while marginalizing others. Indeed, every generation must be vigilant with regard to who has and who does not have power, especially in a polis that purports to be a democracy. I say this because citizens in a "democracy" may believe that because people have the right to vote, there are not numerous citizens who are shuffled to the fringe of the polis's space of appearances. The belief in democracy can serve as a motivator to ensure

110. Some readers might raise concerns about violence vis-à-vis people released from prison. According to the Bureau of Justice, four out of five people released from state prisons are nonviolent offenders who are predominantly convicted of drug offenses (United States Department of Justice, "Profile of Nonviolent Offenders"). The programs identified above would significantly reduce the recidivism rate of this group (by 70 percent), reducing drug offenses and related crimes.

democracy for all citizens, while at the same time the belief can function as a soporific, numbing us to the voices and needs of politically and economically excluded and marginalized persons in the polis.

In this coda, I briefly address the politics of exclusion in the U.S., by which I mean the exclusion or marginalization of individuals and groups from the polis's space of appearances. This is a concern for a political pastoral theology because people who are on the fringe of the polis's space of appearances not only lack a voice in the public sphere but also struggle to access resources to meet needs for survival and flourishing. The politics of exclusion distorts and disrupts both care and justice. I contend that the politics of exclusion violates principles of democracy and eschews the principles of inclusion and acceptance associated with the biblical notion of the kingdom of God[111]—a notion that calls a polis to be one in which care and justice for all are realized.

To grasp the politics of exclusion in the U.S., one must first understand the realities of political-economic power. In his book *Democracy Incorporated*, Sheldon Wolin describes how the intersection of political and economic organizations results in a complex matrix of power, making it difficult for anyone to clearly identify who is responsible.[112] Wolin calls this current state of political-economic sovereignty an inverted totalitarianism, wherein the economic symbol system "dominates politics—and with that domination comes different forms of ruthlessness."[113] This inverted totalitarianism is unlike other forms of totalitarianism that subordinate economics to politics. Instead, inverted totalitarianism occurs when economics dominates politics. As in any totalitarian system, there is a significant distortion of the space of appearances. We have democratic beliefs, practices, and political institutions, yet large corporations, which are hierarchical and nondemocratic, and the wealthy hold tremendous political-economic power on both sides of the political spectrum.[114] For instance, the American Legislative Exchange Council, which represents the interests of large corporations, has for decades worked behind the scenes to influence and create

111. Two points can be made here. First, I am not equating the kingdom of God with democracy. No human political organizations can be equated with the kingdom of God precisely because of human finitude and sin. However, we can attempt to embody the principles of love, mercy, inclusion, care, and justice, even as we realize that we fall short. And this falling short should give us a motivation to be wary of any complacency about having arrived. Second, Wolfart Pannenberg uses the term "prolepsis" to indicate that the kingdom of God is partially realized in the present whenever love, justice, and mercy are present. See Pannenberg, *Theology and the Kingdom of God*.

112. Wolin, *Democracy Incorporated*.

113. Ibid., 58.

114. See Gasparino, *Bought and Paid For*.

legislation at state and national levels—beyond the scrutiny of the American public and at odds with the common good. Lisa Dugan's intriguing book examines and highlights the numerous covert ways wealthy Republican and Democrat neoliberals have used social issues to screen political moves to privatize public sectors, such as public education and the penal system mentioned above.[115] Echoing Dugan's analysis, Joseph Stiglitz, a Nobel laureate, expressed concern that huge disparities in economic equality, which have been growing in the last three decades, threaten democracy.[116] What is clear is that plutocrats and oligarchs in a neoliberal economy are interested in neither the common good nor democracy, though they publicly espouse democracy. Understandably, because they operate out of neoliberal capitalistic values and principles, they are interested in expanding their control of political-economic space to achieve what is good for them—namely, greater wealth and political power. Inverted totalitarianism, then, leads to an increase in nondemocratic use of political institutions; politicians are lured to find more ways to privatize public sectors (e.g., schools, prisons, the military), more ways to reduce public (not corporate) entitlements, more ways to reduce or eliminate government bureaucracies that administer social programs, more ways to expand profits through redistribution upward, more ways to undermine unions, and more ways to shrink federal regulations from agencies such as the Occupational, Safety, and Health Administration and the Environmental Protection Agency. Echoing Wolin's notion of inverted totalitarianism, Henry Giroux argues that "State sovereignty has been replaced by corporate sovereignty, producing new forms of authoritarianism in the United States in which economics dominates and drives politics, producing a neoliberal militarized culture of misery, cruelty, and ruthlessness."[117]

The prevalence of plutocrats and oligarchs in influencing and wielding political power means that the actual political space of appearances vis-à-vis regular citizens has diminished, though the illusion of democracy remains. By this I mean that only a very small segment of the populace possesses the political means and power to effect legislation, which indicates that this small percentage has secured the space of appearances for themselves, operating together with other plutocrats to secure political agency and power. Evidence for this claim is seen in the extensive Princeton study by Martin Gilens and Benjamin Page. Examining the years from 1981 to 2002, they found "the nearly total failure of median voter and other Majoritarian

115. Dugan, *The Twilight of Equality.*

116. Stiglitz, *The Price of Inequality.*

117. Giroux, *Dangerous Thinking*, 50.

Electoral Democracy theories. When the preferences of economic elites and the stands of organized interest groups are controlled for, the preferences of the average American appear to have only a minuscule, near-zero, statistically non-significant impact on public policy."[118] They note further that "the preferences of economic elites have far more independent impact upon policy change than the preferences of average citizens do."[119] Indeed, whenever "the majority of citizens disagrees with economic elites or with organized interests, they generally lose."[120] We can better understand, then, why the pressing matters discussed above are ignored by political-economic elites who are in favor of a neoliberal state. Moreover, this means that even though citizens have the right to vote, they are marginalized from political and economic power.

The people who experience the full effect of the neoliberal economic and political restriction on the space of appearances are people who are poor, whose numbers have risen since the economic crisis of 2008.[121] The dominant neoliberal capitalistic state constructs poor people as burdens to society. Neoliberals believe the poor do not contribute to wealth. The poor are believed to be drains on the economy. By not adding to social economic value, the poor are perceived to possess little if any value—intrinsic or social. They are often restricted from public spaces or segregated from other class groups.[122] In some cases, the poorest among us (e.g., the homeless) are criminalized[123] or relegated to zones of economic apartheid.[124] In terms of the politics of exclusion, the poor have little voice (or representation) in the political arena and are materially deprived of resources they need to survive and flourish. Indeed, in previous chapters, I mentioned Chris Hedges and Joe Sacco's notion of sacrifice zones where poor and working class people suffer deep poverty and economic and environmental devastation. They are clearly excluded by the media—an exclusion that is a symptom of deeper political exclusion. We could add Henry Giroux's notion of "zones of abandonment" to this discussion: these zones of abandonment include inner cities, where large numbers of poor people of color are subject to police

118. Gilens and Page, "Testing Theories of American Politics," 575.

119. Ibid., 576.

120. Ibid.

121. See University of Michigan, "Poverty in the United States: Frequently Asked Questions."

122. See Hooks, *Where We Stand*.

123. See Ehrenreich, "On Turning Poverty into an American Crime."

124. See Desmond, *Evicted*.

control and lack access to education, jobs, and healthy food.[125] To the poor, care and justice are empty concepts in a polis that excludes them from the space of appearances.

Yet, the poor are not the only ones subject to the politics of exclusion. In 1965, the Voting Rights Act was passed. This act, passed in response to Jim Crow laws, aimed at keeping mainly southern states from enacting laws that restricted voters' rights. Dana Liebelson reviewed the data that "shows that the law really did work at preventing voting restrictions: Between 1982 and 2006, the Justice Department blocked more than 700 voting changes on the basis that the changes were discriminatory."[126] In 2013 the Supreme Court overturned a key section of this law, basically eviscerating the Voting Rights Act and allowing states to enact restrictive voter legislation. Liebelson "found that 8 of the 15 states, or 53 percent, passed or implemented voting restrictions since June 25."[127] Reduced early voting days, onerous voter identification requirements, voter registration restrictions, and a reduction in the number of polling stations are just some of the attempts to make voting more difficult, especially for marginalized populations (e.g., the poor, the working class, and the elderly). Consider one of the worst offenders in restricting the space of appearances, North Carolina. Ari Berman writes that North Carolina passed legislation (after only three days of debate) that "mandates strict voter ID to cast a ballot (no student IDs, no public employee IDs, etc.), even though 318,000 registered voters lack the narrow forms of acceptable ID according to the state's own numbers and there have been no recorded prosecutions of voter impersonation in the past decade. The bill cuts the number of early voting days by a week, even though 56 percent of North Carolinians voted early in 2012. The bill eliminates same-day voter registration during the early voting period, even though 96,000 people used it during the general election in 2012 and states that have adopted the convenient reform have the highest voter turnout in the country. African-Americans are 23 percent of registered voters in the state, but made up 28 percent of early voters in 2012, 33 percent of those who used same-day registration and 34 percent of those without state-issued ID."[128] North Carolina is merely one example of a neoliberal state that aims to reduce the space of appearances to maintain political and economic power for the elite.

125. Giroux, *Dangerous Thinking*, 152. I would also point to the previous chapter that addressed how the poor are punished and disciplined in a neoliberal market society.

126. Liebelson, "The Supreme Court Gutted the Voting Rights Act."

127. Ibid.

128. Breman, "North Carolina Passes Country's Worst Voter Suppression Law."

The Supreme Court's decision to gut the Voting Rights Act was not the only decision that aids the politics of exclusion and so leads to a further reduction in the demos's space of appearances. In 2010, the Supreme Court, overturning over a century of precedents, ruled that corporations are persons who have the right to free speech, which means the right to spend whatever amount of money they deem necessary. Grounded in a philosophical and theological fallacy that corporations are persons (are they registered to vote?), this decision opened the floodgates of money into the political realm. Liz Kennedy outlines ten negative consequences of this decision, not the least of which is that ordinary citizens' voices are drowned out by the increasing power of corporations vis-à-vis influencing and corrupting politicians and the democratic system.[129] Of course, citizens continue to have the right to vote and have been known to have political successes,[130] but voter suppression laws and the influence of corporate money make it more difficult to vote and are clearly examples of the politics of exclusion.

The close ties between corporate and political leaders, the vast amounts of money corrupting politics, voter suppression laws, and evidence that government policies are shaped by economic elites lead to voter depression and apathy. The politics of exclusion, in other words, works by undermining the motivation of citizens of lower classes to engage in the polis's space of appearances. Consider that 72 to 77 percent of people who make over $75,000 vote, compared to 44.2 percent of poor and uneducated people.[131] It is significant that 55 percent of people in the lower classes exclude themselves from the political process. I recall one gentleman who said he does not vote because it never does any good. When he looks at political elites, he sees men and women who are not concerned about his or his family's needs and interests. There are, of course, other reasons why people do not vote, but people absent themselves from the space of appearances when their interests and needs are excluded from the discourse and concerns of political leaders.

In the previous chapters I wrote about *alterempire* and *altercapitalist* communities of faith (secular and religious). Given the current level of the

129. Kennedy, "Ten Ways Citizens United Endangers Democracy."

130. One example is Richmond, California, where Chevron backed their candidates, placing more than three million dollars into the campaign to control the city council. Chevron for years had controlled this small town, but the tide turned after an explosion that sent fifteen thousand residents fleeing, as well as a report indicating the negative health effects associated with Chevron's plant emissions. Despite the lack of money, local townspeople organized to defeat Chevron's candidates. See McCormick, "Small Town Beats Big Oil."

131. See "Voter Turnout."

politics of exclusion, these *altercommunities* by contrast are inclusive, especially toward those on the fringe of the polis's space of appearances. They seek to give voice to and represent the voices, needs, and concerns of people marginalized by the neoliberal capitalist polis. Even better, these communities bring their voices to local and national politics, demanding to be heard and speaking truth to power. I am thinking of Saint Sabina Catholic Church on the south side of Chicago. This African American church, led for decades by Father Michael Pfleger, has sought to be inclusive of those who are marginalized in society. They have challenged local political leaders, and their members work tirelessly to address the needs of the local community. In so doing, this community, with all of the normal human problems of living and working together, incarnates, if only partially, the polis of the kingdom of God wherein all are recognized, equally receiving the love and compassion of God.

CONCLUSION

Human beings face many pressing matters of care and justice throughout the world, today and in the future. Political pastoral theologians are tasked with understanding these complex matters relying on the hermeneutical lenses of care and justice. This includes critical and constructive micro and macro analyses of systemic political, economic, and social structures and systems that negatively or positively impact citizens in the polis (and throughout the world). Put differently, pastoral theologians and theologians of all stripes pay attention to the polis and its pressing political-economic matters, for it is in the polis where persons are born and created: It is a good enough polis where persons are recognized, where their voices heard, and where their needs for survival and flourishing are met. A good enough polis is dynamic, yet without constant care and critical attention, it will devolve into a dystopia of carelessness, cruelty, and oppression. A political-pastoral theological critical analysis aims to foment actions that heal, reconcile, sustain, and liberate, enabling the polis and its people to survive and thrive.

BIBLIOGRAPHY

Alder, Nancy, and Katherine Newman. "Socioeconomic Disparities in Health: Pathways and Policies." *Health Affairs*. http://content.healthaffairs.org/content/21/2/60.full/.

Alexander, Michelle. *The New Jim Crow: Mass Incarceration in the Age of Colorblindness*. New York: New Press, 2010.

American Civil Liberties Union. "Racial Disparities in Sentencing." Hearing on Reports of Racism in the Justice System of the United States. Submitted to the Inter-American Commission on Human Rights, 153rd Session, October 27, 2014. https://www.aclu.org/sites/default/files/assets/141027_iachr_racial_disparities_aclu_submission_0.pdf/.

American Psychological Association. Socioeconomic Status Office. "Ethnic and Racial Minorities & Socioeconomic Status." http://www.apa.org/pi/ses/resources/publications/minorities.aspx/.

Andre, Claire, and Manuel Velasquez. "A Healthy Bottom Line: Profits or People?" Markkula Center for Applied Ethics, November 15, 2015. https://www.scu.edu/ethics/focus-areas/bioethics/resources/a-healthy-bottom-line-profits-or-people/.

Arendt, Hannah. *The Human Condition*. Charles R. Walgreen Foundation Lectures. Chicago: University of Chicago Press, 1958.

———. *The Origins of Totalitarianism*. New York: Harvest, 1968.

———. *The Promise of Politics*. New York: Schocken, 2005.

Babin, Janet. "New York Skyscraper's Separate 'Poor Door' Called a Disgrace." *Morning Edition*, July 30, 2014, National Public Radio. http://www.npr.org/2014/07/30/336322608/new-york-skyscrapers-separate-poor-door-sparks-outrage/.

Bacevich, Andrew J. *American Empire*. Cambridge: Harvard University Press, 2002.

———, ed. *The Imperial Tense: Prospects and Problems of American Empire*. Chicago: Dee, 2003.

Baier, Annette. "The Need for More Than Justice." In *Justice and Care: Essential Readings in Feminist Ethics*, edited by Virginia Held, 47–60. Boulder, CO: Westview, 1995.

Baldwin, James. *The Fire Next Time*. New York: Dial, 1963.

———. *Notes of a Native Son*. Beacon Paperback. Boston: Beacon, 1984.

Barker, Ernest, Sir, ed. *The Politics of Aristotle*. London: Oxford University Press, 1971.

Barton, Stephen. "Money Matters: Economic Relations and the Transformation of Value in Early Christianity." In *Engaging Economics: New Testament Scenarios and Early Christian Reception*, edited by Bruce Longenecker and Kelly Liebengood, 37–59. Grand Rapids: Eerdmanns, 2009.

Bauerschmidt, Frederick. "Aquinas." In *The Blackwell Companion to Political Theology*, edited by Peter Scott and William Cavanaugh, 48–61. Blackwell Companions to Religion. Malden, MA: Blackwell, 2007.

Baxter, Michael. "John Courtney Murray." In *The Blackwell Companion to Political Theology*, edited by Peter Scott and William Cavanaugh, 150–64. Blackwell Companions to Religion. Malden, MA: Blackwell, 2007.

Becker, Gary. *The Economic Approach to Human Behavior*. Chicago: Chicago University Press, 1976.

Beebe, Beatrice, et al. "Mother-infant Interactions: Structures and Presymbolic Self and Object Representations." *Psychoanalytic Dialogues* 7/2 (1997) 133–82.

Beebe, Beatrice, and Frank Lachmann. *Infant Research and Adult Treatment: A Dydactic Systems Approach*. Hillsdale, NJ: Analytic Press, 2002.

Bell, Daniel. *The Cultural Contradictions of Capitalism*. New York: Basic Books, 1996.

———. "State and Civil Society." In *The Blackwell Companion to Political Theology*, edited by Peter Scott and William Cavanaugh, 423–38. Blackwell Companions to Religion. Malden, MA: Blackwell, 2007.

Bell, Larry. *Climate of Corruption: Politics and Power behind the Global Warming Hoax*. Austin: Greenleaf, 2011.

Bender, Peter. "The New Rome." In *The Imperial Tense: Prospects and Problems of American Empire*, edited by Andrew J. Bacevich, 81–92. Chicago: Dee, 2003.

Benhabib, Seyla. "The Generalized Other and the Concrete Other: The Kohlberg-Gilligan Controversy and Feminist Theory." In *Feminism as Critique: Essays on Politics and Gender*, edited by Seyla Benhabib and Drucilla Cornell, 158–72. Feminist Perspectives. Cambridge, : Polity, 1987.

———. *Situating the Self: Gender, Community, and Postmodernism in Contemporary Ethics*. New York: Routledge, 1992.

Berkman, Lisa, and Arnold M. Epstein. "Beyond Health Care—Socioeconomic Status and Health." *New England Journal of Medicine* 358 (June 5, 2008) 2509–10.

Bion, Wilfred. *Attention and Interpretation: A Scientific Approach to Insight in Psychoanalysis and Groups*. London: Tavistock, 1970.

Boer, Roland. *Criticism of Heaven: On Marxism and Theology*. Historical Materialism Book Series 18. Chicago: Haymarket, 2009.

———. *In the Vale of Tears: On Marxism and Theology, V*. Chicago: Historical Materialism Book Series 52. Chicago: Haymarket, 2014.

———. *Marxist Criticism of the Hebrew Bible*. 2nd ed. London: Bloomsbury, 2015.

Boff, Leonardo. *Essential Care: An Ethics of Human Nature*. Translated with notes by Alexandre Guilherme. Waco, TX: Baylor University Press, 2008.

Boggs, Carl. *The Crimes of Empire: Rogue Superpower and World Domination*. London: Pluto, 2010.

Bollas, Christopher. *Being a Character: Psychoanalysis and Self Experience*. New York: Hill & Wang, 1992.

Boorstin, Daniel. *The Image: A Guide to Pseudo-Events in America*. 25th ann. ed. with a new foreword. New York: Vintage, 1987.

Bowlby, John. *A Secure Base: Parent-Child Attachment and Healthy Human Development*. New York: Basic Books, 1988.

Bradford, Harry. "Warren Buffett: 'My Class Has Won' and 'It's Been A Rout.'" *Huffington Post*. Business. November 15, 2011. http://www.huffingtonpost.com/2011/11/15/warren-buffett-tax-code-l_n_1095833.html/.

Breger, Louis. *Freud: Darkness in the Midst of Vision*. New York: Wiley, 2000.

Breman, Ari. "North Carolina Passes Country's Worst Voter Suppression Law." *Nation*, July 26, 2013. http://www.thenation.com/article/north-carolina-passes-countrys-worst-voter-suppression-law/.

Brown, Wendy. *States of Injury: Power and Freedom in Late Modernity*. Princeton: Princeton University Press, 1995.

———. *Politics Out of History*. Princeton: Princeton University Press, 2001.

———. *Undoing the Demos: Neoliberalism's Stealth Revolution*. New York: Zone Books, 2015.

Bubeck, Diemut Elisabet. *Care, Gender, and Justice*. Oxford: Clarendon, 1995.

Buber, Martin. *I and Thou*. With a Postscript by the Author Added. Translated by Ronald Gregor Smith. New York: Scribner, 1958.

Buthelezi, Manas. "Toward Indigenous Theology in South Africa." In *The Emergent Gospel: Theology from the Underside of History*, edited by Sergio Torres and Virginia Fabella, 56–75. Maryknoll, NY: Orbis, 1976.

Butler, Smedley. *War Is a Racket*. Port Townsend, WA: Feral House, 2003.

Canon, Gabrielle. "Here's the Latest Evidence on How Private Prisons Are Exploiting Inmates for Profits." *Mother Jones*, June, 17, 2015. http://www.motherjones.com/mojo/2015/06/private-prisons-profit/.

Capper, Brian. "Virtuoso Religion, and the Community of Goods." In *Engaging Economics: New Testament Scenarios and Early Christian Reception*, edited by Bruce Longnecker and Kelly Liebengood, 60–80. Grand Rapids: Eerdmans, 2009.

Carrette, Jeremy, and Richard King. *Selling Spirituality: The Silent Takeover of Religion*. New York: Routledge, 2005.

Carter, J. Kameron. "Between W. E. B. Du Bois and Karl Barth: The Problem of Modern Political Theology." In *Race and Political Theology*, edited by Vincent W. Lloyd, 83–111. Stanford: Stanford University Press, 2012.

Center for Disease Control and Prevention. National Center for Health Statistics, Office of Analysis and Epidemiology. "Health, United States, 2015—Poverty." https://www.cdc.gov/nchs/hus/poverty.htm/.

Chari, Anita. *A Political Economy of the Senses: Neoliberalism, Reification, Critique*. New Directions in Critical Theory. New York: Columbia University Press, 2015.

Chomsky, Noam. *Hegemony or Survival: America's Quest for Global Dominance*. New York: Metropolitan, 2003.

———. *Imperial Ambitions*. The American Empire Project. New York: Metropolitan Books, 2005.

Clebsch, William, and Charles Jaekle. *Pastoral Care in Historical Perspective*. Northvale, NJ: Aronson, 1994.

Coates, David. *A Liberal Tool Kit: Progressive Responses to Conservative Arguments*. Westport, CT: Praeger, 2007.

Cone, James. *A Black Theology of Liberation*. Maryknoll, NY: Orbis, 1970.

———. *The Cross and the Lynching Tree*. Maryknoll, NY: Orbis, 2011.

Connolly, William. *The Fragility of Things: Self-Organizing Processes, Neoliberal Fantasies, and Democratic Activism*. Durham: Duke University Press, 2013.

Cook, Carol. "Empathy: A Bridge between Two Worlds, A Landscape of Care." *Family Ministry* 28 (2006) 29–38.

Coontz, Stephanie. *The Social Origins of Private Life: A History of American Families, 1600-1900*. The Haymarket Series. London: Verso, 1988.

Corradi Fiumara, Gemma. *The Other Side of Language: A Philosophy of Listening*. London: Routledge, 1990.

Corrigan, Edward and Pearl-Ellen Gordon. "The Mind as an Object." In *The Mind Object: Precocity and Pathology of Self-Sufficiency*, edited by Edward Corrigan and Pearl-Ellen Gordon, 1–22. Northvale, NJ: Aronson, 1995.

Couldry, Nick. *Why Voice Matters: Culture and Politics after Neoliberalism*. London: Sage, 2010.

Coulter, Ann. *Godless: The Church of Liberalism*. New York: Three Rivers, 2007.

———. *Guilty: Liberal "Victims" and Their Assault on America*. New York: Crown Forum, 2008.

———. *Treason: Liberal Treachery from the Cold War to the War on Terrorism*. New York: Three Rivers, 2004.

Critchley, Simon. *Infinitely Demanding: Ethics of Commitment, Politics of Resistance*. London: Verso, 2007.

Crossan, John Dominic. *God and Empire: Jesus against Rome, Then and Now*. San Francisco: Harper-SanFrancisco, 2007.

———. *Jesus: A Revolutionary Biography*. New York: HarperOne, 1995.

Crossette, Barbara. "Iraq Sanctions Kill Children." *New York Times*, December 1, 1995. http://www.nytimes.com/1995/12/01/world/iraq-sanctions-kill-children-un-reports.html/.

Curtis, Michael, ed. *The Great Political Theories*. 2 vols. 1961–62. Reprint, New York: HarperPerennial, 2008.

Cushman, Phillip. *Constructing the Self, Constructing America*. Boston: Addison-Wesley, 1995.

Cvetkovich, Ann. *Depression: A Public Feeling*. Durham: Duke University Press, 2012.

Damasio, Anthony. *Descartes' Error: Emotion, Reason, and the Human Brain*. New York: Avon, 1994.

Danner, Mark. *Stripping Bare the Body: Politics, Violence, War*. New York: Nation Books, 2009.

Dardot, Pierre, and Christian Laval. *The New Way of the World: On Neoliberal Society*. London: Verso, 2013.

Davenport, Coral. "Pentagon Signals Security Risks of Climate Change." *New York Times*, October 13, 2014. http://www.nytimes.com/2014/10/14/us/pentagon-says-global-warming-presents-immediate-security-threat.html?_r=1/.

Davenport, Coral, and Michael Connelly. "Most Republicans Say They Back Climate Change, Poll Finds." *New York Times*, January 30, 2015. http://www.nytimes.com/2015/01/31/us/politics/most-americans-support-government-action-on-climate-change-poll-finds.html?_r=0/.

Dean, Howard, and Judith Warner. *You Have the Power: How to Take Back Our Country and Restore Democracy in America*. New York: Simon & Schuster, 2004.

Deleuze, Giles, and Felix Guittari. *Anti-Oedipus: Capitalism and Schizophrenia*. Minneapolis: University of Minnesota Press, 1983.

D'Entreves, Maurizio. *The Political Philosophy of Hannah Arendt*. London: Routledge, 1994.

Derber, Charles, and Yale Magrass. *Bully Nation: How the American Establishment Creates a Bullying Society*. Lawrence: University of Kansas Press, 2016.

Desmond, Matthew. *Evicted: Poverty and Profit in the American City*. New York: Crown, 2016.

D News. "Climate Change Has Raised Ocean Acidity by a Quarter." Tech. Seeker, October 8, 2014. https://www.seeker.com/climate-change-has-raised-ocean-acidity-by-a-quarter-1769155275.html/

Drysdale, Peter. "America's Pivot to Asia and Asian Akrasia." *East Asia Forum*, November 26, 2012. http://www.eastasiaforum.org/2012/11/26/americas-pivot-to-asia-and-asian-akrasia/.

Dufour, Dany-Robert. *The Art of Shrinking Heads: On the New Servitude of the Liberated in the Age of Total Capitalism*. Cambridge: Polity, 2008.

Dugan, Lisa. *The Twilight of Equality? Neoliberalism, Cultural Politics, and the Attack on Democracy*. Boston: Beacon, 2003.

Duménil, Gérard, and Dominique Lévy. *The Crisis of Neoliberalism*. Cambridge: Harvard University Press, 2011.

Dumouchel, Paul. *The Barren Sacrifice: An Essay on Political Violence*. Translated by Mary Baker. Studies in Violence, Mimesis, and Culture. East Lansing: Michigan State University Press.

Dussel, Enrique. *A Philosophy of Liberation*. 1985. Reprint, Eugene, OR: Wipf & Stock, 2003.

Eagleton, Terry. *After Theory*. New York: Basic Books, 2003.

———. *Why Marx Was Right*. New Haven: Yale University Press, 2011.

Easterly, William. *The Tyranny of Experts: Economics, Dictators, and the Forgotten Rights of the Poor*. New York: Basic Books, 2013.

The Effects of Poverty on Health. "The Relationship between Poverty and Health." http://theeffectsofpovertyonhealth.weebly.com/relationship-between-poverty-and-health.html/.

Ehrenreich, Barbara. *Bright-Sided: How Positive Thinking Is Undermining America*. New York: Picador, 2009.

———. "On Turning Poverty into an American Crime." *Truthout*, 9 August, 2011. http://www.truth-out.org/opinion/item/2579:barbara-ehrenreich-on-turning-poverty-into-an-american-crime/.

Engster, Daniel. *The Heart of Justice: Care Ethics and Political Theory*. Oxford: Oxford University Press, 2007.

Erikson, Erik. *Childhood and Society*. New York: Norton, 1963.

Estey, Ken. "Protesting Classes through Protestant Glasses: Class, Labor, and the Social Gospel in the United States." In *Religion, Theology, and Class: Fresh Engagements after Long Silence*, edited by Joerg Rieger, 121–42. New York: Palgrave Macmillan, 2013.

Familiaris Consortio. http://www.catholic.net/RCC/Indices/subs/by-subject.html/.

Fanon, Frantz. *Black Skin, White Masks*. 1952. Reprint, New York: Grove, 2008.

Farley, Edward. *Good and Evil: Interpreting a Human Condition*. Minneapolis: Fortress, 1990.

———. *Divine Empathy: A Theology of God*. Minneapolis: Fortress, 1996.

Federal Safety Net. http://federalsafetynet.com/welfare-budget.html/.

Ferguson, Niall. *Colossus: The Rise and Fall of the American Empire*. New York: Penguin, 2004.

———. *The War of the World: Twentieth-Century Conflict and the Descent of the West*. New York: Penguin, 2006.

Fingarette, Herbert. *Self-Deception*. Berkeley: University of California Press, 1969.

Fish, Charles. *The Path of Empire: A Chronicle of the United States as a World Power*. Yale Chronicles of America Series 46. New York: United States Publishers, 1978.

Flores, Rosa. "In Chicago, Less Than 1 Percent Saw a Lawyer after Arrest." *CNN*, May 25, 2016. http://www.cnn.com/2016/05/25/us/chicago-police-arrests-civil-rights/index.html/.

Fonagy, Peter. "Male Perpetrators of Violence against Women: An Attachment Theory Perspective." *Journal of Applied Psychoanalytic Studies* 1/1 (1999) 1–27.

Fonagy, Peter, and Mary Target. "Attachment and Reflective Function: Their Role in Self-Organization." *Development and Psychopathology* 9/4 (1997) 679–700.

Fonagy, Peter, et al. *Affect Regulation, Mentalization, and the Development of the Self.* New York: Other Press, 2002.

Foucault, Michel. *The Birth of Biopolitics: Lectures at the Collége de France, 1978–1979*, Edited by Michel Senellart. Translated by Graham Burchell. New York: Picador, 2010.

———. *Power/Knowledge: Selected Interviews and Other Writings*. New York: Pantheon, 1980.

Francis, Pope. *Evangelii Gaudium*. 2013. http://w2.vatican.va/content/francesco/en/apost_exhortations/documents/papa-francesco_esortazione-ap_20131124_evangelii-gaudium.html.

Frank, Jerome D. *Persuasion and Healing: A Comparative Study of Psychotherapy*. New York: Shocken, 1961.

Frank, Thomas. *One Market under God: Extreme Capitalism, Market Populism, and the End of Economic Democracy*. New York: Anchor, 2000.

Fussell, Paul. *Class*. New York: Ballantine, 1983.

Freeberg, Ernest. *Democracy's Prisoner: Eugene V. Debs, the Great War, and the Right to Dissent*. Cambridge: Harvard University Press, 2008.

Freud, Sigmund. "The Dissolution of the Oedipus Complex." In *The Standard Edition of the Complete Psychological Works of Sigmund Freud*, 19:171–80. London: Hogarth, 1924.

———. "The Future of an Illusion." In *The Standard Edition of the Complete Psychological Works of Sigmund Freud*, 21:5–58. London: Hogarth, 1927.

———. *Group Psychology and the Analysis of the Ego*. New York: Norton, 1959.

———. "Inhibitions, Symptoms and Anxiety." In *The Standard Edition of the Complete Psychological Works of Sigmund Freud*, 20:87–175. London: Hogarth, 1926.

Friedman, Marilyn. "Beyond Caring: The De-Moralization of Gender." In *Justice and Care: Essential Readings in Feminist Ethics*, edited by Virginia Held, 61–78. Boulder, CO: Westview, 1995.

Friedman, Milton. *Capitalism and Freedom*. Chicago: University of Chicago Press, 2002.

Fullbright, William. *The Arrogance of Power*. New York: Random House, 1966.

Ganis, Richard. *The Politics of Care in Habermas and Derrida*. New York: Lexington, 2011.

Garland, Sarah. "When Class Becomes More Important to a Child's Education Than Race." *Atlantic*, August, 28, 2013. http://www.theatlantic.com/national/archive/2013/08/when-class-became-more-important-to-a-childs-education-than-race/279064/.

Gasparino, Charles. *Bought and Paid For: The Hidden Relationship between Wall Street and Washington*. New York: Portfolio/Penguin, 2012.

Gay, Peter. *Freud: A Life for Our Time*. New York: Norton, 1988.

Gilligan, Carol. *In a Different Voice: Psychological Theory and Women's Development*. Cambridge: Harvard University Press, 1982.

Gilligan, James. *Why Some Politicians Are More Dangerous than Others*. Cambridge: Polity, 2011.

Gingrich, Newt, with Joe DeSantis. *To Save America: Stopping Obama's Secular-Socialist Machine*. Washington DC: Regnery, 2010.

Gilens, Martin, and Benjamin I. Page. "Testing Theories of American Politics: Elites, Interest Groups and Average Citizens." *Perspectives on Politics* 12/3 (2014) 564–81.

Giroux, Henry A. "America's Addiction to Torture." *Truthout* (December 17, 2014). http://www.truth-out.org/news/item/28055-torture-and-the-violence-of-organized-forgetting/.

———. *Dangerous Thinking in the Age of the New Authoritarianism*. Boulder, CO: Paradigm, 2015.

———. *Disposable Youth, Racialized Memories, and the Culture of Cruelty*. Framing 21st Century Social Issues. New York: Routledge, 2012.

———. *Zombie Politics and Culture in the Age of Casino Capitalism*. New York: Lang, 2011.

Go, Julian. *Patterns of Empire: The British and American Empires, 1688 to the Present*. New York: Cambridge University Press, 2012.

Goizueta, Roberto. "Gustavo Gutiérrez." In *The Blackwell Companion to Political Theology*, edited by Peter Scott and William Cavanaugh, 288–301. Blackwell Companions to Religion. Malden, MA: Blackwell, 2007.

Goldberg, David Theo. *The Threat of Race: Reflections on Racial Neoliberalism*. Malden, MA: Wiley-Blackwell, 2009.

Goleman, Daniel. *Emotional Intelligence*. New York: Bantam, 1997.

———. *Social Intelligence: The New Science of Human Relationships*. New York: Bantam, 2006.

Gottschalk, Marie. *Caught: The Prison State and the Lockdown of American Politics*. Princeton: Princeton University Press, 2015.

Graham, Elaine. "Feminist Theology, Northern." In *The Blackwell Companion to Political Theology*, edited by Peter Scott and William Cavanaugh, 210–26. Blackwell Companions to Religion. Malden, MA: Blackwell, 2007.

Graham, Larry. *Care of Persons, Care of Worlds: A Psychosystems Approach to Pastoral Care and Counseling*. Pastoral Care and Counseling. Nashville: Abingdon, 1992.

———. "From Relational Humanness to Relational Justice: Reconceiving Pastoral Care and Counseling." In *Pastoral Care and Social Conflict: Essays in Honor of Charles V. Gerkin*, edited by Pamela D. Couture and Rodney J. Hunter, 220–34. Nashville: Abingdon, 1995.

Gray, John. *False Dawn: The Delusions of Global Capitalism*. New York: New Press, 1998.

Gutiérrez, Gustavo. *Essential Writings*. Edited by James B. Nickoloff. Maryknoll, NY: Orbis, 1996.

———. *On Job: God-talk and the Suffering of the Innocent*. Translated by Matthew J. O'Connell. Maryknoll, NY: Orbis, 1987.

———. "Option for the Poor." In *An Eerdmans Reader in Contemporary Political Theology*, edited by William Cavanaugh et al., 174–93. Grand Rapids: Eerdmans, 2012.

———. *A Theology of Liberation: History, Politics, and Salvation*. Translated by Sister Caridad Inda and John Eagleson. Maryknoll, NY: Orbis, 1985.

Hagopian, Jesse. "Schooling Arne Duncan." *Common Dreams*, 21 July, 2010. http://www.commondreams.org/views/2010/07/21/schooling-arne-duncan/.

Hamilton, John T. *Security: Politics, Humanity, and the Philology of Care*. Translation/Transnation. Princeton: Princeton University Press, 2013.

Hamington, Maurice. *Embodied Care: Jane Addams, Maurice Merleau-Ponty, and Feminist Ethics*. Urbana: University of Illinois Press, 2004

Hardt, Michael. *Multitude: War and Democracy in the Age of Empire*. New York: Penguin, 2005.

Hardt, Michael, and Antonio Negri. *Commonwealth*. Cambridge: Belknap, 2009.

———. *Empire*. Cambridge: Harvard University Press, 2000.

Harvey, David. *A Brief History of Neoliberalism*. Oxford: Oxford University Press, 2005.

———. *The Enigma of Capital: And the Crises of Capitalism*. Oxford: Oxford University Press, 2010.

Hauerwas, Stanley. "Dietrich Bonhoeffer." In *The Blackwell Companion to Political Theology*, edited by Peter Scott and William Cavanaugh, 136–49. Blackwell Companions to Religion. Malden, MA: Blackwell, 2007.

Hayek, F. A. *The Road to Serfdom: Texts and Documents*. Edited by Bruce Caldwell. Chicago: University of Chicago Press, 2007.

Hedges, Chris. "The Prison State of America." *Truthdig*, December 28, 2014. http://www.truthdig.com/report/page2/the_prison_state_of_america_20141228/.

Hedges, Chris, and Joe Sacco. *Days of Destruction, Days of Revolt*. New York: Nation Books, 2012.

Held, Virginia. *The Ethics of Care: Personal, Political, and Global*. Oxford: Oxford University Press, 2006.

———, ed. *Justice and Care: Essential Readings in Feminist Ethics*. Boulder, CO: Westview, 1995.

Hendricks, Obery M., Jr. *The Universe Bends toward Justice: Radical Reflections on the Bible, the Church and the Body Politic*. Maryknoll, NY: Orbis, 2011.

Herring, George C. *From Colony to Superpower: U.S. Foreign Relations since 1776*. Oxford: Oxford University Press, 2011.

Hesse, Edward, and Mary Main. "Second-Generation Effects of Unresolved Trauma in Non-maltreating Parents: Dissociated, Frightened, and Threatening Parental Behavior." *Psychoanalytic Inquiry* 19/4 (1999) 481–540.

Hetherington, Marc, and Jonathan Weiler. *Authoritarianism and Polarization in American Politics*. Cambridge: Cambridge University Press, 2009.

Hewitt, Marsha. "Critical Theory." In *The Blackwell Companion to Political Theology*, edited by Peter Scott and William Cavanaugh, 455–70. Blackwell Companions to Religion. Malden, MA: Blackwell, 2007.

Hill, Steven. "Not-For Profit vs. Profit Health Care." *Washington Monthly* May 27, 2011. http://www.washingtonmonthly.com/ten-miles-square/2011/05/nonprofit_vs_forprofit_health029839.php/.

Hochschild, Arlie. *The Managed Heart: Commercialization of Human Feeling*. Berkeley: University of California Press, 2012.

Hollerich, Michael. "Carl Schmidt." In *The Blackwell Companion to Political Theology*, edited by Peter Scott and William Cavanaugh, 107–22. Blackwell Companions to Religion. Malden, MA: Blackwell, 2007.

Holthaus, Eric. "Poll: Americans Don't Believe Climate Change Will Affect Them Personally." Slatest. *Slate,* April 6, 2015. http://www.slate.com/blogs/the_slatest/2015/04/06/new_climate_change_poll_shows_americans_believe_in_global_warming.html/.

hooks, bell. *Where We Stand: Class Matters.* New York: Routledge, 2000.

Horsley, Richard. *Jesus and Empire: The Kingdom of God and the New World Disorder.* Minneapolis: Fortress, 2003.

———. *Jesus and the Power: Conflict, Covenant, and the Hope of the Poor.* Minneapolis: Fortress, 2011.

Howard, Jason. "Appalachia Turns on Itself." *New York Times,* July 8, 2012. http://www.nytimes.com/2012/07/09/opinion/appalachia-turns-on-itself.html?_r=1&/.

Hudis, Peter. *Marx's Concept of the Alternative to Capitalism.* Historical Materialism Book Series 36. Chicago: Haymarket, 2015.

Hudis, Peter, and Kevin Anderson, eds. *The Rosa Luxemburg Reader.* New York: Monthly Review Press, 2004.

Huntington, Samuel. *Who Are We? The Challenges to America's National Identity.* New York: Simon & Schuster, 2004.

Illouz, Eva. *Cold Intimacies: The Making of Emotional Capitalism.* Cambridge: Polity, 2007.

———. *Saving the Modern Soul: Therapy, Emotions, and the Culture of Self-Help.* Berkeley: University of California Press, 2008.

Imam, Jareen. "NASA: 10,000-Year-Old Antarctic Ice Shelf Will Disappear by 2020." Space and Science. *CNN,* May 17, 2015. http://www.cnn.com/2015/05/16/us/antarctica-larsen-b-ice-shelf-to-disappear/index.html/.

Intergovernmental Panel on Climate Change. *Climate Change 2007: Synthesis Report; Summary for Policymakers.* A document approved at the twenty-seventh IPCC Plenary in Valencia, Spain, November 12–17, 2007.

"Intergovernmental Panel on Climate Change." *Wikipedia.* https://en.wikipedia.org/wiki/Intergovernmental_Panel_on_Climate_Change/.

Johnson, Cedric C. *Race, Religion, and Resilience in the Neoliberal Age.* New York: Palgrave Macmillan, 2016.

Johnson, Chalmers. *Blowback: The Costs and Consequences of American Empire.* An Owl Book. New York: Holt, 1999.

———. *Sorrows of Empire: Militarism, Secrecy, and the End of the Republic.* An Owl Book. New York: Holt, 2004.

Jones, Daniel Stedman. *Masters of the Universe: Hayek, Friedman, and the Birth of Neoliberal Politics.* Princeton; Princeton University Press, 2012.

Jurist, Eliot. "Mind and Yours: New Directions for Mentalization Theory." In *Mind to Mind: Infant Research, Neuroscience, and Psychoanalysis,* edited by Eliot Jurist et al., 88–114. New York: Other Press, 2008.

Kaiser Family Foundation. The Kaiser Commission on Medicaid and the Uninsured, "Key Facts about the Uninsured Population." September 29, 2016. http://kff.org/uninsured/fact-sheet/key-facts-about-the-uninsured-population/.

Kaplan, Amy. *The Anarchy of Empire in the Making of U.S. Culture.* Convergences. Cambridge: Harvard University Press, 2002.

Karlin, Mark. "Banishing the Poor, Unemployed and Working Class from the Mainstream Media Implies They Are Worthless." *Truthout,* 17 June 2013. http://truth-out.org/buzzflash/commentary/item/18031-banishing-the-poor-unemployed-and-working-class-from-the-mainstream-media-implies-that-they-are-worthless/.

———. "Runaway Capitalism Is Crushing American Workers: An Interview with Steven Hill." *Truthout*, 27 December, 2015. http://www.truth-out.org/progressivepicks/item/34181-runaway-capitalism-is-crushing-american-workers/.

Kennedy, Liz. "Ten Ways Citizens United Endangers Democracy." *Demos*, January 19, 2012. http://www.demos.org/publication/10-ways-citizens-united-endangers-democracy/.

Kerbel, Matthew. *Get This Party Started: How Progressives Can Fight Back and Win.* Lanham, MD: Rowan & Littlefield, 2006.

Kertzer, David I. *Ritual, Politics, and Power*. New Haven: Yale University Press, 1988.

King, Martin Luther, Jr. *The Autobiography of Martin Luther King, Jr.* Edited by Clayborne Carson. New York: Intellectual Properties Management in association with Grand Central Publishing, 1998.

———. "The Southern Christian Leadership Conference Presidential Address." August 16, 1967. *World History Archive*, published by Hartford Web Publishing. http://www.hartford-hwp.com/archives/45a/628.html/.

King, Michael. "Greenspan: Crisis Prompted Re-examination of Economic Beliefs. *MoneyNews*, October 23, 2013. http://www.moneynews.com/newswidget/Greenspan-crisis-financial-bubbles/2013/10/23/id/532650?amp&&/.

Kinzer, Stephen. *Overthrow: America's Century of Regime Change from Hawaii to Iraq*. New York: Times Books, 2006.

Kirkpatrick, Frank G. *Community: A Trinity of Models*. Washington DC: Georgetown University Press. 1986.

Kittay, Eva. *Love's Labor: Essays on Women. Equality, and Dependency.* New York: Routledge, 1999.

Klein, Melanie. "The Importance of Symbol Formation in the Development of the Ego." In *The Selected Melanie Klein*, edited by Juliet Mitchell, 95–111. New York: Free Press, 1986.

Klein, Naomi. *This Changes Everything: Capitalism vs. the Climate*. New York: Simon & Schuster, 2014.

Kolbert, Elizabeth. *The Sixth Extinction: An Unnatural History*. New York: Holt, 2014.

Krieg, Robert A. *Catholic Theologians in Nazi Germany*. New York: Continuum, 2004.

Kuecker, Aaron. "The Spirit and the 'Other,' Satan and "Self': Economic Ethics as a Consequence of Identity Transformation in Luke-Acts." In *Engaging Economics: New Testament Scenarios and Early Christian Reception*, edited by Bruce Longnecker and Kelly Liebengood, 81–103. Grand Rapids: Eerdmans, 2009.

Kujawa-Holbrook, Sheryl A., and Karen B. Montagno. *Injustice and the Care of Souls: Taking Oppression Seriously in Pastoral Care*. Minneapolis: Fortress, 2009.

LaCugna, Catherine. *God for Us: The Trinity and Christian Life*. New York: HarperCollins, 1991.

LaMothe, Ryan. "The Colonizing Realities of Neoliberal Capitalism." *Journal of Pastoral Psychology*, 65 (2016), 23–40.

———. "Empire Matters: Implications for Pastoral Care." *Journal of Pastoral Care and Counseling* 61 (2007) 421–38.

———. "Imaginary Love: Patriotism as Transitional Phenomena." In *Intricacies of Patriotism: Towards a Complexity of Patriotic Allegiance*, edited by Maciej Hulas and Stanislaw Fel, 81–104. Frankfort: Lang, 2015.

———. "The Spirits of Capitalism and Christianity and Their Impact on the Formation of Healthcare Leaders." *Journal of Religion and Health* 52/1 (2013) 3–17.

———. *Missing Us: Re-visioning Psychoanalysis from the Perspective of Community.* Lanham, MD: Aronson, 2013.

———. "Neoliberal Capitalism and the Corruption of Society: A Pastoral Analysis." *Journal of Pastoral Psychology* 65/1 (2016) 5–22.

Landen, Rachel. "Another Year of Pay Hikes for Non-Profit Hospital CEOs." *Modern Healthcare*, August 9, 2014. http://www.modernhealthcare.com/article/20140809/MAGAZINE/308099987/.

Lane, Melissa. *The Birth of Politics: Eight Greek and Roman Political Ideas and Why They Matter.* Princeton: Princeton University Press, 2014.

Lane, Tim. "Desertification: Land Degradation Under a Changing Climate." *Climatica*, June 17, 2014. http://climatica.org.uk/desertification-land-degradation-changing-climate/.

Langer, Susan. *Philosophy in a New Key: A Study in the Symbolism of Reason, Rite, and Art.* Cambridge: Harvard University Press, 1979.

Lartey, Emmanuel. *Postcolonizing God: An African Practical Theology.* London: SCM, 2013.

Lear, Jonathan. *Radical Hope: Ethics in the Face of Cultural Devastation.* Cambridge: Harvard University Press, 2006.

Lemke, Thomas. "The Risks of Security: Liberalism, Biopolitics, and Fear." In *The Government of Life: Foucault, Biopolitics and Neoliberalism*, edited by Vanessa Lemm and Miguel Vatter, 59–76. Forms of Living. New York: Fordham University Press, 2014.

Leo XIII, Pope. *Rerum Novarum.* 1891. http://w2.vatican.va/content/leo-xiii/en/encyclicals/documents/hf_l-xiii_enc_15051891_rerum-novarum.html

———. *Sapientiae Christianae.* 1890. http://w2.vatican.va/content/leo-xiii/en/encyclicals/documents/hf_l-xiii_enc_10011890_sapientiae-christianae.html/

Levin, Mark R. *Men in Black: How the Supreme Court Is Destroying America.* With an introduction by Rush Limbaugh. Washington DC: Regnery, 2005.

Levinas, Emmanuel. *Totality and Infinity: An Essay on Exteriority.* Translated by Alphonso Lingis. Duquesne Studies. Philosophical Series. Pittsburgh: Duquesne University Press, 1969.

———. *Otherwise Than Being, or, Beyond Essence.* Translated by Alphonso Lingis. Pittsburgh: Duquesne University Press, 1998.

Lewis, Renee. "'Disaster after Disaster' Hits Marshall Islands as Climate Change Kicks in." Environment. May 18, 2015. *Al Jazeera America.* http://america.aljazeera.com/articles/2015/5/18/disaster-after-disaster-in-low-lying-marshall-islands.html/.

Library of Congress. *Thomas Jefferson.* Letter from Thomas Jefferson to James Madison, April 27, 1809. http://www.loc.gov/exhibits/jefferson/149.html/.

Liebelson, Dana. "The Supreme Court Gutted the Voting Rights Act." *Mother Jones*, April 8, 2014. http://www.motherjones.com/politics/2014/04/republican-voting-rights-supreme-court-id/.

Lippman, Pauline. "Neoliberal Education Restructuring." *Monthly Review* 63/1. http://monthlyreview.org/2011/07/01/neoliberal-education-restructuring/.

Longenecker, Bruce, and Kelly Liebengood, eds. *Engaging Economics: New Testament Scenarios and Early Christian Reception.* Grand Rapids: Eerdmanns, 2009.

Lord, Carnes. "Aristotle." In *History of Political Philosophy*, edited by Leo Strauss and Joseph Cropsey, 118–54. 3rd ed. Chicago: University of Chicago Press, 1987.

"Louisiana Purchase." *Monticello*. https://www.monticello.org/site/jefferson/louisiana-purchase/.

Lukács, Georg. *History and Class Consciousness: Studies in Marxist Dialectics*. Translated by Rodney Livingstone. Cambridge: MIT Press, 1968.

Lundestad, Geir. *The American "Empire": and Other Studies of U.S. Foreign Policy in a Comparative Perspective* Oxford: Oxford University Press, 1900.

Lyotard, Jean. *The Postmodern Condition: A Report on Knowledge*. Theory and History of Literature 10. Minneapolis: University of Minnesota Press, 1999.

MacDonald, Jeffery. *Thieves in the Temple: The Christian Church and the Selling of the American Soul*. New York: Basic Books, 2010.

MacIntyre, Alasdair. *After Virtue: A Study in Moral Theory*. 2nd ed. Notre Dame, IN: Notre Dame University Press, 1984.

Macmurray, John. "The Conception of Society." In *John Macmurray: Selected Philosophical Writings*, edited by Esther McIntosh, 95–108. Exeter: Imprint Academic, 2004.

———. *Conditions of Freedom*. London: Humanities, 1993.

———. *Person in Relation*. London: Humanities, 1991.

———. *Reason and Emotion*. New York: Humanity Books, 1935.

Mander, Jerry. *The Capitalism Papers: Fatal Flaws in an Obsolete System*. Berkeley: Counter Point, 2012.

Mangan, Dan. "Medical Bills Are the Biggest Cause of U.S. Bankruptcies: Study." CNBC, June, 25, 2013. http://www.cnbc.com/id/100840148/.

Mann, Geoff. *Disassembly Required: A Field Guide to Actually Existing Capitalism*. Edinburgh: AK Press, 2013.

Marris, Peter. *The Politics of Uncertainty: Attachment in Private and Public Life*. London: Routledge, 1996.

May, Rollo. *The Meaning of Anxiety*. New York: Pocket Books, 1979

Mayeroff, Milton. *On Caring*. World Perspectives. New York: Harper & Row, 1971.

McCarty, Nolan, et al. *Polarized America: The Dance of Ideology and Unequal Riches*. The Walras-Pareto Lectures. Cambridge: MIT Press, 2008.

McCormick, Kate. "Small Town Beats Big Oil." Interview with Jovanka Beckles. Compass, March 16, 2015. Sierra Club. http://www.sierraclub.org/compass/2015/03/small-town-beats-big-oil/.

McNeill, John. *A History of the Cure of Souls*. Harper Torchbooks. New York: Harper, 1951.

McLaren, Peter. *Pedagogy of Insurrection: From Resurrection to Revolution*. Education and Struggle 6. New York: Lang, 2015.

Mercer, Joyce. "Economics, Class, and Classism." In *The Wiley-Blackwell Companion to Practical Theology*, edited by Bonnie J. Miller-McLemore, 432–42. Wiley-Blackwell Companions to Religion. Maiden, MA: Wiley-Blackwell, 2012.

Middleton, Robert. "Created in the Image of a Violent God? The Ethical Problem of the Conquest of Chaos in Biblical Creation Texts." In*terpretation* 58 (2004) 341–55.

Mills, C. Wright. *The Sociological Imagination*. Oxford: Oxford University Press, 1959.

Miller, Mary. "In the 'Image' and 'Likeness' of God." *Journal of Biblical Literature*, 91 (1972) 289–304.

Miller, David. *Market, State, and Community*. Oxford: Clarendon, 1989.

Miller-McLemore, Bonnie J. *Also a Mother: Work and Family as a Theological Dilemma.* Nashville: Abingdon, 1995.

———. "Children and Religion in the Public Square." *Journal of Religion* 86 (2006) 385–401.

Min, Anselm Kyongsuk. *The Solidarity of Others in a Divided World: A Postmodern Theology of a Postmodern World.* New York: T. & T. Clark, 2004.

Mintz, Steven, and Susan Kellogg. *Domestic Revolutions: A Social History of American Family Life.* New York: Free Press, 1988.

Moltmann, Jürgen. *The Coming of God: Christian Eschatology.* Translated by Margaret Kohl. Minneapolis: Fortress, 1996.

———. *The Gospel of Liberation.* Translated by H. Wayne Pipkin. Waco, TX: Word, 1973.

———. "Political Theologies in Ecumenical Contexts." In *Political Theology: Contemporary Challenges and Future Directions,* edited by Michael Welker et al., 1–12. Louisville: Westminster John Knox, 2013.

Mounier, Emmanuel. *Personalism.* Notre Dame, IN: University of Notre Dame, 1952.

Murphy, Katie. "Fact Sheet: The Value of Unions and the Consequences of 'Right-to-Work' Laws." Economy. *Center for American Progress.* December 13, 2012. https://www.americanprogress.org/issues/economy/news/2012/12/13/48031/fact-sheet-the-value-of-unions-and-the-consequences-of-right-to-work-laws/.

Murray, John Courtney. *We Hold These Truths: Catholic Reflections on the American Proposition.* New York: Sheed & Ward, 1960.

Myers, Robin. *Spiritual Defiance: Building a Beloved Community of Resistance.* New Haven: Yale University Press, 2015.

Nandy, Ashis. *The Intimate Enemy: Loss and Recovery of Self under Colonialism.* Oxford: Oxford University Press, 1983.

National Aeronautics and Space Administration. "A Blanket around the Earth." Facts. *Global Climate Change: Vital Signs of the Planet.* https://climate.nasa.gov/causes/.

———. "Climate Change: How Do We Know?" Facts. *Global Climate Change: Vital Signs of the Planet.* Website. https://climate.nasa.gov/evidence/.

———. "Scientific Consensus: Earth's Climate Is Warming." Facts. *Global Climate Change: Vital Signs of the Planet.* https://climate.nasa.gov/scientific-consensus/.

———. "Child Poverty." http://www.nccp.org/topics/childpoverty.html/.

Nealon, Jeffery T. *Alterity Politics: Ethics and Performative Subjectivity.* Durham: Duke University Press, 1998.

Nelson, Robert H. *Economics as Religion: From Samuelson to Chicago and Beyond.* University Park: University of Pennsylvania Press, 2001.

Niebuhr, H. Richard. *Faith on Earth.* New Haven: Yale University Press, 1989.

———. *The Meaning of Revelation.* New York: Macmillan, 1941.

———. *The Purpose of the Church and Its Ministry: Reflections on the Aims of Theological Education.* New York: Harper, 1956.

———. "War as Crucifixion." *Christian Century* 60 (1943) 512–15.

———. "War as the Judgment of God." *Christian Century* 59 (1942) 630–33.

Niebuhr, Reinhold. *Love and Justice: Selections from the Shorter Writings of Reinhold Niebuhr.* Edited by D. B Robertson. Philadelphia: Westminster, 1957.

Noddings, Nel. *Caring: A Feminine Approach to Ethics & Moral Education.* Berkeley: University of California Press, 1984.

———. *Starting at Home: Caring and Social Policy*. Berkeley: University of California Press, 2002.

Nouwen, Henri J. M. *Reaching Out: The Three Movements of the Spiritual Life*. London: Collins, 1976.

Novak, Michael. *The Spirit of Democratic Capitalism*. New York: Simon & Schuster, 1982.

———. *Toward a Theology of the Corporation*. Rev. ed. Studies in Religion, Philosophy, and Public Policy. Washington DC: AEI Press, 1987.

Nussbaum, Martha C. *Political Emotions: Why Love Matters for Justice*. Cambridge: Belknap, 2013.

Oakes, Peter. "Methodological Issues in Using Economic Evidence in Interpretation of Early Christian Texts." In *Engaging Economics: New Testament Scenarios and Early Christian Reception*, edited by Bruce Longenecker and Kelly Liebengood, 9–36. Grand Rapids: Eerdmanns, 2009.

O'Donovan, Oliver. "Political Theology, Tradition, and Modernity." In *The Cambridge Companion to Liberation Theology*, edited by Christopher Roland, 268–84. 2nd ed. Cambridge Companions to Religion. Cambridge: Cambridge University Press, 2007.

Oliner, Pearl M., and Samuel P. Oliner. *Toward a Caring Society: Ideas into Action*. Westport, CT: Praeger, 1995.

Orfield, Gary. "Race and Schools: The Need for Action." Research Brief from the NEA Research Visiting Scholars Series, Spring 2008, vol. 1b. National Education Association. http://www.nea.org/home/13054.htm/.

Orr, Judith L. "Ministry with Working-Class Women." *Journal of Pastoral Care* 45/4 (1991) 343–53.

Ortega y Gasset, José. *Man and People*. Translated by Willard R. Trask. New York: Norton, 1957.

Osiek, Carolyn. *Rich and Poor in the Shepherd of Hermas: An Exegetical-Social Investigation*. Catholic Biblical Quarterly. Monograph Series 15. Washington DC: Catholic Biblical Association of America, 1983.

Pannenberg, Wolfart. *Theology and the Kingdom of God*. Edited by Richard John Neuhaus. Philadelphia: Westminster, 1969.

Panousi, Vasia, et al. "Inequality Rising and Permanent over Past Two Decades." *Brookings Paper On Economic Activity*, Spring 2013. http://www.brookings.edu/about/projects/bpea/latest-conference/2013-spring-permanent-inequality-panousi/.

Parenti, Christian. *The Tropic of Chaos: Climate Change and the New Geography of Violence*. New York: Nation Books, 2011.

Perkins, Whitney T. *Denial of Empire: The United States and Its Dependencies*. Leyden: Sythoff, 1962.

Petras, James, and Henry Veltmeyer. *Power and Resistance: U.S. Imperialism in Latin America*. Leiden: Brill, 2016.

Piketty, Thomas. *Capital in the Twenty-First Century*. Translated by Arthur Goldhammer. Cambridge: Belknap, 2014.

Pitt, William Rivers. "A Corrupt CEO Busted? Well, Merry Christmas." *Truthout*, December 20, 2015. http://www.truth-out.org/opinion/item/34110-a-corrupt-ceo-busted-well-merry-christmas/.

Poling James N. *Render unto God: Economic Vulnerability, Family Violence, and Pastoral Theology*. 2002. Eugene, OR: Wipf & Stock, 2012.

Pulcini, Elena. *Care of the World: Fear, Responsibility, and Justice in the Global Age*. Translated by Karen Whittle. Studies in Global Justice 11. Dordrecht: Springer, 2013.

Putnam, Robert D. *Bowling Alone: The Collapse and Revival of American Community*. New York: Simon & Schuster, 2000.

———. *Our Kids: The American Dream in Crisis*. New York: Simon & Schuster, 2015.

Ramsay, Nancy J. "Compassionate Resistance: An Ethic for Pastoral Care and Counseling." *Journal of Pastoral Care* 52/3 (1998) 217–26.

———. "When Race and Gender Collide." In *Women Out of Order: Risking Change and Creating Care in a Multicultural World*, edited by Jeanne Stevenson-Moessner and Teresa Snorton, 331–48. Minneapolis: Fortress, 2010.

Ransom, John S. *Foucault's Discipline: The Politics of Subjectivity*. Durham: Duke University Press, 1997.

Rawls, John. *A Theory of Justice*. Cambridge: Harvard University Press, 1971.

Reich, Robert B. *Saving Capitalism: For the Many, Not the Few*. New York: Vintage, 2015.

———. *Supercapitalism: The Transformation of Business, Democracy, and Everyday Life*. New York: Vintage, 2007.

Rieger, Joerg. *Christ & Empire: From Paul to Postcolonial Times*. Minneapolis: Fortress, 2007.

———. *No Rising Tide: Theology Economics, and the Future*. Minneapolis: Fortress, 2009.

———. *Opting for the Margins: Postmodernity and Liberation in Christian Theology*. AAR Reflection and Theory in the Study of Religion. New York: Oxford University Press, 2003.

———, ed. *Religion, Theology, and Class: Fresh Engagements after Long Silence*. New York: Palgrave Macmillan, 2013.

———. "Why Class Matters in Religious Studies and Theology." In *Religion, Theology, and Class: Fresh Engagements after Long Silence*, 1–26. New York: Palgrave Macmillan, 2013.

Rieff, David. "Liberal Imperialism." In *The Imperial Tense: Prospects and Problems of American Empire*, edited by Andrew J. Bacevich, 10–28. Chicago: Dee, 2003.

Robinson, Fiona. *The Ethics of Care: A Feminist Approach to Human Security*. Global Ethics and Politics. Philadelphia: Temple University Press, 2011.

———. *Globalizing Care: Ethics, Feminist Theory, and International Relations*. Feminist Theory and Politics. Boulder, CO: Westview, 1999.

Rogers-Vaughn, Bruce. "Blessed Are Those Who Mourn: Depression as Political Resistance." *Journal of Pastoral Psychology* 63/4 (2014) 503–22.

———."Powers and Principalities: Initial Reflection toward a Post-Capitalist Pastoral Theology." *Journal of Pastoral Theology* 25/2 (2015) 71–92.

Ruddick, Susan. "Injustice in Families: Assault and Domination." In *Justice and Care: Essential Readings in Feminist Ethics*, edited by Virginia Held, 203–23. Boulder, CO: Westview, 1995.

Rumscheidt, Barbara. *No Room for Grace: Pastoral Theology and Dehumanization in the Global Economy*. 1998. Reprint, Eugene, OR: Wipf & Stock, 2012.

Ryan, Alan. *On Politics: A History of Political Thought from Herodotus to the Present.* New York: Liveright, 2012.

Ryn, Claes G. *America the Virtuous: The Crisis of Democracy and the Quest for Empire.* New Brunswick, NJ: Transaction, 2003.

Samuels, Andrew. "Politics on the Couch? Psychotherapy and Society—Some Possibilities and Limitations." *Psychoanalytic Dialogues*, 14/6 (2004) 817–34.

Sandel, Michael J. *Justice: What's the Right Thing To Do?* New York: Farrar, Straus, and Giroux, 2009.

———. *Public Philosophy: Essays on Morality in Politics.* Cambridge: Harvard University Press, 2005.

———. *What Money Can't Buy: The Moral Limits of Markets.* New York: Farrar, Straus and Giroux, 2012.

Sass, Louis A. *Madness and Modernism: Insanity in the Light of Modern Art, Literature and Thought.* Cambridge: Harvard University Press, 1992.

Sassen, Saskia. *Expulsions: Brutality and Complexity in the Global Economy.* Cambridge: Belknap, 2014.

Sayer, R. Andrew. *The Moral Significance of Class.* Cambridge: Cambridge University Press, 2005.

Scahill, Jeremy. *Dirty Wars: The World Is a Battlefield.* New York: Nation Books, 2013.

Scheib, Karen D. *Challenging Invisibility: Practices of Care with Older Women.* St. Louis: Chalice, 2004.

Schore, Alan N. *Affect Regulation and the Repair of the Self.* Norton Series on Interpersonal Neurobiology. New York: Norton, 2003.

Scott, Peter and William Cavanaugh. "Introduction." In *The Blackwell Companion to Political Theology*, 1–4. Blackwell Companions to Religion. Malden, MA: Blackwell, 2007.

Segal, Hanna. "Notes on Symbol Formation." In*ternational Journal of Psychoanalysis* 38 (1957) 391–97.

Segundo, Juan Luis. *The Liberation of Theology.* Translated by John Drury. Maryknoll, NY: Orbis, 1985.

Sevenhuijsen, Selma. *Citizenship and the Ethics of Care: Feminist Considerations on Justice, Morality, and Politics.* Translated from Dutch by Liz Savage. London: Routledge, 1998.

Silva, Jennifer M. *Coming up Short: Working-Class Adulthood in the Age of Uncertainty.* Oxford: Oxford University Press, 2013.

Shapiro, Ari. "Sotomayor Differs with Obama on 'Empathy' Issue." National Public Radio, July, 14, 2009. http://www.npr.org/templates/story/story.php?storyId=106569335/.

Shoen, Cathy, et al. "America's Underinsured: A State-by-State Look at Health Insurance Affordability Prior to the New Coverage Expansions." The Commonwealth Fund, March 25, 2014. http://www.commonwealthfund.org/publications/fund-reports/2014/mar/americas-underinsured/.

Skiba, Russell. "The Failure of Zero Tolerance." *Reclaiming Children and Youth* 22/4 (2014) 27–33. http://eric.ed.gov/?q=%22%22&ff1=subEarly+Intervention&ff2=subParent+Participation&id=EJ1038609/.

Smiley, Tavis, and David Ritz. *Death of a King: The Real Story of Dr. Martin Luther King Jr.'s Final Year.* New York: Little, Brown, 2014.

Smith, Archie, Jr. *The Relational Self: Ethics & Therapy from a Black Church Perspective.* Nashville: Abingdon, 1982.

Sobrino, Jon. *The True Church and the Poor.* Translated by Matthew J. O'Connell. Maryknoll, NY: Orbis, 1984.

Solomon, Andrew. *The Noonday Demon: An Atlas of Depression.* New York: Scribner, 2001.

Sommers, Benjamin et al. "Mortality and Access to Care among Adults after State Medicaid Expansions." New England Journal of Medicine 367 (2012) 1025–34. http://www.nejm.org/doi/full/10.1056/NEJMsa1202099#t=article.

Soss, Joe, et al. *Disciplining the Poor: Neoliberal Paternalism and the Persistent Power of Race.* Chicago Studies in American Politics. Chicago: University of Chicago Press, 2011.

Squires, David. "The U.S. Health System in Perspective: A Comparison of Twelve Industrialized Nations." *Issues in International Health Policy*, July 2011. http://www.commonwealthfund.org/~/media/Files/Publications/Issue%20Brief/2011/Jul/1532_Squires_US_hlt_sys_comparison_12_nations_intl_brief_v2.pdf/.

Sroufe, L. Alan. *Emotional Development: The Organization of Emotional Life in the Early Years.* Cambridge Studies in Social and Emotional Development. Cambridge: Cambridge University Press, 1995.

Stern, Daniel. *The Interpersonal World of the Infant.* New York: Basic Books, 1985.

Stevenson-Moessner, Jeanne, and Teresa Snorton. *Women Out of Order: Risking Change and Creating Care in a Multicultural World.* Minneapolis: Fortress, 2010.

Stiglitz, Joseph E. *The Great Divide: Unequal Societies and What We Can Do about Them.* New York: Norton, 2015.

———. *The Price of Inequality.* New York: Norton, 2012.

Stone, Oliver, and Peter Kuznick. *The Untold History of the United States.* New York: Gallery Books, 2012.

Strauss, Leo, and Joseph Cropsey. "Introduction." In *History of Political Philosophy*, edited by Leo Strauss and Joseph Cropsey, 1–6. 3rd ed. Chicago: University of Chicago Press, 1987.

Sung, Jung Mo. *Desire, Market, and Religion.* London: SCM, 2007.

Taylor, Charles. *Modern Social Imaginaries.* Public Planet Books. Durham: Duke University Press, 2007.

Taylor, Mark. *The Executed God: The Way of the Cross in Lockdown America.* 2nd ed. Minneapolis: Fortress Press, 2015.

Tillich, Paul. *Love, Power, and Justice: Ontological Analyses and Ethical Applications.* New York: Oxford University Press, 1954.

Tocqueville, Alexis de. *Democracy in America.* A Bantam Classic. New York: Bantam, 2004.

Tronto, Joan. *Moral Boundaries: A Political Argument for an Ethic of Care.* New York: Routledge, 1993.

Turse, Nick. *Kill Anything that Moves: The Real American War in Vietnam.* New York: Metropolitan Books/Henry Holt, 2013.

Tuttle, Ian. "Predatory Government Burdens the Vulnerable." *The National Review*, March 6, 2015. http://www.nationalreview.com/article/415041/injustice-doj-uncovered-ferguson-wasnt-racism-ian-tuttle/.

Tutu, Desmond. *No Future without Forgiveness.* New York: Doubleday, 1999.

Tyrrell, Ian, and Jay Sexton. *Empire's Twin: U.S. Anti-imperialism from the Founding Era to the Age of Terrorism*. United States in the World. Ithaca: Cornell University Press, 2015.

Union of Concerned Scientists. "Causes of Drought: What's the Climate Connection?" http://www.ucsusa.org/global_warming/science_and_impacts/impacts/causes-of-drought-climate-change-connection.html#.WO49kVMrLIF/.

———. "Early Warning Signs of Global Warming: Coral Reef Bleaching." http://www.ucsusa.org/global_warming/science_and_impacts/impacts/early-warning-signs-of-global-2.html#.WO1WoFPyvIF/.

———. Global Warming. "Global Warming Impacts: The Consequences of Climate Change Are Already Here." http://www.ucsusa.org/our-work/global-warming/science-and-impacts/global-warming-impacts#.WO4031MrLIF/.

United States Conference of Catholic Bishops. *Economic Justice for All: A Pastoral Letter on Catholic Social Teaching and the U.S. Economy*. U.S. Catholic Conference of Bishops, 1986.

United States Department of Justice, Office of Justice Programs, Bureau of Justice Statistics. "Key Statistic: Total Correctional Population, 1980–2015." https://www.bjs.gov/index.cfm?ty=kfdetail&iid=487/.

———. "Profile of Nonviolent Offenders Exiting State Prisons." Bureau of Justice Statistics Fact Sheet, October 2004. https://bjs.gov/content/pub/pdf/pnoesp.pdf/.

University of California, Davis, Center for Poverty Research. "How Is Poverty Related to Access to Care and Preventive Healthcare?" http://poverty.ucdavis.edu/faq/how-poverty-related-access-care-and-preventive-healthcare/.

University of Michigan, Gerald R. Ford School of Public Policy, National Poverty Center. Poverty Facts. "Poverty in the United States: Frequently Asked Questions." http://npc.umich.edu/poverty/.

Van Alstyne, Robert. *The Rising American Empire*. New York: Oxford University Press, 1960.

Vauhini, Vara. " Tom Perkins and Schadenfreude in Silicon Valley." *New Yorker*, January 27, 2014. http://www.newyorker.com/business/currency/tom-perkins-and-schadenfreude-in-silicon-valley/.

Vidal, Gore. *Perpetual War for Perpetual Peace: How We Got to Be So Hated*. New York: Nation Books, 2002.

Volf, Miroslav. *Exclusion and Embrace: A Theological Exploration of Identity, Otherness, and Reconciliation*. Nashville: Abingdon, 1996.

Volland, Adam. "Global Temperature Records in Close Agreement." Features. January 17, 2011. *Global Climate Change: Vital Signs of the Planet*, by the National Aeronautics and Space Administration. https://climate.nasa.gov/news/468/global-temperature-records-in-close-agreement/.

Vatican Council II. *Gaudium et Spes*. In *Vatican Council II: The Conciliar and Post Conciliar Documents*, edited by Austin Flannery, 903–1001. Vatican Collection 1. Collegeville, MN: Liturgical, 1975.

"Voter Turnout in the United States Presidential Elections." *Wikipedia*. https://en.wikipedia. org/wiki/Voter_turnout_in_the_United_States_presidential_elections.

Vries, Hent de. "Introduction: Before, Around, and Beyond the Theologico-Politico." In *Political Theologies: Public Religions in a Post-Secular World*, edited by Hent de Vries and Lawrence Sullivan, 1–90. New York: Fordham University Press, 2006.

Wacquant, Loic J. D. *Punishing the Poor: The Neoliberal Government of Social Insecurity*. Politics, History, and Culture. Durham: Duke University Press, 2009.

Wagner, Gernot, and Michael L. Weitzman. *Climate Shock: The Economic Consequences of a Hotter Planet*. Princeton: Princeton University Press, 2015.

Waldman, Peter. *Being Right Is Not Enough: What Progressives Must Learn from Conservative Success*. Hoboken, NJ: Wiley, 2005.

Walzer, Michael. *In God's Shadow: Politics and the Hebrew Bible*. New Haven: Yale University Press, 2012.

Weber, Max. *The Protestant Ethic and the Spirit of Capitalism*. Translated by Talcott Parsons. London: Routledge, 1992.

Welch, Sharon D. *After Empire: The Art and Ethos of Enduring Peace*. Minneapolis: Fortress, 2004.

Werpehowski, William. "Reinhold Niebuhr." In *The Blackwell Companion to Political Theology*, edited by Peter Scott and William Cavanaugh, 180–93. Blackwell Companions to Religion. Malden, MA: Blackwell, 2007.

West, Cornel. *Democracy Matters: Winning the Fight against Imperialism*. New York: Penguin, 2004.

Williams, Cheryl. "Perceptions of Public Schools . . . Fiction Trumps the Truth." *Learning First Alliance*, October, 12, 2012. http://www.learningfirst.org/perceptions-public-schools-fiction-trumps-truth/.

Wimberly, Edward P. *African American Pastoral Care and Counseling: The Politics of Oppression and Empowerment*. Cleveland: Pilgrim, 2006.

———. *Counseling African American Marriages and Families*. Louisville: Westminster John Knox, 1997.

Winnicott, D. W. *Home Is Where We Start From: Essays by a Psychoanalyst*. Compiled and edited by Clare Winnicott et al. New York: Norton, 1986.

———. *Playing and Reality*. New York: Routledge, 1971.

Wolterstorff, Nicholas. *Justice in Love*. Grand Rapids: Eerdmans, 2011.

Wolff, Richard D. *Democracy at Work: A Cure for Capitalism*. Chicago: Haymarket, 2012.

———. *Occupy the Economy: Challenging Capitalism*. San Francisco: City Lights Books, 2012.

Wolff, Richard D., and Stephen A. Resnick. *Contending Economic Theories: Neoclassical, Keynesian, and Marxian*. Cambridge: MIT Press, 2012.

———. *Economics: Marxian versus Neoclassical*. Baltimore: Johns Hopkins University Press, 1987.

Wolin, Sheldon S. *Democracy Incorporated: Managed Democracy and the Specter of Inverted Totalitarianism*. Princeton: Princeton University Press, 2008.

Woodruff, Paul. *Reverence: Renewing a Forgotten Virtue*. Oxford: Oxford University Press, 2001.

X, Malcolm, with the assistance of Alex Haley. *The Autobiography of Malcolm X*. New York: Ballantine, 1964.

Young, Iris Marion. *Justice and the Politics of Difference*. Princeton: Princeton University Press, 1990.

Young, Marilyn B. "Imperial Language." In *The New American Empire: A 21st Century Teach-In on U.S. Foreign Policy*, edited by Lloyd C. Gardner and Marilyn B. Young, 32–49. New York: New Press, 2005.

Young-Bruehl, Elisabeth. *Why Arendt Matters*. Why X Matters. New Haven: Yale University Press, 2006.

Zinn, Howard. *A People's History of the United States*. New York: HarperPerrenial, 2005.

Zinn, Howard, with Anthony Amove. *Voices of a People's History of the United States.* 10th anniversary 3rd ed. New York: Seven Stories, 2014.

Zizioulas, John D. *Being as Communion: Studies in Personhood and the Church.* Contemporary Greek Theologians 4. Crestwood, NY: St. Vladimir's Seminary Press, 1985.

———. *Communion and Otherness: Further Studies in Personhood and the Church.* Edited by Paul McPartlan. New York: T. & T. Clark, 2006.

INDEX

Made in the USA
Columbia, SC
01 November 2018